Principles of Classroom Management

A Professional Decision-Making Model

Second Canadian Edition

James Levin
Pennsylvania State University

James F. Nolan
Pennsylvania State University

James W. Kerr
Brock University

Anne E. Elliott
Brock University

PEARSON

Toronto

For Linda and Richard

Library and Archives Canada Cataloguing in Publication

Principles of classroom management : a professional decision-making model / James Levin ... [et al.]. — 2nd Canadian ed.

Includes bibliographical references and index.
ISBN 978-0-205-53716-7

1. Classroom management—Problems, exercises, etc. 2. Teaching—Problems, exercises, etc.
I. Levin, James, 1946–

LB3013.P74 2008   371.102'4   C2007-904727-0

ISBN-13: 978-0-205-53716-7
ISBN-10: 0-205-53716-2

Vice-President, Editorial Director: Gary Bennett
Executive Acquisitions Editor: Christine Cozens
Marketing Manager: Toivo Pajo
Developmental Editor: Charlotte Morrison-Reed
Production Editors: Joe Zingrone, Söğüt Y. Güleç
Copy Editor: Joe Zingrone
Proofreaders: Tara Tovell, Trish O'Reilly
Production Manager: Peggy Brown
Composition: Laserwords
Photo Research: Sandy Cooke
Art Director: Julia Hall
Cover Design: Anthony Leung
Cover Image: Masterfile

5   12 11 10

Printed and bound in USA.

Contents

4 *Philosophical Approaches to Classroom Management*   78

PART II • *Prevention*

5 *The Professional Teacher*   105

PART III • *Interventions for Common Behaviour Problems*

PART IV • *Interventions for Chronic Behaviour Problems*

Preface

In the second Canadian edition of *Principles of Classroom Management: A Professional Decision-Making Model*, we have updated the case studies, many of which now contain perspectives from various points of view. We have used the metaphor of the kaleidoscope to refer to this type of case study because in a kaleidoscope, as the lens is rotated, the same pieces realign in new ways to form a new image. Thus, in our kaleidoscope cases, we have described situations through the eyes of all of the participants who are engaged in the scenario, thereby offering the reader a variety of perspectives that may provide broader insights into complex issues.

Educators have indicated that it would be helpful for teachers to acquire a list of strategies that have proven effective when dealing with various disruptive classroom behaviours. Therefore, we have developed a memorable model of sequential strategies for managing inappropriate classroom behaviours. To this model, we have aptly applied the following acronym: **CALM** (**consider**, **act**, **lessen**, **manage**). This model provides a series of steps (Levels I through IV), which should serve to help teachers make logical decisions and avoid responding to problem classroom behaviours entirely from an emotional point of view.

The central theme of *Principles of Classroom Management* remains consistent with the first edition. We believe that teachers and students share responsibility for classroom behaviour, that teachers must adjust their behaviour if they expect student behaviour to change, and that students in constructive relationships with adults are more likely to engage in positive social behaviour and be successful academically.

In continuing to adapt the text for the Canadian educator, we acknowledge that Canadian society, culture, and education are distinct from those of our US neighbours in several important ways. Our historical underpinnings, immigration policies, small population in a vast geographical expanse, as well as provincially controlled educational systems make us distinct from our friends south of the border. In the officially bilingual Canadian culture, there exists a deep tradition of tolerance in which diversity and multilingualism are valued. Canadians and Americans also differ in their views about violence, security, and relationships with other nations.

In order to reflect these Canadian differences, in this edition we continued to make structural changes to the text. Specifically, we added Canadian references to reflect current educational research and practices across the country. We also created new case studies and added more detail to others. It was our intention to make these cases typically Canadian in nature. Our kaleidoscope cases also reflect real issues in Canadian schools and show multiple viewpoints of a given situation. In order to make comprehension easier for the reader, the key ideas in each chapter were emphasized in a number of ways. We placed prereading questions related to content at the beginning of each chapter. Key terms were also identified and highlighted throughout the text and defined at the conclusion of each chapter. Weblinks were updated, and questions for discussion were placed immediately after each classroom case study throughout the text.

As we considered the principles central to the text, we realized the critical nature of the language we chose. Rather than label students as "discipline problems" or "disruptive students," it was more consistent with our beliefs to separate the student from his or her problematic behaviour. Therefore, we identified the situation, rather than the student, as being problematic. As a result, the onus was placed on teachers to modify either their behaviour or the situation that impinged on a student who exhibited disruptive behaviour. This is a subtle but critical difference which implies that teachers need to avoid negative personal labels and strive to maintain and build positive relationships with students who cause classroom disruptions.

Students can now find online testing and additional cases to go with the second Canadian edition of *Principles of Classroom Management*. Features of the Companion Website include chapter objectives, online testing, study questions, additional cases, and links to interesting material and information from other websites that will reinforce and enhance the content of each chapter in this book. To enter, simply visit the site at **www.pearsoned.ca/levin**.

Iterative Case Study Analyses

The Iterative Case Study Analyses offer descriptions of three classroom situations involving behavioural problems at different grade levels. We suggest that one or more of the case studies be analyzed four times.

The first analysis should be completed prior to reading and studying the text. This initial analysis will serve as a baseline from which you can reflect upon your growth of understanding and ability to analyze complex student behaviours as you study the text and reanalyze the cases.

The second analysis is to be completed after you have read and studied Part I, Foundations, which includes Chapters 1 through 4. The third analysis should incorporate the concepts discussed in Part II, Prevention, which includes Chapters 5 and 6. The fourth and final analysis should use the concepts found in Part III, Interventions for Common Behaviour Problems, and IV, Interventions for Chronic Behaviour Problems, which include Chapters 7 through 10.

For each reanalysis, consider what has changed and what has stayed the same from the previous analysis.

Iterative Case Study Analysis

First Analysis

Select one or more of the case studies below. Before studying the text, how would you analyze the situation(s)? In your analysis, consider why the students may be choosing to behave inappropriately and how you might intervene to influence them to stop the disruptive behaviour and resume appropriate on-task behaviour.

Elementary School Case Study

During silent reading time in my grade 4 class, I have built in opportunities to work individually with students. During this time, the students read to me and practice word work with flash cards. One student has refused to read to me but instead wants only to work with the flash cards. After a few sessions, I suggested we work with word cards this time and begin reading next time. He agreed. The next time we met, I reminded him of our plan, and he screamed, "I don't remember! I want to do word cards!" At this point, I tried to find out why he didn't like reading and he said, "There's a reason, I just can't tell you," and he threw the word cards across the room, some of them hitting other students. What should I do?

Middle School Case Study

I can't stop thinking about a problem I'm having in class with a group of 12-year-old boys. They consistently use vulgar language toward one another and some of the shyer kids in the class, especially the girls. In addition, they are always pushing and shoving each other. I've tried talking to them about why they keep using bad language when they know it's inappropriate. The response I get is that "it makes me look cool and funny in front of my friends." I have asked them to please use more appropriate language in the classroom but that has not worked. I haven't even started to address the pushing and shoving. What should I do?

High School Case Study

This past week, I had a student approach me about a problem he was experiencing in our class. The grade 11 student had recently "come out" as being gay. He said he was tired and upset with the three boys who sit near him. These boys frequently call him a "homo" and a "fag" every time they see him, both in and out of class. What should I do?

1

The Foundations

Focus on the Principles of Classroom Management

1. What is the single most important influence on the classroom learning environment?
2. What range of professional responsibilities do teachers need to accept in the classroom?
3. What ideas and strategies must teachers develop if they are to have a classroom that is characterized by a high level of on-task student behaviour?
4. If students are to display appropriate behaviour in class, what preplanning is necessary for teachers?

Introduction

In Canadian faculties of education, there are many courses that address issues critical to effective instruction. No course or program that focuses on instructional strategies can be complete without discussing the parameters of teaching—a topic that is closely tied to the topic of **classroom management**. Teacher candidates receive guidelines that help them plan meaningful learning experiences for students in all curriculum areas (e.g., language, mathematics, science and technology, arts, physical education). Teacher education programs include instruction for designing and writing effective student outcome expectations after instruction. Teacher education programs also prepare teacher candidates for the task of creating lesson plans, unit plans, long-term plans, and supportive instructional material. Provincial ministries of education require that the faculties provide courses that prepare teacher candidates in teaching methods, special education, educational psychology, history of education, and educational law.

Although we have all taken and taught courses on classroom management at the preservice, in-service, and graduate levels of education, we, the authors, have noted a dearth of research, especially in Canada, on this issue. However, the most thoroughly prepared and well-designed lesson has no chance of success if the instructor is not able to manage the classroom and her students' behaviour effectively.[1] Extreme cases of poor management, in fact, lead to poor learning. Therefore, we begin by setting forth a definition of teaching and explaining how and why classroom management is such a critical part of the teaching process. The rest of this chapter

---

[1]To foster equality without being cumbersome, gender pronouns will be alternated by chapter. Chapter 1 will have female pronouns; Chapter 2, male; Chapter 3, female; and so forth.

presents a structural overview of the book. First, we present the principles of management that form the book's foundation. Second, we provide an explanation of the decision-making hierarchical approach to management. Last, we offer a flow chart of the knowledge, skills, and techniques that make up a management hierarchy and result in successful classrooms in which teachers are free to teach and students are free to learn.

Defining the Process of Teaching

Each year, universities educate and graduate thousands of students who then enter the teaching profession. After completing their professional teacher education program, graduates enter the classroom and, in Canada, typically teach for 30 to 35 years. Many teachers are unable to provide an adequate operational definition of teaching. Some argue that a formal definition is not necessary because they have been teaching for years and whatever they do seems to work. However, for those of us who consider teaching a professionally sophisticated endeavour, experience—although invaluable in many teaching situations—is not the only thing that should be relied on to develop and plan instruction. Furthermore, this "gut-reaction" approach is sorely limited when the old "proven methods" seem not to work, and there is then a need for modifying the existing instructional or management strategies, or for developing new strategies. When asked, some people define teaching as the delivery, transference, or giving of knowledge or information. Definitions like these give no clue as to how knowledge is transferred and what strategies are used to deliver it; they limit teaching to the cognitive domain only, thus failing to recognize the extraordinary level of competence needed to make hundreds of daily decisions based on content and pedagogical knowledge in complex and dynamic classroom environments. Teaching has always emphasized the cognitive domain. For instance, many educators currently adhere to Piaget's constructivist theory, which argues that individuals construct new knowledge from their experiences through assimilation and accommodation (Boudourides, 2003; von Glasersfeld, 1996). However, when teachers view teaching as being concerned solely with cognitive development, they limit their effectiveness in managing students who exhibit disruptive behaviour. Troublesome students often need to grow in the affective domain as well as the cognitive. For instance, many need guidance to help them develop essential interpersonal and societal skills—such as co-operating with peers, respecting others, and contributing positively to their community. Teachers who understand the critical nature of the affective domain are in a much better position to work with disruptive students (Keating and Matthews, 1999).

Vygotsky (1978) and Piaget (1975) have influenced educators with their belief that social interactions enhance children's cognitive development. Vygotsky specifically asserted that social interactions need to include meaningful language opportunities that enable children to negotiate and experiment with new learning. This belief suggests that children's social interactions need to be structured and managed effectively by teachers if learning is to be maximized (Dixon-Krauss, 1996).

Through careful lesson planning, teachers can design strategies that have an increased probability of gaining students' interest and preventing behavioural problems.

Indeed, many exceptional teachers approach their work with the attitude that the reason students need teachers is because some young people exhibit behaviours that seriously interfere with teaching and learning (Haberman, 1995). Teachers with this attitude are better prepared to work effectively with disruptive students. They do not get as frustrated or feel as if they are wasting their time because they understand that teaching helps students to mature not only cognitively but also to develop *emotional intelligence*. Emotional intelligence has been recognized as a separate competency from cognitive aptitude (Goldman, 1996). The ability to be emotionally self-aware is an important skill for success in life and an area where teachers have to help children grow stronger. Its development is a central component of good classroom management and teachers who address emotional intelligence explicitly with their students are generally more successful in the classrooms.

When teaching is properly defined, teachers are more likely to have a clear perception of what the best practices are for their profession. A related issue is teachers' self-efficacy, which is confidence in their ability to promote students' learning and to achieve instructional goals (Bembenutty and Chen, 2005). Self-efficacy is a teacher characteristic related to student achievement and has direct implications for classroom-management skills. Teachers are more likely to engage in effective management behaviours when they believe they are capable of using those behaviours successfully, so they need to possess an effective repertoire of management strategies for a huge variety of classroom scenarios. Additionally, one of the major tenets of Adlerian psychology is that each individual makes a conscious choice to behave in certain ways, either desirable or undesirable (Sweeney, 1981; Watts, 2003). Building on this tenet, we believe that individuals cannot be forced to change their behaviour; they must choose to do so. In other words, teachers do not control student behaviour; students control their own behaviours. If this idea is accepted fully by instructors, it follows that they can change student behaviour only by *influencing* the change through modifications in their own behaviour, which is the only behaviour they can control directly. In the classroom, then, a teacher is continually involved in a process in which student behaviour is monitored and compared with the teacher's idea of appropriate behaviour for any given instructional activity. When actual student behaviour differs from an appropriate standard, teachers attempt to influence a change in the behaviour by changing their own behaviour. The behaviour the teacher decides to use should be one that maximizes the likelihood that student behaviour will change in the appropriate way.

Fortunately, most human behaviour is learned observationally through modelling—from observing others, a person can form an idea of how new behaviours are performed and then replicate them. This phenomenon, called *social learning theory* (Bandura, 1977), explains human behaviour in terms of interactions among cognitive, behavioural, and environmental influences. As it encompasses attention, memory, and motivation, social learning theory spans both cognitive and behavioural frameworks and is also related to developing a series of classroom-management competencies. The probability of choosing the most effective behaviour increases when teachers have a **professional knowledge** of instructional techniques, cognitive psychology, and child development—and when they use this knowledge to guide the modification of their own behaviour (Anderson, 2002; Brophy, 1988; Keating and Matthews, 1999; Murdoch-Morris, 1993).

With this background, we can define *teaching* as the use of pre-planned behaviours—founded in learning principles and child development theory and directed toward both instructional delivery and classroom management—that increase the probability of effecting a positive change in student behaviour. The significance of this definition in trying to change any student's behaviour is threefold: First, teaching is concerned with what teachers are able to control—their own behaviour—and this behaviour is pre-planned. Teaching is not a capricious activity. Second, the pre-planned behaviours are determined by the teacher's professional knowledge. This knowledge guides the teacher in selecting appropriate behaviours. It is the application of this specialized body of professional knowledge and knowing why it works that makes teaching a profession (Tauber and Mester, 1994). Third, many teaching behaviours are well founded in professional knowledge. The teacher's challenge is to select those behaviours that increase the probability of a corresponding behavioural change in the student. For this to occur, the teacher must not only know students' initial behaviours but also have a clear picture of the desired student behaviours for any given instructional activity.

The emphasis on the use of professional knowledge to inform teacher behaviour is critical. If teachers are asked why they interacted with students in a particular manner or why they used a particular instructional strategy, their response should be based on pedagogical or psychological research, theory, or methodology.

Case 1.1, "Getting Students to Respond" (on page 8), illustrates how a teacher applies the definition of teaching to instructional delivery. Ms. Chong, a grade 10 teacher, was aware of the current student behaviour and, after questioning, had a clear picture of what she wanted the behaviour to become. To effect this change, she analyzed her behaviours and how they affected her students. Because changes in teacher behaviour influence changes in student behaviour, the former is often termed *affecting behaviour* and the sought-after student behaviour is termed *target behaviour* (Morgan and Saxton, 1991; Boyan and Copeland, 1978). Using her professional knowledge, Ms. Chong modified her behaviour to improve her practice of teaching to bring about the target behaviour. The behaviours she chose to employ were well founded in the educational literature on questioning methodology (see Chapter 5, "The Professional Teacher"). Ms. Chong performed as a professional.

Case 1.2, "'Why Study? We Don't Get Enough Time for the Test Anyway'" (on page 9), illustrates the relationship between teacher behaviour and targeted student behaviour in classroom management.

Like Ms. Chong, Mr. Casimir changed his behaviour to one that reflected a well-accepted educational practice. With this change came corresponding changes in student behaviour with his grade 6 class.

Although not as plentiful as the information available on effective teaching practices, there is now a body of knowledge concerning effective classroom management (Anderson, 2002; Emmer, Evertson, Clements, and Worsham, 1997; Evertson, Emmer, Clements, and Worsham, 1997; Martin and Sugarman, 1993; Redl and Wineman, 1952). As stressed throughout this book, effective classroom management is inseparable from effective instruction. Without effective instructional practices, teachers are unlikely to be able to maintain successfully appropriate student behaviour. However, although effective instruction is absolutely necessary, it is not in itself sufficient to guarantee that classrooms are free from disruptive behaviour. Even the best teachers may occasionally experience some disruptive behaviour.

Principles of Classroom Management

As a result of the research on classroom management, a number of well-accepted principles governing teacher behaviour (to prevent and manage disruptive behaviour) have emerged. Some of these principles are quite specific to a particular philosophical underpinning (see Chapter 4, "Philosophical Approaches to Classroom Management"), whereas others are philosophically generic. This book presents 38 generic principles of classroom management developed through years of experience, research, and study. Each of the remaining nine chapters emphasizes some of these principles and discusses in detail how the teacher may incorporate them into effective management practices.

In the following section, we summarize the contents of each chapter and its relevant principles. These paragraphs are followed by an explanation of the decision-making hierarchical approach to managing classroom behaviour. Just as it is good

CASE 1.1 • *Getting Students to Respond*

Ms. Chong believes that students must actively participate in class activities for learning to take place. She prides herself on her ability to design questions from all levels of the cognitive domain; she believes that students benefit from and enjoy working with questions that require analysis, synthesis, and evaluation. However, she is sorely disappointed because very few students have been volunteering to answer questions, and those who have responded have given very brief answers.

Observation of Ms. Chong's class indicates a fairly regular pattern of behaviours during questioning. Standing in front of the class, she asks the first question: "Students, we have been studying the settling of the Canadian West in the late 1800s and early 1900s. Why do you think so many people picked up and moved thousands of miles to a strange land knowing that they would face incredible hardship and suffering during the long trip?" Two hands shoot up. Ms. Chong immediately calls on Judy. "Judy, why do you think they went?" "They wanted new opportunities," Judy answers. Ms. Chong immediately replies, "Great answer. Things where they lived must have been so bad that they decided it was worth the hardships they would face. In a new country, they would have a new beginning and be given free land. Another thing is that some of the pioneers might not have realized how difficult the trip would be. Do you think that the hardships continued even after the pioneers arrived in the Prairies? Ameer?"

After discussion, Ms. Chong realizes how her behaviours are affecting student behaviour. Instead of increasing participation, they actually hinder participation. After conducting further classroom discussions and reading about questioning strategies, Ms. Chong decides to change her approach. She begins to ask questions from different locations throughout the room. She also waits three to five seconds before calling on any student. After a student answers, she again waits at least three seconds and then points out the salient parts of the response, rephrases another question using the student's response, and directs this question to the class.

As before, her behaviours affect student behaviour. However, this time more students volunteer initially, responses are longer, and additional students are willing to expand on initial answers.

Questions to Consider

1. Why did Ms. Chong increase her wait time before accepting an answer to her question?
2. Which teacher behaviour encouraged student discussion?
3. Which behaviour inhibited student discussion?

classroom practice to provide the learner with an anticipatory set of expectations before in-depth instruction, these chapter summaries provide the reader with an indication of the scope, sequence, and structure of this text.

In Chapter 2, "The Nature of Behavioural Problems," we examine the details of behavioural problems. First, we review the limitations of trying to classify behaviours and their subsequent possible association with discipline problems. Offering a new operational definition of the term **behavioural problem** rectifies these limitations.

CASE 1.2 • *"Why Study? We Don't Get Enough Time for the Test Anyway"*

Mr. Casimir has a rule that test papers will not be passed out until all students are quiet and in their seats with all materials, except a pencil, in the desk. He explains this to the class before every test. Without fail, he has to wait 5 to 10 minutes before everyone in the class is ready. Typically, some students complain, "Why do we have less time just because a few other kids are slow to get ready?" Sometimes, students will get visibly angry, saying, "This isn't fair"; "This is stupid"; or "Why study? We don't get enough time for the test anyway." He almost always resorts to arguing with the students. He is aware that his students begin their test in a negative environment and he wonders if this negativity has a serious impact on test results. Mr. Casimir dreads test days.

During a discussion of this situation with another teacher, Mr. Casimir is introduced to the concept of logical consequences—in other words, allowing students to experience a logically related consequence of their behaviour. Employing this concept, Mr. Casimir announces to the class that he will pass out tests on an individual basis. "Once you are ready, you receive a test." He walks down the aisles giving a test paper to students who are ready and passing by without comment those who are not. As a result of his changed behaviour, student behaviour changes. Complaining stops, and in a few minutes, more students are ready to take the test.

Questions to Consider

1. Are there other ways Mr. Casimir could have solved this behavioural problem?
2. Explain the fairness inherent in the decision to use logical consequences in this situation.
3. Can Mr. Casimir use another approach that would give all students the same amount of time to write the test?
4. What classroom routines do you think a teacher should establish to promote an effective test-writing environment for students?

This definition is then used to classify common classroom behaviours. Second, we analyze misbehaviour historically by frequency and type to determine what schools are like today. Third, we present research concerning the effect of disruptive behaviour on both teachers and students. The related principles of classroom management are the following:

1. A problem exists whenever a behaviour interferes with the teaching act, interferes with the rights of others to learn, is psychologically or physically unsafe, or destroys property.
2. For effective teaching to take place, teachers must be competent in managing student misbehaviour so as to maximize the time spent on learning.
3. Teachers who manage their classrooms effectively enjoy teaching more and have greater confidence in their ability to affect student achievement.

Chapter 3, "Understanding Why Children Misbehave," explores the underlying complex causes of misbehaviour and provides multiple reasons for why children misbehave. Societal changes have created an environment vastly different from the one that children of previous generations grew up in. How these out-of-school changes have influenced children's attitudes and behaviours is examined first.

Like adults, children have strong personal, social, and academic needs. At the same time, they undergo rapid cognitive and moral development. We go on in Chapter 3 to describe typical behaviours associated with children's attempts to meet their needs, as well as normal developmental behaviours. We also detail behaviours that may appear when the home or school fails to recognize and respond to those needs and developmental changes.

It must be understood that teachers do not have control over the changes that occur in society and in children. However, teachers *do* have total control over their instructional competence. Excellent instruction and classroom management is a significant way to lessen the effects of uncontrollable factors and to prevent misbehaviour.

The following principles are endorsed in Chapter 3:

1. An awareness of the causes of misbehaviour enables teachers to use positive control techniques rather than negative ones that stem from erroneously viewing misbehaviour as a personal affront.
2. Basic human needs such as food, safety, belonging, and security are prerequisites for appropriate classroom behaviour.
3. The need for a sense of significance, competence, virtue, and power influences student behaviour.
4. Societal changes beyond schools' control greatly influence student behaviour.
5. Cognitive and moral developmental changes result in student behaviour that often is disruptive in learning environments.
6. Instructional competence can lessen the effects of negative outside influences as well as prevent the misbehaviour that occurs as a result of poor instruction.

In Chapter 4, "Philosophical Approaches to Classroom Management," we describe three theoretical models of classroom management. A series of nine questions helps teachers to define their beliefs about the subject. These questions are then used to analyze, compare, and contrast the three models. It is a teacher's underlying beliefs concerning how children learn and develop and who has the primary responsibility for controlling a child's behaviour that determines which model provides the best fit.

Different management strategies are presented as either compatible or incompatible with certain schools of thought. When teachers employ behaviours that are inconsistent with their beliefs about children, they feel emotionally uncomfortable and usually do not see the desired change in student behaviour.

Teachers exert influence through the use of five different social power bases. In Chapter 4, we place each power base along a continuum, which begins with those power bases most likely to engender students' control over their own behaviour, and proceeds to those bases that foster increasing teacher management over student

Many teachers keep up to date on the latest techniques by attending professional development workshops.

behaviour. The chapter concludes with a discussion of teacher behaviours that are congruent with the various power bases.

These are the principles of classroom management discussed in Chapter 4:

1. Theoretical approaches to classroom management are useful to teachers because they offer a basis for analyzing, understanding, and managing student and teacher behaviour.
2. As social agents, teachers have access to a variety of power bases that can be used to influence student behaviour.
3. The techniques a teacher uses to manage student behaviour should be consistent with the teacher's beliefs about how students learn and develop.

In Chapter 5, "The Professional Teacher," we explore the effective instructional techniques used by the professional teacher. Effective teaching prevents most discipline problems. Our discussion here is divided into two parts. The first part, "The Basics of Effective Teaching," gives an overview of the knowledge experts have gained from research on teacher effects. This research focuses on teacher behaviours that facilitate student achievement on lower-level cognitive tasks as measured by paper-and-pencil tests. The second section of the chapter, "Beyond the Basics," covers more recent conceptualizations of teaching and learning that focus on student cognition and higher-order cognitive learning tasks.

Chapter 5 foregrounds the following two principles:

1. Student learning and on-task behaviour are maximized when teaching strategies are based on what educators know about student development, how people learn, and what constitutes effective teaching.
2. Understanding and using the research on effective teaching enhance the teacher's instructional competence and help to prevent classroom-management problems.

Chapter 6, "Structuring the Environment," details how to structure the environment to minimize disruptive behaviour. Many classroom-management problems arise because students are either unaware of or unclear about what types of behaviours are expected of them or why certain procedures must be followed in the classroom. This lack of awareness usually occurs when teachers are unclear about how they want their students to behave. Thus, developing meaningful classroom guidelines is a key to success.

We present the procedures for designing classroom guidelines with an emphasis on the importance of having both a rationale and stated consequences for each rule. We offer techniques to communicate guidelines to students in a way that maximizes understanding and acceptance.

This chapter also discusses the influence of cultural background on teacher and student values, norms, and expectations for appropriate behaviour. Also in Chapter 6, we advocate using co-operative learning activities and teaching social skills to create classroom group norms that support prosocial behaviour and engage students in learning activities.

The principles discussed in Chapter 6 include the following:

1. When environmental conditions are appropriate for learning, the likelihood of disruptive behaviour is minimized.
2. Students are more likely to follow classroom guidelines if the teacher models appropriate behaviour and explains the relationship of the guidelines to learning, to mutual respect between student and teacher, and to protection and safety of property and individuals.
3. Clearly communicating guidelines to students and obtaining their commitment to following them enhances appropriate classroom behaviour.
4. Enforcing teacher expectations by using natural and logical consequences helps students to learn that they are responsible for the consequences of their behaviour and thus are responsible for controlling their own behaviour.
5. When classroom guidelines and rules match the culture of students' homes and communities, the likelihood that students will behave appropriately is increased.
6. When the teacher creates group norms that are supportive of engagement in learning activities, the likelihood that students will behave appropriately is increased.

Chapters 7, "Managing Common Misbehaviour Problems: Non-verbal Interventions," and 8, "Managing Common Misbehaviour Problems: Verbal Interventions and Use of Logical Consequences," explore the management of common misbehaviours through the use of a three-tiered hierarchical decision-making model of non-verbal and verbal behaviours called *coping skills*. Research reviewed in Chapter 7 reveals that the majority of misbehaviours are verbal interruptions, off-task behaviour, and disruptive physical movements. The frequency of these surface disruptions can be greatly reduced with proper planning, instructional strategies, environmental structure, and verbal and non-verbal teacher behaviours.

We examine in Chapter 7 the first tier of the decision-making hierarchy. It discusses the appropriate use and limitations of three non-verbal coping skills: planned ignoring, signal interference, and proximity interference. The chapter includes an intervention decision-making model that hierarchically orders non-verbal behaviours teachers can use to manage student behaviour. The hierarchy begins with those non-intrusive techniques that give students the greatest opportunity to control their own behaviours and proceeds to intrusive strategies that give the teacher more responsibility for managing student behaviour. We also present five implementation guidelines.

The following principles are the focus of Chapter 7:

1. Classroom-management techniques need to be consistent with the goal of helping students to become self-directing individuals.
2. Use of a pre-planned hierarchy of remedial interventions improves the teacher's ability to manage misbehaviour.
3. The use of a hierarchy that starts with non-intrusive, non-verbal teacher behaviours gives students the opportunity to exercise self-control, minimizes disruption to the teaching/learning process, reduces the likelihood of student confrontation, protects students' safety, and maximizes the teacher's management alternatives.

In Chapter 8, we discuss in detail the second and third tiers of the decision-making hierarchy: verbal intervention and the application of logical consequences. Twelve verbal-intervention techniques are presented, along with nine guidelines for their appropriate use as well as their limitations. Once again, these techniques are ordered along a continuum that ranges from non-intrusive student control to intrusive teacher management of behaviour. The use of verbal intervention is founded on the assumption that teachers do have effective alternatives to angry, personal, sarcastic confrontations with students. Such alternatives typically defuse rather than escalate misbehaviour. The third tier of the decision-making hierarchy, the use of logical consequences, is a powerful technique in managing student behaviour. The concept of logical consequences is explained in detail along with the guidelines teachers use to develop effective logical consequences for a wide range of misbehaviour. We also discuss the assertive delivery of logical consequences.

These are the principles dealt with in Chapter 8:

1. When non-verbal teacher intervention does not lead to appropriate student behaviour, the teacher should employ verbal intervention to deal with the misbehaviour.

2. Some forms of verbal intervention defuse confrontation and reduce misbehaviour; other forms of verbal intervention escalate misbehaviour and confrontation.
3. When verbal intervention does not lead to appropriate student behaviour, the teacher needs to apply logical consequences to the student's misconduct.

Chapter 9, "Classroom Interventions for Chronic Problems," looks at classroom interventions for students with chronic problems. Two long-term problem-solving strategies—relationship building and disrupting the cycle of discouragement—are presented, along with three techniques for managing behaviour. Most strategies used with chronic behavioural problems involve referral outside the classroom. However, there are three effective field-tested, in-classroom techniques: self-monitoring, behaviour contracting, and anecdotal record keeping. The effective use of these three techniques assumes that the teacher's classroom behaviours have met the prerequisites discussed in previous chapters and outlined here. The step-by-step implementation of these techniques is explained specifically and followed by a detailed discussion of the critical communication skills that can make the difference in successful management of chronic misbehaviour. Lastly, we explain teacher-controlled exclusion from the classroom, an interim step between in-classroom management and outside referral.

The following principles are a part of Chapter 9:

1. When dealing with students who pose chronic behavioural problems, teachers should use strategies to resolve the problems within the classroom before seeking outside assistance.
2. Finding positive qualities in students who have chronic behavioural problems and building positive relationships with those students increase the possibility that the problems can be resolved within the classroom.
3. Breaking the cycle of discouragement in which most students with chronic behavioural problems are trapped increases the likelihood that the problems can be resolved within the classroom.
4. When teachers conduct private conferences and use effective communication skills with students who have chronic behavioural problems, the likelihood that the problems can be resolved within the classroom increases.
5. Interventions that require students to recognize their inappropriate behaviour and its impact on others increase the likelihood that the problems can be resolved within the classroom.
6. Interventions that require students with chronic behavioural problems to be accountable for trying to control their behaviour on a daily basis increase the likelihood that the problems can be resolved within the classroom.
7. Interventions that call for gradual but consistent improvement in behaviour increase the likelihood that chronic problems can be resolved within the classroom.

Chapter 10, "Seeking Outside Assistance," offers outside-the-classroom advice. When in-classroom techniques have been exhausted and have not resulted in appropriate student behaviour, it is necessary to seek outside assistance. Teachers are offered guidelines to follow when deciding whether or not outside consultation is warranted. The concept of a success–failure ratio is explained, and how this ratio contributes to persisting misbehaviour is discussed.

Other students may need outside referral even though they do not display any forms of chronic misbehaviour. These students may exhibit signs of emotional stress or family dysfunction. We discuss six warning signs of these problems. A referral process that stresses multidisciplinary team consultation is offered as an effective means of working with these students. The roles of the counsellor, parents, administrator, and school psychologist are presented along with the legal issues that must be considered when making outside referrals.

Parental support and co-operation with the school is critical when working with students who misbehave chronically. The authors set out specific guidelines that teachers can use to decide when parents need to be contacted; we also discuss techniques on how to conduct parent conferences to facilitate and enhance parental support and co-operation.

These are the classroom management principles underlined in Chapter 10:

1. Professional teachers recognize that some chronic behavioural problems are not responsive to treatment within the classroom or are beyond their expertise and necessitate specialized outside assistance.
2. When outside assistance must be sought to manage a chronic misbehaviour problem adequately and appropriately, the use of a multidisciplinary team is the most effective approach.
3. Parental support and co-operation with the school is critical when attempting to manage a student who chronically misbehaves. Careful planning and skilled conferencing techniques are essential in developing a positive working relationship between home and school.

Professional Decision-Making Hierarchy

In the teaching profession, hierarchies, taxonomies, and classification systems are used to organize vast amounts of isolated bits of data into manageable, comprehensible bodies of knowledge. Hierarchies may be used for more than just organizing information. They may also be used to guide professional decisions. The advantages of using a hierarchical approach are twofold: (1) it allows for the systematic implementation of the knowledge that informs the practice of a given profession, and (2) it provides the practitioner with a variety of approaches rather than a limited few. Thus, the hierarchical approach increases the likelihood that successful outcomes will result. The hierarchical strategies are based on professional knowledge, and if early strategies are ineffective, there are numerous other strategies that may produce positive results.

Applying a hierarchical approach to classroom-management decisions allows teachers to employ knowledge effectively in order to understand, prevent, and

CASE 1.3 • *The Vice-Principal Wants to See Whom?*

Ms. Iannizi decides that one way to maintain discipline in her grade 8 class is to be firm and consistent with the enforcement of classroom rules and procedures, right from the beginning of the school year. One of her rules is that students must raise their hands to be called on before answering questions. She explains this rule to the class: "By grade 8, I'm sure you all understand that everyone has an equal chance to participate. For this to happen, all students must raise their hands to be called on. I hope I will have to tell you this only once."

During the year's first question-and-answer session, Jill calls out the answer. Ms. Iannizi reminds her, "Jill, you must raise your hand if you want to answer. I do not expect this to happen again." However, it isn't much longer until Jill calls out again in an enthusiastic and energetic manner. This time Ms. Iannizi says, "Jill, please leave the room and stand in the hallway. When you feel that you can raise your hand, come back and join us."

In a few minutes, Jill returns to class and, as before, calls out an answer. This time Ms. Iannizi says, "Go to the office and speak with the vice-principal." Within minutes, Jill is sent back to class and apologizes to Ms. Iannizi, saying that she keeps forgetting because her previous teacher never commented on this behaviour. Later that day, Ms. Iannizi receives a message in her mailbox requesting her to set up a meeting with the vice-principal to discuss the matter.

Questions to Consider

1. Why was Ms. Iannizi's attempt to be consistent problematic?
2. What new problems did she create for herself and for her students by removing Jill from the classroom?
3. What could she have done when Jill called out the second time? The third time?
4. How can Ms. Iannizi help Jill develop appropriate answering behaviours?
5. What message do you think that Ms. Iannizi is attempting to send to her students? How do you think they are interpreting that message?

---

manage student behaviour. When such an approach is not used, teachers may find themselves with few alternatives for managing student behaviour. Consider, for example, Case 1.3.

Needless to say, Ms. Iannizi's approach to managing a common student behaviour was a gross overreaction. It not only led to an administrator-initiated meeting, but also would probably result in increased student misbehaviour as students recognize the discrepancy between the minimal student behaviour and the maximal teacher response. Furthermore, Ms. Iannizi's approach left her with few if any alternatives in managing other students who called out answers in the future. It is highly unlikely that parents, students, administrators, or other teachers would support this approach. The technique of exclusion from class is usually reserved for use after many less intrusive strategies have been attempted. In other words, classroom management is best accomplished when the teacher employs management strategies in a hierarchical order.

TABLE 1.1 A Hierarchical Approach to Successful Classroom Management

Part I. Foundations (Chapters 1–4)	Part II. Prevention (Chapters 5–6)	Part III. Interventions for Common Behaviour Problems (Chapters 7–8)	Part IV. Interventions for Chronic Behaviour Problems (Chapters 9–10)
Conceptualizing the process of teaching	Developing effective teaching strategies	Using proactive coping skills	Relationship building
Understanding classroom management principles	*Lesson design*	Using preplanned, remedial non-verbal intervention	Disrupting the cycle of discouragement
Understanding the decision-making hierarchical approach	*Student motivation: teacher variables*	*Planned ignoring*	Using self-monitoring
Defining a behavioural problem	*Teacher expectations*	*Signal interference*	Using anecdotal record procedure
Understanding the extent of behavioural problems in today's schools	*Classroom questioning*	*Proximity control*	Using behavioural contracts
Understanding how behavioural problems affect teaching and learning	*Time-on-task*	*Touch control*	Understanding the nature of persisting misbehaviour
Understanding societal change and its influence on children's behaviours	Teaching for understanding	Using preplanned verbal intervention	Recognizing when outside assistance is needed
Recognizing student needs	Authentic instruction	*Adjacent reinforcement*	Making referrals
Understanding developmental changes and accompanying behaviours	Thinking and problem-solving skills	*Calling on the student*	*Counsellors*
Recognizing the importance of instructional competence	Creating learning communities	*Humour*	*Administrators*
Understanding and employing different power bases of teachers	Teaching for multiple intelligences	*"I message"*	*School psychologists*
Referent	Student motivation: student cognition	*Direct appeal*	Working with parents
Expert	Designing the physical environment	*Positive phrasing*	Protecting student rights
Legitimate	Establishing classroom guidelines	*"Are not for"*	
Reward/Coercive	*Determining procedures*	*Reminder of rules*	
Understanding theories of classroom management	*Determining rules*	*Glasser's triplets*	
Student-directed	*Determining consequences*	*Explicit redirection*	
Collaborative	natural • logical • contrived	*Canter's "broken record"*	
Teacher-directed	*Communicating rules*	Applying logical consequences	
	Obtaining commitments		
	Teaching rules		
	Understanding cultural embeddedness of behaviour		
	Creating positive group norms		
	The CALM model		

When teachers use a professional body of knowledge to make decisions, the decisions are usually professionally acceptable and defendable, and result in desired changes in students' behaviours. When teachers make "gut" or emotional decisions, sometimes called *reactions*, the decisions more often than not result in unexpected and undesirable student behaviours, as Ms. Iannizi discovered. The principles of classroom management and the decision-making hierarchy of coping skills presented in this book have served many educators well in making effective decisions concerning the management of student behaviour.

We have also developed a model of sequential strategies, which we have named **CALM** (see the four keywords—*consider*, *act*, *lessen*, and *manage*—in the levels outlined below), for managing inappropriate classroom behaviours. The rationale for developing this model emerged from our discussions with educators who indicated that it would be helpful for beginning teachers, in particular, to acquire a list of strategies that have proven effective when dealing with various disruptive classroom behaviours. We believe that a layered method for analyzing and managing behavioural concerns is a superior approach to trying to anticipate all classroom challenges and providing methods for coping with each challenge separately. After carefully considering the types of questions that educators, from teacher candidates to experienced classroom teachers, raise about classroom management, we have developed CALM as a flexible, hierarchical model for examining and managing challenges that may affect the classroom environment.

CALM will be discussed fully in Chapter 6, and we will refer to it throughout the text where appropriate. For now, we will provide the essential steps to the model.

An additional two hierarchies are presented in *Principles of Classroom Management*. The first is a summary of how classroom management should be viewed. The chapters are grouped into four parts that represent this hierarchy (see the Contents on pages iii–vi). The first part, "Foundations"—comprising Chapters 1 through 4—presents the foundational knowledge base. Part Two, "Prevention"—Chapters 5 and 6—examines the prevention of management problems. Part Three, "Interventions for Common Behaviour Problems"—Chapters 7 and 8—deals with the management of common misbehaviour problems. The fourth and final part, "Interventions for Chronic Behaviour Problems"—Chapters 9 and 10—addresses the issues related to managing chronic misbehaviour problems.

The second hierarchy, which is a subset of the CALM model, includes the introduction and implementation of management strategies once the teacher determines that it is necessary to proceed to Level III. This hierarchy is a decision-making model that uses specific techniques called coping skills. Entering the decision-making model, the teacher finds a variety of non-intrusive coping skills that provide students with the opportunity to manage their own behaviour while at the same time curbing the common forms of classroom misbehaviour efficiently and effectively (Shrigley, 1985). As the teacher moves through the coping skills, the techniques become more and more intrusive, with the teacher playing an increasingly larger role in managing student behaviour.

The CALM Model

The **CALM** strategy provides the following steps as a general guide for handling classroom-management issues. It can become automatic and be applied as needed. When these levels become an instinctive part of the teacher's repertoire of strategies, along with other components of the effective classroom (including the development of a positive rapport), the successful teacher should be able to determine quickly the suitable level to apply in order to avoid serious disruptions to the learning environment.

Level I—Consider

When a student's behaviour becomes disruptive, the teacher should **consider** the following question to initiate a response process. "Does the behaviour change, affect, or disrupt the classroom learning environment, teacher, or students?"

Level II—Act

Once the behaviour has become a "distracting" force for the teacher, the next level of intervention is introduced. This occurs when it becomes necessary to **act**.

Level III—Lessen

Since it is important to minimize distraction and not give undue attention to inappropriate behaviour, it is important to **lessen** the use of invasive responses in dealing with a situation that requires action.

Level IV—Manage

Manage the milieu to quickly return to an effective learning environment.

The overall hierarchy of *Principles of Classroom Management* is illustrated in Table 1.1 on page 17.

Summary

In this chapter, we first discussed a critical premise concerning successful classroom management that the reader should understand clearly before continuing: teaching (which is defined as "the use of pre-planned behaviours—founded in learning principles and child-development theory and directed toward both instructional delivery and classroom management—that increase the probability of effecting a positive change in student behaviour") and classroom management are really the same process. Therefore, by deliberately changing their own behaviour, teachers can help to bring about positive changes in students' behaviours. We then explained the principles and the decision-making hierarchical approach to classroom management on which this entire book is based. These serve as the foundation on which specific management techniques are developed throughout the rest of the book.

Key Terms

behavioural problem (or inappropriate behaviour): in the opinion of the teacher, when a student interferes with the act of teaching or with the rights of others to learn, or causes psychological or physical harm, or destroys property.

CALM model: a flexible, hierarchical model for examining and managing challenges that may affect the classroom environment.

CALM Level I—Consider: When a student's behaviour becomes disruptive, the teacher should **consider** the following question to initiate a response process. "Does the behaviour change, affect, or disrupt the classroom learning environment, teacher, or students?"

CALM Level II—Act: Once the behaviour has become a "distracting" force for the teacher, the next level of intervention is introduced. This occurs when it becomes necessary to **act**.

CALM Level III—Lessen: Since it is important to minimize distraction and not give undue attention to inappropriate behaviour, it is important to **lessen** the use of invasive responses in dealing with a situation that requires action.

CALM Level IV—Manage: Manage the milieu to quickly return to an effective learning environment.

classroom management: a teacher's ability to establish and maintain an environment that is suited to teaching and learning. The teacher possesses a repertoire of procedures to ensure optimal learning for all students.

professional knowledge: pedagogical and practical knowledge related to teaching and learning.

Exercises

1. Many teachers define *teaching* as the delivery of knowledge or the giving of information. In your opinion, are these definitions adequate? If so, why? If not, what are the limitations?

2. What problems may arise when teachers base most of their decisions on "gut reactions"? Give specific examples.

3. In recent years, there has been much discussion over whether or not teaching is a profession. In your opinion, is teaching a profession? If yes, why? If no, why not? What must occur to make it a profession?

4. Review the definition of *teaching* presented in this chapter. Do you agree with the definition, or should it be modified? If you agree, explain why. If not, explain what should be changed.

5. The definition of teaching in this chapter focuses on teachers changing their behaviour to manage discipline problems because that is the only behaviour over which they have

control. Given this, how might you reply to a principal who believes that teachers should be able to control their students' behaviour?

6. We discuss in Chapter 1 how teacher behaviours (affecting) influence changes in student behaviour (targeted). For each targeted behaviour that follows, suggest an appropriate affecting behaviour and explain why such a behaviour would increase the likelihood of a positive change in the student's behaviour.

Situation	Targeted Behaviour	Affecting Behaviour
calling out answers	raising hand	
not volunteering	volunteering	
daydreaming	on task	
forgetting textbook	prepared for class	
short answers to questions	expanded answers	
few students answer	more participation questions	
passing notes	on task	
walking around room	in seat	
noisy during first five minutes of class	on task from start of class	

7. Suggest some ways that busy teachers can keep up with the latest research on effective teaching.

8. This book offers principles of classroom management. Principles are usually very broad statements. How can teachers use these principles to guide their teaching practices and specific management techniques?

9. The authors of this book support the use of a decision-making hierarchical approach to classroom management. Discuss the advantages as well as the disadvantages to such an approach.

Weblinks

Health Canada
www.hc-sc.gc.ca
The federal government's health site, designed to help Canadians maintain and improve their health, with advice and resources for issues like behavioural problems.

The Learning Disabilities Association of Canada
www.ldac-taac.ca
The LDAC is a non-profit voluntary organization founded in 1963 that acts as a voice for persons with learning disabilities and those who support them.

The Ontario College of Teachers
www.oct.ca
The OCT licenses, governs, and regulates the practice of teaching in Ontario.

California Department of Education
www.cde.ca.gov/ls/ss
This website provides information about safe schools and violence-prevention programs in California.

CanTeach: Classroom Management
www.canteach.ca/elementary/classman1.html
This webpage takes a positive approach to classroom management by listing ways to
encourage good behaviour.

2

The Nature of Behavioural Problems

Focus on the Principles of Classroom Management

1. When does a behaviour become a problem?
2. For teaching to be effective, what skills must teachers possess?
3. What are the benefits to both students and teachers when classrooms are well managed?

Introduction

When educators, public officials, or parents with school-age children discuss schooling, the topic of classroom behaviour inevitably arises. Behaviour and classroom management are topics that have been widely discussed by both professionals and the public for a considerable period of time. Canadian researchers recently reported that more of a classroom teacher's time is spent managing behavioural and social problems than actually teaching. One-quarter of teacher respondents to a survey in Nova Scotia said they had faced physical violence in their schools ("A Quarter of Nova Scotia teachers . . . ," 2003).

In these discussions, it is generally assumed that everyone knows what is meant by a behavioural problem and that inappropriate behaviour poses major problems for some educators. However, when pre- or in-service teachers are asked, "What is a behavioural problem?" there is no overall agreement in their responses. Contrary to popular belief, there does not seem to be a professional consensus about which behaviours negatively affect teaching and learning in the classroom.

Almost everyone agrees that it is important for students to behave properly in classrooms. What are the actual effects of misbehaviour on students and their learning and on teachers and their teaching? In this chapter, we will (1) develop a working definition of what constitutes a behavioural problem in a classroom; (2) assess the magnitude of behavioural problems in Canadian schools today; and (3) determine the effect of misbehaviour on both students and teachers.

Defining a Behavioural Problem

Teachers often describe students who have behavioural problems as lazy, unmotivated, belligerent, aggressive, angry, or argumentative. These words at best are imprecise, judgmental, and descriptive of a wide range of behaviours. After all, a student can be lazy or angry and yet not be a disruptive factor in the classroom. Furthermore, attribution theory (Weiner, 1980; Winzer, 2002) tells us that our thoughts guide our feelings, which in turn guide our behaviour. Therefore, when teachers describe children using negative labels and react to children negatively, these same children may seek to continue this type of response because a negative reaction is better than no reaction (Taylor, 1996). Also, negative teacher reaction is ineffective in helping children learn appropriate behaviour (Martin, Dworet, and Davis, 1997). Thus, for a definition of a behavioural problem to be useful to a teacher, it must clearly differentiate student behaviour that requires immediate corrective action from that which does not.

Surprisingly, the most basic question—"What types of student behaviours constitute classroom problems?"—has rarely been considered in recent literature. Having a clear understanding of which behaviours are inappropriate in the classroom is a prerequisite for effective classroom management. Without this understanding, it is impossible for teachers to design rational and meaningful classroom guidelines and communicate them to their students, to recognize misbehaviour when it occurs, or to employ management strategies effectively and consistently.

In developing an operational definition, it is helpful to examine the most comprehensive definition offered by Shrigley (1979), who states that any behaviour that disrupts the teaching act or is psychologically or physically unsafe constitutes a disruptive behaviour. This definition includes behaviours that do not necessarily interfere with the teaching act but are psychologically or physically unsafe, such as running in a science lab, using unsafe tools or laboratory equipment, threatening other students, and constantly bullying classmates. However, there are problems with this definition. For instance, if a student defaces school property, under this definition it would not be considered a behavioural problem because the act does not interfere with teaching and classroom safety.

It should be clear from this discussion that any definition of the term *behavioural problem* must provide teachers with the means to determine instantly whether or not any given behaviour requires discipline or intervention. Once this identification has been made, the teacher can then decide which specific **teacher intervention** should be used.

Consider the following six scenarios. For each one, ask yourself the following questions:

1. Is there a behavioural problem?
2. If there is a behavioural problem, who is exhibiting it?
3. Does the behaviour require discipline or intervention?

Scenario 1: Marisa quietly enters the room and takes her seat. The teacher requests that students take out their homework. Marisa does not take out her homework but instead

When teachers are not prepared to start classes on time, behavioural problems can result.

takes out a magazine and begins to flip quietly through the pages. The teacher ignores Marisa and involves the class in reviewing the homework.

Scenario 2: Marisa quietly enters the room and takes her seat. The teacher requests that students take out their homework. Marisa does not take out her homework but instead takes out a magazine and begins to flip quietly through the pages. The teacher publicly announces that there will be no review of the homework until Marisa puts away the magazine and takes out her homework.

Scenario 3: Marisa quietly enters the room and takes her seat. The teacher requests that students take out their homework. Marisa does not take out her homework but instead takes out a magazine and begins to flip quietly through the pages. The teacher begins to involve the class in reviewing the homework and at the same time moves closer to Marisa. The review continues with the teacher standing in close proximity to Marisa.

Scenario 4: Marisa quietly enters the room and takes her seat. The teacher requests that students take out their homework. Marisa does not take out her homework but instead takes out a magazine and begins to show the magazine to the students who sit next to her. The teacher ignores Marisa and begins to involve the class in the review of the homework. Marisa continues to show the magazine to her neighbours.

Scenario 5: Marisa quietly enters the room and takes her seat. The teacher requests that students take out their homework. Marisa does not take out her homework but instead takes out a magazine and begins to show the magazine to the students who sit next to her. The teacher does not begin the review and, in front of the class, loudly demands that Marisa put the magazine away and get out her homework. The teacher stares at Marisa for the two minutes that it takes her to put the magazine away and find her homework. Once Marisa finds her homework, the teacher begins the review.

Scenario 6: Marisa quietly enters the room and takes her seat. The teacher requests that students take out their homework. Marisa does not take out her homework but instead takes out a magazine and begins to show the magazine to the students who sit next to her. The teacher begins the homework review and, at the same time, walks toward Marisa. While a student is answering a question, the teacher, as privately as possible, assertively asks Marisa to take out her homework and put the magazine away.

If you are like many of the teachers to whom we have given these same six scenarios, you probably have found answering the questions that preceded them difficult. Furthermore, if you have taken time to discuss your answers with others, you undoubtedly have discovered your answers differ from theirs.

Much of the difficulty in determining an appropriate teacher response can be avoided using our following definition of the term **behavioural problem**, which recognizes that classroom problems are multifaceted: "A behavioural problem is behaviour that (1) interferes with the teaching act, (2) interferes with the rights of others to learn, (3) is psychologically or physically unsafe, or (4) destroys property." This definition not only covers calling out, defacing property, or disturbing other students, but also other common behaviours that teachers confront every day. Note, however, that the definition does not limit behaviour to student behaviour. This is very important, for it means teachers must consider their own behaviour as well as their students' behaviour.

Using our definition, review the six scenarios again and compare your analysis with ours. In scenario 1 there is no need for discipline or intervention because neither Marisa's nor the teacher's behaviour is interfering with the rights of others to learn. The teacher has decided to ignore Marisa for the time being and focus on involving the class with the homework review.

In scenario 2, the teacher has caused a problem because he has interrupted the homework review to reprimand Marisa, who isn't interfering with any other student's learning. In this situation, it is the teacher who is interfering with the rights of the students to learn.

In scenario 3, there is no evident problem. Neither Marisa's nor the teacher's behaviour is interfering with the other students' right to learn. The teacher has not decided to ignore Marisa but has wisely chosen an intervention strategy that allows the homework review to continue.

In scenario 4, both Marisa and the teacher are displaying problematic behaviours. Marisa is interfering with the other students' right to learn, and, by ignoring her, the teacher also interferes with the other students' right to learn.

In scenario 5, Marisa and the teacher are again displaying problematic behaviour. Marisa's sharing of the magazine is disruptive, but the teacher's choice of intervention is also a problem. In fact, it is the teacher's behaviour—not Marisa's—that is actually interfering more with learning.

In scenario 6, Marisa's behaviour is distinctly problematic. However, the teacher's intervention strategy enables the class to continue to learn and simultaneously manages Marisa's behaviour.

The guidelines provided by the definition make it far easier to determine whether or not a behavioural problem exists, and, if it does, who has the problem. Most misbehaviour can be managed at some later time, after the other students have begun their work, during a break, or before or after class. When a behaviour becomes problematic for the **learning environment**, however, the teacher must intervene immediately, because by definition there exists a behaviour that is interfering with other students' rights or safety. When teachers inappropriately or ineffectively use management strategies that result in interference with the learning of others, they in fact become the disruptive factor.

Let's examine Case 2.1. Did Tobias's late opening of his book interfere with teaching or his classmates' learning? Was it unsafe or did it destroy property? Was it not Mr. Karis's behaviour that caused the escalation of a minor problem that would have corrected itself? Using our definition, Mr. Karis's behaviour escalated the problem. It is doubtful that any teacher intervention was necessary at all. See Chapter 7, "Managing Common Misbehaviour Problems: Non-verbal Interventions," for a full discussion of when teacher intervention is appropriate. Note that under the terms of the definition of behavioural problems, inappropriate or ill-timed classroom procedures, public address announcements, and school policies also tend to disrupt the teaching and/or learning process.

CASE 2.1 • *Can a Teacher's Behaviour Be the Disruptive Factor?*

Usually when the bell rings, the students in Mr. Karis's grade 9 class have their books out and are quietly waiting to begin work. Today, when Mr. Karis finishes taking attendance and is asking a few questions to review the previous day's work, he notices that Tobias is just starting to get his book out and appears to be unmotivated and lethargic. Mr. Karis feels annoyed and asks abruptly why he isn't ready. Tobias replies in a somewhat surly manner that he has a lot on his mind. Mr. Karis then reminds Tobias in a strong tone that when the bell rings he is to be ready to start. Tobias replies in a way that makes it very clear that he, too, is annoyed,

"Look, you don't know what my morning's been like!" Mr. Karis feels embarrassed and that his authority is being threatened in front of the other students. He tells Tobias sharply that he "is not to be spoken to in that tone of voice."

The rest of the students are now either talking or laughing quietly among themselves and deeply involved in the outcome of the confrontation. By the time Tobias decides it probably is not in his best interest to continue the escalating conflict, at least five minutes of class time has elapsed and no teaching or learning has taken place and the rest of the class is unfocused. Mr. Karis is left feeling disempowered.

Problem Student Behaviour Outside the Definition

By now, some readers have probably thought of many student behaviours that are not covered by our definition: for example, students who refuse to turn in homework, who are not prepared for class, or who are daydreaming, as well as those who give the teacher "dirty looks." A careful analysis of these behaviours will reveal that under the terms of the definition, they are not problems that require teacher intervention. Rather, they may be **motivational problems**.

Motivational problems can occur because of low levels of self-confidence, low expectations for success, lack of interest in academics, lost feelings of autonomy, achievement anxieties, or fears of success or failure (Novak and Purkey, 2001; Stipek, 1998). Thus, working with students who have motivational problems often involves long-term individualized intervention and/or referrals to professionals outside the classroom.

Although in-depth coverage of motivational problems is beyond the scope of this book, we must recognize that some of the very strategies used to manage these problems—problems that themselves generally do not interfere with other students' learning—actually disturb the learning of others or reduce the time spent on learning. Therefore, it is best to work with students who have motivational problems individually, *after* involving the rest of the class in the day's learning activities. Doing so allows the teacher to protect the class's right to learn and to maximize the time allocated for learning.

Even though the strategies presented later in this book are usually used to manage behavioural problems, some of them, particularly coping skills and anecdotal record keeping, can be used quite successfully for motivational problems (Duquette, 2001). We cannot stress enough, however, that motivational problems must be properly addressed, usually by focusing on students' expectations of success and the value students place on the learning activity, so that they do not develop behavioural problems (see Chapter 5, "The Professional Teacher"). Case 2.2 illustrates how one teacher ensures that this does not occur.

Ms. Polinski recognized that Rahul's behaviour did not interfere with the teaching and learning act and so did not need immediate action. She used effective strategies that protected the class's right to learn. The strategies were the beginning of a long-term effort to build up Rahul's interest and confidence in mathematics and to have him

CASE 2.2 • *Solving a Motivational Problem*

Ms. Polinski teaches grade 4. She believes that she is a good teacher and spends a great deal of time preparing interesting units of study and motivational activities to enhance her students' learning experiences. She is concerned about one of her students, Rahul, who rarely participates in class and often is the last one to begin classwork. She has observed him closely and believes that he is shy and lacks self-esteem. He is not a problem in class and the other students treat him with respect, although he is often ignored when plans are made for recess and after-school activities.

One day, the class is assigned math problems for seatwork. After a few minutes, Ms. Polinski notices that Rahul has not started. She CALMly walks over to Rahul, kneels down beside his desk, and asks him if he needs any help. This is enough to get Rahul to begin his math problems. Ms. Polinski waits until three problems are completed; she then tells Rahul that since he understood them so well, he should put them on the board. Rahul complies and neatly presents his on the board but accomplishes the task with little enthusiasm. After the class has finished the assignment, Ms. Polinski begins to review the answers, stressing the correct procedures Rahul used to solve the problems and thanking him for his board work. There is little reaction from Rahul.

Questions to Consider

1. Describe Rahul's feelings about this incident.
2. What do you think Rahul's behaviour will be a week later?
3. What is Ms. Polinski's belief about behavioural problems in her class?
4. How can Ms. Polinski build on this beginning without being too obvious and thus risking embarrassing Rahul?

become an active, participating member of the class. Probably, many readers have witnessed similar situations in which the teacher, unfortunately, chose to deal with the student's behaviour in ways that were disruptive to the entire class.

Extent of the Problem

When Canadians were asked how they felt about their education system, 57 percent said that they were satisfied with the education system in their province. The most satisfied were residents of the Prairies (72 percent), Quebecers (68 percent), and 18- to 24-year-olds (74 percent). Except in British Columbia (45 percent), more than 50 percent of residents of other regions said they were satisfied with the education system in their province: Alberta (59 percent), Atlantic provinces (55 percent), and Ontario (52 percent) (Leger, 2002). However, according to an Ipsos-Reid (1999) survey of 1515 Canadian adults, 40 percent of the respondents had concerns about student violence and behavioural problems in the public school system. To some extent, these concerns may reflect current fears resulting from the high media coverage of school shootings in both Canada and the United States in the last few years. Recent shootings in Toronto high schools have prompted the Ontario government to issue a new school health and safety initiative in the 2007–08 school year (www.labour.gov.on.ca/english/news/2007/07-103.html).

Certainly, Canada has not escaped from the headlines associated with severe violence in schools. The most serious incident was in December 1989, when Marc Lépine killed 14 women engineering students at l'École Polytechnique in Quebec. In 1999, a high school student was killed and another wounded in Tabor, Alberta, by a fellow student. In 2000, a 15-year-old Ottawa student stabbed four other students and a computer technician. More recently, in 2006 a gunman entered Dawson College in Montreal and began a shootout with the police. While these were shocking, high-profile cases of extreme violence, they are, fortunately, quite uncommon in Canada.

The media's focused reporting on violent youth crime stories may contribute to a distortion of facts and, as well, it may accentuate the amount of youth crime. "An Ontario study found that 94 percent of youth crime stories in the media were about violent offences when less than 25 percent of Ontario's youth court cases actually involved violent crime" (Statistics Canada, 2004). In reality, violent youth crime was down by 2 percent in 2002 (Statistics Canada, 2004). Of the 84 592 youth cases heard in youth court in 2002–03, just under 75 percent involved non-violent offences such as mischief and theft—and minor assaults accounted for more than half of the violent crimes committed by youth. Even though homicides and other serious crimes committed by youth are still very rare, they are almost always portrayed as a growing trend. In reality, the opposite is true. "In 2002, there were 42 youths charged with homicide: 7 fewer than the average over the past decade" (Statistics Canada, 2004). None of these crimes were committed on school property.

It has to be acknowledged that even with the most recent drop, the 2002 youth violent crime rate was still 7 percent higher than a decade earlier. Still, the fact remains that young people ages 12 to 17 are less likely to be charged with violent crimes than adults. Also, our schools are safer than many believe—youth crime on school property is relatively rare.

Even though only a small percentage of Canadian youth are charged with very serious offences (Statistics Canada, 2002, 2004), and even though well-behaved students greatly outnumber those who exhibit inappropriate behaviour, educators require skills to help them deal with serious behaviour challenges. Numerous authors argue that school boards should establish and implement policies and provide programs that help teachers develop strategies to manage behaviours not appropriate for the classroom (e.g. Holt, 2007; Benn, 2002; Bonta and Hanson, 1994; Fitzpatrick, 1994; Crux, 1993; James, 1993; MacDougall, 1993; Patus, 1993; Roy, 1993). This is an important professional issue, because the reasons teachers give for exiting early from the profession are that they have become dissatisfied with student behaviour or the working environment (Canadian Teachers' Federation, 2002).

Students themselves are usually aware of the frequency of disruptive behaviour. According to a national poll of teenagers, conducted just prior to the Littleton,

Daydreaming students are not interfering with teaching or the rights of others to learn. Therefore, the teacher should first involve the rest of the class in the learning activity before individually influencing the daydreamer.

Colorado, and Taber, Alberta, school shootings, one-third of Canadian teens said that violence had increased in their schools over the previous five years. Younger teens, ages 12 to 15, are more likely than older teens to say that violence has escalated in their schools. Teens living in BC (40 percent), Alberta (39 percent), and Ontario (37 percent) appear more likely to say that the incidence of violence in their schools has increased recently. Female teens are also more likely to say that violence has been on the rise in the last five years. On the other hand, 23 percent of teens feel that violence in schools has decreased over the past five years, while 41 percent say that there has been no change (Angus Reid Group, 1999).

In attempting to assess the magnitude of the discipline problem in the past, Doyle (1978) has pointed out that serious historical investigation of student behaviour is lacking and the studies that are available use data that are typically incomplete and, in some cases, unreliable. Doyle has reviewed evidence from the few available sources and has found that crime (violence and vandalism) was not a serious concern among school officials from the late 1800s to the early 1900s. However, there is evidence that juvenile crime outside of school was a problem during this period. In the early 1900s, less than 50 percent of the school-age population was enrolled in school. Of this group, only 40 percent finished grade 8, and approximately 10 percent graduated from high school. Thus, the children most likely to commit crimes were not in school (Hawes, 1971; Mennell, 1973; Schlossman, 1977).

Since the early 1980s, researchers have made a concerted effort to distinguish between crime (violence and vandalism) and common misbehaviour (off-task and disruptive classroom behaviours). Such a distinction is essential because crime and routine classroom misbehaviour are inherently different problems that require different solutions administered by a variety of professionals both inside and outside the school. Whereas teachers are responsible for managing routine classroom misbehaviour, crime often must come under the control of the school administration and outside law-enforcement agencies.

By the mid-1980s, Wayson was able to state that "most schools never experience incidents of crime and those that do seldom experience them frequently or regularly" (1985, 129), but disruptive behaviour of "the kinds that have characterized schoolchildren for generations . . . continue to pose frequent and perplexing problems for teachers" (1985, 127).

These conclusions were supported by numerous studies reporting that teachers and administrators consistently ranked common classroom misbehaviours (excessive talking, failure to do assignments, disrespect, lateness) as the most serious and frequent disturbances, whereas they ranked crime (vandalism, theft, assault) as the least serious disturbances to their teaching or the least frequently occurring (Huber, 1984; Levin, 1980; Thomas, Goodall, and Brown, 1983; Weber and Sloan, 1986).

The schools of the late 1980s and early 1990s were perceived as experiencing less crime than the schools of the 1970s, and even though classroom misbehaviour continued to be a major problem, it too was perceived as lessening in frequency. By the late 1990s, however, there were indications that these trends were reversing, and students agreed that violence in school was increasing (Angus Reid Group, 1999).

One form of violence that is causing great concern among parents and in Canadian schools is bullying. Bullying has received much attention in the past few years and, unfortunately, is a common problem in Canadian schools, starting in the earliest months of schooling (Pepler and Craig, 1995). Bullying refers to the physical and/or psychological abuse of power by peers (usually children against other children) and can occur verbally and/or physically; directly (face to face) and/or indirectly (gossip or exclusion) (Olweus, 1991). The result of bullying is that the victims often suffer from severe anxiety, intimidation, and chronic fear (Marini, Spear, and Bombay, 1999). A 1997 survey of Canadians revealed that 6 percent of children admitted to bullying others over a six-week span and that 15 percent of children reported they had been victimized in the same way (O'Connell, Pepler, and Craig, 1999). Systematic observations of children on playgrounds note that some type of bullying occurs every 7 minutes. When children are in the classroom, bullying occurs once every 25 minutes (O'Connell, Pepler, and Craig, 1999). Boys and girls are equally likely to report being bullied (Charach, Pepler, and Ziegler, 1995). Further studies have indicated that 30 to 40 percent of children who bully grow up to have problems with violence later in life (Craig, Peters, and Konarski, 1998).

The Canadian federal government's National Strategy on Community Safety and Crime Prevention was established in 1998 to help people deal with crime and victimization. This program placed particular emphasis on children, youth, women, and Aboriginal people. The strategy supports schools' efforts to encourage resiliency in children and build healthy learning environments. Specifically, the program is raising the consciousness of teachers and children alike to establish grassroots initiatives to combat bullying. This strategy also supports the current belief that if schools are to provide a safe place for learning, the issue of bullying needs to be addressed explicitly. Currently in Canada, schools are adopting clear policies regarding bullying and consistently applying consequences. For many school boards, this means adopting a zero-tolerance policy.

Thus, as the new millennium progresses, every successful teacher will have to be able to recognize the genesis of potentially violent situations and manage disruptive classroom behaviours properly. Teachers must be proficient in defusing such situations and directing students toward more prosocial means of conflict resolution (Novak and Purkey, 2001).

The Effect of Classroom-Disruptive Behaviour on Teaching and Learning

When classrooms are characterized by disruptive behaviour, the teaching and learning environment can be adversely affected. The amount of interference in the teaching and learning environment is related to the type, frequency, and duration of the disruptive behaviour. Disruptive behaviour also affects students' psychological safety, readiness to learn, and future behaviours.

In the course of the last decade, we have had the opportunity to interact with thousands of teacher candidates as well as with many in-service teachers and school administrators who want to improve their classroom-management skills. One of the first questions we always ask is, "Why do students have to behave in a classroom?" At first, we were somewhat embarrassed to ask such a basic question because we felt there was a universally obvious answer. To our surprise, however, the answer was not obvious to others. The answer, of course, involves the widely accepted learning principle that the more time spent on learning (time on task, or engaged time), the more learning will take place (Brophy, 1988; Winzer, 2002). In other words, disruptive, off-task behaviour takes time away from learning.

CASE 2.3 • *Discipline: A Costly Waste of Time*

Mr. Kay, a grade 9 science teacher and head of the science department in the high school, teaches four classes a day. Sometimes, his departmental duties cause him to be a couple of minutes late for class. He is content to allow his students, on entering the room, to stand around and talk rather than prepare their materials for class. As a result, each time the class convenes it usually does not begin until five minutes after the bell has rung.

Case 2.3 touches on a very common problem in classrooms: namely, the tremendous amount of time that can be wasted over the course of a school year by some very minor off-task behaviours. Over a period of a week, 25 minutes that could have been directed toward learning are wasted. Over the 40-week school year, 1000 minutes are consumed by off-task behaviour. This amounts to more than 22 class periods, or approximately one-ninth of the school year, that could have been directed toward learning goals. If the calculations also consider the 120 students Mr. Kay teaches per day, 2640 "student class periods" were not spent on learning science.

It has been reported that some teachers spend as much as 30 to 80 percent of their time addressing discipline problems (Walsh, 1983). This figure simply highlights a previously mentioned basic fact of teaching: to be successful, teachers must be competent in managing student behaviour to maximize the time spent on learning.

CASE 2.4 • *The Ripple Effect*

Rebecca is a well-mannered, attentive grade 5 student. For the first time since starting school, she and her two best friends are in the same class. Unlike Rebecca, her friends are not attentive and are interested more in each other than in class activities. The teacher often has to reprimand them for passing notes, talking to each other, and giggling excessively during class.

One day, Rebecca is tapped on the shoulder and is handed a note from her friend across the room. She accepts the note and sends one back. With this, her friends quickly include her in their antics. The teacher, who has been observing this increasingly distracting behaviour decides that it is necessary to remove Rebecca from her friends' influence in the classroom and to reduce the off-task behaviours of the other two girls.

Questions to Consider

1. According to the CALM model, the teacher has already identified a concern. Discuss this case from the perspective of the next three steps in the model.
2. How might this teacher reduce Rebecca's off-task behaviour?
3. How can a teacher effectively prevent friends in the same classroom from letting their friendship interfere with their learning?

Case 2.4 shows how disruptive behaviour can result in a *ripple effect*. In other words, students learn misbehaviour from observing misbehaviour in other children (Baker, 1985). The off-task behaviours of Rebecca's friends draw her off task. This type of observational learning is often accelerated when a student notices the attention a disruptive student gains from both the teacher and his classmates.

Ripple effects are not limited to the initial misbehaviour. The methods the teacher uses to curb the misbehaviour and the targeted student's resultant behaviour can cause a second ripple effect (Kounin, 1970). Research has shown that threatening teacher behaviour can lead to student anxieties—these anxieties can cause additional disruptive behaviours. Students who see disruptive classmates comply with the teacher's management technique and who tend to rate their teacher as fair, are less distracted from their classwork than when they observe unruly students defying the teacher (Smith, 1969). Clearly, the dynamics that come into play with even minor classroom disruptions are quite complex.

Common day-to-day off-task student behaviours such as talking and leaving seats without permission exist in all classrooms to some degree. Although less common, some classrooms, indeed some entire schools, are plagued by threats, violence, and vandalism. In Ontario, a survey conducted by the Ontario English Catholic Teachers' Association (OECTA) in 1992 revealed an increase in biting, kicking, and the use of weapons, and a 50 percent increase in minor incidents, such as verbal abuse, over a three-year period (Roher, 1993). Much of this aggression was perpetrated against students, although teachers and other adults in the school also fell victim. The OECTA survey also reported that the number of verbal assaults increased 6.1 percent and 20.5 percent in elementary and secondary schools respectively. In terms of student-to-teacher incidents, verbal assaults were more likely to occur with less experienced teachers (Department of the Solicitor General of Canada, 2002). This same report indicates that there are a number of initiatives at the board and school levels to identify and implement effective solutions to school-based violence. A large majority of school boards have policies or programs to address these issues. School boards also generally delegate to administrative staff and teachers responsibilities related to communicating policy information and promoting a positive school climate. Unfortunately, staff members are often not provided with the support needed to familiarize themselves with these policies and programs.

Teachers are also identifying the need for well-defined policies and programs in the increasingly used communication technologies. For example, 88 percent of elementary students and 97 percent of secondary students in Canada attended a school that had internet access for instructional purposes (Statistics Canada, 1999). In another paper, Statistics Canada (2003) reported that, according to data gathered by the Programme for International Student Assessment (PISA) and in a paper presented at the Pan-Canadian Education Research Agenda conference (2002), 88 percent of 15-year-old Canadian students had access to a home computer. This number placed Canada 11th among 32 countries that belong to the Organisation for Economic Co-operation and Development (OECD). Of the 88 percent who had home computers, 69 percent also had internet access from home. Similar students in the United States and Australia had home internet access at levels of 69 and 67 percent respectively. It was also reported that the probability of having a computer in the home increased by 18 percent and internet in the home increased by 15 percent for every additional year of education that parents had.

The ubiquitous internet and the use of email have led to many benefits and some potential behavioural problems for those who have access to new media technologies. Advantages include almost instantaneous access to information and contact with colleagues, friends, and family. The internet has also become a useful tool for those who are adept at anticipating and creating business opportunities. Unfortunately, it has also provided a conduit for those who wish to prey on children. Young people may be less sophisticated or unaware of the possible dangers that exist when dealing with unscrupulous people who are motivated by profit or worse. And there are some students who might, initially, use the internet to complete assignments by plagiarizing or downloading complete documents for submission. In addition, students may be tempted to use the internet to download music and visit pornographic sites. Some of the less serious, but still troubling, issues involving the internet and email occur during instructional or assigned work periods during school hours when the students log on to chat with virtual friends. Teachers are not always able to monitor a large class of students to make sure that they are on task. Therefore, increasingly, many schools are setting up filters to limit access to the internet as well as inappropriate uses of communication technology.

In conclusion, minor *and* major misbehaviour reduces learning time for both disruptive students and their peers. And less learning time equals less learning. Although not a clear cause-and-effect relationship, there is a positive correlation between poor grades and all types of misbehaviour (Holt 2007; DiPrete, Muller, and Shaeffer, 1981).

Classroom behavioural problems also have a negative impact on teacher effectiveness and career longevity. We believe that the overwhelming majority of teachers choose to enter the profession because they enjoy working with children and are intrinsically motivated when they know that their efforts have contributed to children's academic growth. Therefore, teachers are emotionally vulnerable to behavioural problems. They put long hours of preparation into what they hope will be interesting, motivating, and meaningful lessons. When uninterested, off-task students undermine these efforts, teachers begin to feel discouraged and often "burned out." The result is that, currently, 20 to 25 percent of Canadian teachers quit in their first five years of teaching. In urban settings, closer to 50 percent of all teachers who initially enter the profession leave the classroom within their first three years of teaching (Canadian Teachers' Federation, 2002).

No matter how carefully teachers control their personal feelings, it is inevitable that some of these feelings will influence their interactions with disruptive students. Indeed, studies have shown that teachers interact differently with disruptive students than they do with non-disruptive students (Walker, 1979; Winzer, 2002). Such differential treatment is fuelled by the negative beliefs many teachers have about disruptive students, the negative feelings many teachers harbour toward them, and the disparaging labels they often assign to these students (Brendtro, Brokenleg, and Van Bockern, 1990).

Unfortunately, differential treatment serves only to escalate inappropriate student behaviour. Even the most chronic disruptive student spends *some* time showing appropriate behaviour. However, teachers may sometimes become so angry with certain students that they overlook the appropriate behaviour and focus only on the disruptive behaviour. When this occurs, teachers miss the few opportunities they have to begin to change disruptive behaviours to acceptable ones. At least two studies have concluded that teachers are much more likely to reprimand inappropriate behaviour than to acknowledge appropriate behaviour when interacting with disruptive students (Walker and Buckley, 1973, 1974). As a result, students soon learn that when they behave appropriately, nothing happens, but when they misbehave, they are the centre of both the teacher's and other students' attention.

Management problems are a major cause of job-related stress for teachers.

Any teacher can attest that students easily realize when rules and expectations are not consistently enforced or obeyed by either the teacher or the students. Even so, because teachers are so emotionally tied to the disruptive students, they often set and enforce standards for these students that are different from those for the rest of the class. Often, these standards are so inflexible and unrealistic that they actually reduce the chances of the disruptive student behaving appropriately.

Since disruptive students have a history of inappropriate behaviours, they must be given the opportunity to learn new behaviours. The learning process is usually best accomplished in small, manageable steps that enable problem students to have a high probability of success. This process requires that behavioural standards be realistic and the same as those set for the rest of the class. The teacher must recognize and encourage what at first may be infrequent and short-lived appropriate behaviours. When behavioural standards are stricter for some students than for others, the teacher risks losing the confidence and support of even the non-disruptive students while the disruptive student gains peer support. In such circumstances, all students will view the teacher as being unfair.

Teachers, when they begin to experience more and more discipline problems, will sometimes lose their motivation to teach and assume a laissez-faire attitude. If conditions do not improve, this attitude may develop into a "get-even" approach. When a get-even attitude overrides a teacher's motivation to assist students in learning, supportive and effective teacher behaviours are replaced by vengeful behaviours. Once a teacher operates from a basis of revenge, teaching effectiveness ceases and power struggles between teachers and students become commonplace. Such power struggles often further fuel and escalate disruptive behaviour and place the teacher in a no-win situation (Dreikurs, 1964).

Children who display disruptive behaviours are constant reminders to teachers that the classroom environment is not what they would like it to be. The time and energy needed to cope with some disruptive students can be both physically draining and emotionally exhausting. Stress related to classroom management is one of the most influential factors in failure among novice teachers (Housego, 1990; Levin, 1980; Vittetoe,

Teachers who are effective managers have greater job satisfaction.

1977) and a major reason why they leave the profession (Canter, 1989). Those instructors who do persist through their first few years of teaching report that students who continually misbehave are the primary cause of job-related stress (Feitler and Tokar, 1992).

Teachers who manage their classrooms effectively, on the other hand, report that they enjoy teaching and feel a certain confidence in their ability to affect student achievement (Levin, Hoffman, Badiali, and Neuhard, 1985). Such feelings of efficacy lead to improvements in the teaching–learning process and job satisfaction, which ultimately result in gains in student achievement.

Summary

This chapter has answered three questions that are critical for an understanding of discipline and classroom management: Is there a behavioural problem? If there is a behavioural problem, who is exhibiting it? Is the behaviour a discipline problem or is it another kind of problem?

After a discussion of the contemporary definitions of the term *behavioural problem* and their shortcomings, an operational definition was provided: a behavioural problem is any behaviour that (1) interferes with the teaching act; (2) interferes with the rights of others to learn; (3) is psychologically or physically unsafe; or (4) destroys property. According to this definition, teachers as well as students are responsible for ensuring appropriate behaviour.

In response to the second question ("If there is a behavioural problem, who is exhibiting it?"), we explored the belief that today's schools are plagued by violence, crime, and disruptive classroom behaviour. Recent Canadian studies indicate that schools since the late 1990s may have experienced not only an increase in disruptive classroom behaviour but also an increase in student violence.

Finally, we showed that disruptive behaviour reduces the time spent on learning, encourages misbehaviour in onlooking students because of a ripple effect, and may cause fear in other students, with a resultant decrease in school attendance and academic achievement. Teachers are also adversely affected by disruptive behaviour—they often suffer through reduced in-class effectiveness, a rise in job-related stress, and decreased career longevity.

Key Terms

behavioural problem: An action that distracts from an effective learning environment.

learning environment: a setting in which teaching and learning can occur.

motivational problems: student difficulty in initiating, participating in, and/or persevering with learning or classroom activities.

teacher intervention: teacher actions—which may include verbal response, proximity, or silence—that lead to desired student behaviour.

Exercises

1. Is it important that all teachers have a consistent definition of what types of student behaviours constitute behavioural problems? Why or why not?

2. Do you agree with the definition of a behavioural problem stated in this chapter? If so, why? If not, how would you modify it?

3. Give several examples of teacher behaviour that would cause a classroom-management problem.

4. Using the definition of a behavioural problem stated in this chapter, categorize each of the following behaviours as a behavioural problem or a non-behavioural problem and explain your reasoning.

Behaviour	Non-behavioural Problem	Behavioural Problem	Rationale
a. A student consistently tries to engage the teacher in conversation just as class is about to begin.			
b. A student continually comes to class one minute late.			
c. A teacher stands in the hallway talking to fellow teachers during the first three minutes of class.			
d. A student does math homework during social studies class.			
e. A student interrupts a lecture to ask permission to go to the bathroom.			
f. A student often laughs at answers given by other students.			
g. A student doesn't wear safety goggles while welding in industrial arts class.			
h. A grade 1 student continually volunteers to answer questions but never has an answer when he is called on.			
i. A grade 4 student refuses to wear a jacket during recess.			
j. A grade 7 student constantly pulls the hair of the girl who sits in front of him.			
k. A boy in grade 8 spends half of the time allotted for group work encouraging a girl to go out with his friend.			

Behaviour	Non-behavioural Problem	Behavioural Problem	Rationale
l. A grade 9 student consistently uses the last two minutes of class for hair combing.			
m. An unkempt student can't get involved in group work because all students refuse to sit near him.			
n. A student continually asks good questions, diverting the teacher from the planned lesson.			
o. A student eats a candy bar during class.			
p. A student flirts with the teacher by asking questions about his clothes and personal life during class.			
q. A student consistently makes wisecracks that entertain the rest of the class.			

5. At this point in your reading, how would you handle each of the 17 behaviours listed in question 4? Why?

6. For each of the 17 behaviours in question 4, give at least one type of teacher behaviour that might escalate the student behaviour.

7. Think back to your days as a student. To what extent would you say that behavioural problems were rampant in your school? What types of behavioural problems were most common?

8. Do you feel that behavioural problems in schools have increased or decreased since you attended high school? On what evidence or information do you base your opinion?

9. Considering what teachers' jobs entail and their relationship with students, why would they be prone to take behavioural problems personally?

10. What are the dangers of personalizing student behaviour? How might doing so affect the instructional effectiveness of a teacher?

11. How can teachers protect themselves from personalizing misbehaviour?

12. Think back on your days as a student. Can you recall instances in which classroom behavioural problems prevented you and others in the class from learning? How did you feel about the situation at the time?

13. When students disrupt a class and take away the right of others to learn, do those students forfeit their right to learn? If you believe they do, what implications does that have for teacher behaviour? If you believe they don't, what implications does that have for teacher behaviour?

14. Do you think that youth violence is on the increase, or is this just a common misperception brought about by the increased coverage of this topic by the media?

15. What would you do as the teacher if a student told you that a member of your class had brought a gun to school?

Weblinks

Canadian Teachers' Federation
www.ctf-fce.ca
A site dedicated to showing and preserving the work of teachers.

Child and Family Canada
www.cfc-efc.ca
Provides valuable resources on children and families.

Ipsos Canada
www.ipsos.ca
Matching science with insight.

Statistics Canada
www.statcan.ca
Produces and reports statistics on Canada's population, resources, economy, society, and culture.

3

Understanding Why Children Misbehave

Focus on the Principles of Classroom Management

1. How does an awareness of the causes of misbehaviour enable teachers to avoid viewing misbehaviour as a personal affront?
2. What basic human needs are prerequisites for appropriate classroom behaviour?
3. How does the need for a sense of significance, competence, virtue, and power influence student behaviour?
4. What societal changes beyond schools' control greatly influence student behaviour?
5. How do cognitive and moral developmental changes result in student behaviour that, while normal, often is disruptive in learning environments?
6. How can instructional competence minimize misbehaviour?

Introduction

Kids aren't the way they used to be. When I went to school, kids knew their place. Teachers wanted to teach, and students wanted to learn. The students respected their teachers, and, believe me, they sure didn't fool around in school like they do today. Adults frequently make statements like this one as they remember the "way it used to be." But are such statements true? Not entirely.

There have always been some behavioural problems in our schools if only because of students' normal developmental changes. There also have always been some schools and homes that have been unable to adequately provide for children's needs. Even so, rapid societal changes have caused new behavioural problems and have compounded existing ones. Significant shifts in the family structure, the pervasiveness of media in children's lives, the cultural and racial makeup of the population, world economies that seem to increasingly segregate the rich from the poor, and rapid advances in technology have made huge impacts on students' thoughts, attitudes, and behaviour. Nonetheless, students still are intrinsically motivated toward skill acquisition and competency (Stipek, 1993), and teachers still want to teach (Knowles and Cole, 1994).

If, however, teachers want to maximize their teaching time, they must minimize the effect of societal changes on student behaviour. Teachers must (1) not expect students to think and act the way they did years ago; (2) not demand respect from students solely on the basis of a title or position; (3) understand the methods and behaviours young people use to find their place in today's society; and (4) understand the ongoing societal changes and the influence these changes have on students' lives (Fullan, 1993, 2001; Ng, 2006). To assist teachers in reaching these goals, we describe in this chapter some of the factors that have influenced students to change and we provide an explanation of why students now behave as they do.

Societal Changes

For over 70 years now, schools have been recognized as microcosms of the larger society ("Ontario: where everyone . . . ," 1999; Kindsvatter, 1978; Dewey, 1916). Therefore, discipline problems in the schools reflect the problems that face society. The social climate of the nation, city or town, and the community that surrounds each school has profound effects on students' perceptions of the value of education and on their behaviour in school (Menacker, Weldon, and Hurwitz, 1989).

   Our society is plagued by the ills of drug and alcohol abuse, crime violence, unemployment, child abuse, adolescent suicide, and teenage pregnancy. It is no coincidence that as these problems increase, so do a school's behavioural problems. This clear relationship between social problems and school behavioural problems demonstrates that many factors which contribute to behavioural problems are beyond the schools' control (Bayh, 1978). Even if there were no societal problems, disruptive behaviour could still be expected because a school brings together many of the conditions that facilitate misbehaviour. Large numbers of young people, many of whom are still learning socially acceptable behaviours and would rather be elsewhere, are concentrated in one place for long periods of time. Currently, according to Statistics Canada, immigration is responsible for two-thirds of Canada's growth in population (Mahoney, 2007). The greatest growth is in the major cities of Toronto, Vancouver, and Montreal, which grew by 950 000 or 11.1 percent between 2001 and 2006, whereas the country's rural population increased by just 1 percent. This increasingly important demographic has implications for schools, the curriculum, and the way teachers interact with students.

   Young people in our schools now come from a wide range of backgrounds, with different ethnic, racial, and parental attitudes and expectations concerning education. A school exposes all students to **off-task/norm-violating behaviours** and makes failure visible (Elliott and Voss, 1974; Feldhusen, 1978).

   Children no longer grow up in a society that provides them with constant, consistent sets of guidelines and expectations. The intense, rapid technological advancements in mass communication of the last several decades have exposed young people to a multitude of varying viewpoints, ideas, and philosophies (Elliott, Bosacki, Woloshyn, and Richards, 2001). With this exposure, the direct influence of parents, community, and school has begun to wane. Role models have changed. Schools are now faced with children who are exposed to a greater variety of information than ever before. As a result, these children think and act differently than earlier generations.

The Knowledge Explosion

Erosion of Respect for Authority

Since the 1950s, when the Soviet Union launched Sputnik, the first satellite, there has been an unabated explosion in scientific knowledge and technological advancements. This explosion has resulted in products only dreamed of previously: cellular and digital phones, DVDs, iPods, satellite dishes, CD-ROMs, powerful personal computers and laptops, fax machines, the internet, email, PDAs and other telecommunication devices provide instantaneous, worldwide personal communication. And today we have access to an ever-expanding array of databases.

To understand how great the explosion of knowledge has been, consider this: In the early 1970s, less than 20 years after Sputnik's launch, it was estimated that by the time children born in 1980 reached the age of 50 the world's knowledge would have increased by 32 times (Toffler, 1970). With the advances that have been made in as few as the last 10 years, these estimates are probably much too low. Nothing illustrates this better than the emergence of the internet. The internet provides any user of a personal computer with instantaneous access to an almost limitless range and quantity of global information. Such a rapid growth in technology, information and, hence, knowledge appears to create a widening gap between those who "stay current" with these advances and those who do not. For example, by the end of elementary school, many children possess knowledge that their parents only vaguely comprehend. This is poignantly clear in such areas as personal computing, information retrieval, ecology, biotechnology, and astronomy. In addition, because of the almost instantaneous telecommunication of national and world events, children are keenly aware of the state of the present world. They see famine, terrorist attacks, political corruption, drug busts, and chemical spills on a daily basis.

Such knowledge has caused many young people to view adults as being ineffective in managing their own world. These young people perceive past solutions to life's problems as irrelevant to the world in which they live. Therefore, respect, which was once given to adults because of their worldliness and expertise, has eroded, and adults exercise less influence on the young than they once did (Manley-Casimir and Luke, 1987; McMillan and Morrison, 2006). When talking to adolescents, we commonly hear such statements as, "My parents don't understand"; "Why do we have to do it by hand when there are calculators that can do it for us?"; and "Why do I have to be honest when government officials are always lying?"

As the world becomes a more complex and frightening place, and as young people perceive their parents and teachers to be less relevant sources of solutions, the future for these young people becomes more remote, uncertain, and unpredictable. More than 40 years ago, Stinchcombe demonstrated a direct relationship between adolescents' envisioned images of the future and their attitudes and behaviours (1964). Those adolescents who saw little or nothing to be gained in the future from school attendance were likely to exhibit rebellious, alienated behaviour. Unfortunately, there are even more young people today with this pessimistic view of the future. Clearly,

*The unabated knowledge explosion
has influenced the erosion of respect
for traditional authority figures.*

then, a teacher's ability to maximize student success and demonstrate the present and
future usefulness of the material to be learned plays an important role in students'
perceived value of education (Hargreaves, 1994).

Teacher and Student Frustration and the Relevancy of Schooling

Students are not alone in their feelings of frustration. Teachers, too, perceive many
school curricula to be irrelevant to today's world. They are frustrated because of the
almost impossible task of keeping up with the expansion of knowledge and the new
technologies (Hargreaves, 1994; McMillan and Morrison, 2006). Changes in school
curricula occur at a snail's pace compared to the daily expansion of information and
technological advances. The advent of standardized testing for numeracy and literacy
has served to focus teachers' attention on these two subject areas.

Many teachers have said that they find it impossible to keep abreast of
developments in their content areas and the rapidly expanding array of new
pedagogical models, many of which support the use of new technologies. In
addition, many teachers have found it difficult to integrate the new material into
an already overloaded curriculum. While they truly desire to restructure their
curricula in meaningful ways and to integrate technologies into their **instructional
practices** (and **strategies/techniques/methodology**), they often find that their

schools lack the necessary resources or commitment to invest in the latest technologies, training, or teacher release time for curriculum development. Their feelings of frustration lead to job dissatisfaction and poor morale, which can foster less-than-ideal interactions between teachers and students. However, when schools are able to invest in the new technologies and teachers are properly trained in their use, powerful changes can occur for both teachers and students, as illustrated in Case 3.1.

Just as students are positively affected by contemporary and innovative educational programs that meet their needs, they are also negatively affected by those that do not. Frustration is a natural outcome when instructional methodology does not change, and

CASE 3.1 • *"This Is the Greatest Thing That Has Happened to Me in 20 Years of Teaching"*

About five years ago at a national education conference, one of the authors met Mr. Lee, a 20-year veteran high school earth sciences teacher. Clearly somewhat distressed, Mr. Lee said that he felt he was no longer reaching his students—they were uninterested, distracted, and turned off learning in his class. In his opinion, each day was an endless hassle that left him tired and frustrated. This frustration was following him home and he felt he was making his family unhappy too. As a result, he was not sure he wanted to return to the classroom the following year.

A couple of years later, surprisingly, the author met Mr. Lee again at another national conference. When pressed, Mr. Lee said that not only had he remained in the classroom but that he had regained his enthusiasm for teaching and it was currently as high as it had ever been. When he was asked what had prompted the rejuvenation, he replied that he had challenged himself to restructure his course to better reflect contemporary earth sciences.

Specifically, he had used his yearly allotment for resources to purchase a high-speed internet connection to enable his students to access a real-time meteorological–oceanographic database that allowed them to examine the same up-to-the-minute data that scientists used. He said it was the best strategy he had ever implemented. He was delighted to observe that his students responded to this opportunity with interest and enthusiasm. For the first time in many years, visitation night was crowded with parents who had come to see what was going on in their children's earth sciences class. Mr. Lee was gratified to hear that many of his students were going home and talking with their parents about the neat things they were doing in class for the first time ever.

Mr. Lee went on to say that he was so impressed by the educational impact of technology that he had decided to study instructional technology at the graduate level and recently had enrolled in a doctoral program. He was eagerly anticipating learning more about how to motivate his students.

Questions to Consider

1. Describe the steps in Mr. Lee's transformation.
2. What was the most significant component of Me. Lee's new way of teaching?
3. What do you think was more important—Mr. Lee's new-found enthusiasm or the technology that he introduced into his classroom?

students are expected to learn more in shorter periods of time. Using uniformly traditional instructional practices to deliver outdated content is meaningless and boring to youths who are growing up in a world significantly different from that of their parents. What teachers often label as a lack of motivation may actually have more to do with the students' inability to feel any affiliation with what is going on in the classroom (Gabay, 1991). Lack of affiliation leads to boredom and off-task, disruptive classroom behaviours (Green, Campbell, Stirtzinger, DeSouza, and Dawe, 2001).

Teaching just the facts is not sufficient. To prepare them for their futures rather than our past, students must be instructed in ways that facilitate their *learning how to learn* (see Chapter 5, "The Professional Teacher"). Case 3.2 illustrates how students respond to a type of educational experience, depending on its relevancy.

Obviously, Ashley has a much better attitude than Amy about learning capitals. Although neither sister knew the answer to the Nunavut question, Ashley knew one way to find the capital of that territory and was willing to follow through. Could it be that the sisters' different attitudes are related to varying instructional strategies that had been used in the girls' respective classrooms? Unlike Amy, Ashley had an opportunity to use appropriate instructional technology and was taught a skill that facilitates her ability to be a self-learner. In other words, Ashley was learning how to learn.

CASE 3.2 • *Who Really Cares?*

Over the winter holidays, a group of adults and their children played a newly unwrapped board game that involved facts about Canada. The question that would win the game seemed simple: *What is the capital of the territory of Nunavut?* Even so, none of the adults who were playing could remember the answer. Don said, "I'm sure I never saw this in the paper—the place must be very small and unimportant. That's what bothers me about these games; I always end up feeling frustrated and stupid." He turned to his two daughters and said, "Hey, one of you answer this question. I'm sure you said you learned the provincial and territorial capitals in grade 5. So, what's the capital of Nunavut?" Amy, who was now in grade 7, replied by saying, "I hated that stuff. Our teacher made us memorize all 10 provincial capitals for a test. I did it and passed the test, but I have never needed to know the city names again, so I've forgotten them and I'm not sure I ever learned the capital of Nunavut in the first place. Anyway, who really cares about capitals of places? What's the point?" Ashley, who was in grade 6, said, "I don't remember Nunavut's capital either, although I am sure we had to learn it along with the other territories. It's not hard to find out, though. I can go and look it up on the computer now. I'll google it! Just wait one minute while I go to Google and then we'll know.

Questions to Consider

1. What do you consider more important, the content knowledge or the skill to locate it? How can we teach to emphasize the most important learning?
2. What could a teacher do to motivate Amy?
3. Can teachers influence parental attitudes? It so, how?

Media and Violence

Unlike any previous time in human history, people today have instant access to incredible amounts of information and entertainment through the media. As an example of this phenomenon, according to a 2005 Statistics Canada survey, two-thirds of Canadians searched the internet for information during the previous year (Statistics Canada, 2006). A recent study conducted by the Media Awareness Network (2005) showed that 77 percent of senior elementary students chose playing electronic games as their favourite after-school or free-time activity. It would be no surprise to anyone that more than 99 percent of all Canadian homes have at least one television set (Statistics Canada, 2002). It has been reported that the average Canadian child spends approximately 15 hours per week watching television—and many children spend more time than the average (Statistics Canada, 2001). Numerous forms of media have combined to become a major source of information and entertainment and thus an enormous influence on children.

A very big concern is the fact that the inhabitants of the television world and the characters of electronic games often act and think in ways that contrast sharply with the conventional attitudes, behaviours, beliefs, and values of society in general. As a result, many parents and educators feel helpless in trying to convey appropriate behavioural messages in the face of such stiff opposition from the passive and interactive media that dominate so many children's lives (Luke, 1999; Rosenberg and Barbara, 2007). The widespread worry is that children who watch violence on television and in movies, and who are exposed to violent behaviours and attitudes while playing pervasive electronic games, will become more aggressive and desensitized to the horror of violent acts.

These concerns are not new. Many of the same worries surfaced in the 1950s with the advent of mainstream television viewing. Content analysis of television shows in the early 1950s indicated that, on average, there were 11 threats or acts of violence per hour in programming at that time. By the 1990s, however, this number had risen to 32 per hour. While these are US statistics, given the format for most television shows— brief sequences of fast-paced action with frequent interruptions for unrelated commercial messages—and given that most Canadians watch a great deal of US-made television and movies, it can be assumed that Canadian children are exposed to a similarly large amount of violence and mayhem on a regular basis.

All children may not be equally vulnerable to adopting aggressive behaviour. However, a recent study found that Canadian children who watch violent television programs involving characters to whom they can relate and those who view these programs as authentic have a greater chance of becoming physically aggressive young adults (Canadian Press, 2003). Another study found that children who play violent video games are more likely to have engaged in a physical fight in the past year than children who play fewer violent electronic games (Zillman and Weaver, 1999). It has also been noted that the rise in bullying in the schoolyard bullying has coincided with the rise in violent representations in the media (Alphonso, 2003; Rosenberg and Barbara, 2007), and that players of violent electronic games are more likely to perform poorly in school than children who play fewer of those types of games (Zillman and

Weaver, 1999). Another related concern is that regular heavy gaming may inhibit a child's ability to distinguish real life from simulation (Subrahmanyam, Kraut, Greenfield, and Gross, 2000).

Although in the 1950s some psychologists suggested that TV violence had a cathartic effect and reduced a child's aggressive behaviours, by the 1980s, laboratory and field studies had cast serious doubt on the cathartic hypothesis (Pearl, Bouthilet, and Lazar, 1982). In the United States, the 1982 National Institute of Mental Health's report, *Television and Behaviour: Ten Years of Scientific Progress and Implications for the Eighties*, concluded that (1) research findings supported a causal relationship between television violence and aggressive behaviour; (2) there was a consensus among researchers that television violence leads to aggressive behaviour; (3) despite slight variations over the previous decade, the amount of violence on television remained at consistently high levels; and (4) television cultivated television-influenced attitudes among viewers, with those who watch the most television being more fearful and less trusting of others than those who watch very little television (Bouthilet and Lazar, 1982). A poignant statement on the relationship between television viewing and real-life violence was made by the American Psychological Association (APA): "There is absolutely no doubt that higher levels of viewing violence on television are correlated with increased acceptance of aggressive attitudes and increased aggressive behavior" (1993, 33). Psychologists now suggest that the effects of TV violence may extend beyond causing viewers' increased aggressive behaviours to the *bystander effect*, or the desensitization/callousness of people toward violence directed at others (Morgan, Shanahan, and De-Guise, 2001; *Congressional Quarterly*, 1993).

Some researchers have proposed that violence on TV produces stress in children. Exposure to too much violence over too long a time, they say, creates emotional upset and insecurity, leading to resultant disturbed behaviour (Rice, 1981). A 1984 study indicated that heavy television viewing is associated with elementary schoolchildren's belief in a "mean and scary world" and that poor school behaviour—restlessness, disruptiveness, inattentiveness, aggressiveness—is significantly correlated with the home television environment: the number of sets, hours of viewing, and types of programs (Singer, Singer, and Rapaczynski, 1984).

Of course, there have been many theories about the relationship between TV viewing and children's behaviour (Pearl, 1984). The observational modelling theory, which is now over 30 years old, is the most widely accepted. This theory proposes that aggression is learned from the models and real-life simulations portrayed on TV and is practised through imitation (Bandura, 1973). In more recent years, researchers found a correlation between television coverage of violence and our perception of how much violence exists in the world around us ("Seeds of Violence," 2001). In trying to explain the effects of TV on children's behaviour at school, Rice, Huston, and Wright (1982) hypothesized that the stimuli of sound effects, exciting music, and fast-action images generate an arousal reaction, with an accompanying inability to tolerate the typically long conversations, explanations, and delays characteristic of the real world of school.

An overview to this issue is difficult to state definitively, as research is conflicting. Certainly, children view a great deal of violence on television, and young people of this era have been called the "gaming generation" because electronic games have become such a major source of leisure-time entertainment. As mentioned above, many of these games are very violent. According to some researchers, though, the problems may be overstated, as most children still prefer to meet their friends face to face and participate in their favourite activities (Livingstone and Bovill, 1999). For instance, the Canadian Teachers' Federation (2003) found that while boys in higher elementary grades state electronic games as a favoured activity, they still prefer to play sports either in organized leagues or more informally with their friends. The bottom line appears to be that a small portion of children may be at risk for losing sight of reality in the gaming world, but the vast majority return to real life unscathed (Turkel, 1996). The debate continues, however, and parents and educators need to remain vigilant.

The Media and Alternative Role Models

Television, the internet, music, videos, and magazines, and the commercials contained in all of these media, directed at children, also influence their behaviours by presenting a wide range of alternative models and lifestyles. At the same time, they are presenting uniform images about the most desirable attitude, body image, and fashion, putting pressure on young people to conform to these "norms," often dismissed or denigrated by adults. For instance, Canada's popular MuchMusic Television broadcasts 24 hours a day the audio and video imagery of the latest popular music. What once were often indecipherable lyrics have been replaced by visual depictions, many concerning drug and alcohol use, sexual promiscuity, hopelessness, and distrust of school and teachers. Often, these songs become components of other forms of questionable "entertainment" such as video games. Rosenberg and Barbara (2007) argue that "like the worst television shows, the worst video games teach children to associate violence and killing with pleasure, entertainment and feelings of achievement."

The proliferation of talk shows and reality shows present children with a glamorized view of oftentimes dysfunctional lives—and at a critical point in the formative years of such young viewers as they attempt to determine who they are, what they can do, and how far they can go in testing the limits of their parents' and teachers' authority. In addition, the news media's propensity to cover war, violence, and natural disasters with intensive 24-hour saturation-coverage desensitizes immature viewers. For instance, the television coverage of the wars in Afghanistan and Iraq tend to depict these deadly conflicts in a manner that often parallels video-game formats. The media have the power, therefore, to communicate pluralistic standards, changing customs, and shifting beliefs and values. While behavioural experimentation is both a prerequisite for, and a necessary component of, the cognitive and moral developmental growth of young people, today's world is more complicated than it once was, and parents and teachers need to have a working knowledge of the alternative models that they compete with.

Media messages possibly have the most detrimental effects on children who live in poverty. These children usually are aware that they do not possess the things most others have. They also know they lack the opportunities to obtain them in the near future. Thus, television's depiction of the "good life" may compound their feelings of hopelessness, discontent, and anger. Such feelings, coupled with the fact that many of these children feel they hold no stake in the values and norms of the more affluent society, lay the foundation for rage, which is often released in violent or aggressive behaviours directed at others (APA, 1993). It is imperative for teachers to be aware of these outside influences on student behaviours in order to work constructively with, and be supportive of, today's youth.

The Failure to Meet Children's Basic Needs

The Home Environment

Educators have long recognized the significant influence of home life on a child's behaviour and on academic progress. As Case 3.3 illustrates, the home's ability to meet students' basic needs is particularly crucial.

CASE 3.3 • *Hanging on the Corner*

Teresa, a grade 5 student, is on the school playground at 7:45 every morning, even though school doesn't start until 9:00. Often, she is eating a bag of potato chips and drinking a can of soda. On cold, snowy mornings, she huddles in the doorway wearing a spring jacket and sneakers, waiting for the door to be unlocked. She brags to the other students that she hangs out on the corner with the teenagers in her neighbourhood until 12:00 or 1:00 a.m. The home and school coordinator who has investigated her home environment has confirmed this.

Teresa is the youngest of four children. Her father left the family before she started school. Her mother works for a janitorial service and leaves for work by 7:00 a.m. When she returns home in the evening, the mother either goes out with her boyfriend or goes to sleep early, entrusting Teresa's care to her 16-year-old brother, who has recently quit school.

Teresa is two years below grade in both reading and mathematics. She is never prepared for class with the necessary books and materials, never completes homework assignments, and usually chooses not to participate in learning activities. Her classroom behaviour is clearly attention seeking, as she is generally off task, characterized by moving noisily both in and out of her seat, calling out, and disrupting other students by talking to them or physically touching them. Occasionally, Teresa becomes abusive to her fellow students and her teacher, using a loud, challenging voice and vulgarities.

Questions to Consider

1. In your opinion, does Teresa's home situation explain and excuse her disruptive behaviour in class?
2. Discuss three specific things a teacher might do to help Teresa academically and personally.

When considering Teresa's home environment, is it surprising that she has academic and behavioural problems in school? Abraham Maslow's theory of basic human needs predicts Teresa's behaviour. According to Maslow (1968), basic human needs align themselves into a hierarchy of the following levels:

1. physiological needs: hunger, thirst, breathing;
2. safety and security needs: protection from injury, pain, extremes of heat and cold;
3. belonging and affection needs: giving and receiving love, warmth, and affection;
4. esteem and self-respect needs: feeling adequate, competent, worthy; being appreciated and respected by others; and
5. self-actualization needs: self-fulfillment by using one's talents and potential.

If lower-level needs are not met, an individual can experience difficulty, frustration, and a lack of motivation in attempting to meet the higher-order needs.

Maslow's hierarchy also represents a series of developmental levels. Although the meeting of these needs is important throughout an individual's life, a young child spends considerably more time and effort meeting the lower-level needs than an older child. From preadolescence on, assuming the lower-level needs are met, emphasis shifts to the higher-order needs of esteem and self-actualization. (Further discussion of self-esteem is found in the "Children's Pursuit of Social Recognition and Self-Esteem" section later in this chapter.)

Academic achievement and appropriate behaviour are most likely to occur when a student's home environment has met her physiological, safety, and belonging needs. This enables her to begin to work on meeting the needs of esteem and self-actualization both at home and at school. Let's now examine Teresa's home environment in light of Maslow's hierarchy of basic needs. Her breakfast of potato chips and soda; her clothing (a light jacket and sneakers) on cold days; the lack of a father at home and a mother who is rarely present are strong indications that her physiological, safety, and belonging needs are not being met. Because of her inadequate home environment, Teresa has attempted to meet her need for belonging and esteem by bragging about hanging out with teenagers and by using loud, vulgar statements in class and disturbing other students. Given her situation, it is surprising that Teresa still attends school on a regular basis. If Teresa's home environment remains the same, and if she continues to achieve below grade academically and exhibit behavioural problems, she probably will quit school at an early age, still unable to control her own behaviour. This might be disastrous for her, as school may be her only stable and predictable environment.

The results of a longitudinal study of students in grades 3, 6, and 9 (Feldhusen, Thurston, and Benning, 1973) provided clear evidence of the importance of the home environment on school behaviour. Persistently disruptive students differed substantially from persistently prosocial students in a number of home and family variables:

1. Parental supervision and discipline were inadequate, being too lax, too strict, or erratic.
2. The parents were indifferent or hostile to the child. They disapproved of many things about the child and handed out angry, physical punishment.
3. The family operated only partially if at all, as a unit, and the marital relationship lacked closeness and equality of partnership.
4. The parents found it difficult to discuss concerns regarding the child and believed that they had little influence on the child. They believed that other children exerted bad influences on their child.

In its 1993 publication, *Violence and Youth*, the American Psychological Association offered examples of the family characteristics of children with anti-social behaviours that were quite similar to the Feldhusen et al. findings (1973). The examples included

CASE 3.4 • *Marital Conflict*

Seth was a typical grade 11 student from a middle-class suburban home who attended the local high school. He was friendly by nature and enjoyed school activities, particularly sports. Although he was not an outstanding student, he was motivated and attentive enough and his teachers seldom had any real problems with his in-class behaviour. Occasionally, he had to be reminded to stop talking and to take his seat when class started. His grades were typically Bs with a few Cs. Seth had discussed his future with his guidance counsellor and his parents and it was decided that he would attend a small university and major in liberal arts. According to his teachers, they liked Seth and enjoyed having him in their classes.

Now, at the end of grade 11, something is different and Seth appears to have changed. He frequently fails to hand in his homework and is regularly off task in class. It is evident that his usual motivation has disappeared. When questioned, Seth says that he has changed his plans about attending university and now he wants instead to get a job right out of high school. His teachers begin to discuss the observable changes in Seth's behaviour and aspirations; his counsellor reveals that Seth shares the information that

his parents have been discussing divorce.

As the oldest of the three children in the family, Seth is being included in the discussions about how the family will manage in the future. The counsellor also discerns that both of Seth's parents are now asking him for assistance in fulfilling family responsibilities—they are not minimizing the ramifications of the marital breakup for the young man. Clearly, the situation is putting a great deal of stress on Seth and causing him to be distracted from his schoolwork. However, of greater concern is the fact that his aspirations for a university degree, which is well within his academic reach, are also being affected negatively. In addition, the counsellor identifies that Seth is considerably less outgoing with fellow students and appears distracted and unhappy when talking with them.

Questions to Consider

1. What role, if any, should the school play in cases of family breakdown when the child is being affected very negatively?
2. How could a counsellor or teacher help Seth without interfering in matters beyond her control?

parental rejection, inconsistent and physically abusive discipline, and parental support of their children's use of aversive and aggressive problem-solving approaches. The study found lack of parental supervision was one of the strongest predictors of children's later conduct disorders. Case 3.3, Feldhusen's longitudinal study, and the APA's summary describe homes that could be considered abusive or at least neglectful. However, many non-abusive or non-neglectful home environments also create situations that are quite stressful to children. This stress may manifest itself symptomatically as behavioural problems. Consider the example of Seth in Case 3.4.

While Seth's home environment is significantly different from Teresa's, it, too, has a detrimental effect on behaviour in school. Seth's situation is one that an increasing number of children face.

What changes have occurred in the home environment of Canadian children? In 1985, the Divorce Act was revised—this resulted, between 1986 and 1987, in the number of divorces increasing by more than 20 percent. For three consecutive years leading up to 2000, the divorce rate went up. From 1998 to 2000, the divorce rate rose by 3.0 percent, with 71 144 couples finalizing divorce in 2000 (Statistics Canada, 2002). Remarriage often creates additional problems for children (Visher and Visher, 1978). Any form of marital conflict increases the likelihood that children will develop some type of behavioural problem (Rutter, 1978). In a Canadian study, 92 percent of children who had lived with both parents from birth to 15 years of age reported that they had enjoyed a very happy childhood. Of those who had lived through a change in parental structure before age 15, however, only 72 percent said that they had happy memories of their early years (Williams, 2001). In another study by Jenkins et al. (2005), researchers found that not only did marital conflict predict a change in children's behaviour but also children's behaviour predicted an increase in marital conflict.

Divorce not only changes the family structure but also frequently results in a decrease in the family's standard of living, with an increasing number of children and their single mothers moving into poverty status (Levine, 1984). The 1995 General Social Survey reported that 96 percent (22.5 million) of Canadians who were age 15 and older were born into families with two parents. A significant number of children (87 percent) lived with both parents until they were at least 15 years old. Prior to age 15, however, there was a change in family composition for approximately 1.9 million Canadians, or 13 percent (Williams, 2001).

Canadian Council on Social Development (CCSD) research shows that 15 percent of Canadian residents were living in poverty in 1990. This percentage had increased to 16.2 percent by 1999 and represented 4 886 000 persons. Of these, 1 298 000 were children under the age of 18 (Canadian Council on Social Development, 2002). These children are at greater risk than others of developing academic and/or behavioural problems (APA, 1993; Gelfand, Jenson, and Drew, 1982; Parke, 1978). "Education is a fundamental human right and the cornerstone in the battle against poverty. It is critical that bilateral and international institutions work together more closely to ensure that support is increased to national education programs for the poor" ("Canada Says Education Is Key . . . ," 2001).

The School Environment

Physiological Needs. Students are in school to learn. They are continually asked to demonstrate their new understanding and skills. In asking them to do so, schools are attempting to aid students in a process that Maslow calls *self-actualization*. When students successfully demonstrate new learning, they usually are intrinsically and extrinsically positively reinforced, which leads to the development of self-esteem and self-respect. Positive self-esteem motivates students to learn, which results in the further development of self-actualization. The cycle of self-esteem, learning, and self-actualization can be maximized only if the home and schools create environments in which the lower-level needs—physiological, safety and security, belonging, and affection—are met (Novak and Purkey, 2001). Consider Sari's reaction in Case 3.5 when the teacher unintentionally stifles her enthusiasm.

Case 3.5 illustrates how a young child attempts to meet the physiological need of movement and activity. For some young children, no school activity takes more energy than sitting still. When the teacher demanded that Sari sit and then eventually removed recess, her physiological need was no longer being met. This resulted in Sari's excessive movement around the room. When Sari's needs were met, the disruptive behaviours stopped.

The importance of meeting students' physiological needs as a prerequisite to learning should be evident to everyone. Ask any teacher how much learning occurs on the first cold day of fall before the heating system is functional or on the first hot

CASE 3.5 • *Forgetting to Sit Down*

Sari, a grade 2 student, is a bright, happy, active child. She is always the first one ready for recess and the last one to stop playing. When going to or from school, she is often seen skipping, jumping, or doing cartwheels.

Sari's desk is second from the front. When given seat work, she either stands at her desk or half-stands with one knee on the chair. Her teacher always reminds Sari to sit, but no sooner has she sat down than she is back up on her feet.

After a good number of reminders, Sari is kept in from recess. When this occurs, she begins to walk around the room when class is in progress. This leads to further reprimands by her teacher. Finally, her parents are notified.

Sari's parents inform her teacher that at home Sari is always jumping rope, playing catch, dancing, and even standing rather than sitting for piano lessons and practice. She even stands at the table at mealtimes. It is decided that Sari's seat will be moved to the back of the room so that her standing doesn't distract the other students. After this is explained to Sari, she agrees to the move. The reprimands stop. Sari continues to do excellent work, and by the end of grade 2, she is able to sit in her seat while working.

Questions to Consider

1. Do you consider Sari's active behaviour to be a problem? Why? Why not?
2. Why did this solution succeed with Sari?
3. Which teacher behaviours could have led to Sari becoming a behavioural problem?

day of early spring before the heating system has been turned off. At a minimum, every classroom in every school should have adequate space and proper lighting and ventilation.

Somewhat less evident, but no less important, than a school's environmental conditions are concerns about poverty, overcrowding, noise, and frequent interruptions. Teachers have long known that students are less attentive in classes held just before lunch. When schools are overcrowded and/or lunch facilities are inadequate, lunch can span a three-hour period. Some students may eat lunch before 11:00 a.m., whereas others may not eat until after 1:00 p.m. This can produce a group of students whose long wait for lunch leaves them inattentive to learning tasks. In an attempt to improve learning environments and nutritional practices, many boards of education are experimenting with alternative scheduling in their schools. One of the current timetabling implementations is called the *balanced day*.

CASE 3.6 • *"There Must Be a Better Way"*

One university requires its secondary student teachers to follow a student's schedule of classes for an entire day. Teacher candidates must record their reactions to this experience. What follows are a couple of common reactions:

- *No sooner were we in our seats in the first-period class than the VP was on the intercom system. She spent at least five minutes with announcements mostly directed at the teachers. The speaker was loud and very annoying. After the announcements, most of the students were talking among themselves. By the time we got down to work, 15 minutes had passed. Halfway through the period, a student messenger interrupted the class when he brought the morning office notices to the teacher. And believe it or not, five minutes before the end of class, the VP was back on the intercom with additional announcements. It was quite evident to me that these interruptions were a direct cause of inattentiveness and reduction in effective instruction. Much time was wasted during the announcements and in obtaining student on-task behaviour after the interruptions. There must be a better way.*

- *Probably the most eye-opening experience I had was remembering how crowded and noisy schools can be. This was most evident to me when we changed classes. We had three minutes between classes. The halls were very crowded, with frequent pushing, shoving, and just bumping into each other. The noise level was so loud that it really bothered me. On arriving at the next class, all I really wanted to do was sit quietly for a few minutes before starting to work. The changes from hallways to classrooms are dramatic. I can see why it is difficult for some students to settle down and get on task at the beginning of class. As bad as the hallways were, it didn't prepare me for lunch. The lunchroom was even noisier. By the time I waited in line, I had only 15 minutes to eat and then back to the hallways to class. By the end of the day, I was drained.*

Questions to Consider

1. "A noisy, crowded school is a fact of life, and students and teachers just need to accept it!" Comment on this statement.
2. How can a classroom teacher minimize the effects of disruptions and noisy hallways?

The timetable is designed to provide longer periods in each class, two nutritional/activity breaks which replace the structure of two recesses and a lunch break. "Schools that piloted this new schedule have reported an increase in concentration levels of students, more positive play time, more physically active students, and better opportunities for learning through uninterrupted blocks of teaching/learning time" (Waterloo Region District School Board, 2007).

Regardless of students' ages, interruptions, noise, and overcrowding can produce emotional uneasiness that may result in nervousness, anxiety, a need to withdraw, or overactivity. In these cases, emotional uneasiness interferes with on-task behaviour and reduces the effectiveness of the teaching–learning environment (Marini, Spear, and Bombay, 1999). Consider, for example, Cases 3.6 and 3.7. Schools must pay particular attention to minimizing distractions if they want to reduce student off-task behaviour.

CASE 3.7 • *Too Much Noise*

Karen is a quiet, well-behaved grade 3 student who does her work conscientiously and achieves well academically. She sits near the front of the class and seldom interrupts or offers answers to questions. She is always responsive to her teacher Ms. Gray's instructions and Ms. Gray recently told Karen's parents that "she is a pleasure to have in the class."

One day, all the grade 3 classes are taken to the all-purpose room to observe a well-known film on the environment. As the class has been studying this topic for the past week, interest and excitement are unusually high. The teacher has encouraged this excitement by giving the children a sheet of questions that can be answered by watching the film.

All the grade 3 classes happen to enter the hall on the way to the all-purpose room simultaneously and the children in the hallway are very noisy because of increased excitement and expectation about the break in the usual routine to see the movie.

Ms. Gray notices Karen walking down the hall, not interacting with her peers, and holding her hands over her ears. Curiously, Ms. Gray watches Karen enter the all-purpose room heading right for the back corner of the room and sitting down against the wall. Going over to Karen, Ms. Gray asks her what the problem is. Karen replies quietly that the noise hurts her ears and she feels like crying. Clearly distressed, she adds that she doesn't want to be there if the noise is going to be loud.

Ms. Gray quickly moves to the front to quiet the students and Karen appears to relax and enjoy the film. Ms. Gray, though, is troubled by the obvious distress that Karen displayed, so she contacts Karen's parents and suggests a consultation with an ear specialist. Some weeks later, the parents contact Ms. Gray and report that the specialist has confirmed Karen has no problems with her hearing or her ears. They are all baffled by the strange behaviour Karen exhibited on movie day.

Questions to Consider

1. What steps should Ms. Gray take to ensure that Karen does not have a recurrence of this issue?
2. What can be done to help Karen cope when her classmates become noisy and excited?

Safety and Security Needs. For the most part, schools create environments in which students feel safe from physical harm. There are, however, occasions when students, like Keith in Case 3.8, fear for their physical safety (Marini, Spear, and Bombay, 1999; Marini, Fairbain, and Zuber, 2001; Pepler and Craig, 1994). Students in troubled schools are sometimes assaulted, coerced, bribed, or robbed. Violence such as that observed in US schools is becoming increasingly evident in Canadian schools and has been the subject of serious study (MacDonald, 1997; Smith, Bertrand, Arnold, and Hornick, 1995). In 1998, 29 percent of grade 10 male students and 28 percent of grade 10 female students surveyed reported that they had been bullied at school (Health Canada, 2002). This may not be surprising, as more weapons are brought to schools each day and the presence of street gangs at schools is increasing (Chandler, Chapman, Rand, and Taylor, 1998). Also, there are students in all

Concentric Case Study Kaleidoscope

CASE 3.8 • *Afraid of Going to School*

Keith, a grade 8 student, achieves at an average level in his classes. He does best in social studies, which is scheduled for the last period of the day. Keith is generally attentive and has never caused any disruption in class. Approximately midway through the year, Keith's behaviour in social studies begins to change. He goes from being a student who is attentive and participates freely to one who rarely is engaged in the discussion. The teacher notes that he seems distracted and is clearly not paying attention. When asked a specific question that he would normally have been able to answer, Keith appears not to have heard and has to ask the teacher embarrassedly to repeat the question. When the teacher does so, Keith mumbles that he doesn't know the answer. Mystified, the teacher begins to notice that Keith is often watching the clock nervously and is the first to leave his seat and rush through the door at the end of class.

After a few days of observing this behaviour, the teacher asks Keith to stay behind for a few minutes after class to discuss his distracted behaviour. Keith appears upset at being asked to stay and, when questioned, tells the teacher that he has to leave early because his schoolmate Greg will beat him up if he sees him on the street. Keith is fearful of the boy because Greg has threatened him for telling the gym teacher that he was the one throwing Keith's clothing around the locker room after gym class.

Keith's Perspective

I used to like social studies class, but now I can't concentrate on it. I just can't! I keep watching the clock so that I can get my books away and get out the door before Greg does. Then I can run all the way home and avoid getting trapped by him. He is really mad at me and has told everyone that he intends to beat me up. He is bigger than me and much tougher and can easily do it. I bet he could really hurt me. I know that the kids will gather around and some of my friends will feel bad for me, but I also know that they will not be able to help me. I just have to get home before he catches me.

I know he is really mad at me for telling the teacher that he was the one throwing my clothes around the locker room last month. I just wasn't thinking when the teacher asked me who had made a mess and I was really stupid not to have lied. I should have said that I didn't know who had done it. Now I'm in trouble.

I could tell my parents, but they will come over to the school and there will be big fuss. I don't want them to know. The other day when I got home from school all hot and sweaty and out of breath, Mom asked me why I had run so hard. I lied and told her that I wanted to get home so I could watch a program on TV. Also, I don't want the other kids to call me a sissy. I could tell the teacher, but that's what got me into this mess in the first place.

The problem is that this is all I think about. I know my marks are going down and I will get zero for participation this term, but I am so afraid of getting beaten up and being made to look like an idiot. I just have to get out of class quickly and run home as fast as I can. I hope he forgets about me soon. I wish someone else would offend him so he would lay off me.

Things could get really bad now because the teacher asked me to stay late and I did not know what to say when he asked me why my classroom behaviour had changed. I told him about Greg's bullying. I am not sure what he will do now, but I am really afraid Greg will find out that I snitched on him again and get even madder. I am really scared—I wonder if I should tell my parents or call the police. I feel desperate . . .

Greg's Perspective

That little creep Keith keeps leaving class early so he can avoid getting what he deserves. I can see that I have frightened him, though, as he seems to run all the way home. Good! He should have known better than to be a snitch about me throwing the clothes around—it was really only a joke. I hate it when people don't treat me with respect and

I'm going to show everyone what happens when I get mad. I can't wait to get my hands on him and I know that he can't escape me forever. It's just a matter of time—I can wait until he drops his guard.

One thing that does bother me is that today the teacher asked him to stay after class. I bet the creep told him why he leaves early and runs home. Little snitch! I'll make him pay for that, too.

Teacher's Perspective

I wonder what is happening to Keith these days. He seems like a different student and his marks are going to reflect his non-participation in class. I feel sorry about that because I have always enjoyed and valued his input. He looks distracted and inattentive throughout the class, gathers his books up in a hurry, and darts out of the class before I can talk to him. I wonder if I should call his parents or talk to him first.

I have decided to talk to Keith first and managed to hold him back after class, although he was clearly very agitated about not leaving in a hurry. After some persistent questioning, he finally told me that Greg was bullying him by threatening to beat him up for tattling. I am not surprised, as I have noted for some time that Greg appears to be a bully in the classroom. The other kids treat him very carefully and he makes threatening comments quite openly. I wasn't sure whether he was a real threat or just acting like one, but clearly to Keith the treat of violence is very real. Now I have a real issue that I must deal with.

Questions to Consider

1. How can the teacher help Keith cope with being the victim of bullying?
2. How can the teacher help Greg stop being a bully?
3. What is the first step that should be taken by the teacher?

schools who occasionally experience anxiety about walking to and from school, going to the restroom, dressing in locker rooms, or changing classes (MacDonald, 1997). The more that students feel insecure about their physical safety, the less likely they will exhibit the on-task behaviours necessary for learning.

Belonging and Affection Needs. While these needs are most often met by family at home or the students' peers in and out of school, there must be elements of caring, trust, and respect in the interpersonal relationships between teachers and students. In other words, there should be a caring, supportive classroom climate (Novak and Purkey, 2001; Purkey and Novak, 1996). Such a climate is more likely to be created by teachers who subscribe to a referent power base in the classroom. The development of various teacher power bases will be studied in Chapter 4, "Philosophical Approaches to Classroom Management."

Withall (1969) has stressed that the most important variables in determining the climate of a classroom are the teacher's verbal and non-verbal behaviours (see Case 3.9). Appropriate student behaviour can be enhanced when teachers communicate the following to the learners:

Trust: "I believe you are able to learn and want to learn."

Respect: "Insofar as I try to help you learn, you are, by the same token, helping me to learn."

CASE 3.9 • *Turning Off Students*

Ms. Barrie, a high school science teacher, is quite concerned over what she perceives to be a significant decrease in student participation throughout the year. She views the problem as follows: "I ask a lot of questions. Early in the year, many students volunteer, but within a few weeks I find that volunteering has almost ceased and the only way I can get students to participate is to call on them."

Arrangements are made to observe the class to determine the causes of the problem. Teacher questions, student responses, and teacher feedback are recorded. An example of one such interaction follows:

Teacher question: "We know that man is in the family of Hominidae. What is man's taxonomic order?"

Student response: "Mammals."

Teacher feedback: "No, it's not mammals. We had this material last week; you should know it. The answer is primates."

Further observation reveals that about 70 percent of Ms. Barrie's feedback is totally or partially negative. Students note that they don't like being put down because their answers aren't exactly what Ms. Barrie wants. One student states, "I answer only when I know I'm correct. If I don't understand something, I often just let it go rather than be drilled."

Questions to Consider

1. Describe a learning situation that you have been in that has made you reluctant or nervous about answering/asking questions.

2. Reword the teacher's feedback so that the student will be encouraged to contribute again.

Caring: "I perceive you as a unique and worthwhile person whom I want to help to learn and grow." (Withall, 1979)

For students to learn effectively, they must participate fully in the learning process. This means they must be encouraged to ask and answer questions, attempt new approaches, make mistakes, and ask for assistance. However, learners engage in these behaviours only in settings in which they feel safe from being ridiculed or made to feel inadequate. Study Case 3.9. As the year progressed, Ms. Barrie failed to demonstrate her trust, respect, and caring for her students. Thus, her students were discouraged from fully participating in the learning process.

Comments such as, "Why do you ask so many questions?"; "You should know this; we studied it last week"; or "Everyone should understand this; there should be no questions" serve no useful purpose. Indeed, they hinder learner participation, confidence, and motivation and lead to off-task behaviour. Glasser (1978) sees failure as the root of misbehaviour, noting that when students don't learn at the expected rate, they get less "care" and recognition from the teacher. As the situation continues, students see themselves as trapped. Acceptance and recognition, it seems to them, can be gained only through misbehaviour. In sharp contrast to the feelings of Ms. Barrie's students are those of the grade 5 students in Case 3.10.

CASE 3.10 • *"I'm Going to Be Sorry When Grade 5 Is Over"*

One afternoon last May, I was acting as a parent volunteer with my daughter's grade 5 class to supervise at a track and field meet. While we were sitting around waiting for the final event, I overhead a group of grade 5 students talking. I paid very little attention until I heard one of them say, "I'm going to be sorry when grade 5 is over." I observed that the other students appeared to be in agreement, what with the nodding of heads and mutterings of, "Yeah, me too." Interested, I interrupted the conversation and asked if they would be willing to explain to me why they felt this way. Their comments follow.

"She lets us give our opinions."

"If we say something stupid, she doesn't say anything."

"She lets us decide how we are going to do things."

"She gives us suggestions and helps us when we get stuck."

"You can say how you feel."

"She gives us choices."

"She tells us what she thinks, but doesn't want us to think like her. Some teachers tell us their opinions, but you know that they really want you to think the same way."

"We learn a lot."

Questions to Consider

1. Describe this grade 5 teacher's philosophy of education.
2. What were these children learning?
3. Given the teacher's skill, what do you think would be the response from children at the primary level, the intermediate level, or the senior level to such teaching?

Children's Pursuit of Social Recognition and Self-Esteem

Social Recognition

Alfred Adler, the renowned psychiatrist, and Rudolph Dreikurs, Adler's student and colleague, believed that behaviour can be best understood using three key premises:

1. People are social beings who have a need to belong, to be recognized, and to be accepted.
2. Behaviour is goal-directed and has the purpose of gaining the recognition and acceptance that people want.
3. People can choose how they behave; they can behave or misbehave. Their behaviour is not outside their control.

Putting these key ideas together, Adler and Dreikurs theorized that people choose to try a wide variety of behaviours to see which behaviours gain them the recognition and acceptance they want. When socially sanctioned behaviours do not produce the needed recognition and acceptance, people often choose to misbehave in the mistaken belief that socially unacceptable behaviours will produce the recognition they seek.

Applying these premises to children's conduct, Dreikurs, Grundwald, and Pepper (1982) have identified four goals of disruptive behaviours: attention getting, power seeking, revenge seeking, and the display of inadequacy. According to this theory, these goals, which are usually sequential, are strongest in elementary-aged children but are also present in adolescents.

Attention-seeking students make up a large part of the misbehaving population in the schools. These students may ask question after question; use excessive charm; continually need help or assistance; and continually ask for the teacher's approval, call out, or show off. In time, the teacher usually becomes annoyed. When the teacher reprimands or gives these children attention, they temporarily stop their attention-seeking behaviour. In Case 3.11, Kayer is a child who feels that he is not getting the recognition he desires. He sees no chance of gaining this recognition through socially accepted or constructive contributions. He first channels his energies into gaining attention. Like all attention-seeking students, he has the notion that he is important only when others take notice of him and acknowledge his presence. When attention-getting behaviour no longer gives the students the recognition they want, many of them seek recognition through the next goal, power, which is exactly what Kayer does when he begins to confront the teacher openly.

Students who seek power through misbehaviour feel that they can do what they want and that nobody can make them do anything they don't want to do. By challenging teachers, they often gain social acceptance from their peers. Power-seeking students argue, lie, ignore, become stubborn, have temper tantrums, and become disobedient in general to show that they are in command of the situation. Teachers feel threatened or challenged by these children and often feel compelled to force them into compliance. Once teachers enter into power struggles with power-seeking students, the students usually "win." Even if they do not succeed in getting what they want, they succeed in

CASE 3.11 • *Seeking Faulty Goals*

Kayer is a grade 6 student of average academic ability. On the first day of class, when students are asked to choose seats, Kayer chooses the one next to the window in the back of the room. Between classes, he rarely interacts with classmates. Instead he either bolts out of the class first or slowly swaggers out last.

During instructional times, he either nonchalantly leans back in his seat or jumps up and calls out answers. During seat work, he often has to be reminded to begin, and once finished, he taps his pencil, wanders around the back of the room, or noisily moves his chair and desk.

Kayer's behaviour often improves for short periods of time after excessive teacher attention, ranging from positive reinforcement to reprimands. These periods of improvement are followed by a return to disruptive behaviours. Kayer's attention-seeking behaviour continues throughout the first half of the school year.

As time goes on, the teacher usually yells at Kayer, sends him to the principal, or makes comments in front of the class that reflect her extreme frustration.

Eventually, the teacher's behaviour is characterized by threats, such as, "You will stay after school longer every day until you begin to behave," or "Every day that you don't turn in your homework, you will have 20 more problems to do." Kayer sees immediately the impossibility of some of the threats and boldly says, "If I have to stay longer after school each day, in two weeks I'll have to sleep here." There are tremendous amounts of laughter from his classmates at such comments. However, after a week or two, Kayer says, "I'm not coming for your detention," and "You can't make me do homework if I don't want to." The teacher no longer feels annoyed but now feels threatened and challenged.

Whenever problems arise in the classroom, the teacher and students are quick to blame Kayer. Occasionally, he is accused of things that he has not done, and he is quick to shout, "I didn't do it; I'm always the one who gets blamed for everything around here." His classmates now show extreme annoyance with his behaviours, and Kayer resorts to acts directed against individuals. He kicks students' chairs and intentionally knocks over others' books as he walks down the aisles.

One day, one of the boys in the class accuses Kayer of taking his book. Without warning, Kayer flips the student's desk. The student falls backward, lands on his arm, and breaks it. As a result, Kayer is suspended.

When Kayer returns from his suspension, he is told that he will be sent to the office for any violation of a classroom rule. He is completely ignored by his classmates.

For the rest of the year, Kayer comes in, goes to the back of the room, does no work, and bothers no one. At first, the teacher tries to get Kayer involved, but all efforts are to no avail. The teacher thinks to herself that she has tried everything she knows. "If he wants to just sit there, let him. At least he isn't bothering anyone any more," she says.

Postscript: Teachers should be very aware of student behaviour and act quickly to provide feedback that will redirect inappropriate behaviours. In Kayer's case, the teacher could have determined that Level II in the CALM model—act—applied in this scenario. Once it has been decided that acting is necessary, do not hesitate. It is important to realize that prompt action at Level III may have defused the situation without further complications. However, the teacher chose to ignore the situation until it became more confrontational.

Questions to Consider

1. Describe all the strategies used by this teacher to deal with Kayer's negative behaviour.

2. In light of the CALM model, describe what other strategies the teacher might have employed.

3. Should a teacher modify expectations for an exceptional student like Kayer? What impact might modifications have on the rest of the class?

---

getting teachers to fight, thereby giving them undue attention and time as well as control of the situation. If a teacher "wins" the power struggle, the winning reinforces the student's idea that power is what really counts.

With a power-seeking student, reprimands from the teacher result in intensified challenges or temporary withdrawal before new power-seeking behaviours reappear. As power struggles develop between a teacher and a student, both teacher-controlling and student-power-seeking behaviours usually become more severe and the student–teacher relationship deteriorates further (Levin and Shanken-Kaye, 1996). If students see themselves as losing the power struggle, they often move to the next goal—seeking revenge.

When students perceive that they have no control over their environment, they experience an increased sense of inferiority and futility. They feel that they have been treated unfairly and are deeply hurt by what they consider to be others' disregard for their feelings. They seek revenge by hurting others, often not just those who they think have hurt them. For instance, Kayer sought his revenge on random individuals who happened to be sitting along his aisle. Revenge-seeking children destroy property, threaten other students and sometimes the teacher, engage in extremely rough play, and use obscenities.

When working with these students, teachers feel defeated and hurt and have a difficult time focusing on what is best for the student. Teacher reprimands usually result in an explosive display of anger and abusiveness from the student. Over time, the teacher feels a strong desire to "get even."

Unfortunately, revenge-seeking behaviours elicit dislike and more hurt from others. Revenge-seeking students continually feel a deep sense of despair and worthlessness. Their interactions with other people often result in negative feelings about themselves, which eventually move them to the last goal—the display of inadequacy. These students cannot be motivated and refuse to participate in class activities. Their message is clear: "Don't expect anything from me because I have nothing worthwhile to give." They are often heard saying, "Why don't you just leave me alone—I'm not bothering anyone"; "Mind your own business"; "Why try, I'll just get it wrong"; or "I can't do it."

Teachers often feel that they have tried everything with these students. Further attempts usually result in very little, if any, change in the students' refusal to show interest, to participate, or to interact with others. Kayer's teacher actually felt somewhat relieved that he no longer was a disturbing influence in class. However, if the teacher had been able to stop his progression toward the display of inadequacy, Kayer would have had a much more meaningful and valuable grade 6 learning experience, and the teacher would have felt much more professionally competent.

Most of the goals of misbehaviour are pursued one at a time, but some students switch back and forth between goals. Goal-seeking misbehaviours can also be situational. The CALM model, which is the decision-making hierarchical approach to classroom management presented in this book, offers many strategies for working with children seeking these four mistaken goals. In addition, specific management techniques for each goal are discussed in detail in Charles, Senter, and Barr (1995), Dreikurs, Grundwald, and Pepper (1982), Dubelle and Hoffman (1984), and Sweeney (1981).

Self-Esteem

Self-esteem, or a feeling of self-worth, is a basic need that individuals continually strive to meet. Without a positive sense of self-esteem, a child is vulnerable to a variety of social, psychological, and learning problems (Gilliland, 1986).

In his definitive work on self-esteem, Stanley Coopersmith (1967) wrote that self-esteem is made up of four components:

Significance: a learner's belief that she is liked, accepted, and important to others who are important to her.

Competence: a learner's sense of mastery of age-appropriate tasks that have value to her.

Power: a learner's ability to control important parts of her environment.

Virtue: closely akin to significance, a learner's sense of worthiness to another person's well-being because of the care and help she provides to the other person.

If families, teachers, or communities fail to provide prosocial opportunities that allow students to experience a sense of significance, competence, power, and virtue, students are likely to express these four components in negative, distorted ways (Levin and Shanken-Kaye, 1996).

It is possible to express the concept of self-esteem as an equation. Manifested in this way, the equation offers an explanation of why students choose to be disruptive:

$$\text{Self-Esteem} = \text{Significance} + \text{Competence} + \text{Power} + \text{Virtue}$$

Chronically disruptive students have low levels of significance because, typically, they are not liked or accepted by their teachers, peers, and sometimes even their parents. Their levels of competence are depressed because they rarely achieve academically, socially, or extracurricularly. In addition, because these students rarely choose or are rarely selected by the teacher to interact responsibly with others, their sense of virtue is low. Therefore, as the self-esteem equation indicates, the only component left to build a chronically disruptive student's self-esteem is *power*. It is exactly this striving for power, or control of the environment, that is operating when students choose to behave disruptively. In fact, the chronically disruptive student can be viewed as the most powerful individual in the classroom. How she behaves often determines the amount of time spent on learning in the classroom and whether the teacher leaves the classroom with a headache, or, in some cases, leaves the profession. It is, however,

CASE 3.12 • *Just Can't Get Respect!*

Rob, Justin, Ami, Tanya, and Miya, who are all grade 10 students, are talking in the hallway outside their last-period class. They are animated and excited about an upcoming weekend event. Ms. Wertz, who teaches across the hall and knows Rob from last year, comes out of her classroom to see who is making the noise. She raises her voice to a very high level and says, "Rob, get into your class immediately. A struggling student like you should never be standing around wasting time like this. You need all the time in class you can get." Rob replies in a respectful calm tone, "Ms. Wertz, my class is right here and we have another two minutes before we . . . " Before he can finish, Ms. Wertz interrupts, "Don't give me your feeble excuses—you always have excuses." There is a silence among the students in the hall and then Rob replies again

in a calm, respectful manner, "Ms Wertz, this is not an excuse, this is my class and these are the rules in this class. We are allowed to stay in the halls and talk with our friends until the teacher is ready to start." Rob's friends in the hall are angry on his behalf and talk about ways of telling the principal about what they see as inappropriate behaviour on the part of Ms. Wertz.

Questions to Consider

1. What previous events prompted Ms. Wertz's behaviour?

2. How are both Ms. Wertz and Rob damaged by this encounter?

3. What, if anything, do you think the student bystanders should do in response to what they see as an injustice? Do you think that their actions would help or harm Rob?

important to note that this is not prosocial power but distorted power. The display of such power provides the student with a distorted sense of significance and competence that is evident in this type of mindset: "The other kids know that they can count on me to get Mr. Beal to go ballistic and liven this class up a bit."

As Case 3.12 illustrates, when teachers interact with students without considering the students' self-esteem, they increase the likelihood that students will use distorted power to preserve self-esteem. If a student's self-esteem is publicly threatened in front of peers, the likelihood of the young person using distorted power increases.

Stages of Cognitive and Moral Development

Not long ago, it was believed that children thought exactly the same way as adults. Jean Piaget's work in the area of cognitive development, however, has shown that children move through distinct stages of cognitive and moral development. At each stage, children think and interpret their environment differently than children at other stages. For this reason, a child's behaviour varies as she moves from one stage to another. An understanding of the stages of development enables a teacher to better understand student behaviour patterns.

Cognitive Development

Throughout his life, Piaget studied how children interacted with their environment and how their intellect developed. To him, knowledge was the transformation of an individual's experience with the environment, not the accumulation of facts and pieces of information. His research resulted in the formulation of a four-stage, age-related cognitive development theory (Piaget, 1970), which has significantly influenced the manner in which children are educated.

Piaget called the four stages of development *the sensory-motor*, *the preoperational*, *the concrete operational*, and *the formal operational stages*. The sensory-motor stage occurs from birth to approximately 2 years of age. It is characterized by the refinement of motor skills and the use of the five senses to explore the environment. This stage, obviously, has little importance for teachers working with school-age children.

The preoperational stage occurs from approximately 2 to 7 years of age and is the stage most children have reached when they begin their school experience. Children at this stage are egocentric—they are unable to conceive that others may see things differently than they do. Although their ability to give some thought to decisions is developing, the great majority of the time they act only on perceptive impulses. Their short attention span interacts with their static thinking, resulting in an inability to think of a sequence of steps or operations. Their sense of time and space is limited to short duration and close proximity.

The concrete operational stage occurs from approximately 7 to 12 years of age. Children are able to order and classify objects and to consider several variables simultaneously as long as they have experiences with "concrete" content. These children need step-by-step instructions if they are expected to work through lengthy procedures. What can be frustrating to teachers who do not understand the characteristics of this stage is that these children do not attempt to check their conclusions, have difficulty thinking about thinking (how they arrived at certain conclusions), and seem unaware of and unconcerned with inconsistencies in their own reasoning.

At about the age of 12, at the earliest, children begin to move into the formal operational stage. They start to develop independent critical-thinking skills, plan lengthy procedures, and consider a number of possible answers to problems. They no longer are tied to concrete examples but instead are able to use symbols and verbal examples. These children, who are adolescents, begin to think about their own and others' thinking, which leads them to consider motives; the past, present, and future; the abstract; the remote; and the ideal. The methodological implications for teaching students at each stage are straightforward and have been researched and written about extensively (Adler, 1966; Gorman, 1972; Karplus, 1977).

Moral Development

Piaget related his theory of a child's cognitive development directly to the child's moral development. Through his work, Piaget demonstrated that children are close to or at the formal operational stage of cognitive development before they possesses the intellectual ability to evaluate, consider, and act on abstract moral dilemmas. Thus, what an elementary schoolchild thinks is bad or wrong is vastly different from what an adolescent thinks is bad or wrong (Piaget, 1965).

Using Piaget's work as his basis, Laurence Kohlberg proposed that moral development progresses through six levels of moral reasoning: *punishment–obedience, exchange of favours, good boy–nice girl, law and order, social contract,* and *universal ethical principles* (Kohlberg, 1969, 1975).

Between the ages of 4 and 6, children have a punishment–obedience orientation to moral reasoning. Their decisions are based on the physical consequences of an act: will they be punished or rewarded? Outcomes are paramount, and there is very little comprehension of a person's motive or intention. Children's egocentrism at this stage limits their ability to see other points of view or alternatives.

Between the ages of 6 and 9, children move into the exchange of favours orientation. At this level, judgments are made on the basis of reciprocal favours: "You do this for me and I will do this for you." Fulfilling one's own needs comes first. Children are just beginning to understand the motives behind behaviours and outcomes.

Between the ages of 10 and 15, children move into the good boy–nice girl orientation. Conformity dictates behaviour and reasoning ability. Peer review is strong, and judgments about how to behave are made on the basis of avoiding criticism and pleasing others. The drive to conform to peer pressure is so strong that it is quite common for children to follow peers unquestioningly; at the same time, these children always ask *why* when requests are made by adults.

The law-and-order orientation dominates moral reasoning between the ages of 15 and 18. Individuals at this stage of development are quite rigid. Judgments are made on the basis of obeying the law. Motives are understood but not wholeheartedly considered if the behaviour has broken a law. At this stage, teenagers are quick to recognize and point out inconsistencies in expected behaviour. It is quite common to hear them say to adults, "Why do I have to do this? You don't." It is at this stage that adolescents begin to recognize the consequences of their actions.

According to Kohlberg, few people reach the last two levels of moral reasoning. The social contract orientation is reached by some between the ages of 18 and 20. At this level, moral judgments are made on the basis of upholding individual rights and democratic principles. Those who reach this level recognize that individuals differ in their values and do not accept "because I said so" or "that's the way it is" as rationales for rules.

The highest level of moral reasoning is the universal ethical orientation. Judgments are based on respect for the dignity of human beings and on what is good for humanity, not on selfish interests or standards upheld by authority.

As in cognitive development, the ages given above for any of the moral development stages are approximations. Individuals continually move back and forth between stages, depending on the moral situation at hand, especially at transitional points between stages.

Behaviour: The Interaction of Cognitive and Moral Development

In order to understand how children perceive what is right and wrong, what cognitive skills they are able to use, and what motivates their social and academic behaviour, teachers must know the stages of moral and cognitive growth. Teachers must also recognize common developmental behaviours that are a result of the interaction of the

Some misbehaviour can result when instruction is not matched with students' cognitive development stages.

cognitive and moral stages through which the children pass. While this interaction does not and cannot explain all disruptive classroom behaviours, it does provide a basis on which we can begin to understand many disruptive behaviours. Table 3.1 summarizes the cognitive and moral stages of development, their characteristics, and associated behaviours.

At the beginning of elementary school, students are in the preoperational stage cognitively and the punishment–obedience stage morally. Their behaviour is a result of the interplay of such factors as their egocentricity, limited sense of time and space, little comprehension of others' motives, and short attention span. At this stage, children become frustrated easily, have difficulty sharing, argue frequently, believe that they are right and their classmates wrong, and tattle a lot.

From roughly grades 4 to 9, children are in the concrete operational stage cognitively and the exchange of favours to the good boy–nice girl stages morally. Early in this period, students form and re-form cliques, act on opinions based on a single or very few concrete characteristics, and tell secrets. They employ many annoying attention-seeking behaviours to please the teacher. Later in the period, the effects of peer conformity appear. Students are often off task because they are constantly in conversation with their friends. Those who do not fit into the peer group are excluded and ridiculed.

Students still have little patience with long discussions and lengthy explanations. They are unaware of, or unconcerned about, inconsistencies in their own thinking. They are closed-minded, often using such phrases as, "I know!"; "Do we have to discuss this?"; or "I don't care!" with a tone that communicates a nonchalant lack of interest.

TABLE 3.1 *Cognitive and Moral Development with Common Associated Behaviours*

Cognitive Stage	Cognitive Abilities	Moral Stage	Moral Reasoning	Common Behaviours
Sensorimotor (0–2)	use of senses to "know" environment			
Preoperational (2–7)	difficulty with conceiving others' points of view (egocentric) sense of time and space limited to short duration/close proximity difficulty thinking through steps or decisions; acts impulsively	punishment–obedience (4–6)	actions based on physical outcome little comprehension of motives egocentric	inattentiveness easily frustrated difficulty sharing arguments during day
Concrete Operational (7–12)	limited ability to think about thinking often will not check conclusions unaware of and unconcerned with their own inconsistencies	exchange of favours (6–9)	actions based on reciprocal favours fulfilling one's own needs comes first beginning to understand motives	cliques attention-getting behaviour exclusion of certain classmates inattentiveness during periods of discussion "know-it-all" attitude
		good boy–nice girl (10–15)	actions based on poor conformity	
Formal Operational (12–)	able to think about thinking can use independent critical thinking skills can consider motives; the past, present, and future; the abstract; and the ideal	law and order (15–18)	rigid judgments based on following the law motives and consequences recognized	point out inconsistencies between behaviours and rules challenge rules and policies demand rationale behind rules will not unquestioningly accept authority argumentative refuse to change even in face of punishment
		social contract (18–20)	actions based on upholding individual rights and democratic principles	
		universal ethical (few people reach this level)	actions based on respect for human dignity	

Age-specific behaviour often is the result of the interaction of cognitive and moral development.

By the time students are leaving grade 8 and entering high school, most of them are in the formal operational stage cognitively and moving from the good boy–nice girl stage to the law-and-order stage morally. By the end of high school, a few of them have reached the social contract level.

At this stage, students can deal with abstractness and conceive of many possibilities and ideals as well as the reality of their environment. Although peer pressure is still strong, they begin to see the need and rationale for rules and policies. Eventually, they see the need to protect rights and principles. They are now attempting to discover who they are, what they believe in, and what they are competent in.

Because students at this stage are searching for self-identity and are able to think abstractly, they often challenge the traditional values taught in school and home. They need to have a valid reason for why everything is the way it is. They will not accept "because I said so" as a legitimate reason to conform to a rule. Some young people will hold to a particular behaviour, explanation, or judgment—even in the face of punishment—if they feel that their individual rights have been challenged or violated. Unfortunately, many of these behaviours are carried out in an argumentative format.

There have been a number of studies supporting the idea that normal developmental changes can lead to disruptive behaviour. Jessor and Jessor (1977) found that the correlates of misbehaviour in school are (1) growth in independence; (2) decline in traditional ideology; (3) increase in relativistic morality; (4) increase in peer orientation; and (5) increase in modelling problem behaviours. They concluded that the normal course of developmental change leans toward a greater probability of problems. However, Clarizio and McCoy (1983) have found problem behaviours that occur as a developmental phenomenon have a higher probability of being resolved with increasing age. A study of 400 famous 20th-century men and women concluded that four out of five had experienced difficulties and problems related to school and schooling (Goertzel and Goertzel, 1962), which appears to support Clarizio and McCoy's findings.

Instructional Competence

At first glance, it would seem that the teacher has little or no control over the five influences of misbehaviour that have been discussed thus far. While it is true that a teacher cannot significantly alter the course of most of these societal, familial, and developmental events, she can control her instructional competence. Excellent instructional competence can minimize the effects of these ongoing events, maximize the learning potential in the classroom, and prevent misbehaviour caused by poor instructional methodology. Case 3.13 describes the difficult consequences for a teacher who did not understand the *art* of teaching.

In Case 3.13 on the next page, why does Ms. Cook, who is knowledgeable and enthusiastic about her subject matter and enjoys working with young people, have such management problems? Why do otherwise well-behaved students misbehave to such an extent in one particular class? The students' responses indicate a reasonable answer: the teacher's lack of skill in basic instructional methodology.

Because of Ms. Cook's instructional skill deficiencies, her students did not accord to her *expert power*, the social authority and respect a teacher receives because she possesses special knowledge and expertise (French and Raven, 1960). (This and other

This teacher has total control over the use of effective teaching strategies.

authority bases are discussed in depth in Chapter 4, "Philosophical Approaches to Classroom Management.") Her inability to communicate content clearly, evaluate and remediate student misunderstandings, and explain the relevancy of the content to her students' lives caused Ms. Cook's students to fail to recognize her expertise in the field of mathematics.

A teacher's ability to explain and clarify is foremost in developing authority. Kounin (1970) has found that teachers who are liked are described by students as those who can explain the content well, whereas those who are disliked leave students in some state of confusion. Kounin has also noted that when students are fond of their teachers, they are more likely to behave appropriately and are more motivated to learn. As Tanner has stated, "Teacher effectiveness, as perceived by pupils, invests the teacher

CASE 3.13 • *Not Being Able to Teach*

Ms. Cook loves mathematics and enjoys working with young people, which she often does in camp and youth organizations. After graduating with a B.Sc. in mathematics, she goes on to earn a master's degree in math and becomes certified to teach at the secondary level. She obtains a teaching position at a progressive suburban junior high school.

Ms. Cook conscientiously plans for all of her algebra and geometry classes and knows the material thoroughly. Within a few months, however, her classes are characterized by significant discipline problems. Most of her students are out of their seats, talking, throwing paper, and calling out jokes. They come in unprepared and, in a few instances, openly confront Ms. Cook's procedures and competence. Even though she is given assistance, supervision, and support from the administration, Ms. Cook decides not to return for her second year of teaching.

In an attempt to understand the class's behaviour, the students are interviewed at the end of the school year. The following are the most common responses concerning Ms. Cook's methods:

1. Gave unclear explanations

2. Discussed topics having nothing or little to do with the subject at hand
3. Kept repeating understood material
4. Wrote things on the board but never explained them, and her board work was sloppy
5. Would say, "We already did this" when asked for help
6. Did not involve the whole class and called on the same people
7. Had difficulty giving clear answers to questions
8. Didn't explain how to apply the material
9. Always used her note cards
10. Could not determine why the class was having difficulty understanding the material
11. Either gave the answers to the homework or didn't go over it, so no one had to do it

Questions to Consider

1. What is the common theme among Ms. Cook's students' complaints?
2. Describe Ms. Cook's beliefs about teaching.
3. What three suggestions would you have for Ms. Cook?

with classroom authority" (1978, 67). To students, teacher effectiveness translates to "explaining the material so that we can understand it." When this occurs, students regard the teacher as competent, and the teacher is invested with authority.

Summary

Although there are innumerable causes of misbehaviour in schools, this chapter has focused on some of the major ones.

Societal changes, most notably the effects of the knowledge explosion and the media revolution, have created an environment that is vastly different from the one that children of previous generations grew up in. More children now than ever before live in single-parent homes. Also, more children today are living at or below the poverty level than in previous generations. Because of these and other factors, some children's basic needs, including the need for self-esteem, are not met by the home. Such out-of-school experiences are much more significant predictors of school behaviour than children's in-school experiences. When a child's basic need for self-esteem is not met at home and/or is not met at school, discipline problems frequently result.

Throughout the school year, children's cognitive and moral development, as well as their continual need for social recognition, are reflected in their behaviour. Teachers have little or no control over many of these developments. What they can control is their own instructional competence. Excellent instruction can ameliorate the effects of outside influences and prevent the misbehaviour that occurs as a direct result of poor instruction. Effective teaching techniques are covered in detail in Chapter 5, "The Professional Teacher."

*Key Terms*_____

instructional practices/strategies/techniques/methodology: procedures that instructors use to deliver lesson materials.

off-task/norm-violating behaviours: conduct that is deemed inappropriate in the current environment.

on-task behaviours: conduct that is deemed appropriate and productive in the current environment.

*Exercises*_____

1. Look back on your own school experiences. What are some instructional techniques your teachers used that had the potential to change disruptive student behaviours?

2. What if anything can schools and classroom teachers do to help students meet the following basic human needs: (a) physiological, (b) safety and security, and (c) belonging and affection?

3. Self-esteem can be conceptualized mathematically as follows:

   Self-Esteem = Significance + Competence + Power + Virtue

   How does the self-esteem equation help to explain why students behave disruptively inside and outside the classroom?

4. How does the self-esteem equation provide insight into the types of interventions that can lead to decreasing a student's disruptive behaviour?

5. How does self-esteem or lack of self-esteem relate to success or failure?

6. Even though they are beyond the school's control, changes in society can influence student behaviour in school. What changes in society during the last 15 years do you feel have had negative influences on classroom behaviour?

7. In your opinion, can television programs and films cause students to misbehave in the classroom? If so, list some specific examples to support your opinion. If not, explain why.

8. Explain why some educational researchers believe that cognitive development is a prerequisite for moral development.

9. Considering students' cognitive development, how might an instructor teach the following concepts in grades 3, 7, and 11?

   a. volume of a rectangular solid = L W H
   b. civil rights and equality
   c. subject–predicate agreement
   d. gravity

10. How might inappropriate teaching of these concepts for the cognitive level of the students contribute to classroom discipline problems?

11. Considering students' moral development, what can we expect as typical reactions to the following events at each of the following grade levels?

Event	First	Fourth	Seventh	Twelfth
a. A student from a poor family steals the lunch ticket of a student from a wealthier family.				
b. A teacher gives the entire class a detention because of the disruptive behaviour of a few.				
c. A student destroys school property and allows another student to be falsely accused and punished for the vandalism.				
d. A student has points subtracted from her test score for talking after her test paper was already turned in.				

12. What are some normal behaviours for elementary students or high school students (considering their developmental level) that can be disruptive in a classroom?

13. What might a teacher do to allow the normal behaviours (listed in the answer to question 12) to be expressed, while at the same time preventing them from disrupting learning?

14. Disruptive students often rationalize their inappropriate behaviour by blaming it on the teacher: "I'll treat Mr. Lee with respect when he treats me with respect." Unfortunately, teachers often rationalize their negative behaviour toward a student by blaming it on the student: "I'll respect Nicole when she respects me." Using the levels of moral development, explain why the student's rationalization is understandable but the teacher's is not.

Weblinks

Behavioural Planning
www.edu.gov.mb.ca/k12/specedu/beh
Helps educators develop a range of responses to students with behaviour problems.

Media Awareness Network
www.media-awareness.ca/english/resources/research_documents/statistics/
television/tv_viewing_habits.cfm
A Canadian website that addresses television and violence.

Students with Challenging Behaviours: A Bibliography for K–12
www.sasked.gov.sk.ca/curr_inst/iru/bibs/speced/t-dh.html
Provides a list of documents that give information about students with challenging behaviours.

TeacherNet
www.teachernet.gov.uk
A UK site packed with resources designed to help teachers in the many aspects of teaching.

4

Philosophical Approaches to Classroom Management

Focus on the Principles of Classroom Management

1. How are theoretical approaches to classroom management useful to teachers as they manage their own and their students' behaviour?
2. What are the power bases that teachers can access in order to influence student behaviour?
3. Why is it important that the techniques a teacher employs to manage student behaviour be consistent with the teacher's beliefs about how students learn and develop?

Introduction

Teaching can be a threatening and frustrating experience, and all of us at some time entertain doubts about our ability to maintain effective classroom learning environments. For many teachers, however, these normal self-doubts, which are especially common early in a teaching career (Housego, 1992), lead to a frantic search for gimmicks, techniques, or tricks that they hope will allow them to survive in the real classroom world (Fast, Elliott, Hunter, and Bellamy, 2002). This is indeed unfortunate, as Case 4.1 on pages 79 and 80 illustrates. When classroom-management problems are approached with a frenetically sought-after bag of tricks instead of a carefully developed systematic plan for decision-making, teachers are likely to find themselves behaving in ways they later regret. The teachers who are most successful at creating a positive classroom atmosphere that enhances student learning are those who employ a carefully developed plan for classroom management. Clearly, any such plan must be congruent with their basic beliefs about the nature of the teaching and learning process. When teachers use this type of plan, they avoid the dilemma that Ms. Knepp encounters in Case 4.1.

There are multiple models or systems of classroom management and hundreds of techniques for promoting positive student behaviour within these models. Most of these techniques are effective in some situations, but not others; for some students, but not others; and for some teachers, but not others. "What most of the experts fail to mention is that the efficacy of a technique is contextually dependent. Who the teacher teaches and who the teacher is dictates which technique will have the greatest potential for addressing the complex management problems evidenced in classrooms" (Lasley,

1989). Because every technique is based implicitly or explicitly on some belief system concerning how human beings behave and why, classroom teachers must find prototypes of classroom management that are consistent with their beliefs and use them under appropriate circumstances.

CASE 4.1 • *The Tricks-of-the-Trade Approach*

Judy Knepp is a first-year teacher at Armstrong School. Although most of her classes are going well, she is having a great deal of difficulty with her grade 6 developmental reading class. Many of the students seem uninterested, lazy, immature, and rebellious. As a result of the class's continuous widespread chattering, Ms. Knepp spends the vast majority of her time yelling at and reprimanding individual students. She has considered using detention to control students, but there are so many disruptive students that she doesn't know whom to give detentions to first. The class has become such a battlefield, that she finds herself hating to go to school in the morning.

After struggling on her own for a couple of long weeks, Ms. Knepp decides that she had better ask somebody for help. She is reluctant to go to any of the administrators because she thinks that revealing the problem will result in a low official evaluation for her first semester's work. Finally, she decides to go to Ms. Hoffman, a veteran teacher of 14 years with a reputation for striking fear into the hearts of her grade 6 students.

After she tells Ms. Hoffman all about her horrendous class, Ms. Knepp waits anxiously for some words of wisdom that will help her to get the class under control. Ms. Hoffman's advice is short and to the point: "I'd just keep the whole class in for detention. Keep them until about 4:30 p.m. for a one day, and I guarantee you won't have any more trouble with them. These kids think they're tough, but when they see that you're just as mean and tough as they are, they'll melt pretty quickly."

Ms. Knepp is dismayed. She immediately thinks, "That's just not fair. What about those four or five kids who don't misbehave? Why should they have to stay in, too?" She does not voice her objections to Ms. Hoffman, fearing the veteran teacher will see her as rude and ungrateful. She does ask, "What about parents who object to such punishment?" Ms. Hoffman assures her that she has never had any trouble from parents and that the principal, Dr. Kropa, will support the disciplinary action even if any parents do object.

Ms. Knepp feels trapped. She knows that Ms. Hoffman expects her to follow through, and she fears that her colleague will tell the other veteran teachers if she doesn't take the advice. Like most newcomers, Ms. Knepp longs to be accepted.

Despite her misgivings, then, Ms. Knepp decides to follow the advice and to do so quickly before she loses her nerve. The next day, she announces that one more disruption—no matter who is the culprit—will bring detention for the entire class. For five minutes, silence reigns and the class actually accomplishes some work. Ms. Knepp has begun to breathe a long sigh of relief when suddenly she hears a loud "You pig!" from the back corner of the room. She is positive that all the students have heard the epithet and knows that she cannot ignore it. Ms. Knepp also fears that an unpoliced barb will mean disaster for her reading class.

"That does it. Everyone in this class has detention tomorrow after school." Immediately, the air is filled with "That ain't fair"; "I didn't do nothing"; "You wish"; and "Don't hold your breath." Naturally, most of these complaints come from the biggest troublemakers. However, several students who never cause trouble also complain bitterly that the punishment is unfair. Deep down, Ms. Knepp agrees with them, but she feels compelled to dismiss their complaints with a faint-hearted, "Well, life just isn't always fair, and you might as well learn that now." She stonewalls it through the rest of the class and is deeply relieved when the class is over.

When Ms. Knepp arrives at school the next morning, there is a note from Dr. Kropa in her box stating that the Palmers are coming in during her free period to talk about the detention vis-à-vis their son, Fred. Fred is one of the few students who rarely causes trouble. Ms. Knepp feels unable to defend her action. It contradicts her beliefs about fairness and how students should be treated. The conference is a disaster. Ms. Knepp begins by trying to convince the Palmers that she is right but ends by admitting that she, too, feels Fred has been dealt with too harshly. After the conference, she discusses the punishment with Dr. Kropa, who suggests that it is best to call it off. Ms. Knepp drags herself, half in tears, to her class. She is going to back down and rescind the punishment. Ms. Knepp believes that the kids will see this as a sign of weakness, and she is afraid of the consequences.

Questions to Consider

1. What might Ms. Knepp have done to avoid her dilemma with regard to following Ms. Hoffman's advice?
2. Why did the detention idea fail?
3. Should Ms. Knepp have rescinded the punishment? What should she have said to the class?
4. Most important, what can Ms. Knepp learn from the experience?

How can teachers ensure that their behaviour in dealing with classroom-management problems will be effective and will match their beliefs about students, teachers, and learning? First, they can understand their own basic beliefs about classroom management. Second, they can develop, based on their beliefs, a systematic plan for promoting positive student behaviour and dealing with inappropriate behaviour. Chapters 6 through 9 in this text, which provide multiple options for dealing with any single classroom-management problem, are designed to help teachers develop a systematic plan. We provide numerous options to allow teachers to develop a personal plan for encouraging appropriate student behaviour and for dealing with unacceptable behaviour in a manner that agrees with their own basic beliefs about management. Because there are numerous options, teachers can prioritize them in a hierarchical format.

To help teachers and future teachers lay the philosophical foundation for their own classroom-management plan, we offer in this chapter an overview of a variety of philosophical approaches to classroom management. So that they may be considered in a more systematic and orderly fashion, the approaches are grouped under two major headings: *teacher power bases* and *theories of classroom management*. The first section discusses the four power bases—the types of power or influence that are available to teachers to promote appropriate student behaviour. In the second section, we explain three theories of classroom management and their underlying beliefs—we also include models and techniques for each of the theoretical approaches.

It is important to be aware of the inherent connection between the four power bases and the three theories. Each of the three theories relies on the dominant use of one or two power bases. Teachers can examine the foundations on which their own classroom-management plans rest by comparing their beliefs with those inherent in each of the various teacher power bases and theories of classroom management.

It is appropriate here to emphasize that teachers should reflect on the levels that the CALM model recommends for dealing with issues of classroom management. For a more detailed description, please refer to Chapter 1 of this book.

The CALM model comprises the following four levels:

Level I: *Consider* the question of whether student behaviour has become disruptive in your classroom.

Level II: *Act* only when it becomes necessary.

Level III: *Lessen* your invasive responses to deal with the disruptive situation.

Level IV: *Manage* the milieu to quickly return to an effective learning environment.

Teacher Power Bases

Although it has been expanded to include other elements (Erchul, Raven, and Whichard, 2001), the foundational work of French and Raven remains relevant for teachers (1960). They have identified four different types of power that teachers, as social agents, may use to influence student behaviour. The effective teacher is aware of the type of power he wants to use to influence student behaviour and is also aware of the type of power that is implicit in each of the techniques available. It cannot be emphasized enough that when teachers' beliefs and behaviours are consistent, they are more likely to be successful than when a teacher functions inconsistently. When beliefs and behaviours are congruent, teachers usually follow through and are consistent in dealing with student behaviour. Students usually perceive such teachers as genuine; they practise what they preach. As you read the descriptions of the four types of power bases, ask yourself which type or types fit your beliefs and which ones you could use comfortably. Although teachers likely use each of the four types of power at some time or other, most tend to have a dominant power base.

The four teacher power bases are presented in a hierarchical format, beginning with those more likely to foster student control over their own behaviour and proceeding to those that bring forth increasing teacher control. If teachers believe, as we do, that one of the important long-range goals of schooling is to encourage student self-direction, then their use of those power bases at the top of the hierarchy becomes paramount. For teachers who do not share the goal of achieving student self-direction, the hierarchical arrangement of power bases will not be as important. Whatever teachers believe about the long-range goals of education, they must understand the four teacher power bases—no single one is effective for all students, all classrooms, or all teachers. Thus, effective classroom management requires the use of a variety of power bases.

Referent Power

Consider Case 4.2. The type of power Mr. Emig uses to influence student behaviour has been termed *referent power* by French and Raven (1960). When a teacher has **referent power**, students behave as the teacher wishes because they like the teacher as a person. Students view the teacher as a good person who is concerned about them, cares about their learning, and demands a certain type of behaviour because it is in their best interests.

CASE 4.2 • *The Involved Teacher*

Mr. Emig is a grade 8 teacher in Prince Philip School, which has a reputation of being a rough inner-city school where it is difficult to teach because so many students are unruly. Mr. Emig teaches English to all the grade 8 students, and his classes are admired by administrators and teachers alike. He is admired because he never sends misbehaving students to the principal's office, never gives detentions, and never needs to call parents to discuss student behaviour. Rather, Mr. Emig is able to concentrate on his lessons and spend his time pinpointing novels to study that will engage his students in discussions of issues related to social justice. Other teachers, who often have problems with the very same students who participate quite enthusiastically in Mr. Emig's lessons, are openly envious of the fact that Mr. Emig seldom suffers any behavioural problems with his students—they actually enjoy his classes.

The principal, Mr. Karr, and the vice-principal have most of their days filled with the behavioural problems of students in other classes. They begin to wonder if other teachers could learn something from Mr. Emig's teaching style and techniques. Accordingly, Mr. Karr decides to ask some of the students why they behave so well in Mr. Emig's class. The students are willing to share their reasons openly. They agree that they like Mr. Emig because he is often involved in extracurricular school activities with them. They point out that he sponsors the school newspaper, goes skiing with the ski club each Friday night in the winter, always shows up at their athletic events, chaperones school dances on a regular basis, and is the staff advisor to the student council. He is friendly and encouraging in all these situations and the students say they know him well and like him. Students also say they feel Mr. Emig is "real" and that he never talks down to them. One of the boys adds that Mr. Emig respects them as people. They do not see him just as a teacher, but also as a well-rounded and really good person who is interested in them and their activities. "He really seems to care about kids." They add that, as a result, no one ever feels like hassling him in class, they actually do their homework, and class members enjoy some good discussions about the novels they're reading for assignments.

Questions to Consider

1. How important is it to be liked by your students?
2. Should students view their teachers as "cool"? Why or why not?
3. Explain which is more important in the student–teacher relationship: being respected or being liked?
4. Describe the responsibilities and role of teachers in student activities beyond the classroom.

There are two requirements for the effective use of referent power: (1) teachers must perceive that the students like them, and (2) teachers must communicate that they care about and like the students. They do this through positive non-verbal gestures; positive oral and written comments; extra time and attention; and displays of sincere interest in students' ideas, activities, and, especially, learning. Teachers with referent power are able to appeal directly to students to act a certain way. Examples of such direct appeals are, "I'm really not feeling well today. Please keep the noise level at a minimum," and "It really makes me angry when you hand assignments in late. Please have your assignments ready on time." These teachers might handle Ms. Knepp's problem with a statement such as, "You disappoint me and make me very angry when you misbehave and disrupt class time. I spend a great deal of time planning activities that you will enjoy and that will help you to learn, but we lose so much time to misbehaviour that we don't get to them. I would really appreciate it if you would stop the antics."

Referent power must not be confused with attempts to be the students' friend. Teachers who want to be friends with students usually are dependent on students to fulfill their personal needs. This dependency creates an environment in which students are able to manipulate teachers. Over time, teacher and students become equals, and the teacher loses the ability to influence students to behave appropriately. In contrast, teachers who use referent power are authority figures and do make demands on students. Students carry out the teacher's wishes because they like the teacher as a teacher, not as a friend.

It is neither possible nor wise to use referent power all the time with all students. In any classroom, it may be difficult to establish referent power with some students. In these cases, a different technique must be selected because the foundation for using referent power cannot be built. However, when students make it clear, through their general reactions before, during, and after class, that they like the teacher, and when the teacher has communicated caring and concern to students, the use of referent power can make classroom management easy.

Expert Power

Ms. Sanchez in Case 4.3 is a teacher who uses **expert power** to influence student behaviour. When a teacher enjoys expert power, students behave as the teacher wishes because they view that teacher as someone who is good and knowledgeable and who can help them to learn. This is the power of professional competence. To use expert power effectively, two important conditions must be fulfilled: (1) students must believe the teacher has both special knowledge and the teaching skills to help them acquire that knowledge, and (2) students must value learning what the teacher is teaching. Students may value what they are learning for any number of reasons—the subject matter is inherently interesting, they can use that knowledge in the real world, they want good grades, or they want to reach some personal goal such as college or a job.

Teachers who use expert power successfully communicate their competence through mastery of content material, the use of motivating teaching techniques, clear explanations, and thorough class preparation. In other words, such teachers use their professional knowledge to help students learn. When expert power is employed

CASE 4.3 • *Her Reputation Precedes Her*

Ms. Sanchez is a chemistry teacher at Lakefront High School. Each year, she teaches an academic chemistry course for university-bound students. For the past five years, none of her students has failed the final chemistry exam. All failing students have studied in one of two other classes with different chemistry teachers. This fact has become obvious to students, parents, administrators, and other teachers in the school. They've all noticed that students in Ms. Sanchez's class not only habitually pass the final exam in the course relatively easily but that they also have a strong foundation for achieving a university credit in chemistry as well.

Because of her reputation as an excellent teacher, students who are serious about their academic futures, strive to get into Ms. Sanchez's classes. They recognize that she knows a lot about chemistry and also has a large repertoire of teaching skills and strategies. In addition, Ms. Sanchez has a reputation for really caring about the success of each student and is available for

extra help early in the morning before class starts. She treats each student as an individual learner and encourages all of them to seek help when they feel they need it.

When people walk past Ms. Sanchez's classroom or when administrators enter it, they consistently notice the same thing: students are thoroughly engaged in class activities with very little off-task behaviour. The administrators have noted for five years that Ms. Sanchez almost never needs to send behaviourally challenged pupils to the office.

Questions to Consider

1. What did Ms. Sanchez likely do over the past five years to build such a positive reputation?

2. How could Ms. Sanchez's skills and attitudes be useful for other staff members?

3. Imagine a new student attempting to undermine Ms. Sanchez. How do you think the teacher would respond?

successfully, students make comments similar to these: "I behave because he is a really good teacher"; "She makes biology interesting"; and "He makes you really want to learn." A teacher with an expert power base might say to Ms. Knepp's disruptive class: "I'm sure you realize how important reading is. If you can't read, you will have a rough time being successful this year. You know that I can help you learn to read and to read well, but I can't do that if you won't behave as I've asked you to behave."

As is the case with referent power, a teacher may be able to use expert power with some classes and some students but not with others. A math teacher may be able to use expert power with an academic calculus group but not with a remedial math group; an auto mechanics teacher may be able to use expert power with the vocational-technical students, but not with students who take auto mechanics to fill up their schedules.

One final caveat concerning this type of power: whereas most primary teachers are perceived as experts by their students, expert power does not seem to be effective in motivating these students to behave appropriately. Thus, unlike the other three power bases, which can be employed at all levels, the appropriate use of expert power seems to be confined to students beyond the primary grades.

Legitimate Power

The third type of power identified by French and Raven and used by Mr. Kumar in Case 4.4 is **legitimate power**. The teacher who seeks to influence students through legitimate power expects students to behave appropriately because the teacher has the legal and formal authority for maintaining appropriate behaviour in the classroom. In other words, students behave because the teacher is the teacher, and inherent in that role are a certain authority and power.

Teachers who wish to use a legitimate power base must demonstrate through their behaviour that they accept the responsibilities, as well as the power, inherent in the role of teacher. They must be viewed by students as fitting the stereotypical image of teacher (e.g., in dress, speech, and mannerisms). Students must believe that teachers and school administrators are working together. School administrators help teachers gain legitimate power by making clear, through words and actions, that students are expected to treat teachers as legitimate authority figures. Teachers help themselves gain legitimate power by following and enforcing school rules and by supporting school policies and administrators.

Students who behave because of legitimate power make statements such as, "I behave because the teacher asked us to. You're supposed to do what the teacher says." A teacher who employs legitimate power might use a statement in Ms. Knepp's class such as, "I do not like the way you people are treating me. I am your teacher. I will not

CASE 4.4 • *"School Is Your Job"*

Mr. Kumar looked at his grade 4 class noting that many of them were talking to friends or else staring into space rather than doing the assignment that he had just passed to them. He felt a surge of anger coupled with frustration. He said, "You are really disappointing me as you sit there wasting precious time. School is not a place for wasting time. School is your job just as your parents have jobs. It is *my* job to see that you work hard and learn something during my classes." As he continued, Mr. Kumar noticed some students were listening intently while others appeared bored. "Your parents pay taxes so that you'll have the chance to come to school and learn. You and I both have a responsibility to do what we are supposed to do. Now, cut out the daydreaming and talking and do your math." When he finished, there was a silence in the class and most students did appear to be doing their math assignment.

Questions to Consider

1. How long do you think Mr. Kumar's rant will keep the students focused on the math assignment?
2. Explain the effectiveness of this strategy.
3. What else could Mr. Kumar have said that might have been more effective in keeping his students focused?
4. Using your own "rant" technique and words, try role-playing to emulate the actual classroom scenario where one of the players is the teacher and the others are the students.

put up with disrespectful behaviour. I am responsible for making sure that you learn, and I'm going to do that. If that means using the principal and other school authorities to help me do my job, I'll do just that."

Because of the societal changes that we discussed in Chapter 3, most teachers rightly believe that today's students are less likely to be influenced by legitimate power than students of 30 or 40 years ago were. However, it is still possible to use legitimate power with some classes and some students.

Reward and Coercive Power

Notice how the teacher in Case 4.5 is using **reward and coercive power** to influence student behaviour. Although they may be considered two separate types of teacher authority, reward and coercive power are really two sides of the same coin. They are both based on behavioural notions of learning, they both foster teacher control over student behaviour, and they are both governed by the same principles of application.

There are a number of requirements for the effective use of this power base: (1) the teacher must be consistent in assigning and withholding rewards and punishments; (2) the teacher must ensure that students see the connection between their behaviour and a reward or punishment; (3) the rewards or punishments must be perceived as rewards or punishments by the student (many students view a three-day, out-of-school suspension as a vacation, not a punishment).

CASE 4.5 • *Going to Recess*

"Okay, grade 2s, it's time to put your spelling books away and get ready for recess. Now, we must all remember that we get ready by putting all our books and materials neatly and quietly in our desks and then we fold our hands on the desk and look quietly at me. Let's see which row is ready first." There was a pause and a flurry of activity and then the class began to settle down. The teacher said, "I see that Tammy's row was ready first. Okay, Tammy's row can get their coats and boots and go quietly out to the playground." As everyone in Tammy's row rose to leave, the teacher spoke sharply, "Oh, no, wait a minute. Where are you going Joe? You're not to enjoy recess this week because of your poor behaviour on the bus. Instead, you are to go to Mr. Li's room and do an additional math assignment. I will be in to check it after recess."

Questions to Consider

1. Name three strategies being used by this teacher.
2. Explain why you agree or disagree with Joe's punishment and the teacher's reminder to him in this context.
3. If Joe misbehaved on the bus, what other penalty might the teacher have chosen for the student?
4. Describe how the consequences might be different if Joe's misbehaviour happened when the teacher was
   a) on the bus, too.
   b) not on the bus.

Teachers using the reward and coercive power base rely on a variety of rewards—e.g., oral or written praise, gold stars, free time, "good news" notes to parents, and release from required assignments—and a mix of punishments—e.g., verbal reprimands, loss of recess or free time, detention, in-school suspension, and out-of-school suspension.

Students who behave appropriately because of reward and coercive power are apt to say, "I behave because if I don't, I have to write out a stupid 'I will not . . . ' line 50 times and get it signed by my parents." A teacher using reward and coercive power to solve Ms. Knepp's problem might say, "I've decided that for every five minutes without a disruption this class will earn one point. At the end of each week, for every ten points it has accumulated, the class may buy one night without homework during the following week. Remember, if there are any disturbances at all, you will not receive a point for the five-minute period." This point system is an example of a behaviour-modification technique. You can obtain more information on the use of behaviour modification in the classroom from many sources (e.g., Boekaerts and Corno, 2005; Alberto and Troutman, 1999; Kerr and Nelson, 1998; Axelrod, 1983; Winter, 1983).

As is true for the other three power bases, reward and coercive power cannot be used all the time. As students become older, they often resent obvious attempts to manipulate their behaviour through rewards and punishments. It is also difficult with older students to find rewards and punishments under the classroom teacher's control that are powerful enough to motivate them (see Chapter 6, "Structuring the Environment"). Still, some teachers have found their control of student time during school has allowed them to use reward and coercive power successfully with some students and some classes at all levels of schooling.

It should be noted that there are some inherent dangers in the use of reward and coercive power. Research has indicated that when students are rewarded for engaging in an activity, they are likely to perceive the activity as less inherently interesting in the future and are less likely to engage in that activity without external rewards (Ryan and Deci, 2000; Lepper and Green, 1978). Also, overuse of punishment is likely to engender in students negative attitudes toward school and learning.

It is important for a teacher to recognize what power base he uses to influence students in a given situation and to recognize why that base is appropriate or inappropriate. It is also important for the teacher to recognize the power base he uses most frequently as well as the power base he is comfortable with and would like to use. For some teachers, the two things may be quite different. Examining your beliefs about teacher power bases is one important step toward ensuring that your beliefs about classroom management and your actions are congruent. Table 4.1 offers a brief comparison of the four power bases on several significant dimensions.

Of course, most teachers use a combination of power bases in the classroom, depending on the types of classes and students they tend to have. They may even need to use a variety of power bases with the same students. This approach may, indeed, be the most practical and effective one, although combining certain power bases—for example, coercive and referent—can be difficult to do.

TABLE 4.1 *Teacher Power Bases*

	Referent	Expert	Legitimate	Reward/ Coercive
Motivation to behave	Student likes teacher as a person	Teacher has special knowledge	Teacher has legal authority	Teacher can reward and punish
Need for teacher management of student behaviour	Very low	Very low	Moderate	High
Requirements for use	Students must like the teacher as a person	Teacher expertise must be perceived and valued	Students must respect legal authority	Rewards and punishments must be effective
Key teacher behaviours	Communicates caring for students	Demonstrates mastery of content and teaching skills	Acts as a teacher is expected to act	Has and uses knowledge of student likes and dislikes
Age limitations	Useful for all levels	Less useful at primary level	Useful at all levels	Useful at all levels but less useful at senior high level
Caveats	Teacher is not the student's friend	Heavily dependent on student values	Societal changes have lessened the usefulness of this power base	Emphasizes extrinsic over intrinsic motivation

Theories of Classroom Management

In this section, we will describe three theories of classroom management. In order to make the differences clear among the three theories, we will describe each one as if it were completely independent of the others. In reality, however, the theories are more like three points on a continuum, moving from student-directed toward teacher-directed practices. On such a continuum, collaborative models represent a combination of the two end points. Of course, the classroom behaviour of most teachers represents some blending of the three theories. According to Martin and Sugarman, "There inevitably is a big gap between theory and practice. Even when theory (principles) is supported by research . . . , it still does not tell teachers exactly what to do in any classroom situation" (1993, 12). As Bob Strachota has noted, "Theories about how to best help children learn and change have to be broad enough to encompass the vitality and ambiguity that come with life in a classroom. If relied on too exclusively, behaviourism or constructivism end up living awkwardly in school" (1996, 133). Still, if a teacher's behaviour is examined over time, it is usually possible to classify his general approach

Punishment and rewards are often used by teachers; however, they may not be the most effective means to manage student behaviour.

to working with students and goals for classroom management into one of the theories on a fairly consistent basis.

Before reading the specific theories, determine your answers to the following nine basic questions about classroom management. Inherent in each theory are answers, either implicit or explicit, to these questions. If you are aware of your own beliefs about classroom management before you begin, you will be able to identify the theory that is aligned most closely with those beliefs.

1. Who has primary responsibility for managing student behaviour?
2. What is the goal of classroom management?
3. How do you view time spent on management issues and problems?
4. How would you like students to relate to each other within your management system?
5. How much choice will you give students within your management system?
6. What is your primary goal in handling misbehaviour?
7. What interventions will you use to deal with misbehaviour?
8. How important to you are individual differences among students?
9. Which teacher power bases are most compatible with your beliefs?

Readers of other versions of this text will recognize that the labels of the three theories have changed from *non-interventionist* to *student-directed*, from *interventionist* to *teacher-directed*, and from *interactionalist* to *collaborative*. We believe the new labels describe the theories more clearly than the former labels, which were taken from

Wolfgang and Glickman (1995). Because the student-directed approach is used less frequently in schools than the other two approaches and may be unfamiliar, more specific details are provided for it than for the other two.

Student-Directed Management

Advocates of the **student-directed classroom management** theory believe that the primary goal of schooling is to prepare students for life in a democracy, which requires citizens—who are able to—to control their behaviour, to care for others, and to make wise decisions. Previously, student-directed models of classroom management were drawn primarily from counselling models. Gordon's teacher-effectiveness training (1989), Berne's and Harris's transactional analysis (1964 and 1969 respectively), and Ginott's communication model (1972) relied almost exclusively on one-to-one conferencing between teacher and student to deal with behaviour issues. Such models were difficult to implement in the reality of a classroom filled with 25 to 30 students, each with a variety of talents, needs, interests, and problems. As a result, **teacher-directed management** models dominated most classrooms. In recent years, however, there has been considerable progress in developing student-directed management models that can be employed effectively within classrooms. Alfie Kohn (1996), Bob Strachota (1996), Ruth Charney (1992), Martin and Sugarman (1993), Putnam and Burke (1992), and Schwartz and Pollishuke (2002) have provided a variety of practical strategies that classroom teachers can use effectively.

The student-directed theory of classroom management, which Ms. Koskowski in Case 4.6 uses to handle David's behaviour, rests on two key beliefs: (1) students must have the primary responsibility for controlling their behaviour; and (2) students are capable of controlling their behaviour if given the opportunity to do so. Given these beliefs, student-directed models of management advocate the establishment of classroom learning communities, which are designed to help students become more self-directed, more responsible for their own behaviour, more independent in making appropriate choices, and more caring toward fellow students and teachers. The well-managed classroom is one in which students care for and collaborate successfully with each other, make good choices, and continuously strive to do high-quality work that is interesting and important to them.

When viewed from a student-directed perspective, time spent on management is seen as time well spent on equipping students with skills that will be important to them as adult citizens in a democracy (Novak, 2002). "Learning to behave in manners consistent with the goal of accepting individual responsibilities within a democratic social context is a functional strategy for individual development" (Martin and Sugarman, 1993, 33). In attempting to develop a student-directed learning environment in which students develop self-regulation skills, collaborative social skills, and decision-making skills, the teacher relies heavily on several major concepts: *student ownership*, *student choice*, *community*, and *conflict resolution* and *problem solving*.

Concentric Case Study Kaleidoscope

CASE 4.6 • *Handling Disruptive David*

Ms. Koskowski, Ms. Sweely, and Mr. Green teach grade 4 at Longmeadow School. Although they work well together and like each other, they have very different approaches to classroom discipline. To illustrate their differing approaches, let's examine their behaviour as each one deals with the same situation.

In the classroom, there are three students at the reading centre in the far right-hand corner and two students working quietly on insects at the science interest centre near the chalkboard located at the front of the room. Five students are correcting math problems individually, and ten students are working with the teacher in a reading group. David, one of the students working alone, begins to mutter out loud, "I hate this math. It's too hard to do. I never get fractions right. Why do we have to learn about them anyway?" As his monologue continues, David's voice begins to get louder and clearly becomes a disruption for the other students.

Ms. Koskowski

Ms. Koskowski recognizes that David, who is not strong in math, is really frustrated by the problems on fractions. She walks over to him and quietly says, "You know, David, the other night I was trying to learn to play tennis, and I was getting really frustrated. It helped me to take a break and get away from it for a minute, just to clear my head. How about if you do that now? Go get a drink of water; when you come back, you can get a fresh start." When David returns to his seat and begins to work, Ms. Koskowski helps him to think through the first problem and then watches and listens as he does the second one on his own.

Ms. Sweely

As soon as she sees that David is beginning to interrupt the other students, Ms. Sweely gives the reading group a question to think about and walks toward David's desk. She quietly approaches David until she is right beside him, but the muttering continues. She says, "David, you are disrupting others; please stop talking and get back to math." David stops for about five seconds but then begins complaining loudly again. "David, since you can't work with the group without disrupting other people, you will have to go back to the castle [a desk and rocking chair partitioned off from the rest of the class] and finish your math there. Tomorrow, if you believe that you can handle it, you may rejoin your math group."

Mr. Green

As soon as David's muttering becomes audible, Mr. Green says, "David, that behaviour is against our class rules. Stop talking and concentrate on your math." David stops talking momentarily but begins again. Mr. Green walks calmly to David's desk and removes a small, round, blue chip. As he does, he says, "Well, David, you've lost them all now. That means no more recess for the rest of the week and no good-news note to your mom and dad."

Questions to Consider

1. Whose approach would likely receive the best learning response from David? Why?

2. What would the other students be learning by observing each of the teachers interact with David?

Student ownership is established in several ways. Although the teacher takes responsibility for the arrangement of the classroom and for the safety of the environment, students are often responsible for deciding how the room should be decorated, for creating the posters, pictures, and other works that decorate the walls, and for maintaining the room. In fact, sharing the responsibility of establishing a positive learning environment can empower students to take control of their own learning (Schwartz and Pollishuke, 2002). Throughout the school year, students rotate through committees (the art supplies committee, the plants and animals committee, the cleanup committee, and so forth) that are responsible for various aspects of the class's work. Often, these committees are structured so that students gain experience in planning, delegating, and evaluating their own work in a fair and equitable manner.

Students are also given a great deal of responsibility for determining classroom rules. Typically, the teacher and students hold a class meeting to discuss how they want their classroom to be. Students are asked to think about the ways they are treated by others that make them feel good or bad. These experiences are then used as a springboard for a discussion about how the students want to treat each other in the classroom. The students' words become the guidelines for classroom behaviour.

Choice plays a key role in student-directed learning environments because it is believed that a student can learn to make good choices only if he has the opportunity to make choices (Ryan and Deci, 2000). In addition to making choices about the physical environment of the room and the expectations for behaviour, students are given choices about classroom routines and procedures, topics and questions to be studied in curriculum

Co-operative learning activities can help students realize that they have responsibilities to both themselves and the class.

units, learning activities, and the assessment of their learning—including assessment options and criteria. Creating rubrics together, prior to a learning task, is a good example of providing students with meaningful choices about their own learning. Classroom meetings, which are viewed as important vehicles for establishing and maintaining a caring classroom community, provide more opportunities for choices. Agendas for the meetings, which may be planning and decision-making meetings, check-in meetings, or problem-solving and issues-oriented meetings, are often suggested by the students.

Through the physical arrangement of the room, class meetings, and planned learning activities, the teacher attempts to build a community of learners who know and care for each other and work together productively. A great deal of time is spent at the beginning of the year helping students to get to know each other through get-acquainted activities, meetings, and small group activities. Throughout the year, the teacher uses co-operative learning activities stressing individual accountability, positive interdependence, face-to-face interaction, social-skill development, and group processing (see Chapter 6). These types of activities are emphasized because student-directed theorists believe that students learn more in collaborative activities. Theorists say that when students know and care for those in their classroom community, they are more likely to choose to behave in ways that are in everyone's best interest.

Student-directed teachers see interpersonal conflict as a teachable moment. They realize that conflict is inevitable when individuals are asked to work closely together. In fact, the absence of conflict is probably a good indication that individuals are not working together very closely. Thus, these teachers believe that helping students to deal with interpersonal conflict productively is an important goal of classroom management. Conflict resolution, peer mediation, and interpersonal problem-solving skills are taught just as academic content is taught. Students are encouraged to use these skills when conflicts arise. Issues that concern the class as a whole—conflicts concerning the sharing of equipment, class cliques, and relationship problems—become opportunities for using group problem-solving skills during class meetings. Some teachers even use class meetings to involve the entire class in helping to improve the behaviour of a particular student. It is important to note that encouraging caring relationships and teaching ways to deal with conflict productively go hand in hand and demand ongoing efforts and consistency on the part of the teacher. If students do not know or care about each other, conflict is hard to resolve. Conversely, if students do not acquire the ability to resolve conflict productively, they are unlikely to build caring relationships with each other.

Student misbehaviour is seen not as an affront to the teacher's authority but rather as the student's attempt to meet needs that are not being met. In response to misbehaviour, the teacher tries to determine what motivates the child and to find ways to meet those unmet needs. A student-directed teacher would view the behaviour problems in Ms. Knepp's class, in Case 4.1 on pages 79 and 80, as a clear indication that the learning activities and curriculum were not meeting the student needs. The teacher probably would hold a class meeting to address the problem behaviours in the classroom. He would articulate his feelings and reactions to the class and would elicit student feelings about the class as well. Through a discussion of their mutual needs and interests, the teacher and the class would develop a solution to the problem that would probably include some redesign of the tasks that students were asked to perform.

Kohn (1996) suggests that the first questions the teacher should ask when a child is off task are (1) What is the task? and (2) Is it really a task worth doing? Many teachers try to identify with the child. Strachota (1996) calls this "getting on their side." This strategy seems especially appropriate when coping with students who seem out of control and unable to behave appropriately. If a teacher can identify experiences in which *he* has felt out of control, he is usually more empathetic and helpful (see Chapter 9, "Classroom Interventions for Chronic Problems"). In Case 4.6 on page 91, Ms. Koskowski employs this strategy with David.

Student-directed teachers also believe in allowing students to experience the consequences of their behaviour. Natural consequences (consequences that do not require teacher intervention) are the most helpful because they allow the student to experience the results of his behaviour directly. However, sometimes the teacher must use logical consequences. The teacher's role in using consequences is neither to augment nor to alleviate the consequences but rather to support the child or the class as the consequences are experienced. This can be a difficult role for teachers and parents to play. Even when a teacher can predict that a given choice is going to lead to negative consequences, student-directed theorists argue, the student should experience the consequence unless it will bring great harm to the child. According to the theorists, students learn to make wise choices by recognizing that their behaviour inevitably has consequences for themselves and others.

Some student-directed theorists also believe that restitution is an important part of dealing with misbehaviour when a behaviour has hurt other students. In order to emphasize that the classroom is a caring community and that individual behaviour has consequences for others, a student whose behaviour has hurt others is required to make amends to those harmed. One strategy used by some teachers is called "an apology of action" (Forton, 1998; see Chapter 8, "Managing Common Misbehaviour Problems: Verbal Interventions and Use of Logical Consequences"). In this strategy, the student who has been hurt is allowed to decide what the offending student must do to make restitution. The strategy not only helps students to recognize that inappropriate behaviour hurts others but also can be a powerful way to mend broken relationships.

Referent and expert teacher power bases seem most compatible with student-directed management theory. Each power base emphasizes students' control over their own behaviour. At the same time, the student-directed perspective adds a new dimension to the notion of expert power. Students must recognize the teacher's specialized knowledge and his ability to build a caring classroom community in which students are given the opportunity to make choices and take responsibility for directing their own behaviour. Putting this philosophy into practice demands highly competent and committed teachers who truly believe that enabling students to become better decision-makers who are able to control their own behaviour is an important goal of schooling.

These teachers must be committed to establishing more democratic classrooms that are true caring communities (Novak, 2002). A teacher who is not committed to these beliefs will be unwilling to invest the time and effort needed to establish a student-directed learning environment. Long-term commitment is one key to success.

It is important to note that student-directed classrooms are not laissez-faire situations or classrooms without standards. In fact, the standards for student behaviour in most of these classrooms are exceptionally high. When student efforts fall short of meeting agreed-upon standards for behaviour and work, the teacher plays the role of encourager, helping students to identify ways to improve. The teacher's role is not to punish the student with behaviour or academic problems but rather to find ways to help the student overcome the problems.

Student-directed strategies are effective in all teaching situations and are especially well-suited for self-contained early childhood and elementary settings—for several reasons. First, students and teachers in these settings typically spend a large portion of the day together, which gives them the opportunity to build close relationships with each other. Second, because the classes are self-contained, it is possible to build a community in which students really know and care about one another. Finally, teachers in these settings have greater control over the allocation of time during the day than most secondary teachers. Because they are not "bell bound," they are free to spend more time dealing with classroom-management issues with individual students or the class as a whole. The current practice of *teacher looping*, in which teachers stay with one group of students for two or three years (for example, from grades 1 through 3), provides an outstanding opportunity to create a student-directed environment because teachers and students work together for an extended period of time. Secondary schools would seem to be well served by adopting similar structures to personalize the environment and make it more student-directed—i.e., by using an integrated curriculum (Drake, 1998). At present in many secondary schools, students and teachers spend about 80 minutes together per day, and an individual teacher may teach 120 students or more per day. In such environments, although it may be more difficult, it is still possible to get to know each other personally, to understand each other's needs, and to establish a caring community.

Collaborative Management

The collaborative theory of classroom management is based on the belief that the control of student behaviour is the joint responsibility of the student and the teacher. Although those who adopt the collaborative approach to management often believe in many of the tenets of the student-directed theory, they also believe that the number of students in a class and the size of most schools make it too hard to put a student-directed philosophy into practice. With the current provincial trends toward standardized testing and prescriptive and extensive curriculum, the time required to work collaboratively with students under this model is becoming more difficult for teachers to attain (Elliott and Woloshyn, 1996). In fact, many secondary teachers feel that the size of their classes and the limited time they have with students make it imperative for them to place the needs of the group above the needs of any individual student. Under the collaborative theory, then, students must be given some opportunity to control their own behaviour because a long-range goal of schooling is to enable students to become mature adults who can control their own behaviour; but the teacher, as a professional, retains primary responsibility for managing student behaviour because the classroom is a group learning situation.

In Case 4.6 on page 91, Ms. Sweely represents the **collaborative management** theory in action. Note that she tries to protect the reading group activity and, at the same time, deal with David. While the group is occupied, she uses proximity interference (see Chapter 7, "Managing Common Misbehaviour Problems: Non-verbal Interventions") to signal to David that he should control his behaviour. When he cannot, she emphasizes the effect of his behaviour on others and separates him from the rest of the group to help him recognize the logical consequences of being disruptive in a group situation. Thus, the teacher oriented toward the collaborative theory promotes individual control over behaviour but sometimes subordinates this goal to the right of all students to learn. From the collaborative perspective, the goal of classroom management is to develop a well-organized classroom in which students are (1) engaged in learning activities; (2) usually successful; (3) respectful of the teacher and fellow students; and (4) co-operative in following classroom guidelines because they understand the rationale for the guidelines and see them as appropriate for the learning situation. From the collaborative point of view, then, students become capable of controlling their own behaviour not by simply following rules but, rather, by understanding why rules exist and then choosing to follow them because they make sense. Neither blind obedience to rules nor complete freedom in deciding what rules should exist is seen as the best route toward self-regulated behaviour.

In collaborative classrooms the teacher and students develop rules and procedures jointly. Some teachers begin with a minimum list of rules, those that are most essential, and allow students to develop additional ones. Other teachers give students the opportunity to suggest rules but retain the right to add rules or veto suggested rules. Both of these techniques are intended to help the teacher maintain the ability to use his professional judgment to protect the rights of the group as a whole.

Teachers who adopt a collaborative approach to classroom management often give students choices in other matters as well. Typically, the choices are not as open-ended as those provided by student-directed advocates. For example, instead of allowing students to develop the criteria for judging the quality of their work, a collaborative teacher might present a list of ten potential criteria and allow students to choose the five criteria that will be used. Thus, the students are provided with choices, but the choices are confined to some degree by the teacher's professional judgment. This same system of providing choice within a given set of options may be followed in arranging and decorating the classroom or selecting topics to be pursued during academic units.

Advocates of a collaborative approach see time spent on classroom-management issues as potentially productive for the individual but not for the class as a whole unless there is a major problem interfering with the learning of a large number of students. Thus, collaborative teachers, whenever possible, do not take time away from group learning to focus on the behaviour of an individual or a few students. Interpersonal conflicts are treated in a similar way. They are not dismissed, but collaborative teachers usually do not use classroom time to deal with them unless they involve many students. When an interpersonal conflict arises, the teacher deals with the individuals involved when there is a window of time to do so. Class meetings are used to deal with management issues or conflicts involving large numbers of students. Collaborative teachers tend to view a class meeting as a means for solving problems as a way to maintain the classroom community.

While collaborative management advocates believe that outward behaviour must be managed to protect the rights of the group, they also believe the individual's thoughts and feelings must be explored to get at the heart of the behaviour. Therefore, collaborative teachers often use *coping skills* (see Chapter 7) to manage student behaviour in a group situation and then follow up with a conference with the student. Because collaborative theorists believe that relating behaviour to its natural or logical consequences helps students learn to anticipate the consequences of their behaviour and thus become more self-regulating (see Chapters 6 and 8 for discussions of consequences), they advocate consequences linked as closely as possible to the misbehaviour itself. A student who comes to school five minutes late, for example, might be required to remain five minutes after school to make up work.

The teacher power bases most compatible with collaborative management theories are the expert and legitimate bases. Each of these power bases rests on the belief that the primary purpose of schools is to help students learn important processes and information. Therefore, the teacher must protect the rights of the group while still nurturing the learning of individual students. A collaborative teacher running Ms. Knepp's class might decide to hold a class meeting to review the classroom expectations and the rationale for them, to answer any questions or concerns regarding those expectations, and to remind students that the expectations will be enforced through the use of logical consequences. The teacher might also allow the class to make some choices concerning upcoming activities and events from a presented list of options. Three well-known collaborative-management models come from the work of Dreikurs, Grundwald, and Pepper (1998), Glasser (1992), and Curwin and Mendler (1988).

Teacher-Directed Management

Advocates of the teacher-directed management theory believe that students become good decision-makers by internalizing the rules and guidelines for behaviour that are given to them by responsible and caring adults. The teacher's task, then, is to develop a set of guidelines and rules that will create a productive learning environment, to be sure that the students understand the rules, and to develop a consistent system of rewards and punishments that make it likely that students will follow the guidelines and rules. The goal of the teacher-directed theory is to create a learning environment, in which management issues and concerns play a minimal role, to discourage misbehaviour and to deal with it as swiftly as possible when it does occur. In this theory, the teacher assumes primary responsibility for managing student behaviour. Time spent on management issues is not seen as productive because it reduces time for teaching and learning. The well-managed classroom is seen as one in which the management system operates efficiently and students are co-operative and consistently engaged in learning activities. The primary emphasis in teacher-directed classrooms is on academic content and processes. Current Canadian trends are prompting more teachers to adhere to this model of management in light of increased curriculum expectations and standardized testing. Pressure from the public—exerted through the media—as well as from provincial ministries of education for increased teacher accountability, is also contributing significantly to this trend (e.g., Alberta Department of Education, 2003; Newfoundland and Labrador Department of Education, 2003; Ontario Ministry of Education, 2003).

In teacher-directed environments, the teacher makes almost all of the major decisions, including room arrangement, seating assignments, classroom decorations, academic content, assessment devices and criteria, and decisions concerning the day-to-day operation of the classroom. Students may be given a role to play in implementing teacher decisions—for example, they could be asked to create a poster—but they are usually restricted to implementing the teacher's decisions. Advocates of teacher-directed models view the teacher as a trained professional who understands students, teaching, and the learning process and therefore is in the best position to make such choices.

Usually, the teacher presents rules and a system of consequences or punishments for breaking those rules to students on the first or second day of school. Often, students are asked to sign a commitment to obeying the rules, and frequently their parents are asked to sign a statement declaring that they are aware of the rules. Punishments for misbehaviour are typically not directly related to the misbehaviour itself but rather are universal consequences that can be applied to a variety of transgressions. For example, the student's name may be written on the board, a mark may be made in the grade book, or a call may be made to the student's parents. Teachers may also establish a set of rewards that are provided to the class as a whole if everyone follows the rules consistently. Punishments and rewards are applied consistently to ensure that the management system and rules are internalized by all.

Although teachers who follow teacher-directed approaches do use co-operative learning strategies, their management techniques usually are not focused on the creation of a democratic classroom community in which caring is a primary motivator for choosing to behave appropriately. In a teacher-directed classroom, the primary relationship is usually the one between the teacher and individual students. Students tend to be seen as a collection of individuals who should not interfere with each other's right to learn or with the teacher's right to teach. Self-control is often viewed as a matter of will. If students want to control their own behaviour, they can.

Given this, conflict is seen as threatening, non-productive, and disruptive of the learning process. The teacher deals swiftly with any outward manifestations of a conflict, but usually not with the thoughts and feelings that have led to the conflict. Students have a right to feel upset, it is argued, but not to act in inappropriate ways.

Using the predetermined list of punishments or consequences, the teacher redirects the misbehaving student to appropriate behaviour by applying the appropriate consequence. For the most part, punishments are sequenced so that second or third offences bring more stringent consequences than first offences. While individual differences may play an important part in the academic aspects of classroom work, they do not play a major role in the management system. Consider the actions of Mr. Green in Case 4.6 on page 91. As an advocate of teacher-directed management, he moves quickly to stop the misbehaviour, emphasizes classroom rules, employs blue chips as rewards, and uses punishments in the form of loss of recess privileges and good-news notes.

Clearly, reward and coercive power is the teacher power base that is most compatible with the teacher-directed theory. Advocates use clear, direct, explicit communication, behaviour contracting, behaviour modification, token economy systems, consistent reinforcement of appropriate behaviour, and group rewards and punishments. A teacher following this theory might handle Ms. Knepp's dilemma by setting up a group management plan in which the group earns points for appropriate behaviour. The points could then be exchanged for meaningful rewards. At the same time, the teacher uses a predetermined set of punishments for any students who misbehave.

The teacher who wants to use a teacher-directed approach should be aware of some important considerations. A thorough understanding of the principles of behavioural psychology is necessary in order to apply a behaviour-modification approach appropriately. Individual student differences do play a role in the management system because they must be considered in developing rewards and punishments. After all, a reward to some individuals may be a punishment to others. Thus, most teacher-directed theorists are concerned with students' thoughts and emotions; however, the primary goal in dealing with misbehaviour is management of the student's outward behaviour, not inner feelings. Therefore, individual differences do not play a role in determining which behaviours are acceptable. Some well-known authors of classroom-management systems derived from the teacher-directed perspective are Axelrod (1983), Canter and Canter (1992), Cangelosi (1997), and Valentine (1987).

TABLE 4.2 *Theories of Classroom Management*

Question	Student-Directed	Collaborative	Teacher-Directed
Primary responsibility for management	Student	Joint	Teacher
Goal of management	Caring community focus and self-direction	Respectful relationships, academic focus	Well-organized, efficient, academic focus
Time spent on management	Valuable and productive	Valuable for individual but not for group	Wasted time

Continued

TABLE 4.2 *continued*

Question	Student-Directed	Collaborative	Teacher-Directed
Relationships within management system	Caring, personal relationships	Respect for each other	Non-interference with each other's rights
Provision of student choice	Wide latitude and freedom	Choices within teacher-defined options	Very limited
Primary goal in handling misbehaviour	Unmet need to be explored	Minimize in group; pursue individually	Minimize disruption; redirect
Interventions used	Individual conference, group problem solving, restitution, natural consequences	Coping skills, natural and logical consequences, anecdotal record keeping	Clear communication, rewards and punishments, behaviour contracting
Individual differences	Extremely important	Somewhat important	Minor importance
Teacher power bases	Referent, expert	Expert, legitimate	Reward/coercive
Theorists	Charney, Faber and Mazlish, Gordon, Kohn, Strachota, Putnam and Burke	Curwin and Mendler, Dreikurs, Glasser	Axelrod, Cangelosi, Canter and Canter, Valentine

Table 4.2 provides a summary of the three theories of management in terms of their answers to the nine basic questions about classroom management introduced at the beginning of this "Theories of Classroom Management" section.

Summary

In the first section of the chapter, with the CALM model in mind, we provide an explanation of the four teacher power bases: referent, expert, legitimate, and reward and coercive. Each base is presented in terms of the underlying assumptions about student motivation to behave, the assumed need for teacher control over student behaviour, the requirements for employing the base effectively, the key teacher behaviours in using the base, and limitations and caveats concerning its use.

In the second section, we discuss nine basic questions that are useful for articulating beliefs about classroom management:

1. Who has primary responsibility for managing student behaviour?
2. What is the goal of classroom management?
3. How do you view time spent on management issues and problems?

4. How would you like students to relate to each other within your management system?
5. How much choice will you give students within your management system?
6. What is your primary goal in handling misbehaviour?
7. What interventions will you use to deal with misbehaviour?
8. How important to you are individual differences among students?
9. Which teacher power bases are most compatible with your beliefs?

Articulating one's beliefs is the initial step toward developing a systematic plan for managing student behaviour. These nine basic questions are used to analyze three theories of classroom management: student-directed, collaborative, and teacher-directed.

Teachers may use the information and questions provided in this chapter to develop a plan for preventing classroom-management problems and for dealing with disruptive student behaviour that is congruent with their basic beliefs about teaching and learning.

Key Terms

collaborative management: the belief that the control of student behaviour in the classroom is the joint responsibility of the student and the teacher.

expert power: where students view the teacher as a good, knowledgeable teacher who can help them to learn; the power of professional competence.

legitimate power: where students behave because the teacher is the teacher; inherent in that role are a certain authority and power.

referent power: where students behave as the teacher wishes because they like the teacher as a person and they feel the teacher cares about them.

reward and coercive power: where students behave to avoid some form of punishment or to gain a predetermined reward.

student-directed management: where the primary goal of schooling is to prepare for life in a democracy; students are allowed to make many decisions in the classroom.

teacher-directed management: the belief that students become good decision-makers by internalizing rules and guidelines for behaviour that are provided by a responsible and caring teacher.

Exercises

1. If one of the long-term goals of classroom management is for students to gain control over their own behaviour, what are some advantages and disadvantages of using each of the four teacher power bases to help students achieve that goal?

2. Given your knowledge of cognitive and moral development, what factors facilitate or limit the use of each of the four teacher power bases at (a) the primary elementary grades, (b) the intermediate elementary grades, (c) the junior high level, and (d) the senior high level?

3. Do you think there is any relationship between teacher job satisfaction and the power base the teacher uses most frequently to influence student behaviour?

4. Which specific teacher behaviours would indicate to you that a teacher was trying to use (a) referent power and (b) expert power?

5. Using referent authority successfully requires the teacher to convey his caring nature to students. (a) How can a teacher communicate caring without initiating personal friendships? (b) As you see it, is there a danger in initiating personal friendships with students?

6. How would teachers operating at each of the four authority bases respond to the following situations?

Behaviour	Referent	Expert	Legitimate	Reward and Coercive
a. A student throws a paper airplane across the room.				
b. A student publicly shows disrespect for the teacher.				
c. A student makes funny noises while another student is giving an oral report.				

7. If one of the long-range goals of classroom management is to help students gain control over their own behaviour, what are the advantages and disadvantages of each of the three theories of classroom management in helping students meet that goal?

8. Given your knowledge of cognitive and moral development, what factors facilitate or limit the use of each of the three theories of classroom management at (a) the primary elementary level, (b) the intermediate elementary level, (c) the junior high level, and (d) the senior high level?

9. How would teachers using each of the theories of classroom management respond to the following situations?

Behaviour	Student-Directed	Collaborative	Teacher-Directed
a. A student uses power equip ment in a dangerous way.			
b. A student chews gum loudly and blows bubbles.			
c. A student draws moustaches and beards on all the pictures in a textbook.			

10. Is there any danger in using techniques to manage student behaviour that are not consistent with your basic beliefs about student learning and behaviour?

11. Think of the best teacher that you have ever had when you were a student. Which authority base and classroom-management theory was this teacher using the majority of the time?

12. Think of the worst teacher you have ever had. Which authority base and classroom-management theory was this teacher using the majority of the time?

Weblink _____

The Really Best List of Classroom Management Resources
drwilliampmartin.tripod.com/reallybest.htm
This site has links to many resources that may help teachers with classroom-management challenges.

Iterative Case Study Analysis

Second Analysis

Considering the concepts discussed in Part I's Foundations section, Chapters 1 through 4, reanalyze your first analysis. What has changed and what has stayed the same since your last analysis? Once again, consider why the students may be choosing to behave inappropriately and how you might intervene to influence the students to stop the disruptive behaviour and resume appropriate on-task behaviour.

Elementary School Case Study

During silent reading time in my grade 4 class, I have built in opportunities to work individually with students. During this time, the students read to me and practice word work with flash cards. One student has refused to read to me but instead wants only to work with the flash cards. After a few sessions, I suggested we work with word cards this time and begin reading next time. He agreed. The next time we met, I reminded him of our plan, and he screamed, "I don't remember! I want to do word cards!" At this point, I tried to find out why he didn't like reading and he said, "There's a reason, I just can't tell you," and he threw the word cards across the room, some of them hitting other students. What should I do?

Middle School Case Study

I can't stop thinking about a problem I'm having in class with a group of 12-year-old boys. They consistently use vulgar language toward one another and some of the shyer kids in the class, especially the girls. In addition, they are always pushing and shoving each other. I've tried talking to them about why they keep using bad language when they know it's inappropriate. The response I get is that "it makes me look cool and funny in front of my friends." I have asked them to please use more appropriate language in the classroom but that has not worked. I haven't even started to address the pushing and shoving. What should I do?

High School Case Study

This past week, I had a student approach me about a problem he was experiencing in our class. The grade 11 student had recently "come out" as being gay. He said he was tired and upset with the three boys who sit near him. These boys frequently call him a "homo" and a "fag" every time they see him, both in and out of class. What should I do?

5

The Professional Teacher

Focus on the Principles of Classroom Management

1. How can a teacher maximize student learning and on-task behaviour?
2. What is the importance of the research on **effective teaching** for classroom teachers?

Introduction

Frequently, classroom management is conceptualized as a matter of control rather than as a dimension of curriculum, instruction, and overall school climate (Duke, 1982; Martin and Sugarman, 1993; Mastropieri and Scruggs, 2005). In reality, classroom management is closely intertwined with effective instruction: "Research findings converge on the conclusion that teachers who approach classroom management as a process of establishing and maintaining effective learning environments tend to be more successful than teachers who place more emphasis on their roles as authority figures or disciplinarians" (Brophy, 1988a, 1). In the hierarchical decision-making model of classroom management presented in this text, teachers must ensure that they have done all that they can to prevent problems from occurring before using coping techniques (Anderson, 2002; Mazurek, 2002; Laughlin, Hartoonian, and Berci, 1999). The teacher's classroom instructional behaviours, therefore, must match the behaviours defined as best professional practices—that is, those behaviours most likely to maximize student learning and enhance appropriate student behaviour. If there is no match, employing techniques to remediate misbehaviour is likely to prove fruitless since the behavioural problems will inevitably recur.

Unfortunately, one of the problems that has long plagued classroom teachers has been identifying the yardstick that should be used to measure their teaching behaviour against best professional practices. Fortunately, there is now a reliable knowledge base that, when used appropriately, can help teachers to ensure that their behaviour will enhance student learning and encourage appropriate behaviour. In this chapter, divided into two parts, we present a synopsis of that knowledge base. In the first section, "The Basics of Effective Teaching," we describe and explain research that endorses teacher behaviours promoting student achievement as measured by low-level, paper-and-pencil tests. In the second section, "Beyond the Basics," we examine more recent conceptualizations of teaching that focus primarily on student cognition and student performance on higher-level cognitive tasks.

As you'll see, a major difference between the first and second sections of this chapter concerns the drastic shift in emphasis over the decades on teacher behaviour vis-à-vis student behaviour. Early research on effective teaching was based primarily on the premise that the teacher is the most important person in the classroom. Thus, this research focused on the overt behaviour of the teacher during instruction. In the mid-1980s, however, researchers began to see the student as the most important person and the student's thought processes as the key elements during instruction. As a result, the focus of the research switched from the overt behaviour of the teacher to the covert behaviour of the learner during instruction. This shift in mindset is most obvious in the research on student motivation. Indeed, it has led to the inclusion of two sections on student motivation in this chapter. In the first section, "The Basics of Effective Teaching," we focus on student motivation as influenced by teacher behaviour; in the second section, "Beyond the Basics," we examine student motivation as influenced by student cognition.

The Basics of Effective Teaching

Most of the research findings discussed here were derived from studies of teacher behaviours that were effective in promoting student achievement as defined by lower-level cognitive objectives, which are efficiently measured by paper-and-pencil tests (Akey, 2006; Taylor and Blunt, 2001; Brophy, 1988b). It appears that general principles for teaching behaviour derived from these studies apply to "instruction in any body of knowledge or set of skills that has been sufficiently well organized and analyzed so that: (1) it can be presented systematically, and then (2) practiced or applied during activities that call for student performance that (3) can be evaluated for quality and (4) can be given corrective feedback (where incorrect or imperfect)" (Rosenshine and Stevens, 1986, 49).

The research findings that general principles have been drawn from are the result of various long-term research projects that usually followed a three-step process. In step 1 of the process, teams of researchers observed classroom teachers who were considered to be either very effective or very ineffective. Effectiveness was most often defined as enhanced student achievement on paper-and-pencil tests and higher results on standardized tests. From the observations, it was possible to develop a list of teaching behaviours that were used frequently by the effective teachers but not by the ineffective teachers. Researchers hypothesized that at least some of these teaching behaviours were responsible for the success of the effective teachers.

In step 2, correlational studies were conducted to find positive relationships between the use of these "effective" teaching behaviours and student behaviour or student learning as measured by paper-and-pencil achievement test scores. The correlational studies indicated that some of the effective teaching behaviours were positively related to student behaviour and achievement, whereas others were not. Thus, the result of step 2 was to narrow the list of effective teaching behaviours to those that were used by effective teachers *and* had a positive relationship with student behaviour or student achievement test scores.

In step 3, experimental studies were conducted. The researchers trained an experimental group of teachers to use the narrowed-down list of effective teaching behaviours consistently in their teaching. The achievement scores and classroom behaviour of their students were then compared with the achievement scores and behaviour of students taught by a control group of teachers who had not been trained to use the effective teaching behaviours. The results of these experimental comparison studies showed that students of the experimental teachers had significantly higher achievement scores or significantly better classroom behaviour.

Lesson Design

During the 1970s and '80s, Madeline Hunter (1982), Barak Rosenshine (Rosenshine and Stevens, 1986), and other researchers spent a great deal of time trying to identify the type of **lesson** structure that was most effective for student learning. Although the various researchers tend to use their own specialized vocabulary, they agree that lessons which include the following components are the most effective in helping students to learn new material: a lesson introduction, clear explanations of the content, checks for student understanding, a period of coached practice, a lesson summary or closure, a period of solitary practice, and periodic reviews. As you read the discussion of these components that follow, remember that a lesson does not equal a class period. A lesson is defined as the amount of instructional time required for students to achieve a specific learning objective.

1. *Lesson introduction.* A good introduction makes students aware of what they are supposed to learn, activates their prior knowledge of the topic, focuses their attention on the main elements of the lesson to come, and motivates them to be interested in the lesson.

2. *Clarity.* Clear explanations of the content of the lesson proceed in step-by-step fashion, illustrate the content by using concrete examples familiar to the students, and are interspersed with questions that check student understanding (Morgan and Saxton, 1991). "Lessons in which learners perceive links among the main ideas are more likely to contribute to content learning than are lessons in which links among the main ideas are less easily perceived by learners" (Anderson, 1989, 102). Techniques for ensuring that lesson presentations are well organized include (a) using structured overviews, advance organizers, and statements of objectives near the beginning of the presentation; (b) outlining the content, signalling transitions between ideas, calling attention to main ideas, and summarizing subsections of the lesson during the presentation; and (c) summarizing main ideas near the end of the presentation.

3. *Coached practice.* Effective lessons include a period of coached or guided practice during which students practise using the new skill or knowledge, through written exercises, oral questions and answers, or some type of group work. The teacher closely monitors this initial practice so that students receive frequent feedback and correction. Students should experience high amounts of success

(over 75 percent) with the coached practice exercises before moving on to solitary practice. Otherwise, they may spend a large portion of the solitary practice period practising and learning the wrong information or skill.

    Scaffolding, as an additional important aspect of the coached practice portion of lessons, is designed to help students acquire cognitive strategies, such as study skills, problem-solving skills, and critical thinking skills (Brualdi, 1996; Bruner, 1986; Vygotsky, 1978). Scaffolding is a process that underlies all of the elements of lesson design. In other words, the teacher plans instruction to move from modelling and instruction to feedback and coaching, and increasingly transfers control to students.

4. *Closure.* A good lesson summary, or closure, asks students to become actively involved in summarizing the key ideas that have been learned in the lesson and gives students some ideas about where future lessons will take them.

5. *Solitary practice.* Effective lessons also include a period of solitary or independent practice during which students practise the skill on their own and experience significant amounts of success (over 75 percent). This practice often takes the form of independent seatwork or homework. The effectiveness of homework as a tool for promoting learning is directly related to whether it is checked and whether feedback is provided to students.

6. *Review.* Finally, periodic reviews conducted on a weekly and monthly basis help students to consolidate their learning and provide additional reinforcement.

These six research-based components, which are especially effective in lessons designed to impart basic information or specific skills and procedures, should not be viewed as constraints on the teacher's creativity and individuality. Each component may be embellished and tailored to fit the unique teaching situations that confront every teacher. Together, however, the components provide a basic framework that lessens student confusion about what is to be learned and ensures that learning proceeds in an orderly sequence of steps. When students try to learn more different content before they have mastered prerequisites and when they are not given sufficient practice to master skills, they become confused, uninterested, and much more likely to cause behavioural problems in the classroom.

    A more recent approach to lesson planning is **backward design** or **design-down planning**, where planning begins with the end in mind. That is, teachers plan by asking themselves what it is they want their students to know or be able to do as a result of the instruction. This approach to planning is based on the belief that both the students and teacher will understand lesson objectives more clearly if summative assessment is explicitly outlined from the beginning. Beginning with an emphasis on the enduring understandings or concepts that students will learn and be able to apply, and then developing the summative assessment or culminating task will inform the teacher when the students have achieved the objectives. In this approach, teachers plan backwards by designing the culminating task first, followed by the essential subtasks, which are themselves developed in the reverse order from the actual instructional delivery. Student learning and overall concept/skill development is assessed at each stage.

For more information on backward design/design-down planning, please refer to the following PowerPoint demonstration: www.ocup.org/resources/documents/training/ Planner03Design/Planner03Design_2.ppt#533,6,2.2.

Student Motivation: Teacher Variables

Motivation refers to an inner drive that focuses behaviour on a particular goal or task and causes the individual to be persistent in trying to achieve the goal or complete the task successfully. Fostering motivation in students is undoubtedly one of the most powerful tools the teacher has in preventing classroom behavioural problems. When students are motivated to learn, they usually pay attention to the lesson, become actively involved in learning, and direct their energies to the task. When students are not motivated to learn, they lose interest in lessons quickly, look for sources of entertainment, and may direct their energies at amusing themselves and disrupting the learning process of others. There are many variables that a professional teacher can manipulate to increase student motivation to learn. According to a review of research on student motivation (Brophy, 1987), some of the most powerful variables are the following:

1. *Student interest.* Teachers can increase student motivation by relating subject content to life outside of school. For example, an English teacher can relate poetry to the lyrics of popular music, and a chemistry teacher can allow students to analyze the chemical composition of products they like to use. While there is no subject in which every topic can be related to the real world, teachers can often use games, simulations, videos, or group work, and allow students to plan or select activities to increase their interest. Although these strategies can't be used effectively every day, all teachers can employ them at intervals.

2. *Student needs.* Motivation to learn is increased when students perceive that learning activities provide an opportunity to meet some of their basic human needs as identified by Maslow (1968). For example, simply providing students with the opportunity to talk while the whole group listens can be an easy way to help meet students' needs for self-esteem. Also, allowing students to work together with peers on learning activities helps to meet students' needs for a sense of belonging and acceptance by others. At the most basic level, providing a pleasant, task-oriented climate in which expectations are clear helps to meet students' needs for psychological safety and security.

3. *Novelty and variety.* When the teacher has designed learning activities that include novel events, situations, and materials, students are likely to be motivated to learn. The popcorn lesson in Case 5.1 on pages 110 and 111 is an excellent example of using novelty to gain student attention. Once student attention has been captured, a variety of short learning activities will help to keep it focused on the lesson. Human attention spans can be remarkably long when people are involved in an activity that they find fascinating. Most students, however, do not find typical school activities always fascinating—their attention spans can, thus, tend to be rather short. For this reason, the professional teacher plans activities that last no longer than 15 to 20

minutes. A teacher who gives a lecture in two 15-minute halves interspersed with a 5-minute oral exercise is much more likely to maintain student interest than a teacher who gives a 30-minute lecture followed by the 5-minute oral exercise. *Sesame Street* and music videos are good examples of how frequently changing the focus of activity can hold an audience's attention.

4. *Success.* When students are successful at tasks they perceive to be somewhat challenging, their motivation for future learning is greatly enhanced. It is unreasonable to expect students who fail constantly to have any motivation to participate positively in future learning activities. Thus, it is especially important for teachers to create success for students who are not normally successful. Teachers help to ensure that all students experience some success by making goals and objectives clear, teaching content clearly in small steps, and checking to see that students understand each step. Teachers can also encourage success by helping students to acquire the study skills they need when they must work on their own—outlining, note-taking, and using textbooks correctly. The most powerful technique for helping students to succeed is to ensure that the material being covered is at the appropriate level of difficulty. Given the students' prior learning in a particular subject, teachers can make a proper decision on the appropriateness of new material.

5. *Tension.* In teaching, tension refers to a feeling of concern or anxiety on the part of students because they know that they will be required to demonstrate their learning. A moderate amount of tension increases student learning. When there is no tension in the learning situation, students may be so relaxed that no learning occurs. On the other hand, if there is an overwhelming amount of tension, students may expend more energy in dealing with the tension than they do in learning. Creating a moderate amount of tension results in motivation without tension overload. When a learning task is inherently interesting and challenging for students, there is little need for the teacher to add tension to the situation. When the learning task is routine and uninteresting for students, a moderate amount of tension created by the teacher enhances motivation and learning. Teacher behaviours that raise the level of tension include moving around the room, calling on volunteers and non-volunteers to answer questions in a random pattern, giving quizzes on class material, checking homework and seat work, and reminding students that they will be tested on the material they are learning.

CASE 5.1 • *The Popcorn Popper*

As Mr. Armour's students walk into his grade 10 creative writing classroom in their usual desultory manner, they hear an unusual noise. As they look around for the source of the noise, they see that on the teacher's desk an electric popcorn popper is running. As the room fills with the aroma of fresh popcorn, students smile in anticipation. Someone says aloud, "This smells like a movie theatre." Another responds, "Yeah, let's sit back and enjoy. I love the movies."

When the popping is finished, Mr. Armour passes three large bowels around and students help themselves to fistfuls of the popcorn. He admonishes his students that eight people need to get popcorn from each bowl and that they must stay in their seats and take turns. The students comply, appearing to be pleased with the unusual beginning to their lesson.

After giving an appropriate amount of time for students to finish their snack, and after eating some popcorn himself, Mr. Armour starts an oral lesson by asking students to describe the sights, sounds, taste, smell, and feel of the popcorn. Mr. Armour puts each response on the board under the categories of the five senses. The participation is enthusiastic and the descriptive words become increasingly clever and sophisticated. Students laugh over some of the descriptions. This is the introduction to a writing exercise on the five senses.

Questions to Consider

1. What variables for motivating did Mr. Armour achieve with this activity?
2. What other strategies might he have used to introduce this lesson in a motivational manner?

6. *Feeling tone.* Feeling tone refers to the emotional atmosphere or climate in the classroom. According to Madeline Hunter, classroom feeling tone can be extremely positive, moderately positive, neutral, moderately negative, and extremely negative (1982). An extremely positive feeling tone can be so sweet that it actually directs student attention away from learning, a neutral feeling tone is bland and non-stimulating, and an extremely negative feeling tone is threatening and may produce a tension overload. The most effective feeling tone is a moderately positive one in which the atmosphere is pleasant and friendly but clearly focused on the learning task at hand. The teacher can help to create such a feeling tone by making a room comfortable and pleasantly decorated, treating students in a courteous and friendly manner, expressing sincere interest in students as individuals, and communicating positively with students both verbally and non-verbally (Schwartz and Pollishuke, 2002). See how one teacher expresses his interest in students in Case 5.2 on page 112. Although a moderately positive feeling tone is the most motivating one, it is sometimes necessary to create, temporarily, a moderately negative feeling tone. If students are not doing their work and not living up to their responsibilities, it is necessary to shake them out of their complacency with some well-chosen, corrective comments. The wise teacher understands that undesirable consequences may result from a classroom feeling tone that is continuously negative and, therefore, works to create a moderately positive classroom climate most of the time.

CASE 5.2 • *Talking Between Classes*

Mr. Dailey, the grade 8 English teacher, does not spend the time in between classes standing out in the hallway or visiting with friends. Instead he uses the three minutes to chat with individual students. During these chats, he talks with students about their out-of-school activities, hobbies, feelings about school and his class in particular, plans and aspirations, and everyday school activities.

He feels that these three-minute chats really promote a more positive feeling tone in his classroom and allow him to relate to his students as individuals.

Questions to Consider

1. Try to imagine a typical student's feelings about Mr. Dailey and his class.
2. Describe a teacher in your background who was like Mr. Dailey.

7. *Feedback.* Because it provides both information that can be used to improve performance and a yardstick or criterion by which progress can be measured, feedback also increases motivation. Feedback is most effective when it is specific and is delivered soon after or at the time of performance. Teachers usually provide feedback in the form of oral and written comments on tests and assignments. One additional way to use feedback as a motivator is to have students keep track of their own progress over time and to provide periodic opportunities for them to reflect on their progress.

8. *Encouragement.* Encouragement is a great motivator. It emphasizes the positive aspects of behaviour; recognizes and validates real effort; communicates positive expectations for future behaviour; and conveys that the teacher trusts, respects, and believes in the child. All too frequently, teachers and parents point out how children have failed to meet expectations. Pointing out shortcomings and focusing on past transgressions erodes children's self-esteem, whereas encouraging communication enhances self-esteem (Novak and Purkey, 2001). Encouragement emphasizes present and future behaviour, rather than past transgressions, and focuses on what is being learned and done correctly rather than on what has not been learned. For example, consider the way the teacher in Case 5.3 emphasized the negative and the impact it had on the student.

Ms. Lapierre in Case 5.3 would have had a far more positive impact on Heidi's motivation if she had pointed out the positive aspects of Heidi's work in addition to the error in spelling. After all, a child who gets a mark of 68 percent on an exam has learned twice as much as she has failed to learn. For more on encouragement, see Dreikurs's *Children the Challenge* (1964). How can you use these research findings to improve student motivation in your own classroom? Ask yourself the following questions as you plan classroom activities for your students:

CASE 5.3 • *Non-constructive Feedback*

While Ms. Lapierre was handing back the grade 7 students' reports on their library books, Heidi waited anxiously to receive her corrected work from the teacher. She had read a book on archaeology and had really gotten into it. Heidi spent quite a bit of time explaining in her report how neat it must be to relive the past by examining the artifacts people left behind. When she received her book report, Heidi was dejected. The word *artifact*—Heidi had spelled it *artafact*—was circled twice on her paper with *sp* written above it. At the bottom of the paper, Ms. Lapierre had written, "Spelling errors are careless and are not acceptable." The only other mark Ms. Lapierre had made on the paper was a grade of C.

Questions to Consider

1. What has happened to Heidi's motivation for this topic and this assignment?
2. If Heidi's report was going to receive a C, what should the teacher have done to motivate her to continue learning?

---

1. How can I make use of natural student interests in this learning activity?
2. How can I help students to meet their basic human needs in this activity?
3. How can I use novel events and/or materials in this activity?
4. How can I provide for variety in these learning activities?
5. How can I ensure that my students will be successful?
6. How can I create an appropriate level of tension for this learning task?
7. How can I create a moderately pleasant feeling tone for this activity?
8. How can I provide feedback to students and help them to recognize their progress in learning?
9. How can I encourage my students?

This list of nine questions is also an important resource when behavioural problems occur. By answering the questions, the teacher may find ways to increase students' motivation to learn and decrease their motivation to misbehave.

Teacher Expectations

Teacher expectations influence both student learning and motivation. In a famous study entitled *Pygmalion in the Classroom: Teacher Expectations and Pupils' Intellectual Development* (1968), Rosenthal and Jacobson began a line of inquiry that still continues and has yielded powerful insights into the effects of teacher behaviour on student achievement. For their study, Rosenthal and Jacobson told teachers in an inner-city elementary school that they had developed an intelligence test designed to identify "intellectual bloomers"—that is, students who were on the verge of taking a tremendous leap in their ability to learn. They also told these teachers that certain students in their classes had been so identified. This was a total fabrication. There was no such test. However, when Rosenthal and Jacobson checked student achievement test scores at the end of the year, the students identified as intellectual bloomers had actually bloomed. Compared to a matched group of their peers, the researcher-identified bloomers had made much greater gains in achievement. As a result, Rosenthal and Jacobson assumed that the teachers must have treated the bloomers differently in some way in the classroom, but they had no observational data to support this assumption. Although still considered controversial (Wineburg, 1987), the study provided the impetus for further research (Good, 1987).

Beginning in the 1970s, researchers such as Thomas Good and Jere Brophy conducted observational studies of teacher behaviour toward students whom the teachers perceived as high achievers and toward students they perceived as low achievers (Brophy and Good, 1974; Good and Brophy, 1972). Multiple research studies found that teachers often unintentionally communicate low expectations toward students whom they perceive as low achievers. These lower expectations are communicated by behaviours such as

1. calling on perceived low achievers less often to answer questions;
2. giving perceived low achievers less think time when they are called on;
3. providing fewer clues and hints to perceived low achievers when they have initial difficulty in answering questions;
4. praising correct answers from perceived low achievers less often;
5. criticizing wrong answers from perceived low achievers more often;
6. praising marginal answers from perceived low achievers but demanding more precise answers from high achievers;
7. staying farther away physically and psychologically from perceived low achievers;
8. rarely expressing personal interest in perceived low achievers;
9. smiling less frequently at perceived low achievers;
10. making eye contact less frequently with perceived low achievers; and
11. complimenting perceived low achievers less often.

Some of these behaviours may be motivated by good intentions on the part of the teacher, who, for example, may give perceived low achievers less think time to avoid embarrassing them if they don't know an answer. However, the cumulative effect is the communication of a powerful message: "I don't expect you to be able to do much." This message triggers a vicious circle, wherein students begin to expect less of themselves, produce less, and confirm the teacher's original perception of them. While in many cases, the teacher may have a legitimate reason to expect less from some students, communicating low expectations produces only negative effects. Researchers have demonstrated that when teachers equalize response opportunities, feedback, and personal involvement, student learning can improve. The message is clear: communicating high expectations to all learners appears to influence low achievers to learn more, whereas communicating low expectations, no matter how justified, has a debilitating effect (Good and Brophy, 2000).

Although empirical research in this area has been limited to the effects of teacher expectations on achievement, we believe that the generalizations hold true for student behaviour as well. Communicating high expectations for student behaviour is likely to bring about increased positive behaviours; communicating low expectations for student behaviour is likely to bring about increased negative behaviour (Janes, 1996). A teacher who says, "I am sure that all of you will complete all of your homework assignments carefully because you realize that doing homework is an important way of practising what you are learning" is more likely to have students complete homework assignments than a teacher who says, "I know you probably don't like to do homework, but if you fail to complete homework assignments, it will definitely lower your grades."

As Brophy has noted,

> consistent projection of positive expectations, attributions and social labels to the students is important in fostering positive self-concepts and related motives that orient them toward prosocial behaviour. In short, students who are consistently treated as if they are well-intentioned individuals who respect themselves and others and desire to act responsibly, morally, and prosocially are more likely to live up to those expectations and acquire those qualities than students who are treated as if they had the opposite qualities. (1988a, 11)

Given the powerful research results in this area, all teachers should step back and reflect on the expectations they communicate to students through their verbal and non-verbal classroom behaviour. For instance, when a teacher has in her class a challenging and continually disruptive student, the other students may receive a low-frequency messages that it is acceptable behaviour to ostracize that child. The teacher sends such messages by modelling anger, making cutting remarks, and showing dismissive behaviour toward the problem student. Another example of low-frequency communication to the class pertains to Aboriginal education in non-Aboriginal settings. Even though research points to variations in the way that Aboriginal and non-Aboriginal people learn (Castellano, Davis and Lahache, 2000), the majority of Aboriginal students are taught in traditional provincial schools with methods that are not meaningful to them (Auditor General, 1999).

> Traditional Native education relies upon ways of knowing, ways of interacting and ways of using language which are not normally exploited in formal education. (Battiste and Barman, 1995)

Canada's auditor general also reveals that Aboriginal students do not achieve academic success to the same level as non-Aboriginal students and some of this outcome may be related to teacher expectations.

Classroom Questioning

Whatever the desired instructional outcome, "effective teaching depends primarily upon the teacher's skill in being able to ask questions which generate different kinds of learning" (Morgan and Saxton, 1991, 3). Of all the instructional tools and techniques classroom teachers possess, the art of effective questioning is perhaps the most versatile and important for learning (Cecil, 1995; Good and Brophy, 1997; McKenzie, 2002; Mollica, 1994; Millar, 1991; Sloan and Toews, 1984). In addition, the use of

Effective questioning techniques increase student participation.

good questioning skills is a powerful means of keeping students actively involved in lessons and thus minimizing disruptive behaviour. In order to develop this skill, teachers need to be thoughtful about the kinds of questions they ask, be patient as they wait for answers to be formulated, and listen in order to continue the discussion with another effective question. All questions are not equal, and the skill of asking good questions does not develop without conscious effort and careful personal reflection and evaluation.

Good questioning skills depend upon teachers asking themselves what kind of thinking their questions are producing as well as whether their questions are helping students engage with new learning. Morgan and Saxton (1991) have created what they call a "Taxonomy of Personal Engagement" that identifies a variety of questions:

Interest: questions that promote curiosity about what is being presented.

e.g., "What can I ask to gain their attention and interest?"

Engaging: questions that promote a desire to be involved in the task.

e.g., "What questions can I ask that will draw them into active involvement and encourage them to willingly share their ideas?"

Committing: questions that cause a sense of responsibility toward the task.

e.g., "What questions shall I ask that will invite them to accept some responsibility for this inquiry?"

Internalizing: questions that enable students to grasp concepts or new ideas for long-term understanding.

e.g., "What questions can I ask that will create an atmosphere where they will reflect upon their personal thoughts, feelings, points of view, experiences, and values in relation to this lesson?"

Interpreting: questions that encourage students to express the new understanding in their own words or in order to communicate with others.

e.g., "What questions shall I ask to encourage them to express their understanding of their world, their peers' world, and the world of the lesson?"

Evaluating: questions that enable students to put their new understandings to the test in a personal application.

e.g., "What questions shall I ask that will give them an opportunity to test their new thinking or knowledge in a different context?"(Morgan and Saxton, 1991)

Other findings on classroom management indicate that the following behaviours help to promote student learning through questioning:

1. Ask a variety of questions that promote student thinking.
2. Ask good questions that challenge existing thinking and encourage reflection.
3. Ask the kind of question that enables many students to respond before another question is asked. For example, ask for an occasional response from the entire group, ask students to indicate their agreement or disagreement with answers, or redirect the question to obtain several individual answers.
4. After asking a question, allow students three to five seconds of "wait time" before accepting an answer. This time is particularly important when asking higher-level questions that require students to make inferences, connections, and judgments.
5. Vary the type of positive reinforcement you give for a correct or thoughtful response. Save very high praise for exceptional answers. The teacher's intention is not to give praise but to encourage students to share and discuss their ideas.
6. Ask follow-up or probing questions to expand student thinking after both correct and incorrect responses. Some sample types of follow-up questions include (a) asking for clarification, (b) asking a student to recreate the thought process she used to arrive at an answer, (c) asking for specific examples to support a statement, (d) asking for elaboration or expansion of an answer, and (e) asking a student to relate her answer to previous answers or questions.

According to Postman (1979), a basic element of the development of intelligence in children is helping them to learn how to ask productive questions themselves. A skilled teacher encourages her students to ask questions and presents herself as a co-learner with her class. Modelling good questioning and thinking aloud about how to best phrase an important question can accomplish this goal. It can also be accomplished by praising the formation of good questions and identifying why they make everyone (including the teacher) think.

Teachers who use these techniques, which may be adapted to fit their own classroom context, are likely to improve student learning and to increase their involvement in the learning activities, thereby minimizing disruptive student behaviour.

Maximizing Learning Time

One of the variables that affects how much students learn is the amount of time they spend learning. As Lieberman and Denham have found, there is a statistically positive relationship between time devoted to learning and scores on achievement tests (1980). This is not, however, a simple relationship. Other factors, such as the quality of instruction and the kinds of learning tasks, must be considered in assessing the potential impact of increased time spent on learning. In other words, spending more instructional time with a weak teacher or on poorly devised learning tasks will not increase student learning. Results from a similar Canadian study conducted in Alberta suggest that veteran teachers were more effective in fostering improvements in students' skills than less experienced teachers (Lytton and Pyryt, 1998).

Assuming that the teacher is competent and the learning tasks are appropriate, students who spend more time learning will probably learn more and create fewer management problems because they are occupied by the learning activities. Two areas that teachers can control to increase the amount of time students spend learning are the time allocated for instruction and the rate of student engagement in the learning tasks.

Allocated Time. Allocated time refers to the amount of time that the teacher makes available for students to learn a subject. Although elementary school curriculum expectations are clearly defined in Canada, it is at the discretion of the teacher to determine the amount of time that's needed to achieve those expectations. Educators would agree that the time varies from class to class and student to student.

In secondary schools, the amounts of time actually allocated to instruction also vary widely among teachers. The need to deal with routine attendance and housekeeping chores (for example, "Who still owes lab reports?" and "Who needs to write a makeup for Friday's test?") as well as the need to deal with disruptions that can range from behavioural problems to PA announcements can steal large chunks of time from learning activities (see Chapter 2). Usually, both elementary and secondary school teachers need to examine how much time they make available for students to learn the various subjects they teach. Elementary teachers should investigate how they allocate time to their various subjects. Secondary teachers should investigate how to handle routine duties more efficiently and how to minimize disruptions.

Time on Task. In addition to increasing allocated time, teachers need to maximize student time on task (Starnes and Paris, 2000; O'Reilly, 1999).

Research on teaching has established that the key to successful management (and to successful instruction as well) is the teacher's ability to maximize the time students spend actively engaged in worthwhile academic assignments and to minimize the time they spend waiting for activities to get started, making transitions between activities, sitting with nothing to do, or engaging in misconduct. (Brophy, 1988a, 3)

Brophy's statement refers to the percentage of the total time allocated to learning that the student spends actually engaged in learning activities. Once again, research has provided some guidelines to increase student time on task:

1. The use of substantive interaction—a teaching mode in which the teacher presents information, asks questions to assess comprehension, provides feedback, and monitors student work—usually leads to higher student engagement than independent or small group work that is not led by the teacher.
2. Teacher monitoring of the entire class during the beginning and ending portions of a seatwork activity as well as at regular intervals during the activity leads to higher engagement rates.
3. Making sure that students understand what the activity directs them to do, that they have the skills necessary to complete the task successfully, that each student has access to all needed materials, and that each student is protected from disruption by others leads to greater student time on task during seatwork.
4. Giving students oral and written directions concerning how to do a seat-work activity and what to do when they have finished the activity also leads to greater time on task during seat work.
5. Communicating teacher awareness of student behaviour seems to lead to greater student involvement during seat-work activities.
6. "Providing a variety of seat-work activities with concern for students' attention spans helps keep students on task and allows the teacher more uninterrupted small group instruction" (Evertson, 1989, 64).

When students are on task, they are engaged in learning and are less apt to disrupt the learning of others. The effective teacher uses these guidelines to increase student learning and to minimize disruptive student behaviour—in other words, keep them busy, engaged, and productive!

Beyond the Basics

Canadian Response to Educational Change

Since the early 1990s, ministries and departments of education across Canada have been implementing standardized tests and more rigorous curricula in response to concerns that "students are not being educated well enough to compete in a global economy" (Drake, 1998, 3). These changes occurred because of overall dissatisfaction with the current system at the time, as curricula focused almost exclusively on low-level outcomes and teaching and learning strategies, paying little attention to contextual variables and the subject matter being taught. In response, the Canadian Council of Ministers of Education established an agreement called the Pan-Canadian Protocol for Collaboration on School Curriculum. This agreement set out issues that are of common interest for each of the provinces, such as English and French curriculum, student assessment, technology, electronic exchange of information, and curriculum outcomes and standards. More recently, the media focus on global warming and concerns about environmental issues have prompted a mandate to increase curricular attention to the human impact on our planet.

Each province developed its own response to this environment of challenge and change. Most provincial and territorial governments allocated large budgets for funding research and public surveys that were used and endorsed when campaigns were launched by ministries and departments of education to implement new and, in most cases, more stringent curriculum and testing standards. In some cases, educators and the public did not always agree with the latest changes that were recommended by those in charge of policy. In fact, full-scale disputes and unrest in some provinces have resulted in disruptions to education through teachers' work-to-rule actions and strikes because of proposed changes to education. Many teachers were resistant to change and were threatened by suggestions that they were not teaching effectively.

In addition, in 2003 the Newfoundland and Labrador Ministry of Education introduced programs and funding through the province's Stepping into the Future early-childhood-development initiative aimed at increasing childhood and family literacy. This new funding, along with early-childhood literacy grants, targeted children up to age 6. The Government of Newfoundland and Labrador's goal has been to improve literacy within the province to levels comparable to those in the rest of Canada.

In the same year, Nova Scotia, through its Department of Education's Learning for Life plan, announced an investment of $5 million for additional teachers. This funding enabled boards to add teachers to the school system in order to reduce class sizes. This included resource teachers, speech language pathologists, Reading Recovery experts and other special needs professionals. Technological initiatives in reading and writing programs aimed at increasing the number of women in science, trades, technical and technology-related occupations have also been established in Nova Scotia.

Prince Edward Island created a document called the Strategic Plan, 1999–2004, to communicate the strategy and educational guidelines for the coming years. This manuscript outlines the goals for the province's schools and administration and sets out key performance measures for the strategies that have been designed to implement those goals. The Ministry of Education for PEI has also been working on other issues, including approaches to encourage graduates to return to or remain in the province.

In 2003, the premier of New Brunswick announced new spending in an initiative called the Quality Learning Agenda, which was brought in as a ten-year plan to strengthen New Brunswick's education system. The plan included $21.6 million to add 500 teachers to the school system over the next four years. The Quality Learning Agenda continues to concentrate on improving academic achievement, enhancing teaching practices, and guaranteeing increased accountability of the education system to students and parents. The plan calls for New Brunswick students to place in the top three provinces in Canada for academic achievement, high school graduation rates, and advancement to post-secondary institutions.

The province of Quebec developed a long-term document, which is similar to PEI's, called the Strategic Plan of the Ministère de l'Éducation for 2000–2003 (October 23, 2000). The summary for the document lists guidelines for measuring the components of the education system and defines actions to accomplish the objectives. Other programs that are currently offered in Quebec involve special-needs students and technology.

In keeping with other provincial initiatives, Ontario's educational landscape has undergone a great number of changes over the past few years. Ontario faced a major challenge in reducing secondary education by one year. As a result, students in 2003 who graduated from grade 12, and from the last year of the Ontario Academic Credit (OAC)—formerly grade 13—graduated at the same time and became known as the "double cohort." Most of these high school graduates sought admission to tertiary education institutions. Therefore, many new academic and residence buildings were constructed over the years prior to the double cohort year to accommodate the expected influx of first-year students to university and college campuses. Hundreds of millions of dollars were allocated and spent to ready the campuses. Other issues, such as teacher testing, teacher shortage, pressure for more educational funding, and new curricula have added to the educational angst among students, educators, politicians, and the public in Ontario.

Manitoba began its focus on upgrading curriculum with an early years numeracy grant. This grant assisted school divisions/districts to implement early-intervention strategies aimed at improving mathematical skills, knowledge, and attitudes of students from kindergarten to grade 4.

The main issues for Saskatchewan were examining technological methods to further enhance their distance-learning programs. The Evergreen Curriculum is an example of how computer technology provides users who have online access with Saskatchewan's core curriculum guides, bibliographies, links to online resources, and discussion areas; as well, it provides a search function. The province is also examining and revising many areas of the curriculum.

Alberta's Commission on Learning was established in 2002. The commission members visited communities across Alberta and talked with education stakeholders—parents, teachers, and support staff—to determine which educational issues were most important to these groups and to determine the commission's next steps. Alberta had not completed a comprehensive review of education in 30 years, so this process was deemed well overdue.

In 2002, British Columbia also initiated an educational task force to gather perceptions on student achievement, human and social development, and safety. The BC education ministry surveyed students in grades 4, 7, 10, and 12, as well as parents and school staff members in 1582 schools. More than 208 000 people took part in the study. Key findings from the analysis of the survey indicated that 73 percent of parents were satisfied all of the time or most of the time with what their children were learning at school. Eighty-one percent of responding parents felt that school grooms their children for post-secondary education, while 66 percent felt that school prepares children for a job. British Columbia used these results and results from its 2002 administration of the Foundation Skills Assessment (FSA) to set out implications for instruction in reading comprehension, writing, and numeracy in grades 4, 7, and 10.

Canada's territories also participated in educational change with their own initiatives based on perceived needs. For example, the Yukon Ministry of Education is committed to channelling significant resources to projects that use the internet. Several monetary awards were allocated to projects from Canada's SchoolNet grassroots program. In addition to new projects that have received funding, the ministry has a full webpage devoted to projects that have already been completed. Video-conferencing pilots also took place in the 2003–04 school year.

The Northwest Territories (NWT) in 2001 launched a literacy initiative. The purpose of the NWT strategy was to enhance existing literacy programs and to ensure every NWT community has access to literacy training. The government budgeted $2.4 million yearly to encourage partnerships and programs that assist NWT residents to raise their literacy skills and education level. This program, called Towards Literacy: A Strategy Framework, offers literacy programs to all NWT residents through many community-based programs and partnerships with non-governmental organizations (NGOs), individuals, families, communities, and government agencies.

Canada's newest territory, Nunavut, also participates in grassroots programs through SchoolNet. The development of a state-of-the-art technological infrastructure is receiving high priority, along with an emphasis on cultural, literacy, and numeracy skills.

In addition to the advances and positive change that technology can establish, there is also the risk that technology leads to a digital divide. *The New Dictionary of Cultural Literacy* states that *digital divide* is

> a term that describes the division of the world into two camps, those who have access to the Internet and other advanced information technologies and those who don't. The term highlights the issue that those who do not have access to such technology are potentially destined to futures where they will be at an economic disadvantage. (Retrieved online September 2007)

Statistics Canada (2005) presents a number of studies that point to computer use and internet access and, at the same time, highlight the potential widening gap that defines the digital divide. For example, 31.2 percent of Canadians who have less than a high school education use the internet, whereas 89.4 percent of those with a university degree access it. For those who earn $13 000 or less, 58.7 percent use the internet, compared with 83.2 percent of those who earn $46 000 and higher.

Researchers' Responses to Change

The major impetus for the current models of teaching and learning is the rise in popularity of **constructivism** as a philosophical set of beliefs about learning. Until relatively recently, education and its research have been dominated by behaviourist and information-processing views of learning, which, although different in many respects, share a conception of the learner basically as a passive receptor of information received from the outside environment. In contrast, constructivism emphasizes active construction of knowledge by the learner. Thus constructivism places the learner squarely in the centre of the learning paradigm and sees the role of the teacher as one of coaching, guiding and supporting the learner as needed. The tenets of constructivism are the following five points: (1) knowledge is actively constructed, (2) knowledge should be structured around a few powerful ideas, (3) prior knowledge exerts a powerful influence on new learning, (4) restructuring prior knowledge and conceptual change are key elements of new learning, and (5) knowledge is socially constructed (Good and Brophy, 2000). Using the constructivist paradigm, teachers must provide opportunities for students to make new knowledge their own through questions, discussion, debate, and other interactive activities (Brophy, 1993; Scardamalia and Bereiter, 1991).

Another major impetus toward the acceptance of constructivist philosophy in the teaching field lies in research into effective teaching that came from conceptual change research in science (Khalid, 2003; Pintrich, Marx, and Boyle, 1993). This line of research focused on the difficulty science teachers face in attempting to change the misconceptions that students bring to the classroom. For example, most students come to the classroom believing that the explanation for warmer weather in the summer is that the sun is closer to the earth in the summer. The sun, in fact, is actually closer to the earth in the winter. However, research indicates that even after they have the correct explanation, which they are able to reproduce for a test, most students leave the classroom still believing that the sun is closer to the earth in the summer. Researchers have studied student learning of a number of scientific concepts, including photosynthesis, electricity, gravity, and density, with similar results—that is, students enter the classroom with misconceptions, learn the correct explanations for the test, and yet leave the classroom with their basic misconceptions completely unchanged. These studies indicate that we need to pay much closer attention to the prior knowledge that students bring with them to the classroom, as well as to the actual thought processes that take place during instruction.

The research on student cognition, constructivism, conceptual-change teaching, and subject-specific teaching has led to several changes in our thinking about instructional practice. Indeed, such research has led to a *new paradigm for learning* that rests on the following: (1) teaching for understanding as the major goal for teaching; (2) using authentic instructional tasks as the basis for classroom learning; (3) emphasizing teaching frameworks that highlight the importance of thinking skills, problem-solving, and student self-regulation; (4) moving from individual learning to the creation of learning communities; (5) teaching for multiple types of intelligence; and (6) emphasizing student cognitive variables rather than overt teacher behaviour as the key aspect of student motivation in the classroom. In this section of the chapter, these concepts will be described individually, even though they are interwoven and closely related to each other.

Another shift in understanding has come as a result of changing views of the meaning of literacy as it relates to existing communication patterns. The term *multiliteracies* has emerged to describe the increasingly complex world of communication (Cope and Kalantzis, 2000; Elliott, Woloshyn, Bajovic, and Ratkovic, 2007; Ng, 2006). Multiliteracies comprise both the multitude of communication methods through media and the burgeoning cultural and linguistic diversity through globalization (Cope and Kalantzis, 2000). For instance, written communication is changing with MSN, email, social-networking websites such as Facebook and MySpace, and PDA-style text messaging having their own languages and set of ethical behaviours. Thus, educators are starting to respond to this reality by broadening their views of literacy instruction to include critical literacy in order to help children become discerning consumers who are properly prepared to participate in rapidly changing global communication patterns. This particular imperative to change and the overwhelming research support for viewing literacy differently is colliding with the immediacy of standardized testing related to traditional literacy and numeracy skills. Teachers feel they have little time to devote to newer forms of literacy no matter how much they dominate children's lives (Elliott, Woloshyn, Bajovic, and Ratkovic, 2007).

Teaching for Understanding

For much of the history of education in Canada, the goals for classroom learning have focused on the acquisition of factual information and routine skills and procedures. Although still important to some degree, these goals have become increasingly less sufficient for enabling students to function competently in today's technologically sophisticated, information-rich society. In order to function effectively in a global, interactive society, students need to go beyond memorization of content and routine skills to much deeper levels of understanding and interdisciplinary skills. Howard Gardner has asserted that our schools have never really taught for deep understanding (Brandt, 1993). Instead, they have settled for what Gardner calls the "correct answer compromise"—that is, students give agreed-upon answers that are counted as correct, but their real-world behaviour indicates that they have failed to truly understand the material. Gardner believes that we need to enable students to achieve a deep understanding of the material that they encounter in school. **Deep understanding** means being able to do a variety of thought-demanding tasks, such as explaining a topic in one's own words, making predictions, finding exemplars in new contexts, and applying concepts to explain new situations (Brandt, 1993).

The first step in making deep understanding one of our goals for student learning involves the teacher coming to grips with the content-coverage dilemma. Teaching for understanding involves time. Learners' deep understandings of content or skills that transfer across disciplines do not develop overnight. Learners need opportunities to become engaged with the content in different contexts. They need the opportunity to see many examples, ask many questions, discuss ideas with peers and with the teacher, and practise demonstrating their understanding in a variety of situations. If the transfer of skills is to occur, students need explicit prompts by the teacher to remind them to employ a strategy learned in one context to a new situation (Woloshyn and Elliott, 1998). As a result, it is simply not possible to cover the same amount of material that can be covered in a classroom in which student memorization is the goal. The teacher who wants to teach for understanding must be willing to take the time to allow students to become deeply involved with the material.

For those teachers who are willing to cover less material at deeper levels of student understanding, Perkins and Blythe offer a four-part framework that can be used to focus classroom learning on creating deeper understanding (1994). The first part of the framework calls for the teacher to use "generative topics" as the focus for classroom learning. In order for a topic to qualify as generative, it must meet three criteria: (1) it must be an important topic in the discipline; (2) it must be easily enough conveyed by teachers to learners at various developmental levels; and (3) it must be relatable to learners' lives and interests outside of school. The second part of Perkins and Blythe's framework asks the teacher to set learning goals that require students to demonstrate their understanding. For example, students might identify examples of Newton's laws of motion in everyday sports events. The third part of the framework requires students to demonstrate their understanding through classroom activities, such as discussions, debates, experiments, problem-solving, and so forth. The final part of the framework calls for ongoing assessment of student progress using publicly shared criteria for success, frequent feedback by the teacher, and periodic opportunities for students to reflect on their own progress toward demonstrating a deep understanding of the particular topic.

Authentic Instruction

While the concept of teaching for understanding focuses on three separate but related elements (the content selected for instruction, the selected learning goals, and general strategies for assessing student learning), the concept of authentic instruction emphasizes actual classroom activities. When these two concepts are melded together in the classroom, the teacher has a powerful set of ideas for enhancing both student understanding and student interest in the teaching–learning process.

According to Newmann and Wehlage (1993), there are five key elements to authentic instruction. They have developed a continuum for each element that can be used by a teacher or an observer to determine the degree to which authentic instruction is happening in a classroom. The first continuum looks at the emphasis on higher-order thinking versus the emphasis on lower-order thinking. When authentic instruction is in progress, students are asked to manipulate, transform, and use information in new and unpractised ways rather than to receive information and use it in repetitive and routine ways.

The second continuum, depth of coverage, is closely related to the concept of teaching for understanding. When authentic instruction is taking place, students encounter a small number of ideas but are expected to develop a deep level of understanding of the ideas as opposed to encountering many ideas that are dealt with only at surface level.

The third continuum focuses on the connection of school activities to the world outside the classroom. Teachers using authentic instruction present real-world problems as topics of study, and students are expected to apply their knowledge to settings outside the classroom. Information is not seen as useful *only* for continued success in school.

The fourth continuum, substantive conversation, focuses on the nature of the verbal interaction that occurs in the classroom. When authentic instruction takes place, both the learners and the teacher are engaged in dialogue and argumentation that is unscripted and uncontrolled and that builds on participants' understandings, as opposed to verbal interactions that are characterized primarily by lectures and short, pre-planned, predictable conversations and interactions.

The final continuum focuses on the push for achievement in the classroom. When authentic instruction is in place, the classroom environment is marked by mutual respect, intellectual risk taking, and a widely accepted belief that all learners can learn, as opposed to a classroom environment that discourages effort and participation and in which only some students are viewed as capable learners.

Classrooms that use authentic instruction differ from traditional classrooms not only in terms of the problems students are asked to solve but also in terms of the teacher's role in structuring student learning. Because authentic instruction forces students to solve real-world types of problems rather than to simply apply previously learned formulas or concepts to solve textbook problems (Stepien and Gallagher, 1993), the problems are not well-defined and are not usually confined to one specific discipline (Drake, 1998). In order to solve such problems, students must first define the problems, then gather additional information or acquire additional skills.

Consequently, teachers usually introduce these complex, ill-structured problems early in the learning sequence and then allow the instructional sequence to emerge from the way in which the problems are defined. In other words, lower-level knowledge and skills are not introduced as separate topics. The need to develop lower-level skills and acquire lower-level knowledge arises directly from the students' attempt to define and solve the problem that serves as the focus for learning. The old paradigm, which held that students must first acquire a host of prerequisite knowledge before being introduced to problem-solving activities, has been replaced by a new paradigm: it asserts that lower-level knowledge and skills should be acquired as a result of students needing specific information or specific skills in order to solve real-world problems (Drake, 1998). In authentic instruction, the teacher is active early in the learning process, modelling appropriate problem-solving behaviour, providing cues and information to the learner, and structuring the learning process (Woloshyn and Elliott, 1998). However, as time goes on and students acquire a better understanding of the real-world problem and the information and skills needed to solve it, the students become more self-regulated and take an active role in structuring their own learning (Olafson and Field, 1999; Brophy, 1993). As we noted in the section on lesson design, this type of structuring is sometimes referred to as *scaffolding*.

Emphasis on Thinking and Problem-Solving Skills

Clearly, the concepts of teaching for understanding and authentic instruction emphasize student thinking and problem-solving skills. However, because thinking and problem-solving skills are seen as tools for acquiring a deep understanding of content, they play a secondary rather than primary role in the conceptualization of the teaching and learning process. Thinking and problem-solving skills, however, play an important role in the conceptualization of teaching developed by Marzano and his associates (1992). This conceptualization, entitled *dimensions of learning*, provides a comprehensive framework for focusing teaching and learning on the development of higher-order thinking, problem-solving, and understanding. Marzano assumes that the process of learning involves the interaction of five types of thinking, which he has called dimensions of learning.

Dimension 1, which comprises "positive attitudes and perceptions about learning," states that all learning activities are filtered through the students' attitudes and perceptions. Therefore, effective teachers shape their lessons to foster positive attitudes and perceptions. They help to create these positive attitudes by making students feel accepted, providing physical and psychological comfort (see Chapter 3), creating a sense of order and routine in the classroom, helping students to understand what they are required to do in performing classroom tasks, and helping students to believe that they can be successful in completing those tasks.

Dimension 2 concerns the acquisition of new knowledge and skills. According to this dimension, early in the learning process, effective teachers help students to acquire new knowledge by encouraging them to relate the new knowledge to what they already know and by providing them with opportunities to organize the information in ways that will help them to store it in their long-term memory. These teachers aid the acquisition of new skills by structuring the learning sequence: they first help students to build a cognitive model of the new skill, and then gradually shape skill performance to make it more refined, automatic, and internalized. This dimension corresponds nicely to the research on effective teaching described in the first section of this chapter.

Dimension 3 concerns the extension and refinement of knowledge by learners. Effective teachers help learners to refine and extend their knowledge by providing opportunities for them to use such thinking skills as comparing and contrasting information, classifying information and observations, analyzing arguments, constructing support for ideas and arguments, abstracting information, and analyzing diverse perspectives on issues and questions.

The final two dimensions concern using knowledge meaningfully and developing productive habits of mind. These two dimensions remind us that teachers should involve students in long-term, self-directed projects that require investigation, decision-making, research, problem-solving, and invention. Effective teachers should also help their students to develop sensitivity to feedback, a desire for accuracy, persistence in the face of difficulty, an unconventional view of situations, and an ability to avoid impulsive actions. These traits help learners to solve the complex problems and issues that they face both in the classroom and throughout their lives. When used as a framework for planning, implementing, and analyzing instruction, these five dimensions of learning serve as valuable tools for enhancing student thinking, problem-solving, and self-regulated learning.

Creating Communities of Learners

One of the most dramatic changes that has taken place in our thinking about teaching during the last 15 years has been the emphasis we now place on the importance of building learning communities in the classroom. In the past, we emphasized individual student learning and interaction between individual students and the teacher. Note that the research on effective teaching described in the first section of this chapter focuses almost exclusively on interaction between individual students and their teacher. Early research on effective teaching viewed peers as superfluous to the learning process.

However, because of the work on co-operative learning conducted by Johnson, Johnson, and Holubec (1993), Slavin (1989–90), Kagan (1994), and others, we now believe that peers can play a tremendously important role in enhancing student learning and in developing positive classroom environments. For this reason, we now believe that the creation of a classroom learning community in which students engage in dialogue with each other and with the teacher is a critical step toward making classrooms productive learning environments (Prawat, 1993).

Creating communities of learners often begins with designing lessons to involve students in co-operative learning activities. Co-operative learning should not be equated with simply putting students into groups. Co-operative learning activities share a set of common characteristics. Although the number of specific elements in co-operative learning differs among theorists—Johnson, Johnson, and Holubec (1993), for example, favour five elements, while Slavin (1989–90) favours three—there seem to be at least three elements that are critical to its success (Slavin, 1989–90). These are (1) face-to-face interaction, (2) a feeling of positive interdependence, and (3) a feeling of individual accountability.

Face-to-face interaction requires placing students in close physical proximity to each other and ensuring that they are required to talk to each other in order to complete the assigned tasks. If students can complete the task without interacting with each other, they have been engaged in an individual learning activity rather than a co-operative learning activity.

Establishing a feeling of positive interdependence means that students believe each individual can achieve the particular learning goal only if all the learners in the group achieve the learning goal. Johnson, Johnson, and Holubec (1993), who refer to this as "sinking or swimming together," have identified several types of interdependence that the teacher can work to create. Positive reward interdependence occurs when everyone is rewarded or no one is rewarded, and everyone gets the same reward. Positive resource interdependence occurs when each member of the group has only a portion of the information or materials needed to complete the task. A teacher is using positive resource interdependence when each student has only one piece of a puzzle or one section of required reading. Positive task interdependence occurs when a task is broken into a series of steps and is then completed in assembly-line fashion, with each group member completing only one section of the total task. Positive role interdependence is the practice of assigning roles to individual group members—for example, consensus checker, writer, reader, timekeeper, and so on. Obviously, each role must be important to the completion of the task. Finally, positive identity interdependence is established by allowing the group to form its own identity—for example, by creating a group name, decorating a group folder or flag, or developing a group motto or some other symbol that describes the group. The researchers suggest that the teacher build as many of these types of positive interdependence into co-operative learning lessons as possible in order to increase the likelihood of creating feelings of positive interdependence.

Individual accountability refers to each group member's feeling that she is responsible for completing the task and cannot rest on the laurels of the group or allow other members to do the work for her. Feelings of individual accountability can be established in a variety of ways, including assigning individual grades; giving individual tests, worksheets, and quizzes; or structuring tasks so that they must be completed by the group while making it clear that individual group members will be called on at random to answer questions about the task.

In addition to face-to-face interaction, positive interdependence, and individual accountability, the researchers believe two more elements—teaching social skills and processing group functioning—are crucial for the creation of co-operative learning activities. These two elements are described at length in Chapter 6, "Structuring the Environment." As Case 5.4 illustrates, co-operative learning activities can have a positive impact on student motivation and behaviour.

CASE 5.4 • *Co-operative Learning in Biology*

Because of my position as department head, I am often in and out of teachers' classrooms for quick conversations about curriculum and/or students. One day, as I walked into Mr. Higgins's grade 12 biology class, which was filled primarily with vocational technical students, I was surprised to see a variety of specimen samples lying on the lab tables. Mr. Higgins began class by informing his students that they would be having a lab quiz—he referred to it as a "practical"—the next day, which would constitute a major grade for the marking period. The students, who were busily engaged in their own private conversations, met this news with shrugs of indifference. Mr. Higgins continued speaking: "The practical will also be a co-operative learning team activity. Each of your individual scores on the quiz will be added together and averaged to form a team score. Your team score will be counted as part of the scores for our team competition. Just to review team standings so far, we have the Plumbers in first place with 93 points, followed by the Body Fixers with 88 points, the Hair Choppers with 87, and the Electricians in last place with 86 points. Don't forget that we have all agreed that the winning team will be treated to a pizza party by the rest

of the class. Now, you may go ahead and get started studying in teams for tomorrow's practical."

For a brief moment, the room fell completely silent. This was followed by the scrape of chairs and scuffling of feet as students moved into co-operative learning teams. Within minutes, the students were busy looking at the specimens and relating them to the diagrams in their textbook. Students were clearly engaged in helping each other to memorize the various specimen parts that they would need to know for the quiz. Suddenly, one of the students from the Electricians sat down and began to read a comic book. Within a few minutes, however, the other members of the team informed him that he was not going to sit there and do nothing. They assured him that they would help him to obtain a passing grade on the quiz whether he liked it or not. The student got to his feet with a look of resignation and resumed looking at the specimens.

Questions to Consider

1. What beliefs about learning are influencing Mr. Higgins's decisions about administering tests to this class?
2. How could Mr. Higgins also encourage individual accountability in this class?

Teaching Toward Multiple Intelligences

Due to the work of Howard Gardner and his colleagues in the 1980s, many educators have come to realize that success in school has been unnecessarily restricted to those individuals who have talents in the areas of mathematical and verbal intelligence (1983). Many of the tasks and learning activities performed in schools require learners to use verbal and mathematical reasoning while ignoring other ways of expressing talent. One need only look at standardized achievement tests, traditional IQ tests, and the scholastic aptitude tests (SATs) to recognize our overdependence on verbal and mathematical ability. Fortunately, Gardner's theory of multiple intelligences and its application have helped us to recognize how other types of talent can be tapped.

Gardner's theory asserts that there are many types of human intelligence and that it is possible to group the various types into seven comprehensive categories: linguistic, logical/mathematical, spatial, bodily/kinaesthetic, musical, interpersonal, and intrapersonal. Each one of us, according to Gardner, possesses these types of intelligence to some degree. Those who exhibit high degrees of linguistic intelligence are able to use oral and written language effectively. They are often individuals who succeed in areas such as politics, sales, advertising, and writing. Individuals with strengths in the area of logical/mathematical ability work with numbers effectively and tend to use reason and logical arguments well. Such individuals are accountants, lawyers, scientists, and so on. Some individuals—for example, artists, architects, and interior designers—excel at tasks that require them to perceive and transform graphic and visual representations of reality. Athletes, dancers, and craftspeople, such as mechanics, fall into the category of bodily/kinaesthetic intelligence. They are able to use their bodies to express feelings and ideas and are able to use their hands to produce things. Musicians, conductors, music critics, and composers have a special capacity to perceive and express musical form. Thus, they have a high degree of musical intelligence. Individuals who are very sensitive to the feelings, moods, and intentions of others display interpersonal intelligence. They are often quite successful in people-oriented occupations, such as teaching, counselling, and psychology. Finally, there are certain individuals who seem to possess a high degree of self-knowledge and awareness. They understand themselves well and are able to act on that knowledge.

Although good teachers have always been aware of the variety of ways in which students demonstrate high ability, standard classroom practices and assessment devices have not allowed students to demonstrate their knowledge in ways compatible with their strengths. In the last ten years or so, Armstrong (1994), Gibson and Govendo (1999), and others have begun to help teachers figure out how to structure classroom activities and assessments to take full advantage of the range of intelligences that learners possess. According to Armstrong, learners who are linguistically talented benefit from activities such as storytelling, listening to and giving lectures, journal writing, and participating in classroom discussions. Students who have high aptitudes in mathematical/logical ability usually enjoy activities such as problem-solving, observing and classifying, Socratic questioning, and experiments. Students who have strengths in spatial reasoning often profit from visual displays, colour coding and colour cues, and graphic representations, such as semantic maps and webs. Students who are talented in the bodily/kinaesthetic area profit from learning activities that include body movement. Such activities might include acting out stories and concepts, and using manipulatives. Learners who exhibit high degrees of musical ability usually learn more effectively when learning activities include songs, raps, chants, and the use of music as either a teaching tool or a background environment. Learners who are strong in interpersonal intelligence perform best when they are engaged in collegial interactions, such as peer tutoring, co-operative learning, simulations, and board games. Finally, students who possess a high degree of intrapersonal intelligence learn best when provided with opportunities for personal goal setting, for connecting school work to their personal lives, for making choices about learning activities, and for individual reflection on their own learning. These students often are exceptionally good at self-assessment.

Armstrong suggests that teachers ask themselves the following questions when planning a unit of instruction (1994):

1. How will I use the spoken or written word in this unit?
2. How can I bring numbers, calculations, and logic into the unit?
3. How can I use visual aids, colour, and symbolism in the unit?
4. How can I involve movement and create hands-on activities?
5. How can I use music or environmental sounds?
6. How can I involve students in peer tutoring, co-operative learning, and sharing?
7. How can I evoke personal feelings and connections and provide students with the opportunity to make individual choices about the unit?

Student Motivation: Student Cognition

In the first section of this chapter, "The Basics of Effective Teaching," we discussed theories and models of motivation that emphasized factors external to the student. Indeed, the focus of that section was on overt teacher behaviours that have an impact on student motivation. In this section, we will look at motivation from a different perspective—that of student cognition and its impact on motivation to learn. There are at present at least three theories of student motivation—student cognition, attribution, and expectancy value theory—that have interesting implications for teaching.

The primary developer of the social cognition theory of student motivation was Albert Bandura (1986). Bandura took issue with the behavioural notions of motivation that emphasized external reinforcers. He asserted that the individual's thoughts play a central role not only in determining the individual's motivational levels but also in determining how the individual will perceive variables that are intended to be reinforcers. Bandura's research demonstrated that personal evaluation and self-satisfaction are potent reinforcers of behaviour—in fact, probably more potent than reinforcers provided by others. Bandura's research findings showed that involving students in personal goal setting and providing frequent opportunities for students to monitor and reflect on their progress toward these goals can increase student learning efforts. In fact, according to Bandura, external praise can diminish self-evaluation and create dependency on others, thereby reducing an individual's intrinsic motivation to succeed.

Bandura's work on personal evaluation and self-satisfaction led to a related concept that he called **self-efficacy**. Self-efficacy refers to an individual's expectation of success at a particular task. When feelings of self-efficacy are high, individuals are much more likely to exert effort toward task completion than they are when feelings are low, because they believe they have the potential to be successful. When feelings of self-efficacy are low, efforts are diminished. Feelings of self-efficacy develop from judgments about past performance as well as from vicarious observations of others in similar situations. The greater the perceived similarity between the person we are observing (the model) and ourselves, the greater the impact that person's fate will have on our own feelings of self-efficacy.

When social cognition theory is in action in the classroom, the teacher's task is to focus encouragement on the improvement of individual effort and achievement over time. Teachers who wish to use this theory in the classroom should begin by engaging students in setting personal goals that are concrete, specific, and realistic. Teachers should then involve students in monitoring their own performance toward the achievement of these goals. When students are successful, teachers must encourage them to engage in self-reinforcement so that they will build positive feelings of self-efficacy toward the accomplishment of future tasks.

Attribution theory deals with student-perceived causes of success and failure in school tasks. Clearly, students' perceptions of why they succeed or fail at school tasks have a direct impact on their motivation to perform (Tombari and Borich, 1998; Stipek, 1993). Research has identified five factors to which students are likely to attribute success or failure. These factors are ability, effort, task difficulty, luck, and other people, such as the teacher (Ames and Ames, 1984). The only factor that can be controlled directly by the student is effort. When students attribute success to effort, and failure to lack of effort or inappropriate types of effort, they are likely to exert additional effort in the future. "Students who believe that their personal efforts influence their learning are more likely to learn than those who believe that learning depends on teachers or other factors such as task difficulty or luck" (Wang and Palinscar, 1989).

When students attribute failure to lack of ability, the impact on future performance is devastating. Negative feelings of self-efficacy develop, and students see little value in making any effort since they believe that they are not likely to be successful. As negative judgments of ability become more internalized and self-worth more damaged, students stop making any effort as a defence mechanism. Not making the effort allows them to protect their self-concept from further damage. They can simply shrug their shoulders and claim, "I could have done it if I wanted to, but I really didn't think it was worth it." This face-saving device prevents the further ego damage that would result from additional negative ability attributions. To avoid setting up the vicious circle of failure and lack of future effort, teachers need to recognize the danger of placing students in competitive situations in which they do not have the ability to compete, or of asking students to complete tasks that are too difficult for them.

The implications of attribution theory for classroom teaching are clear. Students need to be assigned tasks that are moderately challenging but within their capability. This may mean that the teacher has to break complex tasks into subtasks that the student can handle and provide a great deal of scaffolding for the student, especially early in the learning process. The teacher should encourage students to make the right kind of effort in completing classroom tasks. When students are successful, the teacher can attribute their success to this effort. When students are not successful, the teacher may want to focus attention on the lack of effort or on the use of inappropriate strategies. Research has demonstrated that teacher statements concerning attributions for success or failure are the key variables in influencing students to attribute success or failure to one variable rather than another. Case 5.5 illustrates the impact of changing attributions.

The expectancy value theory proposes that the effort an individual is willing to put forth in any task is directly related to the product of two factors: the belief

CASE 5.5 • *Three Years of History Rolled into One*

Mark was a senior who had failed both grade 10 and grade 11 history and was now taking grade 10, grade 11, and grade 12 history in order to graduate on time. The school guidance counsellor, who was working with him to improve his study skills, began by helping Mark to prepare for a test on Canadian Confederation. When the counsellor asked which material seemed important for the test, Mark replied, "Well, I know that one thing she is going to ask is,—What is the significance to Confederation of building the railroad across Canada?'" With this response, it became clear to the counsellor that Mark was not good at distinguishing important from unimportant material. Over the next couple of weeks, they spent a great deal of time looking at Mark's notes and his textbook, separating important from unimportant material.

Two days before the test, Mark had a list of important material to study and did a reasonably good job learning that material. Immediately after taking the test, Mark went to the guidance counsellor's office and announced, "You know what? I noticed something on the test." "What did you notice?" asked the counsellor. "I noticed that the stuff I studied for, I knew, and the stuff I didn't study, I didn't know."

At first, the counsellor thought that Mark was putting him on. However, as the conversation continued it became clear that Mark was serious. Until this point in his life, Mark had felt that success on tests was simply a matter of luck. If you happened to be paying attention to the right things in class, you did well on tests. If you were unfortunate enough to be daydreaming during key information, you did poorly. It was all a matter of luck in terms of when you were paying attention.

Armed with this information, the guidance counsellor now had a two-pronged approach to working with Mark. Not only did they work on identifying important information but also on attributing both success and failure to personal effort rather than to chance. As

a result of this work, Mark managed to pass (albeit barely) all three histories and graduate on time.

Questions to Consider

1. Why had Mark developed such a dysfunctional belief about tests?
2. The skill of *learning how to learn* is more important than the content being learned. Discuss.

that she will be successful and the value of the outcomes that will be gained through successful completion of the task (Feathers, 1982). A multiplication sign is used to indicate the interaction between the two factors. Note that if either of the two factors is 0, no effort will be put forth. Thus, if a student believes that she has the potential to be successful in academic work and values good grades and the other outcomes that accompany academic success, she will be highly motivated to put forth a strong effort. On the other hand, if the student doubts her ability to perform the academic tasks successfully or does not value good grades and the other outcomes attached to academic success, she is likely to put forth a limited, feeble effort. Teachers can increase a student's effort at success either by encouraging the learner to believe that she can be successful or by increasing the value of the outcomes.

Good and Brophy (1986) have suggested that teachers take the following steps to implement the expectancy value theory in the classroom: (1) establish a supportive classroom climate, (2) structure activities so that they are at the appropriate level of difficulty, (3) develop learning objectives that have personal meaning and relevance for the students, and (4) engage students in personal goal setting and self-appraisal. Finally, for the expectancy value theory to succeed, the teacher needs to help students recognize the link between effort and outcome suggested by attribution theory.

Summary

In the first section of this chapter, we presented an overview of the research on teaching that, as we see it, constitutes the basics of effective teaching. In the second section of the chapter, we described several conceptualizations of teaching that have influenced our current understanding of best teaching practices. These conceptualizations focus on student cognition and higher-order thinking and understanding. Taken together, the two major sections of the chapter provide the reader with a comprehensive understanding of current thinking concerning best teaching practices. All teachers have a professional obligation to examine their teaching behaviour to ensure that it reflects best practices. This is a critical step toward making sure that the teacher has done all that can be done to prevent classroom-management problems. Among the questions teachers should ask in assessing the congruence between their own teaching and best practices are the following:

1. Do the lessons I design include an introduction, a clear presentation of content, checks for student understanding, guided practice, independent practice, closure or summary, and periodic reviews?

2. Have I considered each of the following factors in trying to increase my students' motivation to learn: student interests, student needs, novelty and variety, success, student attributions, tension, feeling tone, feedback, and encouragement?

3. Have I communicated high expectations for learning and behaviour to all students by equalizing response opportunities, providing prompt and constructive feedback on performance, and treating all students with personal regard?

4. Have I used classroom questioning to involve students actively in the learning process by asking questions at a variety of cognitive levels, using questions to increase student participation and to probe for and extend student thinking?

5. Have I maximized student learning by allocating as much time as possible to this objective and increasing the percentage of student engagement in learning activities?

6. Am I teaching to enable students to develop a deep understanding of content rather than a surface-level knowledge?

7. Am I using authentic instruction in terms of the learning activities I plan and carry out?

8. Am I using a comprehensive framework to help students develop thinking skills, problem-solving skills, and the capacity to regulate their own learning?

9. Am I building communities of learners?

10. Am I teaching so that students can demonstrate their learning by using a variety of intelligences?

11. Am I using student cognition to increase student motivation to learn?

The teacher who can answer *yes* honestly to each of these questions has made giant strides toward ensuring that her classroom will be a learning place for students in which behavioural problems are kept to a minimum.

Key Terms

backward design or **design-down planning**: begins with the end in mind, the enduring understanding, then moves further down the planning continuum (please examine other documentation for more complete explanation).

constructivism: learning that is initiated and directed by the learner.

deep understanding: being able to do a variety of thought-demanding tasks

effective teacher/teaching: most often defined as enhanced student achievement on paper-and-pencil tests.

lesson: the amount of instructional time required for students to achieve a specific learning objective.

self-efficacy: an individual's expectation of success at a particular task.

Exercises

1. Select a concept from any discipline with which you are familiar.

    a. Write a series of questions on the concept at each of the following levels: knowledge, comprehension, application, analysis, synthesis, and evaluation.
    b. Would there be any difference in the use of wait time in asking the six questions you wrote? Why?
    c. Why is a hierarchical ordering of questions important in classroom management?

2. Why is it better to ask the question first and then call on someone to answer it? Would there be any justification for doing it the other way around?

3. What specifically can teachers do to communicate high expectations for learning and behaviour to students?

4. What would be the effect on student learning if the following were omitted from the teaching act?

    a. the introduction
    b. a check for understanding
    c. closure or summary

5. What are some things teachers can do to ensure that their explanation of content is clear?

6. Using your knowledge of students' cognitive and moral development, give some important techniques for motivating students at each of the following grade levels:

    a. primary/elementary
    b. junior/elementary
    c. intermediate/elementary

    d. grades 9 and 10
    e. grades 11 and 12

  7. If you were observing a teacher, what specific behaviours would you look for to indicate that the teacher was attempting to maximize student time on task during

    a. a lecture?
    b. a discussion?
    c. a seat-work activity?

  8. How might secondary teachers handle routine chores, such as taking attendance and receiving slips for excuses or early dismissals, to maximize the time allocated for learning? What might elementary teachers do to ensure that all subjects receive the appropriate amount of allocated time?

  9. Make a list of the topics taught in a given unit of instruction and identify those topics that can be considered generative topics to be taught at a deeper level of understanding.

10. Observe a class taught by a colleague or record on video a class that you teach and, using the five key elements for authentic instruction identified by Newmann and Wehlage, assess the class.

11. List three or four habits of mind that you hope to cultivate in your students, and briefly describe what you would do to help students develop them.

12. Take a lesson you have taught using an individual lesson structure and redesign it as a co-operative learning lesson with all three critical elements of co-operative learning. Include as many types of positive interdependence as possible in the lesson.

13. Choose an assignment that you or a colleague has used in the past to assess student learning of a concept or topic. Identify how many types of intelligence were tapped by this assessment. Now, redesign the assignment to include all seven types of intelligence.

14. Carefully review the two bodies of knowledge on teaching presented in the two major sections of this chapter ("The Basics of Effective Teaching" and "Beyond the Basics") and answer the following questions:

    a. In what ways are the two knowledge sets similar?
    b. In what ways are they different?
    c. Can the two approaches be used compatibly in the same classroom?

Weblinks

Pan-Canadian Protocol for Collaboration on School Curriculum
www.cmec.ca/protocol-eng.htm
An agreement set up by the Canadian Council of Ministers of Education that sets out issues of common interest for each of the Canadian provinces.

World Book
www.worldbook.com
The World Book site publishes encyclopedias and references for online use.

Canadian Teachers' Federation / Fédération canadienne des enseignantes et des enseignants
www.ctf-fce.ca
This site contains many good resources for educators. For curriculum documents, please refer to websites for each province or territory. For example (from west to east): British Columbia—www.gov.bc.ca/bced; Alberta—www.education.gov.ab.ca; Ontario—www.edu.gov.on.ca; Quebec—www.meq.gouv.qc.ca; and Newfoundland and Labrador—www.ed.gov.nl.ca/edu. For a complete listing, please see www.oise. utoronto.ca/canedweb/ministries.html.

6

Structuring the Environment

Focus on the Principles of Classroom Management

1. What are the environmental conditions that emphasize learning and minimize disruptive behaviour?
2. What are the teacher behaviours that encourage students to follow classroom guidelines?
3. What can a teacher do to help students learn that they are responsible for the consequences of their behaviour and thus are responsible for controlling their own behaviour?
4. What is the relationship between the culture of the students' home and community and the classroom guidelines?

Introduction

Psychologists have long believed that behaviour is controlled or influenced by the events and conditions—**antecedents**—that precede it as well as by the events, conditions, and consequences that follow it. Antecedents may increase the likelihood that appropriate behaviour will take place, or they may set the stage for the occurrence of misbehaviour. Therefore, when teachers act to prevent or modify inappropriate behaviour, they must examine antecedents carefully before resorting to the delivery of consequences. The start of the school year and the introduction of novel learning activities are two critical times when antecedent variables must be carefully considered. Unfortunately, sometimes teachers give only cursory attention to antecedent variables. While it is understandable that many teachers decide to spend time on designing learning activities, it must be stressed that learning activities are more successful when teachers have pre-planned seating arrangements, supplies, and rules and routines (Brophy, 1988a; Schwartz and Pollishuke, 2002).

As antecedent variables have an impact on student behaviour, teachers should take time to examine the two most crucial variables—the *physical environment* and *classroom guidelines*. Teachers must realize that classrooms are not culturally neutral; it is important to consider how well the culture of the classroom is congruent with the diverse needs of the students. In this chapter, teachers will discover multiple ideas for creating group expectations that are supportive of engagement in learning activities and achievement by students.

Whenever student behaviour is discussed, and because reactions to student (mis)behaviour can vary dramatically, the issue of students' rights and responsibilities

139

must be considered. Most schools and institutions now refer to the Canadian Charter of Rights and Freedoms along with the applicable provincial statutes, as each province designs a charter of students' rights and responsibilities. For example, in Ontario, Confederation College (2004) has a well-defined charter that outlines students' rights and responsibilities.

The Manitoba Human Rights Commission (2007) has prepared a charter entitled Human Rights in the School, which also refers directly to the Canadian Charter of Rights and Freedoms and the United Nations' Universal Declaration of Human Rights. Human Rights in the School details the argument that "human rights education is simply good education."

Although each charter has been individually developed, there are similarities in the content across the provinces because they all develop their approach from the Charter of Rights and Freedoms. The implications of all these documents for educators act as reminders that it is imperative to examine both attitudes and conduct that might threaten the dignity and rights of students. It is therefore necessary for teachers to make a conscious effort to be aware and monitor their own behaviour and reactions to student (mis)behaviour.

Designing the Physical Classroom Environment

Environmental Conditions

The importance of doing as much as possible to create environmental conditions conducive to learning cannot be stressed enough, as students must be physically comfortable before their attention is voluntarily given to learning.

Although there are clear limitations to the physical characteristics of our classroom environments, teachers should ensure that the physical environment of the classroom is the most appropriate one for learning. For instance, teachers can control lighting intensity. Dim lights, a flickering ceiling light, or inadequate darkening of the room for movies or other media presentations causes frustration, a growing lack of interest, and off-task behaviour among students. Given Canada's significant climate differences and because many schools are on predetermined heating schedules, there are usually some days in every season when rooms may be uncomfortably hot or cold. While a teacher may not be able to adjust the thermostat, he can open windows to let in fresh air, turn off unnecessary lights to cool the room, and remind students to bring sweaters.

Depending on the school's location, outside noise may be uncontrollable, but inside noise is manageable. When possible, teachers should insist that noisy repairs be completed either before or after in-school hours. They should also request specific times for public address announcements. Finally, school policy should enforce quiet hallway use by both teachers and students when classes are in session.

Use of Space

Although Canadian teachers have no control over the size of their classrooms and little control over student numbers, they usually can decide how best to utilize space within the classroom. Careful use of physical space makes a considerable difference in classroom behaviour (Andrews and Lupart, 2000; Evans and Lovell, 1979).

Seating Arrangements. A teacher's first concern should be the arrangement of seating. No matter what basic seating arrangement is used, it should be flexible enough to accommodate and facilitate the various learning activities that occur in the classroom. If a teacher's primary instructional strategy involves a lot of group work, the teacher may put three or four desks together to facilitate these activities. On the other hand, if a teacher emphasizes teacher-directed lectures and discussion followed by individual seat work, the traditional rows of desks separated by aisles may be the appropriate seating arrangement. It is quite acceptable, and often warranted, for the teacher to alter the primary seating arrangement to accommodate in-flux instructional activities.

An effective seating arrangement should allow the teacher to gain close proximity to all students, so that he can reach any student in the class without disturbing others. Such a set-up also enables all students to see instructional presentations. An effort should be made to avoid having students face distractions, such as windows or hallways. Finally, seating should not interfere with high-usage areas—those areas where there are pencil sharpeners, sinks, closets, or wastepaper cans. For relevant classroom-layout designs, please use your favourite internet search engine and type the following keywords: *classroom layout design*, *seating*, and *physical arrangements* (National Clearing House of Educational Facilities, 2006; Technology and Instruction, 2006).

Besides planning the location of seats and desks, which occupy most of the classroom space, the teacher must decide where learning centres, computers, storage cabinets, and large work tables are to be placed. Appropriate placement of these things helps the classroom reflect the excitement and variety of the learning that is occurring (Andrews and Lupart, 2000). Because many people find a cluttered area an uncomfortable environment in which to work and learn, classrooms should be neat and tidy. A messy classroom with items strewn about suggests to students that disorganization and sloppiness are acceptable, which may lead to behaviour problems.

Bulletin Boards and Display Areas. The bulletin boards in Mr. Jaffee's room in Case 6.1 on the next page serve two purposes: they publicly recognize students' efforts and provide an opportunity for students to enrich their mathematics learning through their own efforts and ideas. This is in striking contrast to bulletin boards that are packed away unchanged at the end of each school year (only to reappear again in September), or those that have only a few yellowed and outdated notices pinned to them.

The more bulletin boards are used to recognize students effectively, as Ms. White attempts to do in Case 6.2 on pages 142–144, or to provide students with opportunities to actively participate, the more likely they are to facilitate and enhance appropriate student behaviour. Bulletin boards and display areas may also be used to post local or school newspaper articles mentioning students' names and displaying their work. A part of a bulletin board or other wall space may be set aside for a list of classroom guidelines. Remember that decisions about the use of classroom space and decorations may be shared with students sometimes to create a more student-directed learning environment.

CASE 6.1 • *Fourteen to Ten, iPods Win*

Each of Mr. Jaffee's grade 9 math classes has a bulletin board committee, which is responsible for the design of one classroom bulletin board during the year. To be board-worthy, a piece need meet only one of two criteria: the topic has to be related to mathematics or its design must use some mathematical skill.

The period five bulletin board committee is ready to present three ideas to the class. Before the presentation, Mr. Jaffee reminds his students that they can vote for only one idea. Dana presents the first idea: "We would like to make a graph showing iPod sales in 2007." Tina presents the second idea: "I propose that we make bar graphs comparing the 2004 Olympic track and field results to the standing world records." Jamie presents the third idea: "It would be interesting to have a display showing the many careers there are in mathematics."

After the class asks the presenting students questions about each idea, Mr. Jaffee calls for a vote. The iPod sales graph receives 14 votes, the Olympics gets 10, and, not surprisingly, mathematics careers garners a mere 4. Although Mr. Jaffee is inwardly disappointed with the vote, he supports the outcome because he recognizes the importance of modelling the democratic process. So, he begins a dialogue with the class about the process of developing the bulletin board. As a first step, the committee immediately begins its research on iPod sales so that the bulletin board will be completed before parents' back-to-school night.

Questions to Consider

1. Do you think Mr. Jaffee should have tried to influence the vote? Discuss your reasons.
2. What are the risks of giving complete control for decision-making to students?

Concentric Case Study Kaleidoscope

CASE 6.2 • *Having Your Name Placed on the Board Isn't Always Bad*

The Story

One by one, the grade 7 students enter Ms. White's room and cluster around the bulletin board. They are jostling each other and looking at a list to attempt to locate their names. It is evident that students are interested and even anxious about the display. Today is the day after the test and the new Commendable Improvements list has gone up. The list notes those students who have made improvements from one test to another regardless of test grade. Names appear on it in alphabetical order and do not reflect a grade ranking.

Cathy hollers, "Great! I made it!" Rahul says, "Me, too, thank goodness!" Ardra mutters, "My name isn't there." Jimmy pushes and elbows his way to the front of the group and argues, "I think my name should be there, too. I can't understand it." He returns to his desk and slumps in his seat. The enthusiasm and, in a few cases, negative reaction with which students greet this bulletin surprises even Ms. White, and she now realizes that she must carefully consider her comments to the class about the test and the corresponding list.

The Students' Perspectives

Cathy: Cathy enters Ms. White's classroom and notices everyone clustering around the bulletin board. She becomes aware that the Commendable Improvements list is posted and feels her apprehension as well as her excitement rise. As she jostles for a spot near of the list, several thoughts are spinning in her head. "Uh oh, the results are up. I hope I made the list. I think I worked hard enough this term and studied for my tests carefully enough to be on the list. I'll feel really embarrassed in front of my friends if I didn't make it. After all, I decided not to go to a movie on Sunday night just before the big test. I hope my sacrifice was worth it."

Finally, Cathy manages to find her name and in relief she hollers, "Great—I made it!" She takes her seat in the classroom feeling validated, happy, and proud. She thinks, "I can't wait to tell my parents tonight."

Suddenly, Cathy hears Jimmy angrily say that his name is not on the list and that it should be. She also notices that her friend Ardra's name is missing. She looks around the room, noting that Jimmy is slumped in his seat looking very discouraged. "Oh, no," Cathy thinks, "Jimmy looks really unhappy. I feel sorry for him because he must feel stupid. Glancing at Ardra, she notes that eye contact with her friend is impossible because Ardra is busily focused on getting her books out. Cathy reflects, "Too bad everyone can't make the list—but I am glad that I did."

Ardra: Ardra feels apprehension when she enters the classroom and notes the excitement over at the bulletin board. She knows that the much-anticipated Commendable Improvements list is out. Ardra has been worrying about this all week because she feels fairly certain that she will not be on the list. She also feels fairly certain that her best friend Cathy will be on the list. Ardra wonders why learning poses such a challenge for her and yet seems to come so easily for Cathy. She wonders if she had made a bad choice going to the movies the night before the last big test. She also worries that her parents might be angry that she has not done better as Ardra had assured them she knew the material before heading out to the movies. Ardra sighs to herself and wishes that the list had not been posted today.

Jimmy: Jimmy comes to Ms. White's class feeling a mixture of anticipation and dread, although he covers these emotions with a nonchalant air. He knows that the list might be up and, while he believes that he will finally see his name on it, he still feels the usual apprehension. Jimmy knows that he worked hard during the term, partly in response to a contract he had with his parents about doing his homework and studying for tests. He is acutely aware that if he does not achieve at a higher level this term, his parents will suggest that he give up some of his after-school activities in order to take tutoring. He believes, however, that he showed substantial improvement on the recent test, although he is also aware that there were certain sections that gave him problems.

Along with the rest of the students, Jimmy pushes and elbows his way to the front of the group. Finally he gets a look at the list and quickly scans it for his name. Then he reads the list more slowly, feeling a sinking feeling as he realizes that his name is not there. Jimmy feels a surge of anger and blurts out, "I think my name should be there, too. I can't understand it." Now, he realizes that he has drawn attention to the fact that his name, yet again, is not on the list. In discouragement, he returns to his desk and slumps in his seat. When Ms. White moves to the front of the room and begins speaking to the class, Jimmy does not even look up.

Ms. White's Perspective

As Ms. White tacks the new Commendable Improvements list to her bulletin board, she reflects with pride on her students' improvements. "What a good idea the Commendable Improvements list is. It gives everyone a chance to achieve but at his or her own level, by focusing on the improvement rather than on the actual mark. Also, my students seem to really value getting their names on the list."

As the students enter, Ms. White watches with amusement as they jostle each other to see if their names are posted. She notices the enthusiasm among her successful students and thinks about how she can channel their energy into today's class. Suddenly, Jimmy's angry comment about being left off the list shifts Ms. White's focus to his behaviour specifically. She feels disconcerted while observing his negative and frustrated body language as he slumps in his desk. Ms. White then notices that some of the other students appear deflated as well. As all the students take their seats and wait for her to begin the class, Ms. White realizes that she must be very careful about what she says to the class about the results of the test and the posting of the new Commendable Improvements list. For a long moment, Ms. White stands silently in front of her students as she now focuses her thoughts on those who are experiencing a feeling of lack of success.

Questions to Consider

1. What do you think Ms. White should say at this point to the whole class?

2. What do you think she should say to Jimmy, Ardra, and the others who are not on the Commendable Improvements list?

3. How does such a list affect the class positively? Negatively?

4. Is there a better way to handle this list?

5. How can Ms. White help Jimmy and Ardra now?

6. What kind of correspondence should Ms. White send home to the parents or guardians?

Establishing Classroom Guidelines

There is at least one antecedent variable over which the teacher has much control: the development of classroom guidelines, which are necessary for the efficient and effective running of a classroom. The classroom experience is a complex interaction of students, teachers, and materials. Guidelines help to increase the likelihood that these interactions are orderly and the environment is conducive to learning. Properly designed guidelines should support teaching and learning and provide students with clear expectations and well-defined standards, which in turn will give them the feeling of safety, security, and direction. A safe, secure environment often provides students with the motivation and rationale to countermand those peer pressures that oppose behaviours conducive to learning (Jones and Jones, 2003).

Classroom Routines

There are two types of classroom guidelines: routines and rules. Routines are repetitive daily procedures that call for specified behaviours at particular times or during particular activities. They are not meant for managing disruptive behaviour. Examples of routines include methods of handing out and turning in materials, entering and leaving the classroom, and taking attendance. Routines comprise behaviours that are necessary for the smooth operation of the classroom.

Routines are taught to students through examples and demonstrations. Properly designed and learned, routines maximize on-task student behaviour by minimizing the need for students to ask for directions and the need for teachers to give instructions for everyday classroom events. Certain important routines—for example, steps to be followed during fire drills and required heading information that students need to fill in for tests and assignments—may be prominently displayed for all to reference.

Because students often do not learn and use a teacher's routines immediately, feedback and practice must be provided at the beginning of the term. However, the time spent on teaching the routines is well invested and eventually leads to a successful management system (Brophy, 1988b; Elementary Teachers' Federation of Ontario, 2000). Often in art, science, shop, and physical education classes (which require distinct routines), teachers may have students practise the required routines initially until they become habitual. In these situations, it is important that the routines become a consistent and integral part of the classroom/gymnasium dynamic.

Classroom routines have to be taught to students.

The use of natural and **logical consequences** is appropriate for students who fail to follow classroom routines. **Natural consequences** are outcomes of behaviour that occur without teacher intervention. Examples of natural consequences are the inability of a teacher to record a student's grade if an assignment is handed in with no name or if an assignment is not handed in at all.

The use of logical consequences is much more common and has wider applicability in school settings than the use of natural ones. Logical consequences are outcomes that are directly related to behaviour but require teacher intervention to occur. Examples of logical consequences are students having less time for recess because they did not line up correctly to leave the room and students having to pay for the damage to their textbooks because of careless use.

Natural and logical consequences are powerful management concepts because the consequences that students experience are directly related to their behaviour. In addition, because it is only the student who is responsible for the consequences, the teacher is removed from the role of punisher.

Classroom Rules

In contrast to routines, rules focus on appropriate behaviour. They provide the guidelines for those behaviours that are required if teaching and learning are to take place in the classroom. Because they cover a wider spectrum of behaviour than routines, the development of rules is usually a more complex and time-consuming task.

The Need for Rules. Schools in general, and classrooms in particular, are dynamic places. Within almost any given classroom, learning activities vary widely and may range from individual seat work to large group projects that necessitate co-operative working arrangements among students. While this dynamism helps to motivate student learning, human behaviour is highly sensitive to differing conditions across situations as well as to changing conditions within situations (Walker, 1979). Evidence indicates that children in general, and disruptive children in particular, are highly sensitive to changing situations and conditions (Andrews and Lupart, 2000; Johnson, Boadstad, and Lobitz, 1976; Kazdin and Bootzin, 1972). Given this, the need for rules is apparent.

Rules should be directed at organizing the learning environment to ensure the continuity and quality of teaching and learning and not at exerting control over students (Brophy, 1988a). Appropriate rules increase on-task student behaviour, which results in improved learning.

Determining Necessary Rules. A long list of dos and don'ts is one sure way to reduce the likelihood that rules will be effective. Teachers who attempt to cover every conceivable classroom behaviour with a rule place themselves in the untenable position of having to observe and monitor the most minute and insignificant student behaviours. This can interfere with teaching time. Students, especially in upper elementary and secondary grades, view a long list of dos and don'ts as picky and impossible to follow.

They regard teachers who monitor and correct every behaviour as nagging, unreasonable, and controlling.

Teachers must develop on their own or with students a list of rules that is fair, realistic, and can be rationalized as necessary for the development of an appropriate classroom environment (Emmer et al., 2003; Schwartz and Pollishuke, 2002). To accomplish this goal, before meeting a class for the first time, the teacher must seriously consider the question, "What are the necessary student behaviours that I need in my classroom so that behaviour problems will not occur?" To assist in answering this question, teachers must keep in mind that the definition of a behavioural problem is *any behaviour that interferes with the teaching act, interferes with the rights of others to learn, is psychologically or physically unsafe, or destroys property*. Thus, any rule that is developed by the teacher or jointly by the students and the teacher must be vetted as necessary to ensure that (1) the teacher's right to teach is protected, (2) the student's right to learn is protected, (3) the student's psychological and physical safety is protected, and (4) school property is protected (see the section in Chapter 2 entitled, "Defining a Behavioural Problem"). Rules that are so developed and rationalized make sense to students because they are not arbitrary. Such rules also lend themselves to the use of natural and logical consequences when students do not follow them.

Developing Consequences. When students choose not to follow classroom rules, they should experience consequences (Andrews and Lupart, 2000; Canter, 1989; Schwartz and Pollishuke, 2002). The types of consequences and how they are applied may determine whether or not students follow rules and whether or not they respect the teacher. Therefore, the development of appropriate consequences is as important as the development of the rules themselves.

Unfortunately, teachers usually give considerably more thought to the design of rules than they do to consequences. When a rule is not followed, teachers often simply determine the consequence on the spot. Such an approach may lead to inconsistent, irrational consequences that are interpreted by students as unfair, unreasonable, and unrelated to their behaviour. This view of the teacher's behaviour eventually undermines his effectiveness as a classroom manager and leads to more disruptive student behaviour.

Although the teacher should plan consequences in advance, there is some debate about whether or not students should know in advance what the consequences will be. Some teachers feel that sharing potential consequences helps students to live up to teacher expectations and avoids later complaints about the fairness of the consequences. Other teachers believe that announcing consequences in advance gives students the impression that the teacher expects students not to live up to expectations. They prefer to act as if they have no need to think about consequences since they know that all the students will be successful in meeting both behavioural and academic expectations. There is no empirical answer to this debate. It is a matter of teacher beliefs and preferences.

As we have already noted in the discussion of routines, there are two types of consequences: natural and logical. Natural consequences, which occur without anyone's intervention and are the result of a behaviour, are powerful modifiers of the way students act. After all, have you ever

- had an accident because you drove through a red light or a stop sign?
- injured your foot while walking barefoot?
- locked yourself out of your house because you forgot your key?
- lost or broken something because of carelessness?
- missed a bus or train because of lateness?

These events usually lead to a change in behaviour, and they all have certain characteristics. Each is an undesirable consequence, is experienced by all persons equally (regardless of who they are), and comes about without the intervention of anyone else. Dreikurs (1964; Dreikurs et al., 2004) has emphasized that children are provided with an honest and real learning situation when they are allowed to experience the natural consequences of their behaviour.

Although students are more likely to experience natural consequences at home or in general society than at school, allowing them to experience the natural consequences of their behaviour in classroom situations is a very effective learning technique. It clearly communicates a cause-and-effect relationship between a student's chosen behaviour and the experienced consequence, and it removes the teacher from negative involvement with the students. Some examples of natural consequences in schools are

- obtaining a low test grade because of failure to study.
- losing assignments or books because of carelessness.
- ruining a shop project as a result of the inappropriate use of tools.
- losing a ball on a roof or over a school fence because of playing with it inappropriately.

Of course, inherent ethical, moral, and legal restraints prohibit a teacher from allowing some natural consequences to happen. For instance, the natural consequences of failing to follow safety precautions in science laboratories, physical education classes, or industrial arts classes can be serious.

When natural consequences are not appropriate or do not closely follow a given behaviour, the teacher needs to intervene and apply a logical consequence. Have you ever

- been subjected to a finance charge because you were late paying a bill?
- delayed installing the snow tires and skidded into another car during the first snowfall?
- had a cheque returned for insufficient funds because you didn't balance your chequebook?

These are logical consequences because they are directly and rationally related to the behaviour. In school, the teacher ideally administers logical consequences in a calm, matter-of-fact manner. If logical consequences are imposed in anger, they cease to be consequences and tend to become punishments. Children are likely to respond favourably or positively to logical consequences because they do not consider such consequences mean or unfair, whereas they often argue, fight back, or retaliate when punished (Dreikurs, 1964; Dreikurs et al., 2004). Logical consequences may be applied in two different ways. In the first way, the teacher prescribes the logical consequence without giving the student a choice:

"Joe, you spilled the paint; please clean it up."

"Darjeet, you continue to call out. When you raise your hand, you will be called on."

"Antonia, you wrote on your desk. You will have to clean it up during recess."

In the second way, the teacher offers the student a choice of changing his behaviour or experiencing the logical consequence. The use of this technique places the responsibility for appropriate behaviour where it belongs: on the student. If the student chooses to continue the disruptive behaviour, the logical consequence is forthcoming. If the student chooses to cease the disruptive behaviour, there is no negative consequence:

"Phong, you have a choice to walk down the hall without pushing or to hold my hand."

"Heidi, you have a choice to stop disturbing Jeff or to change your seat."

"Mike, you have a choice to raise your hand or not to be chosen to answer."

Notice that in all instances the phrasing clearly identifies the student being addressed and the desired behaviour as well as the logical consequence if the behaviour does not change. Using the words "*you* have a choice" communicates to the student that the teacher is in a neutral position and thus serves to remove the teacher from arguments and power struggles with the student. This is crucial, especially in highly explosive situations. Natural or logical consequences often are not readily apparent to an extremely angry and upset student who has spewed vulgarities at his teacher during class. If, in response to this behaviour, the teacher says, "Your behaviour is unacceptable. If this occurs again, your parents will be contacted immediately," the student is made aware of exactly what will happen if he chooses to continue his behaviour. Furthermore, the teacher remains neutral in the eyes of not only the student but also the rest of the class.

A third form of consequence is *contrived consequence*, more commonly known as punishment. The strict definition of punishment is any adverse consequence of a targeted behaviour that suppresses the behaviour. However in day-to-day school practice, punishment takes on three forms: removal of privileges, which may be applied by the teacher; suspension, which is a decision made by the principal; and expulsion, which is a decision made by the board of education. In days gone by, punishment included painful physical experiences such as giving the strap to students. However, such physical punishments have become increasingly rare since Section 43 of the Criminal Code of Canada was passed by the federal government. Section 43 provides a defence to assault only if the force used is considered "reasonable under the circumstances." It is worded in the following way:

Correction of a Child by Force

Every schoolteacher, parent or person standing in the place of a parent is justified in using force by way of correction toward a pupil or child, as the case may be, who is under his care, if the force does not exceed what is reasonable under the circumstances.

(R.S.C., 1985, c.C-4)

Therefore, currently in Canada, punishment that causes physical pain is not supported by many professional and parental groups including the Canadian Teachers' Federation (O'Brien and Pietersma, 2000). According to an editorial in a national newspaper,

> Legal precedents have interpreted the meaning of reasonable force in Section 43. In actual child abuse trials, courts have decided it is generally impermissible to strike a child under age two, or one older than 12. Blows to the head, even slaps, are typically not allowed. Striking with a closed fist usually constitutes abuse, and using "objects" such as belts, rulers and canes is to be discouraged. Alternatives to spanking, such as "withdrawal of privileges" are to be attempted first. And no form of corporal punishment should be "administered in anger." What is permitted are mild to moderate "smacks" using an open hand to the buttocks or "extremities"—usually a child's hands.
>
> (*National Post*, 2003)

In the past several years, there have been varied reactions to Section 43. Many groups (e.g., World Corporal Punishment Research: www.corpun.com; the Repeal 43 Committee, www.repeal43.org/schools.html; the Canadian Teachers' Federation, www.ctf-fce.ca/archive/docs/en/PRESS/2004/pr04-02.htm) have expressed either concern over or support for Section 43 and have engaged in legal actions to repeal or maintain this component of the Criminal Code. In 1996, Canada received negative feedback from the United Nations Committee on the Rights of the Child based on Section 43. The UN committee argued that Section 43 is contrary to Articles 19, 28, and 37 of the Convention on the Rights of the Child. These three articles are written in a way that is meant to protect children from all forms of violence, punishment, abuse, or cruelty from any person who cares for the child. These articles also require the state to guard the child's human dignity. Even though the Canadian Teachers' Federation disagrees with the use of corporal punishment in public schools, it supports the retention of Section 43 in the Criminal Code. One example that this organization uses for retaining Section 43 is that if teachers are called on to use force to break up a fight between students, assault charges are possible, and without Section 43 teachers would have no legal defence. On balance, it seems that since force is such a contentious issue, teachers should select alternative actions.

If appropriately planned by the teacher, and it is clearly linked to student misbehaviour, the removal of privileges becomes a logical consequence. For example, it is a logical consequence to take away a student's recess time because he has to complete classwork that he missed while he was daydreaming. However, if the teacher cancels a student's participation in next week's trip to the zoo, that is a punishment and not a logical consequence because it is not directly linked to helping the student complete his work.

As we've discussed, punishment should not be physically painful. Psychological punishment, such as yelling, sarcasm, or threats, is also questionable professionally. Other types of punishment often take the form of added assignments (extra homework or writing lines a set number of times). Such punishments are often poorly designed, pedagogically unsound, and are meant only to hurt and get even. The use of painful punishment has been and remains a highly controversial issue on the grounds of morality, ethics, law, and proven ineffectiveness (Jones and Jones, 2003; Hyman and Snook 1999; Kohn, 1999).

Research has indicated consistently that painful punishment suppresses undesirable behaviour for short periods of time without effecting lasting behavioural change (Clarizio, 1980; Curwin and Mendler, 1999). Because avoidance or escape behaviour is often a side effect of painful experiences, frequent punishment may only teach a child how to be "better at misbehaving." In other words, the child will likely continue to misbehave and find ways to avoid detection and, thus, punishment. Because it seldom is logically related to the behaviour and does not point to alternative acceptable behaviour, punishment deprives the student of the opportunity to learn acceptable behaviour. In addition, punishment reinforces a low level of moral development because it models undesirable behaviours. Students come to believe that it is appropriate to act in punishing ways toward others when one is in a position of authority (Clarizio, 1980; Curwin and Mendler, 1999; Jones and Jones, 2003).

As punishment focuses the child's concerns on the immediate effect rather than on the misbehaviour itself, it does not prompt the child to examine the motivation behind the behaviour and the consequences of the behaviour for himself and others, which is important for him to do as he learns to control his disruptive behaviour (Jones and Jones, 2003). Punishment also limits the teacher's ability to help the child in this examination process because the child frequently does not associate the punishment with his or her actions but with the punisher. This often leads to rage, resentment, hostility, and an urge to get even (Dreikurs, Grundwald, and Pepper, 1998; Jones and Jones, 2003).

As we mentioned earlier, there has been an ever-increasing opposition to the use of physical or corporal punishment in schools. Epstein (1979) has stated, "There is no pedagogical justification for inflicting pain. . . . It does not merit any serious discussion of pros and cons" (229–230). Similarly, Canter (1989) has stated, "Consequences should never be psychologically or physically harmful to the students . . . corporal punishment should never be administered" (58). Clarizio (1980) has stated, "There is very little in the way of evidence to suggest the benefit of physical punishment in the schools but there is a substantial body of research to suggest that this method can have undesirable long-term side effects" (141). Both Clarizio (1980) and Epstein (1979) have noted that some of the side effects of physical punishment are a dislike and distrust of the teacher and school; a feeling of powerlessness, with negative effects on a child's motivation to learn; and the development of escape and avoidance behaviours that may take the form of lying, skipping class, or daydreaming.

Those who advocate the use of physical punishment usually cite one of two myths (Smith, Gollop, Taylor and Marshall, 2003; Clarizio, 1980). The first myth advocates punishment as a tried-and-true method that aids students in developing a sense of personal responsibility, self-discipline, and moral character. In reality, however, studies have consistently shown that physical punishment correlates with delinquency and a low development of conscience. The second myth is that it is the only form of discipline some children understand. This has never been shown to be true. Perhaps it is a case of projection on the part of the teacher. In the past, teachers who relied heavily on physical punishment appeared not to know other means of solving classroom-management problems. Teachers must understand that if a technique has not worked in the past, more of the same technique will not produce desirable results.

For teachers who occasionally use mild forms of punishment (not physical), guidelines for minimizing possible harmful side effects are discussed by Clarizio (1980) and Heitzman (1983). Table 6.1 compares natural and logical consequences with punishment.

TABLE 6.1 *Comparison of Consequences versus Punishment*

Natural/Logical Consequence	Punishment
Expresses the reality of a situation	Expresses the power of authority
Logically related to misbehaviour	Contrived and arbitrary connection with misbehaviour
Illustrates cause and effect	Does not illustrate cause and effect
Involves no moral judgment about person— you are okay; your behaviour isn't	Often involves moral judgments
Concerned with the present	Concerned with the past
Administered without anger	Anger is often present
Helps develop self-discipline	Depends on extrinsic control
Choices often given	Alternatives are not given
Thoughtful, deliberate	Often impulsive
Does not develop escape and avoidance behaviours	Develops escape and avoidance behaviours
Does not produce resentment	Produces resentment
Teacher is removed from negative involvement with student	Teacher involvement is negative
Based on the concept of equality	Based on superior–inferior relationship
Communicates the expectation that the student is capable of controlling his own behaviour	Communicates that the teacher must control the student's behaviour

Source: Dreikurs, Grundwald, and Pepper, 1998; Sweeney, 1981.

Communicating Rules. If the teacher decides to develop classroom rules by himself, he must communicate them clearly to the students (Canter, 1989; Evertson and Emmer, 1982; Jones and Jones, 2003; Schwartz and Pollishuke, 2002). Clear communication entails a discussion of what the rules are and a rationale for each and every one of them (Good and Brophy, 1987; Martin and Sugarman, 1993).

When students understand the purpose of rules, they are likely to view them as reasonable and fair, which increases the likelihood of appropriate behaviour (Schwartz and Pollishuke, 2002).

The manner in which rules are worded is important. Certain rules need to be stated so it is clear that they apply to both the teacher and the students. This is accomplished by using the phrase, "We all need to" followed by the behavioural expectation and the rationale. For example, the teacher might say, "We all need to pay attention and not interrupt when someone is speaking because it is important to respect each other's right to participate and voice our views." Such phrasing incorporates the principle that teachers must model the behaviours they expect (Brophy, 1988a; Martin and Sugarman, 1993).

Although it is essential for the teacher to communicate behavioural expectations and the rationales behind them, in many cases, this does not ensure student understanding and acceptance of the rules. A final critical strategy, then, is to obtain from each student a strong indication that he understands the rules as well as a commitment to attempt to abide by them (Jones and Jones, 2003).

Obtaining Commitments. When two or more people reach an agreement, they often finalize it with a handshake or a signed contract to indicate that the individuals intend to comply with the terms of the agreement. While agreements are often violated, a handshake, verbal promise, or written contract increases the probability that the agreement will be kept. With this idea in mind, it is a wise teacher who has his students express their understanding of the rules and their intent to abide by them. In Case 6.3, the teacher uses an interactive approach to develop rules for the classroom.

CASE 6.3 • *"I'm Not Sure If I'll Always Remember"*

At the beginning of the school year, Mr. Merit presents a list of six class rules to his grade 5 students. He explains each rule and gives examples. Mr. Merit then asks if the students have any suggestions for changes to the list—he indicates they could be additions or deletions. After consideration, it is evident that the students are satisfied with the list. He then has a more detailed discussion of the class rules with his students. Members of the class are asked to give the reason for each rule. The class as a whole is encouraged to ask questions about the rules, and Mr. Merit in turn asks questions to assess their understanding of the rules.

After the discussion, Mr. Merit says, "All those who understand our rules please raise your hand." Next, he says, "All those who will attempt to follow our rules please raise your hands." He notices that Helen and Gary do not raise their hands and asks them why. Helen says, "I'm not sure if I'll always remember the rules and if I can't remember I can't promise to follow the rules." Mr. Merit replies, "Helen, I understand your concern, but I have written our rules on a poster, which I am going to place on the front bulletin board. Do you think that this will help you?" Helen answers yes and both she and Gary then raise their hands.

Mr. Merit shows the class the poster of rules, which is entitled, "I Will Try to Follow Our Classroom Rules." One by one, each student comes up and signs his or her name at the bottom of the poster. When all the students have signed it, Mr. Merit asks Helen to staple the poster to the front bulletin board.

Questions to Consider

1. What message does Mr. Merit's approach send to his students?
2. Do you think that signing the rules sheet was important? Give reasons.
3. What rules would you develop for your own class?

Both Mr. Merit and Ms. Lu in Cases 6.3 and 6.4 are attempting to get their students to understand and agree to follow the classroom rules. However, notice that they use different methods because the maturity level of their students is different. Unlike Mr. Merit, Ms. Lu only asks her students to confirm that they understand the rules, not that they will abide by them. This is an important distinction that should be made when working with older students because it reduces the potential of a student confrontation during a time when the development of teacher–student rapport is critical.

CASE 6.4 • *"I'm Not Promising Anything"*

On the first day of class, Ms. Lu explains the classroom rules to her grade 10 mathematics classes. She discusses with each class why these rules are necessary for the teaching and learning of mathematics.

Ms. Lu then says to the class, "I am going to pass out two copies of the rules that we just discussed. You'll notice that at the bottom is the statement,—I am aware of these rules and understand them' followed by a place for your signature. Please sign one copy and pass it up front so I can collect them. Place the other copy in your notebook."

In Ms. Lu's second-period class, Alex raises his hand and says, "I can't make any promises about my future behaviour in this class. I'm not sure what the class is even going to be like." Ms. Lu replies, "Although I can understand your concern, please read what you are

signing." Alex reads, "I am
aware of these rules and understand them" and says out loud, "Oh, I see. I'm not promising anything." Alex then signs the sheet and passes it to the front of the room.

Questions to Consider

1. Compare Ms. Lu's and Mr. Merit's respective approaches and consider the appropriateness of each to its grade level.
2. To what extent do you think that students should participate in establishing classroom rules?
3. How would Ms. Lu's process change if she had required students to sign a promise?
4. Should Ms. Lu follow up with Alex's comment at any time during the term? If so, what should be the nature of the follow-up be?

In Case 6.5, Mr. Martinez models consistency as he works with students to reinforce the classroom rules. Mr. Martinez understands that students often need help learning rules and he indicates he is willing to remind and prompt without showing frustration.

While many experts recommend having classroom rules on display or available for quick reference (Evertson and Emmer, 1982; Jones and Jones, 2003), it should be noted that merely displaying them has little effect on maintaining appropriate student behaviour (Madsen, Becker, and Thomas, 1968). Teachers must refer to and use the displayed rules to assist individual students in learning the rules and developing self-control. Mr. Martinez in Case 6.5 not only displays and teaches the rule to Lowyn but also reinforces the behaviour when she finally does raise her hand. He understands that noting appropriate behaviour and positively encouraging it enhances the likelihood of appropriate behaviour in the future (Clarizio, 1980; Evertson and Emmer, 1982; Madsen, Becker, and Thomas, 1968; Ritchie et al., 1999).

CASE 6.5 • *Calling Out Correct Answers*

Mr. Martinez, a grade 4 teacher, posts his classroom rules on the front bulletin board. One by one, each student signs the poster, thus agreeing to follow the rules.

Mr. Martinez soon notices that Lowyn is having a difficult time remembering to raise her hand before answering questions. Instead, Lowyn just calls out the answers. At first Mr. Martinez ignores her answer. The next time she calls out, he makes eye contact with her and shakes his head in a disapproving fashion. Finally, he moves close to Lowyn and quietly says, "Lowyn, you have great answers, but you must raise your hand so that everyone has an equal chance to answer."

The next lesson begins, and Mr. Martinez asks the class, "Who can summarize what we learned about magnets yesterday?" Enthusiastically, Lowyn calls out, "Every magnet has a north and south pole."

Because Mr. Martinez has half expected that Lowyn will continue to call out answers, he is prepared for the situation and says, "Class, please, put down your hands. Lowyn, please look at the rules on the bulletin board and find the one that you are not obeying." Lowyn answers, "Number four. It says we need to raise our hands to answer a question." Mr. Martinez responds, "Yes it does, and why do we need such a rule?" "So that everyone in the class has a chance to answer questions," she replies. Mr. Martinez then asks, "Lowyn, did you agree to follow these rules when you signed the poster?" "Yes," Lowyn says.

Mr. Martinez asks her to try harder in the future and tells her that he will help her by pointing to the rules if she calls out again. The first time Lowyn raises her hand Mr. Martinez calls on her, and afterwards says, "Lowyn, that was a great answer and thank you for raising your hand."

Questions to Consider

1. How do rules simplify teacher expectations for behaviour?
2. How would this scenario have changed if the rules had not been clearly established?

Teachers also may employ student self-analyses to remind them of appropriate behaviour and to help enhance their self-control. Indeed, self-analysis of one's behaviour can be used by any student, although the actual manner of employment of the technique varies. Whereas Mr. Boudreau's smiley faces in Case 6.6 are appropriate for younger elementary students (see Figure 6.1), older students evaluate their behaviour better by using rating continua. As with younger students, self-analysis is requested of all students or individual students as the need arises. Figure 6.2 on page 158 is an example of a continuum rating scale that was successfully used to manage a grade 7 art class. Similar scales can be developed for self-analysis for group analysis after collaborative learning activities.

Teaching and Evaluating. Teachers do not expect students to learn a mathematical skill on its first presentation because they know students need practice and feedback. Frequently, however, teachers forget this when it comes to rules. They expect students to follow classroom rules immediately (Evertson and Emmer, 1982). But rules, like academic skills, must be taught (Brophy, 1988a; Canter, 1992; Evertson and Emmer, 1982; Jones and Jones, 2003). This entails practice and feedback. The amount of practice and feedback depends on the grade level and the novelty of the routines and rules.

New activities often require new routines and rules. It is customary for teachers to spend up to an entire lesson on how to conduct a debate, co-operatively work on a

CASE 6.6 • *The Smiley Face Self-Analysis*

Mr. Boudreau teaches grade 1. After analyzing the types of behaviours he feels are necessary for the proper running of his class, he shares the rules with the children and explains what he calls the Smiley Face Procedure. "We all know what smiley faces are, and we are going to use smiley faces to help us learn and obey the classroom rules." Holding up a sheet of paper (see Figure 6.1), he continues, "As you can see, this sheet has faces next to each rule for every day of the week. At the end of class each day, you will receive one of these sheets and you will circle the faces that are most like your behaviour for the day."

Each day, Mr. Boudreau collects the sheets and reviews them. When a pattern of frowns is observed or when he disagrees with a student's rating, he is quick to work with the student in a positive, supportive manner.

After a few weeks, Mr. Boudreau discontinues the self-analysis sheets on a regular basis. They are, however, brought back into use whenever the class's behaviour warrants it. Mr. Boudreau also uses the sheets for individual students who need assistance in self-control. When outdoor or new activities such as field trips occur throughout the year, Mr. Boudreau develops new sheets for the students using the same smiley-face format.

Questions to Consider

1. Identify the positive and negative aspects of the smiley-face system.
2. Are there any benefits to the students if they use this procedure?
3. How would you modify Figure 6.1?

FIGURE 6.1 *Smiley Face Self-Analysis*

CIRCLE THE APPLE THAT IS MOST LIKE YOUR BEHAVIOUR TODAY

	MONDAY	TUESDAY	WEDNESDAY	THURSDAY	FRIDAY
Shared with Others					
Listened to the Teacher					
Listened While Others Talked					
Was Friendly to Others					
Worked Quietly					
Joined in Activities					
Stayed in My Seat					
Followed Directions					
Cleaned My Area					
Helped Put Away Materials					

FIGURE 6.2 *Behaviour Self-Analysis for Art Class*

Name _____ Date _____

Class _____

Teacher–Student Evaluation

Class Behaviour

1. Have you worked successfully with minimum supervision during the class period?

0% of the time		50% of the time		All the time
1	2	3	4	5

2. Have you been respectful and considerate to other students and their property?

0% of the time		50% of the time		All the time
1	2	3	4	5

3. Have you been co-operative with your teacher?

0% of the time		50% of the time		All the time
1	2	3	4	5

4. Have you used art materials properly?

0% of the time		50% of the time		All the time
1	2	3	4	5

5. Have you shown a high degree of maturity and responsibility through proper class behaviour?

0% of the time		50% of the time		All the time
1	2	3	4	5

6. Have you been considerate of your classmates and teacher by talking softly, remaining in your seat, and helping classmates if help is needed?

0% of the time		50% of the time		All the time
1	2	3	4	5

7. Have you cleaned your area and put your materials away?

0% of the time		50% of the time		All the time
1	2	3	4	5

group project, safely operate machinery, set up and care for science apparatus, or behave on field trips or outdoor activities. In such cases, specific objectives directed toward the routines and rules are formulated and incorporated into the lesson plans. In these situations, they become an integral part of the course content, and, therefore, their evaluation and consideration in grading decisions are warranted.

Some teachers, particularly those in the elementary grades, evaluate their students' understanding of rules through the use of written exams or student demonstrations (Curwin and Mendler, 1999). Secondary science and industrial arts teachers often insist that students pass safety exams and demonstrate the appropriate use of equipment before being given permission to progress with the learning activities.

To summarize, teachers must communicate to students the importance of the rules for learning and teaching (Ritchie et al., 1999). This is best accomplished through a no-nonsense approach that involves

1. Analyzing the classroom environment to determine the necessary rules and routines needed to protect teaching, learning, safety, and property.
2. Clearly communicating the rules and their rationales to students.
3. Obtaining students' commitments to abide by the rules.
4. Teaching and evaluating students' understanding of the rules.
5. Enforcing each rule consistently with natural or logical consequences.

The Cultural Embeddedness of Rules and Routines

When teachers are establishing and teaching classroom rules and routines, they need to remember that their students come from a variety of cultural backgrounds. *Culture* refers to the knowledge, customs, rituals, emotions, traditions, values, and standards shared by members of a population and embodied in a set of behaviours designed for survival in a particular environment. Because Canadian students come to the classroom from many different cultural backgrounds, they bring with them different values, standards, and behavioural expectations. Some teachers have acted as if everyone shared the same cultural expectations and have ignored cultural differences. However, this does not appear to be a wise strategy. Schools and classrooms are not culturally neutral or culture-free. Some schools still follow the values, standards, and behavioural patterns of middle-class, white, European cultures. As Blades, Johnston and Simmt (2000) have pointed out, however, these values and standards differ in significant ways from the values, standards, and behavioural expectations found in non-dominant cultural groups. This is a particularly prominent issue in Canadian schools, as the Canadian population, particularly in large urban centres, has become increasingly diverse.

Middle-class Canadian culture, which historically tends to hark back to its European roots, continues to be the typical school culture. As a result of differences in values and standards, some behaviour patterns displayed by children who come from a non-dominant culture, while acceptable at home and in the community, often are not as acceptable in schools. Indeed, cultural differences occur in many areas, including language patterns, non-verbal behaviour, amount and freedom of movement, use of personal space, expression of emotions, and dress.

As a result of these cultural differences, many children from under-represented groups experience cultural dissonance or lack of cultural synchronization in school; that is, some teachers and students may be out of step with each other when it comes to their expectations for appropriate behaviour. Cultural synchronization is an extremely important factor in the establishment of positive relationships between teachers and students. According to Jeanette Abi-Nader (1993), one of the most solidly substantiated principles in communication theory is the principle of *homophily*, which holds that the more two people are alike in background, attitudes, perceptions, and values, the more effectively they will communicate with each other and the more similar they will become. A lack of cultural synchronization leads to misunderstandings between teachers and students that can, and often do, result in conflict, distrust, hostility, and possibly school failure (Irvine, 1990).

To illustrate their discussion of the importance of cultural synchronization, Blades, Johnston, and Simmt (2000) have pointed out some of the ways that teachers are modifying courses in an attempt to remove cultural bias. For example, foods and textiles teachers examined food and clothing from many cultures. Those who taught issues related to health and health care discussed various strategies that different cultural groups use to heal or maintain health. Some teachers select multicultural novels for class members to read and direct the discussions to help students develop tolerance and an understanding of the universality of the human condition.

Part of the terrible fallout from the September 11, 2001, attacks in the United States is the rise in North America of Islamophobia. Overgeneralization and paranoia have led to public discourse and anti-terrorist policies that disproportionately and unfairly target Canadians of Arab descent and other Muslims as visible threats to public safety. In response, the Muslim community in Canada is currently undertaking new initiatives to educate the public about Islam through the Muslim Educational Network Training and Outreach Service (MENTORS). This group has developed resource kits for schools (Zine, 2003).

Differences in values, standards, and expectations resulting from cultural differences have several implications for teachers. First, teachers must understand that schools are culturally situated institutions. The values, standards, and behaviours promoted by schools are never culturally neutral. They are always influenced by some particular cultural mindset. Therefore, school and classroom rules and guidelines must be seen as culturally derived. Second, teachers should strive to learn more about the cultural backgrounds of the students they teach. This can be accomplished by observing how students believe in other contexts, by talking to students about their behaviour and allowing them to teach about it, involving parents and community members in the classroom, and participating in community events and learning more about the institutions in the students' home community. "Students are less likely to fail in school settings where they feel positive about both their own culture and the majority culture and are not alienated from their own cultural values" (Cummins, 1986). Third, teachers should acknowledge and intentionally incorporate students' cultural backgrounds and expectations into their classrooms. When teacher rules and expectations are in conflict with student cultural expectations, it may be appropriate to re-examine and renegotiate rules and routines. In a variety of studies in different settings and contexts—and with students from different cultural groups—the findings are remarkably similar. When teachers incorporate language and participation patterns from the home and community into the classroom, relationships and academic learning improve significantly (Banks, 1995). At the very least, students need to be provided with a clear rationale for why the rules and routines are important. It goes without saying that the rationale for the rules should be in keeping with the four guidelines that we articulated earlier in this chapter. Finally, when a student behaves inappropriately, the teacher should step back and examine the misbehaviour in terms of the student's cultural background. Using a different set of cultural lenses to view behaviour may shed a very different light on the teacher's perceptions of individual students. Obviously, misbehaviour that results from differences in cultural background and expectations should be handled quite differently from misbehaviour that signifies intentional disruption on the part of the student.

Creating Group Standards to Structure Appropriate Behaviour

Although students and teachers bring their own cultural backgrounds with them to school, each classroom tends to develop a culture unique to itself. That is, certain standards develop over time that exert a great influence on student behaviour. During the early years of schooling, it is the teacher's wishes and behaviour that create the standards for student behaviour. However, as students grow older, they become the dominant influence in establishing the cultural standards within a given classroom. According to Johnson, Johnson, and Holubec (1993), the relationships that develop among peers in the classroom exert a tremendous influence on social and cognitive development and student socialization. In their interactions with peers, children and adolescents learn attitudes, values, skills, and information that are unobtainable from adults. Interaction with peers provides support, opportunities, and models for personal behaviour. Through peer relationships, a frame of reference for perceiving oneself is developed (Harris, 1998). In both educational and work settings, peers influence productivity. Students' educational aspirations are influenced more by peers than by any other social influence (Johnson, Johnson, and Holubec, 1993).

Traditionally, teachers have ignored the notion of peer culture and group standards in the classroom. They have focused their attention on individual learners and have viewed influencing students to behave appropriately as an issue between the teacher and the individual student. As a result, the development of group standards among students has been left almost completely to chance. However, there is growing evidence that teachers can intervene to create group standards that will promote prosocial behaviour as well as lead to peer relationships that will enhance the four components of self-esteem identified earlier: significance, power, competence, and virtue. Co-operative learning lessons that include face-to-face interaction, positive interdependence, and individual accountability can help to establish positive group standards. When teachers make a concentrated effort to help students develop the social skills necessary to function effectively as group members during co-operative learning activities, they enhance the power of co-operative learning activities to create positive group standards.

Johnson, Johnson, and Holubec (1993) as well as Elliott and Woloshyn (1996) have identified four sets of skills—*forming skills, functioning skills, formulating skills,* and *fermenting skills*—that students need to develop over time in order to function most effectively as a group. When these skills are in place and groups function successfully, group standards develop that lead students to (1) be engaged in learning activities, (2) strive toward learning and achievement, and (3) interact with each other in ways that will facilitate the development of positive self-esteem.

Forming skills are an initial set of management skills that are helpful in getting groups up and running smoothly and effectively. These skills include moving into groups quietly without bothering others, staying with the group rather than moving around the room, using quiet voices that can be heard by members of the group but not by others, and encouraging all group members to participate.

Functioning skills are group-management skills aimed at controlling the types of interactions that occur among group members. These skills include staying focused on the task, expressing support and acceptance of others, asking for help or clarification, offering to explain or clarify, and paraphrasing or summarizing what others have said.

Formulating skills refer to a set of behaviours that help students to process material mentally. These skills include summarizing key points, connecting ideas to each other, seeking elaboration of ideas, finding ways to remember information more effectively, and checking explanations and ideas through articulation.

Fermenting skills are a set of skills needed to resolve cognitive conflicts that arise within the group. These skills include criticizing ideas without deriding people, synthesizing diverse ideas, asking for justification, extending other people's ideas, and probing for more information.

Johnson, Johnson, and Holubec (1993) suggest that educators teach these social skills just as they teach academic content. Therefore, when teachers plan a co-operative learning activity, they must plan social-skill objectives as well as the academic objectives. Making the social skills explicit as lesson objectives helps to focus both student and teacher attention on them. To do this, the teacher should explain the skill before the activity begins and make sure students know what the skill looks like and sounds like as it is expressed in behaviour. Once the teacher is convinced that students understand the meaning of the skill, students may practise the skill during the co-operative learning activity. While the students are practising, the teacher moves from group to group monitoring the use of the skill. When the activity has been completed, the teacher engages each group in reflecting on how successfully the skill was used and in setting goals for improving their use of the skill in the future. Although teaching social skills in addition to academic content takes time, the time is well spent for two reasons. First, many of these skills are exactly the kinds of skills students will need to help them succeed as adults. Second, when students are skilled at interacting with each other in positive ways, group standards develop in the classroom that are supportive of prosocial behaviour and of engagement in appropriate learning activities.

Educators would like to acquire a list of proven and effective strategies for addressing various disruptive classroom behaviours. While such a list would be helpful ideally, the reality is that most classroom mishaps have enough uniqueness that they would render a specific one-size-fits-all solution relatively useless. Therefore, we have decided that a defined method for analyzing and managing behavioural concerns would be a superior approach to trying to anticipate all classroom challenges and providing methods for coping with each challenge separately. After carefully considering the types of questions that educators—from teacher candidates to experienced classroom teachers— raise about classroom management, we have developed a flexible, hierarchical model for examining and managing challenges that may affect the classroom environment.

The CALM Model

The CALM model/strategy provides the following steps as a general guide for handling classroom-management issues. The model can become automatic and be applied as needed. When these levels become an instinctive part of the teacher's repertoire of strategies along with other components of the effective classroom—including the development of a positive rapport—the effective teacher should be able to determine quickly the suitable level in order to avoid serious disruptions to the learning environment.

Level I

When a student's behaviour becomes disruptive, in order to initiate a response process the teacher should **consider** whether the behaviour changes, affects, or disrupts the classroom learning environment, teacher, or students.

When an inappropriate behaviour occurs, the most important and critical question to answer is, does this disruption affect the ability of the teacher to continue teaching and/or the ability of the students to continue learning? If the answer to the above question is no, then the teacher may choose to totally disregard the situation rather than alter the positive focus from the lesson. For example, two students may have a small disagreement in which a few angry gestures are exchanged. If the students resolve the issue and get back to work, there may be no reason for the teacher to disrupt the flow of the lesson and divert the other students' attention. If the learning can continue seamlessly, then there is no need to move to the next level. However, not all situations can be ignored and the teacher may feel that it is best to proceed to the next level. (A general rule: if the situation affects a small group of students, and it is only temporary, then it is usually best to let the students settle themselves down.)

Level II

When it becomes necessary to **act**.

There are situations where it is essential that the teacher respond quickly to avoid jeopardizing the learning environment. If it becomes necessary to respond to a disruption, the teacher decides whether an immediate action is required or if it would be best for him to respond to the situation later. The only question the teacher needs to ask at this level is, "Do I need to act now or can I postpone any action?" For example, if the arguing students described in Level I of CALM escalate their altercation, it may be necessary to direct some attention to the students to be sure that they get back to the task at hand. If the teacher determines that acting is necessary, then he moves to the next level.

Level III

Wherever possible, **lessen** the invasive response in dealing with the situation.

If the teacher determines that the situation will not resolve itself, then a decision needs to be made as to what degree of intervention is necessary. It is very important that whenever an intervention must occur, there should be no doubt in the students' minds that there will be a consequence.

If the teacher decides that a response is needed, then it is critical that any action implemented be the least invasive action possible. For example, if the arguing students from Level I continue to react to each other, "the look" may be enough to refocus their attention. The teacher may choose to use proximity as the management strategy. Maybe a simple tally on the board or just asking the student(s) to come to a conference later will suffice. Possibly, some other unobtrusive technique will be enough to bring the students back to the lesson. On the other hand, if it appears that a more direct response may be essential or that a lack of sufficient response may lead to loss of respect, then the teacher needs to react with a greater presence.

Three broad stages of action and intervention can be identified.

Action Stage A: At this stage, the teacher uses an action that will not affect the flow of the learning environment and will affect only the student(s) involved in the misbehaviour. Usually, a very minimal action is appropriate and other students do not even notice. At this stage, the teacher can proceed without missing a beat.

Action Stage B: Here, the teacher determines that he must make a brief interruption of the learning environment and that a greater degree of intervention is needed. The teacher determines that the disruptive student(s) need attention. At this stage, the misbehaviour requires a more direct approach and the teacher may call the student(s) by name to refocus attention to the task. Other possible actions at this stage include moving the offending student(s) to a different area of the room, giving them a *timeout*, establishing a conference at a time that is convenient for the teacher, using a token economy strategy that has been predefined with the class, or implementing other consequences that the teacher concludes are fitting in this case. Again, this action should be administered quickly and the teacher resumes where he left off without delay. It is important to reiterate: when the students understand that consequences *will* definitely follow misbehaviours, the lesson or task can continue with minimal disruption. The students will understand that is just the way it works with this teacher.

Action Stage C: Hopefully, this stage is needed only in rare cases. To move to this stage, the student(s) has/have misbehaved to the point where the teacher has no option but to interrupt the process to address the misbehaviour. The teacher may again try using the strategies outlined in Action Stage B, but once it is apparent that these relatively moderate techniques are not going to be sufficient, it may be necessary to remove the student(s) from the room using the procedures that are defined within the school and board of education.

Level IV

Manage the milieu to quickly return to an effective learning environment.

Throughout this process, the teacher's demeanour should remain composed and he should refocus as quickly as possible on the effective learning environment that was interrupted. It is imperative that he display a positive demeanour to the rest of the class at this time and avoid commenting on the disruptive situation.

Summary

In this chapter, we first examined two of the critical variables that influence behaviour in the classroom: the physical environment and classroom rules and routines. This discussion was followed by a consideration of the role of culture in the establishment of classroom routines and rules. In the final section of the chapter, we discussed the creation of group standards that are supportive of appropriate behaviour.

Although teachers have no control over of the size of their classrooms, they can control the seating arrangement within the classroom and the use of bulletin boards. The seating arrangement should accommodate the learning activity. It must also permit all students to see instructional presentations and allow the teacher to be close to all students. Bulletin boards should reflect and add to the motivation for learning. Properly used, they can provide students with the opportunity to enrich and actively participate in their learning and allow the teacher to recognize and display students' work and achievements.

When they are well designed, rules and routines provide students with clear expectations. The teacher can increase the effectiveness of rules and routines by (1) analyzing the classroom environment to determine what is needed to protect teaching, learning, safety, and property; (2) communicating the rules and routines and their rationales to students; (3) obtaining student commitments to abide by the rules; (4) teaching and evaluating student understanding of the rules; and (5) enforcing each rule and routine with natural or logical consequences.

Classrooms and schools are never culturally neutral or value free; they are always situated within a particular cultural context. When the culture of the school and the culture of the students are synchronized, positive behaviour increases and positive relationships are established between teachers and students. However, when teachers and students hold differing values, standards, and behavioural expectations, the potential for misunderstanding, conflict, and mistrust is greatly enhanced.

Each classroom also develops its own culture with its own set of group standards and values. Traditionally, some teachers have ignored the communal aspects of classroom life, focusing instead on individual relationships. Evidence now indicates that the use of co-operative learning activities that contain all essential elements combined with the teaching of prosocial skills will lead to the establishment of group standards that are supportive of appropriate student behaviour. The CALM model is used as a guide to help teachers attain such goals in a logical manner.

Key Terms

antecedents: preliminary courses of action that may increase the likelihood that appropriate behaviour will take place, or they may set the stage for the occurrence of misbehaviour.

fermenting skills: a set of skills needed to resolve cognitive conflicts that arise within the group.

forming skills: an initial set of management skills that are helpful in getting groups up and running smoothly and effectively.

formulating skills: a set of behaviours that help students to process material mentally.

functioning skills: group-management skills aimed at controlling the types of interactions that occur among group members.

logical consequences: outcomes that are directly related to the behaviour that require teacher intervention to occur.

natural consequences: outcomes of behaviour that occur without teacher intervention.

Exercises

1. For each of the following activities, design a seating arrangement for 24 students that maximizes on-task behaviour and minimizes disruptions.

   a. teacher lecture
   b. Small-group work (four students per group)
   c. open discussion
   d. individual seat work
   e. class project to design a bulletin board
   f. teacher-led group work and simultaneous individual
   g. seat work
   h. group debate
   i. teacher demonstration

2. Give examples of how a teacher can use the classroom environment (bulletin boards, shelves, walls, chalkboard, and so on) to create a pleasant atmosphere that increases the likelihood of appropriate student behaviour.

3. With your present or future classroom in mind, determine the common activities that do or will regularly occur. Design appropriate routines to accomplish those activities. How would you teach these routines to the class?

4. **a.** With your present or future classroom in mind, determine what general student behaviours are necessary to ensure that learning and teaching take place and that students and property are safe.
   b. State a positive rule for each of the behaviours you previously listed.
   c. For each behaviour, give a rationale you can explain to students that is consistent with the definition of a behaviour problem and appropriate for the age of the students you teach or will teach.

    d. For each behaviour, determine a natural or logical consequence that will occur when the rule is broken.

    e. How will you communicate these rules to students?

    f. How will you obtain student commitment to these rules?

5. Determine a natural, logical, and contrived consequence for each of the following misbehaviours:

    a. grade 4 student who interrupts small group work

    b. grade 11 student who continually gets out of her seat

    c. grade 7 student who makes noises during class

    d. grade 10 student who makes noises during class

    e. grade 12 student who refuses to change her seat when requested to do so by the teacher

    f. grade 1 student who interrupts reading group to tattle on a student who is not doing his seat work

    g. a group of grade 6 students who drop their pencils in unison at a given time

    h. grade 9 student who threatens to beat up another student after class

    i. grade 8 student who continually pushes the chair of the student in front of him

    j. grade 10 student who does not wear goggles while operating power equipment

6. The following are examples of some rules developed for a grade 8 science class. Identify and correct any problems in the rule, rationale, or consequences.

Rule	Rationale	Consequences
a. Don't be late to class	Because we have a lot of material to cover and we need the whole class period	a. Reminder by teacher b. Student required to get a note c. Student writes 100 times, "I will not be late"
b. We all need to work without disrupting others	Because everyone has a right to learn and no one has a right to interfere with the learning of others	a. Reminder by teacher b. Student moved where he cannot disrupt others c. Student removed from class d. Student fails
c. We all have to raise our hands to answer questions or contribute to a discussion	Because I do not like to be interrupted	a. Student ignored b. Reminder by teacher c. Parents notified
d. We must use lab equipment properly and safely	Because it is expensive to replace	a. Pay for broken equipment b. Pay for equipment and additional fine

7. For each of the following scenarios, explain why the student behaved as he or she did:

    a. Juanita, a recently arrived student from Mexico, is being reprimanded by her teacher for not doing her homework. Despite repeated attempts by her teacher to get Juanita to look her in the eye, Juanita refuses to do so.

b. Eunsook, a student from Korea, is obviously upset about something. When Mr. Barber bends close to her and tries to find out what is happening, Eunsook simply clams up and does not say a word.

c. Justin, a Jamaican-born grade 1 student, continually sings along and talks along with his teacher, Ms. Gray, when she is telling stories to the class. Ms. Gray finds Justin's behaviour rude.

8. How do differences in cultural values, standards, and behavioural expectations influence the development of teacher expectations for student achievement?

9. For each of the following social skills, develop an explanation of what the social skill means for students at the grade 3 level, at the grade 7 level, and at the grade 11 level.

   a. encouraging everyone to participate
   b. paraphrasing what others have said
   c. seeking elaboration
   d. asking for justification for ideas

Weblinks

British Columbia Department of Education
www.bced.gov.bc.ca/specialed
This website is designed to address a wide range of issues related to special education.

Ontario Ministry of Education's Violence-Free Schools Policy
www.edu.gov.on.ca/eng/document/policy/vfreeng.html
This one describes the policy devised to develop violence free schools.

Department of Education for Newfoundland and Labrador's Programming for Individual Needs: Policy, Guidelines, and Resource Guide on Discipline, School Violence and Safe Schools Teams
www.ed.gov.nl.ca/edu/dept/safesch.htm
This site describes in general and specific terms how teachers can develop programming that will minimize violence.

The League of Peaceful Schools
www.leagueofpeacefulschools.ns.ca
This site states that it "provides support and recognition to schools that have declared a commitment to creating a safe and peaceful environment for their students."

The Muslim Educational Network, Training and Outreach Service (MENTORS)
www.mentorscanada.com
MENTORS is a website that provides resources for schools that include information and curriculum packages that impart Islamic knowledge, culture and practice.

Iterative Case Study Analysis

Third Analysis

Considering the concepts discussed in Part II, Prevention, reanalyze your second analysis. What has changed and what has stayed the same since your last analysis? Once again consider why the students may be choosing to behave inappropriately and how you might intervene to influence the students to stop the disruptive behaviour and resume appropriate on-task behaviour.

Elementary School Case Study

During silent reading time in my grade 4 class, I have built in opportunities to work individually with students. During this time, the students read to me and practice word work with flash cards. One student has refused to read to me but instead wants only to work with the flash cards. After a few sessions, I suggested we work with word cards this time and begin reading next time. He agreed. The next time we met, I reminded him of our plan, and he screamed, "I don't remember! I want to do word cards!" At this point, I tried to find out why he didn't like reading and he said, "There's a reason, I just can't tell you," and he threw the word cards across the room, some of them hitting other students. What should I do?

Middle School Case Study

I can't stop thinking about a problem I'm having in class with a group of 12-year-old boys. They consistently use vulgar language toward one another and some of the shyer kids in the class, especially the girls. In addition, they are always pushing and shoving each other. I've tried talking to them about why they keep using bad language when they know it's inappropriate. The response I get is that "it makes me look cool and funny in front of my friends." I have asked them to please use more appropriate language in the classroom but that has not worked. I haven't even started to address the pushing and shoving. What should I do?

High School Case Study

This past week, I had a student approach me about a problem he was experiencing in our class. The grade 11 student had recently "come out" as being gay. He said he was tired and upset with the three boys who sit near him. These boys frequently call him a "homo" and a "fag" every time they see him, both in and out of class. What should I do?

7

Managing Common Behaviour Problems: Non-verbal Interventions

Focus on the Principles of Classroom Management

1. What is the ultimate goal of a teacher's classroom-management techniques for individual students?
2. What preplanning is absolutely essential if teachers are to manage misbehaviour?
3. What are the teacher behaviours that are most effective in maximizing management alternatives?

Introduction

In most classrooms, the majority of student misbehaviours are verbal interruptions, off-task behaviour, and disruptive physical movements. These behaviours, which are sometimes called **surface behaviours**, are present in every classroom in every school almost every day. With proper planning, instructional strategies, and environmental structuring, the frequency of surface behaviours can be reduced greatly. However, no matter how much time and energy the teacher directs toward prevention, surface behaviours do not disappear and to some extent are an ever-present fact of life for all teachers.

There are many intervention skills that the successful teacher may use to deal with surface behaviours in a manner that is effective, expedient, and least disruptive to the teaching and learning process. These skills may be divided into three sequenced categories: (1) non-verbal intervention, (2) verbal intervention, and (3) use of logical consequences (see also Figure 8.2 on page 205). Each tier of the sequence consists of a variety of intervention skills, which are themselves sequenced. The degree of intrusiveness and the potential for disruption to the teaching/learning environment determine which skills the teacher employs. When these intervention skills are applied in a pre-planned, systematic manner, they have been shown to be quite effective.

In this chapter, we discuss non-verbal skills, the first tier in the decision-making hierarchy. This group of skills is the least intrusive and has the least potential for disrupting the teaching/learning process while leaving the teacher with the maximum number of management alternatives for future use.

Prerequisites to Management

All too often, teachers are quick to place total responsibility for inappropriate behaviour on their students without carefully analyzing their own behaviour. It is quite common to hear teachers say, "There's nothing I can do. All they want to do is fool around" or "These kids are impossible! Why even try?" Such comments clearly indicate that teachers have assigned all blame for student misbehaviour to the students themselves. However, effective teaching and maximum learning occur in classrooms when teachers and students understand that teaching and learning are the responsibility of both the student and the teacher.

The responsibilities of the students are obvious. Students must prepare for class, study, ask questions to enhance their understanding, and remain on task. Many of the preventive techniques that we've discussed in previous chapters, as well as the management techniques to be discussed in this chapter, assist students in accepting responsibility for their learning. However, students more readily accept their responsibilities when it is clear to them that the teacher is fulfilling her responsibilities. These professional responsibilities, which we have already examined, are the basic minimum competencies that all teachers must possess. They are the prerequisites to appropriate classroom management:

1. The teacher is well prepared to teach. Prior to class, she has designed specific learning objectives and effective teaching strategies based on accepted principles of learning.
2. The teacher provides clear directions and explanations of the learning material.
3. The teacher ensures that students understand evaluation criteria.
4. The teacher clearly communicates, rationalizes, and consistently enforces behavioural expectations.
5. The teacher demonstrates enthusiasm and encouragement and models the behaviours expected from students.
6. The teacher builds positive, caring relationships with students.

When teachers reinforce the concept of shared responsibility for teaching and learning through their behaviour, management techniques, if needed, are more likely to be effective in encouraging appropriate student behaviour.

Surface Behaviours

The most common day-to-day disruptive behaviours are verbal interruptions (talking, humming, laughing, calling out, whispering), off-task behaviours (daydreaming, sleeping, combing hair, playing with something, doodling), physical movement intended to disrupt (visiting, passing notes, sitting on the desk or on two legs of the chair, throwing paper), and disrespect (arguing, teasing/heckling, vulgarity, talking back)

(Huber, 1984; Levin, 1980; Shrigley, 1980; Thomas, Goodall, and Brown, 1983; Weber and Sloan, 1986). These disruptive behaviours, which are usually readily observable to an experienced teacher, are called surface behaviours because they usually are not a result of any deep-seated personal problem but are normal developmental behaviours of children (Ritchie et al., 1999).

Some teachers are able to manage surface behaviours appropriately, almost intuitively. They have a near instinctive grasp of the necessary classroom skills of "overlapping," or attending to two matters at the same time, and "with-it-ness," a subtle non-verbal communication to students that they are aware of all activities within the classroom (Kounin, 1970; Schwartz and Pollishuke, 2002). Other teachers acquire these skills through hard work and experience. Teachers who do not have or do not develop these skills have to cope with abnormally high frequencies of surface behaviours, and in some instances, as in Case 7.1, the absence of these skills actually causes disruptive behaviour.

CASE 7.1 • ... *3, 2, 1, Blast Off!*

The students in Mr. Berk's grade 7 English class have science before English. Today, their science teacher illustrated the concept of propulsion by folding a piece of tin foil around the tip of a match. When he heated the tin foil, the match was ignited and accelerated forward. The students were intrigued and asked him to repeat the experiment.

During English class, Mickey, seated in the back row, decides to try the propulsion experiment for the entertainment of those around him. It is not long before many students are aware of Mickey's activity and are sneaking glances at him. Mickey is enjoying the attention and continues to propel matches across his desk.

It does not take Mr. Berk long to become aware that many of his students are not paying attention. Instead of attempting to determine what the distraction is, he reacts impulsively. He sees Terri turn around to look at Mickey and says sharply, "Terri, turn around and pay attention!" Terri immediately fires back defiantly, "I'm not doing anything." The class begins to laugh, because Mr. Berk is the only person in the room who is unaware of the aerospace activity in the back of the room.

Questions to Consider

1. Why is Mr. Berk unaware of Mickey's activities?
2. When he became aware of the lack of attention, what should Mr. Berk have done?
3. Why was his impulsive discipline of Terri destructive to his classroom management?
4. Consider the levels of the CALM model and discuss how they could be applied in this case. Start with the applicability of Level I to begin the discussion and proceed through all four levels.

Surface behaviours are the most common type of disruptive behaviours that teachers must manage on a day-to-day basis.

Proactive Intervention Skills

Effective classroom managers are experts in the matter-of-fact use of not only *overlapping* and *with-it-ness* skills but also other more specific and narrower **proactive intervention skills**. Their expertise can be seen in the way they employ these skills with little if any disruption in the teaching/learning process. Developing expertise in the use of the following proactive skills should lessen the need for more intrusive management techniques:

1. *Changing the pace of classroom activities.* Rubbing eyes, yawning, stretching, and staring out the window are clear signs that a change of pace is needed. This is the time for the teacher to restructure the situation and involve students in games, stories, or other favourite activities that require active student participation and help to refocus student interests. To reduce the need for on-the-spot, change-of-pace activities, lesson plans should provide for a variety of learning experiences that accommodate the attention spans and interests of the students both in time and in type.

2. *Removing distracting objects.* The skill may be used with little, if any, pause in the teaching act. However, there should be an agreement that the objects will

be returned after class. Teachers who find themselves competing with toys, magazines, or combs may simply walk over to the student, collect the object, and quietly inform the student that it will be available after class.

3. *Interest boosting of a student who shows signs of off-task behaviour.* Rather than using other, less positive techniques, the teacher shows interest in the student's work, thereby bringing the student back on task. Interest boosting is often called for when students are required to do individual or small-group classwork. It is during these times that the potential for chatter, daydreaming, or other off-task behaviours is high. If the teacher observes a student engaging in activities other than the assigned math problems, for example, she can boost the interest of the student by walking over to the student and asking how her work is going or checking the answers of her completed problems. Asking the student to place correct problems on the board is also effective. Whatever technique is decided on, it must be employed in a matter-of-fact supportive manner to boost the student's interest in the learning activity.

4. *Redirecting the behaviour of off-task students.* This skill helps to refocus the student's attention. Students who are passing notes, talking, or daydreaming may be asked to read, do a problem, or answer a question. When this technique is used, it is important to treat the student as if she were paying attention. For instance, if you call on the off-task student to answer a question and the student answers correctly, give positive feedback. If she doesn't answer or answers incorrectly, reformulate the question or call on someone else. A teacher who causes the student embarrassment or ridicule by stating, "You would know where we were if you were paying attention" invites further misbehaviour. The "get-back-on-task" message the teacher is sending is clearly received by the off-task student whether or not she answers the question or finds the proper reading place, and does not require any negative comments.

5. *Non-punitive time out.* This skill should be used for students who show signs of encountering a provoking, painful, frustrating, or fatiguing situation. The teacher quietly asks the student if she would like to get a drink or invites her to run an errand or do a chore. The change in activity gives the student time to regain her control before re-entering the learning environment. Teachers must be alert to the signs of frustration so they can act in a timely fashion to help students cope.

6. *Encouraging the appropriate behaviour of other students.* A statement such as, "I'm glad to see that Andrea and Carl have their books open" reminds off-task students of the behaviour that is expected of them.

7. *Providing cues for expected behaviours.* Cues can be quite effective in obtaining the desired behaviour, but the teacher must be sure the cue is understood by all. For example, a teacher who expects students to be in their seats and prepared for class when the bell rings must make sure that everyone understands that the bell signals the start of class. In schools without bells or other indicators,

A teacher can redirect students to on-task behaviour by the use of interest-boosting techniques.

closing the door is an appropriate cue. Some teachers flick the lights to cue a class that the noise has reached unacceptable levels. Using the same cues consistently usually results in quick student response.

Remedial Intervention Skills

In order to describe and clarify the CALM model further, in the following section we provide an in-depth discussion of the rationale for each level of CALM.

The masterful use of proactive skills diffuses many surface behaviours and causes minimal disruptions of the teaching act. However, there will always be classroom situations that induce misbehaviour or students who continue to display disruptive behaviours.

These behaviours may range from mildly off-task to very disruptive. Mastering the delivery of the intervention skills discussed here and in Chapters 8, "Managing Common Misbehaviour Problems: Verbal Interventions and Use of Logical Consequences," and 9, "Classroom Interventions for Chronic Problems," should help to produce an exceptional classroom in which misbehaviour is minimized and teachers are free to teach and children are free to learn.

Before any intervention may be used, the teacher must have a basis on which to make decisions concerning common inappropriate behaviours in the classroom. To avoid inconsistency and arbitrariness, teachers must also have a systematic intervention plan of predetermined behaviours that clearly communicate disapproval to the student who calls out, throws paper, walks around, passes notes, or in any way interferes with the teaching or learning act (Canter, 1989; Lasley, 1989). This follows our definition of teaching presented in Chapter 1: the conscious use of predetermined behaviours that increase the likelihood of changing student behaviours. Such a systematic intervention plan also follows the levels of the CALM model for examining and managing classroom challenges that are described in Chapter 6.

As outlined in the CALM model, the intervention decision-making approach is a sequence of teacher behaviours. Because we believe that students must learn to control their own behaviour, the initial interventions are subtle, non-intrusive, and very student-centred. Although these behaviours communicate disapproval, they are designed to provide students with the opportunity to control their own behaviour. If the misbehaviours are not curbed, the interventions become increasingly more intrusive and teacher-centred; that is, the teacher takes more responsibility for managing the students' behaviour.

Because we also believe that management techniques should not in themselves disrupt the teaching and learning act (Brophy, 1988; Kerr and Nelson, 2002; Ritchie et al., 1999), early intervention behaviours are almost a private communication between the teacher and the off-task student. They alert the student to her inappropriate behaviour but cause little if any noticeable disruption to either teaching or learning. If these non-verbal interventions, which make up the first level of the CALM decision-making model, are not successful, they are followed by the second, third and fourth levels. These levels are increasingly more teacher-centred, more intrusive, and may cause some interruption to the teaching/learning act. (These techniques are discussed in Chapters 8 and 9.) Please refer to Levels I through IV of the CALM model.

CALM is intended to be a dynamic model, not one that binds a teacher into a lockstep, sequential, cookbook intervention approach. Instead, the model requires the teacher to make a decision as to which intervention in the hierarchy to use first. The decision should depend on the type and frequency of the disruptive behaviour and should be congruent with the five implementation guidelines that follow. These guidelines should help to ensure that any beginning intervention, as well as those that may follow, meets the two foundational precepts of the model: increasing student self-control and decreasing disruptions to the teaching and learning environment.

1. The intervention provides the student with opportunities for self-control of the disruptive behaviours. Self-control is not developed to its fullest in classrooms where teachers immediately intervene with teacher-centred techniques to manage student behaviour. Because we believe that individuals make conscious choices to behave in certain ways and that individuals cannot be forced to learn or exhibit appropriate behaviour, early interventions should not force students but rather *influence* them to manage themselves. Students must be given responsibility in order to learn responsibility.

2. Our CALM model does not cause more disruption to the teaching and learning environment than the disruptive behaviour itself. We have all witnessed teacher

interventions that were more disruptive to the class than the off-task student behaviour. This usually occurs when the teacher uses an intervention too far up the decision-making hierarchy. Use of CALM should reduce the likelihood of such occurrences. For example, a teacher unacquainted with the CALM approach might choose to use a public verbal technique when a private non-verbal intervention would be more effective and less disruptive. When this happens, the teacher becomes a more disruptive factor than the student.

3. The model lessens the probability that the student will become more disruptive or confrontational. Interventions should lessen and defuse confrontational situations. When teachers choose to employ public, aggressive, or humiliating techniques, they increase the likelihood of escalating confrontations and power struggles. Again, deciding where in the decision-making hierarchy to begin has a significant effect on whether a disruptive student will be brought back on task or will become confrontational.

4. CALM can protect students from physical and psychological harm. When a teacher observes behaviours that could be harmful to any student, intervention should be swift and teacher-centred. In such situations, non-verbal techniques are usually bypassed for the assertive delivery of verbal interventions. In all cases, care must be taken that the interventions are not in themselves a source of harm to students or the teacher.

5. Every teacher knows that it often takes more than one type of intervention to manage student behaviour. It is rare that when a disruptive behaviour is noted, a teacher simply intervenes and the student is back on task forever. It is the unwise teacher who sends a student out of the classroom for the first occurrence of a disruptive behaviour. Such an intervention leaves few options available to the teacher if the student continues to misbehave when she returns. By using the CALM model, the savvy teacher reserves many alternative interventions.

It is important to remember that the teacher's goal in employing any remedial intervention skill is to redirect the student to appropriate behaviour. Stopping the misbehaviour may be the initial step in the process, but it is not sufficient in itself. The teacher's goal is not reached until the student becomes re-engaged in learning activities. Thus, whenever the teacher is faced with a disruptive behaviour, one of the questions she should ask is, "What level of the CALM model is likely to be the most effective?"

In Chapter 6, the four levels of the CALM model are outlined. Briefly, those levels are as follows:

Level I—Consider. When a student's behaviour becomes disruptive, the teacher should consider the following question to initiate a response process: "Does the behaviour change, affect, or disrupt the classroom learning environment, teacher or students?"

Level II—Act. Once the behaviour has become a "distracting" force for the teacher, the next level of intervention is introduced. This occurs when it becomes necessary to act.

Level III—Lessen. Since it is important to minimize distraction and not give undue attention to inappropriate behaviour, it is important to lessen the use of invasive responses in dealing with a situation that requires action.

Level IV—Manage. Manage the milieu to quickly return to an effective learning environment.

As is evident, the first three levels of CALM consist of three moderate techniques, which should be considered before resorting to Level IV. These first three techniques could be otherwise described as planned ignoring, signal interference, and proximity interference, which are body-language interventions first identified by Redl and Wineman (1952). When they are used randomly, a teacher is unlikely to manage minor disruptions effectively. However, when they are consciously used in a predetermined logical sequence, they serve to curb milder forms of off-task behaviour (Shrigley, 1985).

Planned Ignoring

Planned ignoring is based on the reinforcement theory that if you ignore a behaviour, it will lessen and eventually disappear. Although this sounds simple, it is difficult to ignore a behaviour completely. That is why *planned* is stressed. When a student whistles, interrupts the teacher, or calls out, the teacher instinctively looks in the direction of the student, thereby giving the student attention and reinforcing the behaviour. In contrast, planned ignoring intentionally and completely ignores the behaviour. This takes practice.

And there are limitations to this intervention. First, according to reinforcement theory, when a behaviour has been reinforced previously, removal of the reinforcement causes a short-term increase in the behaviour in the hope of again receiving reinforcement. Thus, when planned ignoring is first used, there probably will be an increase in the off-task behaviour. Therefore, this technique should be used to manage only the behaviours that cause little interference to the teaching/learning act (Brophy, 1988). Second, other classmates who pay attention to the misbehaving student often are reinforcing the disruptive behaviour. If so, planned ignoring by the teacher has little effect.

The behaviours that usually are managed by planned ignoring include not having materials ready for the start of class, calling out answers rather than raising a hand, mild or infrequent whispering, interrupting the teacher, and daydreaming. Obviously, the type of learning activity has much to do with the behaviours that can or cannot be ignored. If, after a reasonable period of time of ignoring the off-task behaviour, the behaviour does not decrease or the point is reached at which others are distracted by it, the teacher has to move quickly and confidently to the next step in the hierarchy: signal interference.

Signal Interference

Signal interference is any type of non-verbal behaviour that communicates to the student, without disturbing others, that the behaviour is inappropriate. Signal interventions must be clearly directed at the off-task student. There should be no doubt in the student's mind that the teacher is aware of what is going on and that the student is responsible for the behaviour. The teacher's expression should be businesslike. It is ineffective for the teacher to make eye contact with a student and smile. Smiling sends a double message, which confuses students, who may interpret it as a lack of seriousness on the teacher's part.

Examples of signal-interference behaviours are making eye contact with the student who is talking to a neighbour, pointing to a seat when a student is wandering around, head shaking to indicate "no" to a student who is about to throw a paper airplane, and holding up an open hand to stop a student's calling out. Like all coping skills, signal-interference behaviours may be hierarchically ordered, depending on the type, duration, and frequency of off-task behaviour. A simple hand motion might be sufficient for calling out the first time, whereas direct eye contact with a disapproving look may be needed the next time the student calls out.

For disruptive behaviours that continue or for disturbances that more seriously affect others' learning, the teacher moves to the next intervention skill in the hierarchy: proximity interference.

Proximity Interference

Proximity interference is any movement toward the disruptive student. When signal interference doesn't work or when the teacher is unable to gain a student's attention long enough to send a signal because the student is so engrossed in the off-task behaviour, proximity interference is warranted.

Often, just walking toward the student while conducting the lesson is enough to bring the student back on task. If the student continues to be off task, the teacher may want to conduct the lesson in close proximity to the student's desk, which is usually quite effective. This technique works well during question-and-answer periods.

Proximity interference combined with signal interference results in a very effective non-verbal management technique. It's the rare student who is not brought back on task by a teacher who makes eye contact and begins walking toward her desk. Like signal interference, proximity-interference techniques may be hierarchically ordered from nonchalant movement in the direction of the student to an obvious standing behind or next to the student during class.

Effectiveness of Non-verbal Intervention Skills

The use of these three remedial non-verbal intervention skills is considered successful if any one or any combination in the hierarchy leads the student to resume appropriate classroom behaviour.

Notice how Mr. Rothman in Case 7.2 on 180 skilfully uses the three non-verbal remedial-intervention techniques in combination with the proactive skills of removing seductive objects, interest boosting, and redirecting the behaviour to manage the note

CASE 7.2 • *Notes Versus Math*

Mr. Rothman asks each student in his grade 6 class to write one math problem from an assignment on the board. As two students write their problems, he notices, out of the corner of his eye, Leo passing a note to Ben. Mr. Rothman decides to ignore the behaviour, waiting to see if it is a matter of a single occurrence. When all the problems are on the board, Mr. Rothman asks questions about the solutions. During this questioning period, he notices Ben returning a note to Leo. After a few attempts, Mr. Rothman makes eye contact with Leo while at the same time questioning Ben about one of the problems. This technique stops the note passing for the remainder of the questioning activity.

The next activity calls for the use of calculators, and he asks Leo to please pass one calculator to each predetermined pair of students. Leo and Ben are partners, and Mr. Rothman monitors their behaviour from a distance. As he circulates around the room helping students with the classwork, Mr. Rothman makes sure that he stops to look over Leo and Ben's work, encouraging them on its accuracy. Throughout the activity, both boys are on task.

Following the group work, the students separate their desks, and Mr. Rothman begins to review the answers to the problems. He immediately notices that the two boys have begun to pass notes again. He quickly takes a position next to the boys, taps Leo on the shoulder, and holds out his hand for the note. Leo hands Mr. Rothman the note and he puts it in his pocket. Mr. Rothman stands near the boys for the rest of the period, asking questions of the class and reviewing the problems. Both Ben and Leo volunteer and participate for the remainder of the class.

Questions to Consider

1. What are Mr. Rothman's options related to the note he has confiscated? Examine each option and select the one most congruent with the CALM method. Provide a rationale for your choice.

2. Find three ways in which Mr. Rothman adhered to the CALM model.

3. Discuss the appropriateness of each of Mr. Rothman's interventions.

passing between Leo and Ben without noticeably disrupting the teaching/learning act. He is able to do this because the intervention skills are not randomly and haphazardly applied.

Mr. Rothman has a mental flow chart of the intervention sequence so that movement from one behaviour to the next is accomplished quickly, calmly, and confidently. This does not happen overnight. Teachers must pre-plan and practise proactive and remedial-intervention techniques before they need to implement them.

Shrigley studied the efficiency of non-verbal proactive- and remedial-intervention skills when used in a hierarchical sequence. He found that after a few hours of in-service training, 53 teachers were able to curb 40 percent of 523 off-task surface behaviours without having to utter a word or cause any interruption to either teaching or learning. Five percent of the behaviours were corrected by the use of planned ignoring. Signal interference was the most effective technique, rectifying 14 percent of the behaviours. Twelve percent of the behaviours were stopped by proximity. To manage the remaining 69 percent of unresolved behavioural problems, the teachers needed to use verbal intervention (1985). We discuss verbal-intervention skills in Chapter 8.

Remember, however, that the hierarchy is a decision-making model. Depending on the type, frequency, and distracting potential of the behaviour, the teacher may decide to bypass the initial intervention skills in favour of a later technique. There are certain behaviours that need immediate attention—they can neither be ignored nor allowed to continue. This is demonstrated in Case 7.3, in which Ms. Niaz decides to bypass planned ignoring and signal interference in favour of proximity interference to manage a disruption during a test.

Concentric Case Study Kaleidoscope

CASE 7.3 • *Let Your Fingers Do the Walking*

The Story

Ms. Niaz explains the test-taking procedures to her large grade 10 math class. She emphasizes the need for each student to do her own work and in order to expedite this necessity, she asks the students to separate their desks into rows. Ms. Niaz hands out the tests face down. When everyone has a copy, she announces, "Okay, you may begin." All the students turn their tests over and begin to read. For the next 15 minutes, she walks around the room, answers a few questions, and makes sure that her students are aware of her presence.

When Ms. Niaz is at one side of the room, she glances across the class and notices that Danny, a good student, is walking his fingers up Tonya's back in front of him. In a few seconds, Tonya, who is also a good student but has to work harder at it than Danny, turns around and whispers, "Stop it." As soon as she turns back to her test, Danny starts running his fingers up her back again with a slight smile around his lips. Ms. Diaz walks toward Danny and spends the next 10 minutes standing in close proximity to him.

The Students' Perspectives

Danny: "Okay, I get the routine for writing the test. It's the same every time. Let's get started." As he turns the test over, Danny quickly scans the questions and then relaxes, as he knows that he can answer all the questions quite easily. He starts writing and works for about 15 minutes steadily. Looking up, he glances at the time and realizes that he has a lot of time left to do the last couple of questions. He stares at Tonya's back and notes that she is concentrating hard on her work. "I like Tonya", he muses, and remembers dancing with her at the Friday night school dance last week. His mind begins to wander and he feels as though he wants to tease Tonya and get her attention. After all, the test is half over. He slowly and lightly begins to walk his fingers up her back while glancing over to see where the teacher is standing. It's okay because Ms. Niaz is on the other side of the room.

At first, Tonya ignores Danny's touch, so he increases the pressure. He's hoping she'll turn around and smile at him. Instead, she rotates and whispers gently (but firmly), "Stop it!" "I think she's flattered that I'm teasing her," Danny thinks. Again, he starts running his fingers up her back. Glancing up, he notices that Ms. Niaz is now moving purposefully toward him. He quickly returns to focusing on his test and is busily solving the next question when she moves next to him. As Ms. Niaz stays positioned near him for the next few minutes, Danny thinks, "Oh, she obviously saw me touching Tonya and thought I was bothering her or trying to cheat." He keeps his head down and focuses on his test until the end of the allotted time. When Danny hands in the test, he fails to meet Ms. Niaz's eyes and leaves feeling a bit sheepish and anxious to make certain that Tonya is not annoyed with him.

Tonya: "I'm glad Ms. Niaz reminds us about the procedures for writing a test every time. I know tests are important—I really like to study hard beforehand and I need to concentrate hard during the test if I am going to get a good mark. I really like getting good marks and I'm extra prepared for this test. Last night, I didn't even watch *Survivor* and I really wanted to see the next episode. My parents told me what happened but I spent my time in my room with the door closed doing practice questions. I feel much better about myself when I get good marks and my parents are so proud of me."

As Tonya turns her paper over, she feels apprehension, hoping that she has studied well enough to allow her to answer the questions. At first glance, Tonya feels confident, but she knows that she works slowly and methodically and will have to use her time well. No time for daydreaming or distractions. She gets down to work.

"What is that feeling? . . . Oh, no! Danny is running his fingers up my back. I don't have time for this now, although I do like him." She really wishes that he would stop, as he is interfering with her concentration. Finally, she turns around and says gently in a whisper so as not to draw attention to the incident, "Stop it!" For a moment, Danny stops. But then he begins to run his fingers up her back again. Just as Tonya is preparing to speak more sharply to him, she notices the teacher moving toward them. "Thank goodness," she thinks. "Now I don't have to hurt his feelings or deal with the disruption any more." As Tonya refocuses on her paper, she

feels confident and grateful that Ms. Niaz is standing beside them ensuring that Danny leaves her alone. At the end of the test, Tonya hands in her paper feeling confident that she has done well. As they leave the room, she smiles at Danny to let him know that she holds no hard feelings about his disruptive attentions.

Ms. Niaz's Perspective

When Ms. Niaz gives her students a test, she always stresses procedures because she thinks that it helps her students take the work seriously. She also encourages them to study by reminding them of the test in advance and by giving them guidelines about what material to expect on the test. When handing out papers, she further emphasizes the seriousness of the test process by relocating desks and reminding them of the rules. As a result, she prides herself on the serious way her students treat her tests and by the level of preparation many of them engage in. She also believes that her students are young and that she needs to monitor their behaviour carefully. "I am really helping to prepare them for higher education and the way they administer tests in university."

As Ms. Niaz watches the students focus on their test, she feels a sense of pride in the seriousness with which they approach it. "My attention to details is conveyed to them and is part of the reason that my classes always have a slightly higher average mark than the other grade 10 math class." She watches Danny begin to touch Tonya and reflects that Danny is a very capable student who really does not have to spend much time in order to achieve high results on his tests. But Ms. Niaz also knows that Tonya appears to be a very good student but that her efforts are much greater. She often comes in early to ask questions about the previous night's homework if she has difficulty. She also asks questions and volunteers answers readily in class in order to enhance her own learning. Now, Danny is breaking Tonya's focus.

"Oh, no you don't!" Ms. Niaz thinks as she moves over toward Danny. As she moves, she notes that he immediately begins to focus on his work again. In order to make sure that Tonya has uninterrupted time, Ms. Niaz stays beside Danny until the end of the test nears. "They really are good kids," she thought.

"But I bet they'll talk after class!"

Questions to Consider

1. Describe the steps of CALM employed by Ms. Niaz and discuss the effectiveness of her decisions.

2. What should Ms. Niaz have done if Danny bothered Tonya for a third time?

3. Do you think that Ms. Niaz was conducting her tests appropriately? Why or why not?

No matter which technique eventually brings the student back on task, efforts need to be directed toward maintaining the appropriate behaviour. This is most easily accomplished by the teacher, who encourages and attends to the student's new behaviour. The student must realize that she can obtain the same or even more attention and recognition for appropriate behaviour than she did for disruptive behaviour. The student who is ignored when calling out answers should be called on immediately when she raises her hand. The student who ceases walking around the room should be told at the end of the period that it was a pleasure having her in the class. These simple efforts of recognizing appropriate behaviour are often overlooked by teachers, but they are necessary for the teacher who wants to maximize the effectiveness of proactive- and remedial-intervention skills. Frequently, these strategies are referred to as behaviour modification.

Summary

In this chapter, we stressed that teaching/learning is the joint responsibility of the teacher and the students. Students are more willing to accept their responsibilities when it is clear to them that teachers are fulfilling their responsibilities. These responsibilities include being well prepared to teach by developing learning objectives and using effective teaching strategies; providing clear directions and explanations; ensuring that students understand evaluation criteria; communicating and consistently enforcing behavioural expectations; demonstrating enthusiasm and encouragement; and modelling expected behaviour. These behaviours are minimum competencies that all teachers must possess and are considered prerequisites to effective classroom management.

Teachers proficient in classroom management are experts in the use of a variety of proactive intervention skills. Techniques such as changing the pace, removing seductive objects, interest boosting, redirecting behaviour, non-punitive time out, encouraging appropriate behaviour, and providing cues are used to bring students back on task while causing little if any disruption to the teaching/learning process.

The CALM model of remedial-intervention skills provides a means to manage the inappropriate surface behaviours that are not brought on task through proactive-intervention skills. The structure of the hierarchy ranges from non-intrusive techniques that cause little disruption and provide students with the opportunity to control their own behaviour to intrusive techniques that potentially disrupt teaching and learning. The first tier of non-verbal remedial intervention consists of three non-verbal behaviours: planned ignoring, signal interference, and proximity interference. When used systematically, these techniques are effective in managing many surface behaviours.

Key Terms

behaviour modification: a method that involves the use of stimuli through positive and negative reinforcement to change behaviours and reactions. B. F. Skinner is accredited with much of the theoretical work that he referred to as *operant conditioning*.

proactive intervention skills: when an instructor observes the start of, or even anticipates, inattentive behaviour she usually gives a non-intrusive action or verbal cue to indicate to a student or students that they are required to return quickly to the "task at hand."

surface behaviours: the most common day-to-day disruptions, such as verbal interruptions, off-task behaviours, physical movement intended to disrupt, and disrespect.

Exercises

1. Near the beginning of this chapter, we listed six teacher behaviour prerequisites for achieving appropriate student behaviour. Should these teacher behaviours be considered prerequisites? Why or why not?

2. Predict what type of student behaviour may result if the teacher does not meet each of the six prerequisite teacher behaviours.

3. What, if any, deletions or additions would you make to the six prerequisite teacher behaviours? Explain any modification you suggest.

4. Suggest specific techniques a teacher could use that demonstrate each of the following proactive-intervention skills:

   a. changing the pace
   b. interest boosting
   c. redirecting behaviour
   d. encouraging appropriate behaviour
   e. providing cues

5. The hierarchy of remedial-intervention skills is presented as a decision-making model, not as an action model. Explain why.

6. Two effective remedial-intervention skills are signal interference and proximity interference. Suggest specific techniques that would demonstrate their use.

7. What types of student behaviours would cause you to decide to bypass initial remedial non-verbal intervention skills and enter the hierarchy at the proximity interference level?

8. Explain why you agree or disagree with the premise that classroom-management techniques should be used in a manner that provides students with the greatest opportunity to control their own behaviour.

9. Some teachers consider the use of remedial-intervention skills a waste of time. They say, "Why spend all this time and effort when you can just tell the student to stop messing around and get back to work." Explain why you agree or disagree with this point of view.

Weblinks

Saskatchewan's Department of Education—Caring and Respectful Schools Bullying Prevention
www.sasked.gov.sk.ca/branches/pol_eval/school_plus/crse/anti_bully.shtml
Examines how to deal with misbehaviours and bullying and also outlines how to build "caring and respectful schools."

CanTeach
www.canteach.ca/elementary/classman.html
A good classroom resource; it addresses basic issues around behavioural problems and classroom management.

Classroom Management Tips and Beginning of the Year Ideas
www.fvsd.ab.ca/stm/classroom_management_tips_and_be.htm
This site is applicable to primary teachers.

8

Managing Common Behaviour Problems: Verbal Interventions and Use of Logical Consequences

Focus on the Principles of Classroom Management

1. What should a teacher do if non-verbal intervention is ineffective?
2. What are the risks associated with verbal intervention?
3. If verbal intervention is ineffective, what does the teacher need to do?

Introduction

In this chapter, we present 12 verbal intervention techniques in a systematic, hierarchical format. As in the non-verbal intervention skills subhierarchy presented in Chapter 7, the verbal intervention subhierarchy begins with techniques designed to foster students' control over their own behaviour and proceeds to those that foster greater teacher management over student behaviour. Because, as we noted in Chapter 7, this is a decision-making hierarchy, the teacher must decide which particular verbal intervention technique to use with a student who is misbehaving after determining that non-verbal intervention is inappropriate or has not worked. The last section of the chapter discusses the final tier of the management hierarchy, and the use of logical consequences to manage student behaviour.

Case 8.1 is an example of a teacher tirade and its effect upon student behaviour. Although it is true that John has caused many problems for Mr. Hensen and the other students in his class, what does Mr. Hensen accomplish by yelling at him? Although he does get his long-suppressed feelings off his chest, Mr. Hensen does more harm than good. He disrupts any learning that is taking place. He forces the other students to concentrate on John's behaviour rather than on the content of the lesson, and he extends the off-task time by prolonging the reprimand. He reacts negatively and sarcastically to John, who already dislikes him and now is probably more determined than ever to "get Hensen's goat." Finally, by overreacting to a minor incident, Mr. Hensen has probably created some sympathy for John among the other students.

CASE 8.1 • *Blowing His Stack*

"John, you are one of the most obnoxious students I have ever had the misfortune to deal with. How many times have I asked you not to call out answers? If you want to answer a question, raise your hand. It shouldn't tax your tiny brain too much to remember that. I'm sick and tired of your mistaken idea that the rules of this classroom apply to everyone but you. It's because of people like you that we need rules in the first place. They apply especially to you. I will not allow you to deprive other students of the chance to answer questions. Anyway, half of your answers are totally off the wall. I'm in charge here, not you. If you don't like it, you can tell your troubles to the principal. Now sit there and be quiet."

When Mr. Hensen finished his rant and turned to walk to the front of the room, John discreetly "flipped him the bird" and laughed with his friends. John spent the rest of the period drawing pictures on the corner of his desk. The other students spent the remainder of the period in either uncomfortable silence or invisible laughter. Mr. Hensen spent the rest of the class trying to calm down and get his mind back on the lesson.

Questions to Consider

1. How and why did John effectively undermine Mr. Hensen's relationship with the rest of the class?
2. Assuming Mr. Hensen's level of frustration, what could he have said to John to ensure a more effective outcome?
3. Try to imagine the previous relationship between Mr. Hensen and John.
4. Describe John's classroom behaviour over the past year.
5. What can be done to avoid future clashes?

Although we know Mr. Hensen has overreacted, we also know that he is not alone. Many teachers find themselves in Mr. Hensen's position at one time or another. They allow many incidents of relatively minor misbehaviour to build up until one day they just can't take it any more, and they explode. In letting loose their pent-up feelings, these teachers make the situation worse rather than better. Teachers can avoid this by using the CALM intervention skills model (presented in detail in Chapter 6 and outlined in Chapters 1 and 7) to contend with classroom behavioural problems.

Teachers should proceed through the stages from the least to most invasive, as follows: (1) non-verbal intervention skills, (2) verbal intervention, and (3) use of logical consequences. When teachers use this hierarchy to guide their thinking about classroom behavioural problems, they are able to cope with misbehaviour swiftly and effectively. In this chapter, we present the second and third tiers of the hierarchy. **Verbal intervention** is one of the most powerful and versatile tools the teacher has for classroom management. When used effectively, verbal intervention makes classroom management relatively easy and less stressful. When used poorly and thoughtlessly, however, it may create new management problems, make existing problems worse, or turn temporary problems into chronic ones.

Classroom Verbal Intervention

There are, as explained in Chapter 7, four advantages to using non-verbal intervention whenever possible: (1) disruption to the learning process is less likely to occur; (2) hostile confrontation with the student is less apt to happen; (3) the student is provided the opportunity to correct his own behaviour before more teacher-centred, public interventions are used; and (4) a maximum number of remaining alternative interventions is preserved. However, non-verbal intervention is not always possible. When misbehaviour is potentially harmful to any student or potentially disruptive for a large number of students, it should be stopped quickly, and often verbal intervention is the quickest way to do so. Before discussing specific techniques, there are some guidelines teachers should keep in mind when using verbal intervention:

1. Whenever possible, use non-verbal interventions first.
2. Keep verbal intervention as private as possible. This minimizes the risk of having the student become defensive and hostile to avoid losing face in front of peers. Experts suggest that this is one of the most important general principles for disciplinary intervention (Brophy, 1988; Martin and Sugarman, 1993).
3. Make the verbal intervention as brief as possible. Your goal is to stop the misbehaviour *and* redirect the student to appropriate behaviour. Prolonging the verbal interaction extends the disruption of learning and enhances the likelihood of a hostile confrontation.
4. As Haim Ginott suggests, speak to the situation, not the person (1972). In other words, label the *behaviour* as bad or inappropriate, not the person. If, for example, a student interrupts a teacher, "Interrupting others is rude" is a more appropriate response than "You interrupted me. You are rude." Labelling the behaviour helps the student to see the distinction between himself and his behaviour, which in turn helps him to understand that it is possible for the teacher to like him but not his behaviour. If the student is labelled, he may feel compelled to defend himself. Furthermore, the student may accept the label as part of his self-concept and match the label with inappropriate behaviour in the future. This is exactly what Jimmy Dolan decides to do in Case 8.2.
5. As Ginott has urged, set limits on behaviour, not on feelings. For instance, a teacher should tell the student, "It's okay to be angry, but it's not okay to show your anger by hitting" or "It's okay to feel disappointed, but it's not okay to show that disappointment by ripping your test paper up in front of the class and throwing it in the basket." Students need to recognize, trust, and understand their feelings. When teachers and parents tell students not to be angry or disappointed, they are telling them to distrust and deny their genuine and often justified feelings. The appropriate message for teachers and parents to communicate and understand is that there are appropriate and inappropriate ways to express feelings.
6. Avoid sarcasm and other verbal behaviours that belittle or demean the student. Using verbal reprimands to belittle students lowers self-esteem and creates sympathy among classmates.

7. Begin by using a technique that fits the student and the problem and is as close as possible to the student-control end of the decision-making hierarchy.

8. If the first verbal intervention does not result in a return to appropriate behaviour, use a second technique that is closer to the teacher-control end of the hierarchy.

9. If more than one verbal intervention technique has been used unsuccessfully, it is time to move to the next step of the management hierarchy—the use of logical consequences.

Concentric Case Study Kaleidoscope

CASE 8.2 • *Jimmy, the Little Sneak*

The Story

Jimmy Dolan is in a grade 11 mathematics class at Princess Elizabeth High School. He is a fine student who rarely misbehaves and certainly has given none of his teachers any difficulty. His math teacher, Mr. Gamble, has had a long history of difficulty in dealing with classroom misbehaviour. The students are well aware of this reputation and each new class tends to come to Mr. Gamble with a predetermined sense of disrespect based on hearsay gleaned from previous students. This poor reputation makes Mr. Gamble's job very difficult. At times, he feels helpless to break the pattern of misbehaviour that always emerges in his classes.

On the second day of class, as his back is partially turned to the students, Mr. Gamble notices Jimmy talking to a neighbour. In a flash of determination, he turns and pounces on Jimmy, who was only asking Craig Rutler for an easier way to correct a mistake in his homework. "So, you are the one who has been causing all the noise," Mr. Gamble snaps. "You are a little sneak. Since the beginning of class, I thought you were one of the few students I could count on not to cause trouble in here. Well, I've got my eye on you. You'll not get away with any more sneaky behaviour in my class."

For a week or so, Jimmy goes back to his typical good behaviour, but every time something goes wrong or anyone misbehaves, he feels as though Mr. Gamble blames him. After a week or so of unjust blame, Jimmy decides that he may as well start causing some trouble—after all, he's going to get blamed for classrooms mishaps anyway.

In a very short time, Jimmy truly is a great troublemaker who causes all sorts of havoc. Because he is subversive and sneaky about it, he rarely gets caught in the act.

Mr. Gamble's Perspective

Mr. Gamble knows that he has a reputation for suffering through misbehaviour in his classes. He finds teaching very frustrating and difficult and, because of this, often goes home very discouraged. He is aware of students' disrespect for him and that he has been viewed as ineffectual over the years.

Mr. Gamble wonders how he can break the cycle, stop struggling with his students for their attention, and establish himself as a strict disciplinarian.

This year, he has determined to change his behaviour and nip every off-task behaviour in the bud right from the start. He says to himself, "I will have a good class this time and I will do what I have to do to maintain very strict discipline." He determines to watch for every slight deviation from perfect behaviour and make an example of the perpetrator.

In the second class of the semester, Mr. Gamble partially turns his back on the class and then immediately notices Jimmy Dolan talking to his friend. "Aha," he thinks, "now is my opportunity to set this class straight about what I expect from students." He challenges Jimmy very harshly, feeling as though he is addressing all the past disrespectful behaviour that he has endured. It actually feels good to vent.

Jimmy seems surprised, but he does little to rebut the attack by his teacher. Mr. Gamble feels vindicated and believes that he has sent an important message to the class. "Things will be different this year," he thinks.

Over the next couple of weeks, though, Mr. Gamble notices very little change in the class. He constantly tries to recapture the moment of success he felt with Jimmy and blames him for much of the noise in the classroom. Jimmy's behaviour appears to be deteriorating rather than improving, and Mr. Gamble has more and more difficulty actually catching Jimmy in acts of misbehaviour. He begins to dislike Jimmy intensely.

The Students' Perspectives

Jimmy: Jimmy likes school and seldom causes any trouble in his classes. He is a good student who generally listens carefully in class and does his classwork and homework with conscientious diligence. He enters Mr. Gamble's class knowing that this teacher has a reputation for having poor classroom-management skills. This fact does not hold much significance for Jimmy, as it is not his pattern to take advantage of such situations. He does expect some of his friends and fellow classmates to make things difficult for Mr. Gamble, though.

Early in the first week of class, Jimmy is doing an assignment and notices that the homework he has done is not correct. He wonders if he has used the wrong page in his text or if he has actually done the questions incorrectly. To solve this dilemma, he asks his friend Craig Rutler what page the homework is on. Before Craig has an opportunity to answer, Mr. Gamble turns around and starts to attack him verbally. Jimmy is stunned and embarrassed at the same time. He feels unnerved by the threat Mr. Gamble utters to him. He leaves class feeling annoyed, although he notices that his friends are angrily talking about the teacher's unfair behaviour.

The next few classes are very difficult for Jimmy and he becomes increasingly upset at the way he is being made the scapegoat by his teacher. Soon, Jimmy actively begins to dislike and disrespect Mr. Gamble. He feels as though he's getting blamed for all excessive noise in the classroom. "I wonder if I should go and talk to the teacher alone," he thinks. He rejects this idea, as he genuinely feels that the teacher would not be approachable on the subject.

Finally, Jimmy feels angry when he enters the class and becomes determined to get back at Mr. Gamble for his unfairness by causing noise and encouraging other students to misbehave. He does so subtly and successfully. He thinks, "Now you can blame me if you want because I really am doing some things to get under your skin. I don't care because you have been unfair to me and now I will be unfair to you." Jimmy talks to his friends and to other students outside of class about his disrespect for Mr. Gamble and how easy it is to disrupt his classes. He begins to take satisfaction in causing trouble. He doesn't learn much math in the class and soon stops paying attention and neglects his homework.

Craig: Craig has heard about Mr. Gamble's lack of classroom-management skills and he expects this class will be no different. Early in the first week, he answers a question that Jimmy asks about the homework page. He is surprised that Mr. Gamble makes such a big deal about Jimmy's supposed misbehaviour. He feels sorry for the way Mr. Gamble speaks to Jimmy and thinks, "This teacher is really unfair to Jimmy. He did nothing wrong and Gamble is not giving him a chance to explain."

As the days go by, Craig notices that Jimmy starts to get blamed for everything that goes wrong. He talks to Jimmy about the unfairness of the accusations and commiserates with him about the way Mr. Gamble is "picking on" him. In this conversation, Jimmy confides that he is getting really angry and Craig suggests, "Well, you might as well act any way you like because it is clear that you're going to get into trouble whether you do something or not." Jimmy agrees.

Craig watches with some amusement as the weeks pass and Jimmy starts misbehaving for real and encouraging others to do so as well. Craig feels free to talk with his neighbours and ignore the teacher during class and he gets up and walks around the room whenever he feels like it. He reasons that Jimmy will get blamed for everything anyway.

Craig sympathizes with Jimmy and actually feels that his friend is a bit of a hero.

Questions to Consider

1. What do you believe is the overall cause of Mr. Gamble's reputation as a poor manager of his classroom?

2. Why do think Mr. Gamble targeted Jimmy?

3. What will Jimmy's fellow classmates responses be to his new-found "troublemaker" identity?

4. What could Mr. Gamble do to help restore Jimmy as a good student?

5. How can Mr. Gamble's ineffective classroom-management skills be remedied? (Consider the roles of administration, department head, parents, and other colleagues.)

6. How would implementing the CALM model have helped the situation?

Equally as important as these guidelines on how to use verbal interventions is the need for the teacher to be aware of commonly used ineffective verbal interventions. Many of these are instantaneous teacher reactions to disruptive students rather than systematic, pre-planned, professional decisions enhanced by the use and understanding of the hierarchy of remedial-intervention skills. While there are many ineffective verbal interventions, they all share the common characteristics of not speaking directly to the disruptive behaviour and not directing the student toward the appropriate behaviour (Sugai and Horner, 1999; Valentine, 1987). Some ineffective verbal interventions encourage inappropriate behaviour. They may increase the possibility of further confrontation when the student attempts to "save face." With the guidelines in mind and a cognizance of ineffective verbal reactions, let's turn our attention to the hierarchy of effective verbal intervention. Remember that this is a hierarchy of decision-making that begins with verbal interventions that foster student control over their own behaviour and gradually progresses to interventions that call for greater teacher management over student behaviour. The teacher uses the hierarchy as a range of options to consider, not as a series of techniques to be tried in rapid succession. The teacher should begin the intervention at the point on the hierarchy that is likely to correct the misbehaviour and still allow the student as much control and responsibility as possible. It is entirely appropriate to begin with a teacher-centred technique if the teacher believes that it is important to stop the misbehaviour quickly and only a teacher-centred intervention will do so. It is also important to remember that not all of these interventions are appropriate for all types of misbehaviour or for all students. Lasley suggests that teacher-centred interventions are more appropriate for younger, developmentally immature children, and student-centred interventions are more appropriate for older, developmentally mature learners (1989). Therefore, the effective use of this verbal intervention hierarchy requires the teacher to decide which particular intervention techniques are appropriate for both the students and the particular types of misbehaviour that are occurring.

As Figure 8.1 indicates, the verbal intervention hierarchy has been broken into three major categories: *hints*, *questions*, and *requests/demands*. Hints are indirect means of letting the student know that his behaviour is inappropriate. They do not directly address the behaviour itself. Thus, of all the verbal interventions, hints provide the greatest student control over behaviour and are the least likely to result in further disruption or confrontation. Specific techniques that are classified as hints include adjacent or peer reinforcement, calling on students by saying their names, and humour.

The teacher uses questions to ask the student if he is aware of how he is behaving and how that behaviour is affecting other people. The questions are more direct than hints but provide greater student control; and there is less likelihood of confrontation when the teacher questions rather than demands. However, almost any request or demand can be reworded as a question. For example, "Pencils are not for drumming" can be rephrased as "What are pencils for?"

FIGURE 8.1 *Hierarchy of Classroom Verbal Intervention Techniques*

Hints   **(Student-Centred)**
    Adjacent (peer) reinforcement   (less confrontation)
    Calling on student by name   (less disruption)
    Humour

Questions
    Questioning awareness of effect

Requests/Demands
    "I message"
    Direct appeal
    Positive phrasing
    "Are not for"
    Reminder of rules
    Glasser's triplets   (more disruption)
    Explicit redirection   (more confrontation)
    Canter's "broken record"   **(Teacher-Centred)**

The third level of verbal intervention, requests/demands, comprises teacher statements making clear that the teacher wants an inappropriate behaviour stopped. Requests and demands exert greater teacher management over student behaviour and have the potential to be disruptive and confrontational. Despite their disadvantages, it is sometimes necessary for teachers to use these interventions when lower-level interventions have proved unsuccessful. The potential for confrontation can be minimized if the demands are delivered calmly, privately, and assertively rather than aggressively.

No matter which interventions a teacher uses, he must be aware of the limitations and of the implicit message that each intervention conveys about managing student behaviour.

Using Adjacent (Peer) Reinforcement

Adjacent (peer) reinforcement is based on the learning principle that reinforced behaviour is more likely to be repeated. While this usually means reinforcing an individual student's personal behaviour, Albert Bandura has demonstrated through his work on social learning theory that other students are likely to imitate an appropriate behaviour when their peers have been praised for that behaviour (1977). The use of peer reinforcement as a verbal intervention technique focuses class attention on appropriate behaviour rather than on inappropriate behaviour. This intervention technique has been placed first in the hierarchy because it gives the students a chance to control their own behaviour without any intervention on the part of the teacher that calls attention to the students or their behaviour. As you'll remember from Chapter 7, adjacent reinforcement not only can stop misbehaviour but also can prevent other students from misbehaving.

To use this technique effectively, a teacher who notes a disruptive behaviour finds another student who is behaving appropriately and commends that student publicly for the appropriate behaviour. Recall from Case 8.1 Mr. Hensen's anger at John. Mr. Hensen could have handled the problem by saying, "Fred and Bob, I really appreciate that you raise your hands to answer questions" or "I am really glad that most of us remember the rule that we must raise our hands before speaking."

This particular verbal intervention technique is more useful at the elementary level than at the secondary level. Younger students are usually more interested in pleasing the teacher than older students and often vie for the teacher's attention. Thus, public praise by the teacher is a powerful reinforcer of appropriate behaviour. At the secondary level, peer approval is more highly valued than teacher approval; thus, public praise by the teacher is not a powerful reinforcer and indeed may not be a reinforcer at all. For these reasons, it is best to only sparingly use public praise of individuals. Public reinforcement of the group as a whole, however, may be an appropriate intervention at the secondary level.

Calling on the Student by Name

Using this technique, the teacher redirects the student to appropriate behaviour by calling on the student to answer a question or by inserting the student's name in an example or in the middle of a lecture if asking a question is not appropriate. Hearing his name is a good reminder to a student that his attention should be focused on the lesson. This technique may be used to redirect students who are off task but are not disrupting the learning of others (see Chapter 7), as well as students who are overtly disrupting the learning process.

Calling on a student who is misbehaving is a subtle yet effective technique for recapturing the student's attention without interrupting the flow of the lesson or risking confrontation with the student. There are two possible formats for calling on disruptive students. Some teachers state the student's name first and then ask a question; others ask the question and then call on the student. The latter technique, however, invariably results in the student being unable to answer the question because he most likely did not hear it.

Often, the teacher who uses this technique follows the period of embarrassed silence with a comment on why the student can't answer and why it is important to pay attention. Although this procedure may satisfy the teacher's need to say, "I gotcha," it is preferable to call on the student first and then ask the question. Using the name first achieves the goal of redirecting the student's attention without embarrassing him.

In Case 8.1, calling on John to answer or saying John's name are not appropriate techniques for Mr. Hensen to use in dealing with the situation because they encourage John's calling out by giving him recognition. Although inappropriate in that particular case, calling on the student by name is appropriate in a wide range of situations with learners of all ages.

Using Humour

Humour that is directed at the teacher or at the situation rather than at the student can defuse tension in the classroom and redirect students to appropriate behaviour. The use of humour tends to depersonalize situations and can help to establish positive relationships with students (Novak and Purkey, 2001).

If Mr. Hensen wished to use humour to handle John's calling out, he might say something like this: "I must be hallucinating or something. I'd swear I heard somebody say something if I didn't know for sure that I haven't called on anyone yet." In using this technique, teachers need to be very careful not to turn humour into sarcasm. There is a fine line between humour and sarcasm. Used as a verbal intervention, humour is directed at or makes fun of the teacher or the situation, whereas sarcasm is directed at or makes fun of the student. It is important to keep this distinction in mind to ensure that what is intended as humour does not turn into sarcasm.

Questioning Awareness of Effect

Sometimes students who disrupt learning are genuinely not aware of the effect their behaviour has on other people. Our research indicates that even students who have chronic behavioural problems learn to control their behaviour when they are forced to acknowledge both its positive and negative effects (Levin, Nolan, and Hoffman, 1985). Given this, making disruptive students aware of how their behaviour affects other people can be a powerful technique for getting them to control their own behaviour. Usually, a teacher can make a student aware of the impact of his behaviour by asking a rhetorical question, which requires no response from the disruptive student. The teacher who wants to handle Mr. Hensen's problem by questioning the student's awareness of his behaviour's effect might say something like this: "John, are you aware that your calling out answers without raising your hand robs other students of the chance to answer the question?" As soon as the question was asked, the teacher would continue with the lesson without giving John an opportunity to respond.

The informal question not only makes the student aware of the impact of his behaviour but also communicates to other students the teacher's desire to protect their right to learn and may build peer support for appropriate behaviour. In using this intervention, however, especially with students at the junior-high level or above, the teacher must be prepared for the possibility that the student will respond to the question. If the student responds and does so in a negative way, the teacher may choose to ignore the answer, thereby sending the message that he will not use class time to discuss the issue; or the teacher may respond, "John, your behaviour is having a negative impact on other people, and so I will not permit you to continue calling out answers." This option sends the message that the teacher is in charge of the classroom and will not tolerate the misbehaviour. In dealing with a possible negative response from the student, it is important to remember that the teacher's goal is to stop the misbehaviour and redirect the student to appropriate behaviour as quickly as possible. Prolonged confrontations frustrate that goal.

Sending an "I Message"

Thomas Gordon, the author of *Teaching Children Self-Discipline at Home and in School* (1989), has developed a useful technique for dealing with misbehaviour verbally. He terms the intervention an *I message*. The I message is a three-part message that is intended to help the disruptive student recognize the negative impact of his behaviour on the teacher. The underlying assumption of the technique is the same as that for the questioning awareness of effect that we discussed in the previous section: once a student recognizes the negative impact of his behaviour on others, he will be motivated to stop the misbehaviour. The three parts of an I message are (1) a simple description of the disruptive behaviour, (2) a description of its tangible effect on the teacher and/or other students, and (3) a description of the teacher's feelings about the effects of the misbehaviour. Using I messages models for students the important behaviour of taking responsibility for and owning one's behaviour and feelings. There is one important caveat, however, in the use of this technique. Just as the teacher expects students to respect the feelings that are expressed in an I message, the teacher must respect feelings expressed by students.

To use an I message to stop John from calling out, Mr. Hensen might say, "John, when you call out answers without raising your hand (part 1), I can't call on any other student to answer the question (part 2). This disturbs me because I would like to give everyone a chance to answer questions (part 3)." Teachers who enjoy a positive relationship with students, which gives them referent power (see Chapter 4), are usually successful in using I messages. When students genuinely like the teacher, they are motivated to stop behaviour that has a negative impact on the teacher. On the other hand, if the teacher has a poor relationship with students, he should avoid the use of I messages. Allowing students who dislike you to know that a particular behaviour is annoying or disturbing may result in an increase in that particular behaviour.

Using Direct Appeal

Another technique that is useful for instances when a teacher enjoys a referent or expert power base is **direct appeal**. Direct appeal means courteously requesting that a student stop the disruptive behaviour. For example, Mr. Hensen could say, "John, please stop calling out answers so that everyone will have a chance to answer." The direct appeal is not made in any sort of pleading or begging way.

Teachers must not use direct appeal in a classroom in which students seem to doubt the teacher's ability to be in charge. In this situation, the appeal may be perceived as a plea rather than as a straightforward request.

Using Positive Phrasing

Many times, parents and teachers fall into the trap of emphasizing the negative outcomes of misbehaviour more than the positive outcomes of appropriate behaviour. We tell children and students far more frequently what will happen if they don't finish their homework than we tell them the good things that will occur if they do finish. Of course, it is often easier to identify the short-range negative outcomes of misbehaviour than it is to predict the short- and long-range positive impact of appropriate behaviour. Still, when the positive outcomes of appropriate behaviour are easily identifiable, simply stating what the positive outcomes are can redirect students from disruptive to proper behaviour. Shrigley has called this technique **positive phrasing** (1985). It usually takes a form such as this: "As soon as you do X (behave appropriately), we can do Y (a positive outcome)."

In using positive phrasing to correct John's calling out, Mr. Hensen might say, "John, you will be called on as soon as you raise your hand." The long-term advantage of using positive phrasing whenever possible is that students begin to believe that appropriate behaviour leads to positive outcomes. As a result, they are more likely to develop internalized control over their behaviour.

Using "Are Not For"

Of all the verbal interventions discussed in this chapter, the phrase "are not for" (Shrigley, 1985) is the most limited in use. It is implemented primarily when elementary or preschool children misuse property or materials. For example, if a student is drumming on a desk with a pencil, the teacher may say, "Pencils *are not for* drumming on desks; pencils *are for* writing." Although it is usually effective in redirecting behaviour positively at the elementary or preschool level, most secondary students perceive this intervention as insulting. Using "are not for" is not an appropriate technique for Mr. Hensen since John is a secondary student and is not misusing property or material.

Reminding Students of the Rules

When a teacher has established clear guidelines or rules early in the year (see Chapter 6) and students have committed to them, merely reminding disruptive students of the rules may curb misbehaviour. Notice that at this point in the hierarchy, the teacher is no longer relying on the students' ability to control their own behaviour but instead is using external rules to manage behaviour.

In using this technique, Mr. Hensen might say, "John, the classroom rules state that students must raise their hands before speaking" or "John, calling out answers without raising your hand is against our classroom rules." The technique is particularly effective for elementary and junior-high students. Although it may be used in senior high, many students at this level resent the feeling that they are being governed by too many rules. It is important to note that when a reminder of the rules does not redirect the misbehaviour, applying consequences must follow. If this does not occur, the effectiveness of rule reminders will be diminished because students will not see the link between breaking classroom rules and negative consequences.

Asking Glasser's Triplets

In his system for establishing suitable student behaviour, which is outlined in *Schools Without Failure* (1969), William Glasser proposed that teachers direct students to appropriate behaviour through the use of three questions: (1) What are you doing? (2) Is it against the rules? (3) What should you be doing? The use of these questions, which are known as Glasser's triplets, obviously requires a classroom in which the rules have been firmly established in students' minds. To stop John from calling out answers, Mr. Hensen would simply ask Glasser's triplets. The expectation underlying Glasser's triplets is that the student will answer the questions honestly and will then return to the appropriate behaviour. Unfortunately, not all students answer the triplets honestly, and therein lies the intervention's inherent weakness. Asking open-ended questions may result in student responses that are dishonest, improper, or unexpected.

If a student chooses to answer the questions dishonestly or not to reply at all, the teacher responds by saying (in John's case), "No, John, you were calling out answers. That is against our classroom rules. You must raise your hand to answer questions." To minimize the likelihood of an extended, negative confrontation ensuing from the use of Glasser's triplets, it is suggested that teachers use three statements instead of questions: "John, you are calling out. It is against the rules. You should raise your hand if you want to answer."

Using Explicit Redirection

Explicit redirection consists of an order to stop the misbehaviour *and* return to acceptable behaviour. The redirection is a teacher command and leaves no room for student rebuttal. If Mr. Hensen used explicit redirection with John, he might say, "John, stop calling out answers and raise your hand if you want to answer a question." Notice the contrast between this technique and those discussed in the earlier stages of the hierarchy in terms of the amount of responsibility the teacher assumes for managing student behaviour.

The advantages of this technique are its simplicity, clarity, and closed format, which does not allow for student rebuttal. Its disadvantage is that the teacher publicly confronts the student, who either behaves or defies the teacher in front of peers. Obviously, if the student chooses to defy the teacher's command, the teacher must be prepared to proceed to the next step in the hierarchy and enforce the command with appropriate consequences.

Canter and Canter's Broken Record Strategy

Canter and Canter have developed a strategy for clearly communicating to students that the teacher will not engage in verbal bantering and intends to make sure that the student resumes appropriate behaviour (1992). The Canters have labelled their strategy **broken record** because the teacher's constant nagging sounds like a broken record. The teacher begins by giving the student an explicit redirection statement. If the student doesn't comply or if the student tries to defend or explain his behaviour, the teacher repeats the redirection. The teacher may repeat it two or three times if the student continues to argue or fails to comply. If the student tries to excuse or defend his behaviour, some teachers add the phrase, "that's not the point" at the beginning of the first and second repetitions. The following is an example of this technique as applied by Mr. Hensen:

> **HENSEN:** "John, stop calling out answers and raise your hand if you want to answer questions."
>
> **JOHN:** "But I really do know the answer."
>
> **HENSEN:** "That's not the point. Stop calling out answers and raise your hand if you want to answer questions."
>
> **JOHN:** "You let Mabel call out answers yesterday."
>
> **HENSEN:** "That's not the point. Stop calling out answers and raise your hand if you want to answer questions."
>
> Return to the lesson.

We have found the broken record technique to be very good for avoiding verbal battles with students. If, however, the statement has been repeated three times without any result, it is probably time to move to a stronger measure, such as logical consequences.

Comply or Face the Logical Consequences: "You Have a Choice"

Although non-verbal and verbal interventions often stop misbehaviour, sometimes the misbehaviour remains unchecked. When this occurs, the teacher needs to use more overt techniques. The final tier on the decision-making hierarchy is the use of logical consequences to manage student behaviour.

As the reader will recall from Chapter 6, there are three types of consequences: *natural*, *logical*, and *contrived* (Dreikurs, Grundwald, and Pepper, 1998). Natural consequences result directly from student misbehaviour without any intervention by the teacher, although the teacher may point out the link between the behaviour and the consequence. Using natural consequences is a management strategy because the teacher decides to let the natural consequences occur. That is, the teacher decides not to take any action to stop the consequence. Unlike natural consequences, logical consequences require teacher intervention and are related as closely as possible to the behaviour; for example, a student who comes to class five minutes late is required to remain five minutes after school to make up the work. Contrived consequences are imposed on the student by the teacher and are either unrelated to student behaviour or involve a penalty beyond that is fitting for the misbehaviour. Requiring a student who writes on his desk to write 1000 times, "I will not write on my desk" or sentencing a student who comes once to class five minutes late to two weeks of detention are contrived consequences. Since contrived consequences fail to help students see the connection between a behaviour and its consequence and place the teacher in the role of punisher, we do not advocate their use. For this reason, contrived consequences are not part of our decision-making hierarchy. When non-verbal and verbal interventions have not led to appropriate behaviour, the teacher must take control of the situation and use logical consequences to manage student behaviour. To do so, the teacher applies logical consequences calmly and thoughtfully in a forceful but not punitive manner.

Brophy suggests that the teacher who uses logical consequences should emphasize the student changing his behaviour rather than the teacher seeking retribution (1988). When this is done, the teacher makes sure that the student understands that the misbehaviour must stop immediately or negative consequences will result. Often, it is effective to give the student a choice of either complying with the request or facing the consequence. This technique is called "you have a choice." For example, if John continued to call out answers after Mr. Hensen had tried several non-verbal and verbal interventions, Mr. Hensen would say, "John, you have a choice. Stop calling out answers immediately and begin raising your hand to answer or move your seat to the back of the room and you and I will have a private discussion later. You decide." Phrasing the intervention in this way helps the student to realize that he is responsible for the positive as well as the negative consequences of his behaviour and that the choice is his. It also places the teacher in a neutral rather than punitive role. Remember, students do, in fact, choose how to behave. Teachers can't control student behaviour; they can only influence it.

Once the teacher moves to this final level of the hierarchy, the dialogue is over. Either the student returns to appropriate behaviour or the teacher takes action. The manner in which the consequences are delivered is important and provides the teacher with another opportunity to reinforce the idea that the student is in control of his behaviour, that the choice to behave or misbehave is his to make, and that his choice has consequences. In Mr. Hensen's case, if John chose to continue to call out, Mr. Hensen would say, "John, you have chosen to move to the back of the room; please move." There are no excuses, no postponements. The teacher has stated his intentions clearly. Because consistency is crucial, it is imperative that the teacher not move to this final tier on the hierarchy unless he is ready to enforce the consequences that have been specified.

The exact consequence varies with the student misbehaviour. However, one principle is always involved in the formulation of consequences: it should be as directly related to the offence as possible. Consistent application of this principle helps students to recognize that their behaviour has consequences and helps them learn to control their own behaviour in the future by predicting its consequences beforehand.

Because it can be difficult to come up with directly related logical consequences on the spur of the moment (Canter and Canter, 1992), teachers should consider logical consequences for common types of misbehaviour before the misbehaviours occur. Developing one or two logical consequences for each of the classroom rules that we discussed in Chapter 6 is a good way to begin. When misbehaviour occurs for which there is no pre-planned logical consequence, a teacher should ask the following questions to help formulate a consequence directly related to the misbehaviour:

1. What would be the logical result if this misbehaviour went unchecked?
2. What are the direct effects of this behaviour on the teacher, other students, and the misbehaving student?
3. What can be done to minimize these effects?

The answers to these three questions usually will help a teacher to identify a logical consequence. In Case 8.3, note how Ms. Ramonda uses the first of the three questions to formulate the logical consequences for Doug's behaviour.

It must be pointed out that Ms. Ramonda would have to speak to the school principal and obtain approval before allowing Doug to do nothing. Still, while most classroom behavioural problems do not warrant the drastic measures that Ms. Ramonda takes, the case does illustrate a successful use of logical consequences to deal with a difficult classroom situation. Ms. Ramonda's application of logical consequences in a firm but neutral manner helps to redirect Doug to more appropriate behaviour and aids him in recognizing the direct connection between his behaviour and its consequences.

When "You Have a Choice" Doesn't Work

At this point, almost all readers are probably thinking, what if the approach of "you have a choice" doesn't work? Some teachers believe that providing a choice is "not working" when a student chooses the negative consequences rather than choosing to change his behaviour. Remember, teachers cannot force students to behave appropriately, but they

CASE 8.3 • *"I Don't Want to Do Nothin'"*

Doug is a grade 7, learning-disabled student who has serious reading difficulties and poses behavioural problems for many teachers. At the beginning of the year, he is assigned to Ms. Ramonda's remedial reading class. Since Doug hates reading, he is determined to get out of the class and causes all sorts of problems for Ms. Ramonda and the other students. Ms. Ramonda's first reaction is to have Doug removed from her class to protect the other students; however, after talking to Doug's counsellor and his resource room teacher, she comes to believe that it is important for Doug not to get his way and that he desperately needs to develop the reading skills that she can teach him.

Ms. Ramonda decides to try to use Doug's personal interests to motivate him. The next day, she asks, "Doug, what would you like to do?" Doug answers, "Nothin', I don't want to do nothin' in here. Just leave me alone." For the next two days Doug sits in the back of the room and doodles as Ms. Ramonda tries to determine what the next step should be. Finally, Ms. Ramonda asks herself what the logical result is of doing nothing. She decides that the logical result is boredom and resolves to use that to motivate Doug.

On the following day, she announces to Doug that he will get his wish. From then on, he can do nothing as long as he wants to. She explains that he will no longer need books or papers or pencils since books are for reading, and papers and pencils are for writing, and doing nothing means doing none of those things. He will not be allowed to talk to her or to his friends, she explains, since that too would be doing something and he wants to do nothing. "From now on, Doug, you will be allowed to sit in the back corner of the room and do nothing, just as you wish."

For one full week, Doug sits in the back corner and does nothing. Finally, he asks Ms. Ramonda if he can do something. She replies that he can do some reading but nothing else. Doug agrees to try some reading. That breaks the ice. Ms. Ramonda carefully selects some low-difficulty, high-interest material for Doug and gradually pulls him into the regular classroom situation.

Questions to Consider

1. What does Ms. Ramonda's decision to keep Doug in her class tell you about her teaching beliefs?
2. How did Ms. Ramonda approach Doug's problem?
3. Why was her approach relatively successful?

can deliver the logical consequences when students choose them. Beyond this point, teachers can only hope that if they are consistent and follow the guidelines for verbal interventions, students will internalize the relationship between behaviour and its consequences and choose to behave appropriately the next time.

Teachers can increase the likelihood of a student choosing appropriate behaviour by responding assertively when using "you have a choice." Assertiveness is communicated to others by the congruent use of certain verbal and non-verbal behaviours. Do not confuse assertiveness with aggressiveness, which leads to unwanted student outcomes. An aggressive response is one in which a teacher communicates what is expected but in a manner that abuses the rights and feelings of the student. When this happens, students perceive the stated consequences as threats. An aggressive delivery of "you have a choice" would probably be viewed by students as "fighting words" and escalate both hostility and confrontation, leading to further disruptive behaviours. When a teacher uses an assertive response style, the teacher clearly communicates what is expected in a manner that respects a student's rights and feelings. An assertive style tells the student that the teacher is prepared to back up the request for behavioural change with appropriately stated consequences, but is not threatening. We like to describe assertiveness as a style that communicates to the student a promise of action if appropriate behaviour is not forthcoming. Table 8.1 compares the verbal and non-verbal behaviours that differentiate assertive response styles from aggressive ones. Governments, school boards, and other agencies continue to study and promote student rights and responsibilities. Several programs that have received funding from the Human Rights Program at the Department of Canadian Heritage to promote children's rights can be examined at www.pch.gc.ca/progs/pdp-hrp/canada/children_rights_e.cfm. Other examples of students' rights and codes of conduct are available from websites such as the Vancouver School Board (www.vsb.bc.ca/schools/Elementaryschools/03939056/Profile/schoolcodeofconduct.htm) and the Simcoe County District School Board (www.scdsb.on.ca/parents/code_of_conduct.cfm?print=true). The Human Rights Research and Education Centre (www.uottawa.ca/hrrec/links/constitutionalcan_e.html) also provides good resources for further examination of students' rights and responsibilities.

TABLE 8.1 *Comparison of Assertive and Aggressive Response Styles*

	Assertive	Aggressive
Audience	Private only to student	Public to entire class
How student is addressed	Student's name	"You, hey you"
Voice	Firm, neutral, soft, slow	Tense, loud, fast
Eyes	Eye contact only	Narrowed, frowning eyes
Stance	Close to student without violating personal space	Hands on hips, violating personal space
Hands	Quietly approach student or student's desk	Sharp, abrupt gestures

Of course, there will always be some students who do not choose to behave. When the teacher assertively delivers the consequence, these students argue or openly refuse to accept and comply with the consequence. If this happens, the teacher must not be sidetracked by the student and enter into a public power struggle with the student. Instead, the teacher should integrate the use of Canter and Canter's broken record (1992) and a final "you have a choice" in a calm, firm, assertive manner. The following example between Mr. Hensen and John illustrates the integration of these verbal interventions:

1. Mr. Hensen gives John a choice of raising his hand or moving to the back of the room. John calls out again. Mr. Hensen says, "John, you called out; therefore, you have decided to move to the back of the class. Please move."
2. John begins to argue. At this point Mr. Hensen uses the broken record and, if necessary, a final "you have a choice."

JOHN: "You know Tom calls out all the time and you never do anything to him."

HENSEN: "That's not the point. Please move to the back of the room."

JOHN: "I get the right answers."

HENSEN: "That's not the point. Please move to the back of the room."

JOHN: "This is really unfair."

HENSEN: "That's not the point. Move to the back of the room."

JOHN: "I'm not moving and don't try to make me."

HENSEN: "John, you have a choice. Move to the back of the room now, or I will be in touch with your parents. You decide."

As this interaction illustrates, after two or three broken records the teacher issues a final "you have a choice" and then disengages from the student. Some teachers will have the student removed from the classroom by an administrator as the consequence for the final "you have a choice." Whatever the consequence, the teacher must be willing and able to follow through. Thus, teachers must be sure the consequence can be carried out. Since interaction between a student and teacher at this level is likely to be of great interest to the other students in the class, it is imperative for the teacher to remain calm, firm, and assertive. This is a time for the teacher to show the rest of the class that he is in control of his behaviour and that he means what he says. A teacher who remains in control, even if the student refuses to comply, will garner more respect from onlooking students than the teacher who tries to humiliate, is harsh, or lacks control.

Summary

In this chapter, we've presented the final two tiers of the hierarchy introduced in Chapter 7: verbal intervention and the use of logical consequences. We developed the following guidelines for verbal intervention: (1) use verbal intervention when non-verbal is inappropriate or ineffective; (2) keep verbal intervention private if possible; (3) make it as brief as possible; (4) speak to the situation, not the person; (5) set limits on behaviour, not feelings; (6) avoid sarcasm; (7) begin with a verbal intervention close to the student-centred end of the hierarchy; (8) if necessary, move to a second verbal intervention technique closer to the teacher-centred end of the hierarchy; and (9) if two verbal interventions have been used unsuccessfully, move to the application of consequences.

In addition to the nine guidelines, three types of ineffective verbal communication patterns were reviewed: (1) encouraging inappropriate behaviour, (2) focusing on irrelevant behaviours, and (3) abstract, meaningless directions and predictions.

Twelve specific intervention techniques were presented in a hierarchical format, ranging from techniques that foster greater student control over behaviour to those that bring about greater teacher management over student behaviour. The verbal interventions were divided into three categories: hints, questions, and requests/demands. Hints include the following: (1) adjacent or peer reinforcement, (2) calling on the student or name dropping, and (3) humour. The sole questioning intervention that was presented was (4) questioning awareness of effect. We noted that many interventions could be used in a question format. The interventions classified as requests/demands include (5) I messages, (6) direct appeal, (7) positive phrasing, (8) "are not for," (9) reminder of rules, (10) Glasser's triplets, (11) explicit redirection, and (12) Canter and Canter's broken record.

In the last section of the chapter, we discussed the final tier of the hierarchy: the use of logical consequences. We suggested that this intervention should be phrased in terms of student choice and the consequences should be related as directly as possible to the misbehaviour. Three questions were proposed to help teachers formulate logical consequences for those misbehaviours for which the teacher has not developed a consequence hierarchy. The use of an assertive response style and the integration of "you have a choice" with Canter and Canter's broken record were presented as a means to increase the likelihood that a student chooses to behave appropriately.

When taken together with the information presented in Chapter 7, the ideas presented in this chapter constitute a complete hierarchy that teachers can use to guide their thinking and decision-making concerning interventions to cope with classroom misbehaviour. The hierarchy is presented in its complete format in Figure 8.2.

Key Terms

adjacent (peer) reinforcement: based on the learning principle that reinforced behaviour is more likely to be repeated. The use of peer reinforcement as a verbal intervention technique focuses class attention on appropriate behaviour rather than on inappropriate behaviour.

broken record: the use of repetition by a teacher to reinforce a direction to a student.

direct appeal: means courteously requesting that a student stop the disruptive behaviour.

explicit redirection: consists of an order to stop the misbehaviour *and* to return to acceptable behaviour.

positive phrasing: this is done in instances where the teacher states what the potential positive outcomes are for a student who exhibits appropriate behaviour in the classroom; the teacher, thus, aims to redirect a student from disruptive to proper behaviour.

verbal intervention: a systematic hierarchy of spoken techniques that first is designed to foster students' control over their own behaviour and moves to greater teacher management over student behaviour.

FIGURE 8.2 *Hierarchy for Management Intervention*

Level 1: Non-verbal intervention   **(Student-Centred)**
    Planned ignoring   (less confrontation)
    Signal interference   (less disruption)
    Proximity interference

Level 2: Verbal intervention
Hints
    Adjacent (peer) reinforcement
    Calling on student
    Humour
Questions
    Questioning awareness of effect
Requests/Demands
    "I messages"
    Direct appeal
    Positive phrasing
    "Are not for"
    Reminder of rules
    Glasser's triplets
    Explicit redirection
    Canter's "broken record"   (more disruption)
                                                     (more confrontation)

Level 3: Use of logical consequences   **(Teacher-Centred)**
    "You have a choice"

Exercises

1. Which types of student misbehaviour might lead a teacher to use verbal intervention without first trying non-verbal techniques? Justify your answer.

2. Use each of the verbal intervention techniques presented in this chapter to help redirect the student to appropriate behaviour in the following situations:

    a. The student won't get started on a seat-work assignment.
    b. The student pushes his way to the front of the line.
    c. The student talks to a friend sitting on the other side of the room.
    d. The student lies about a forgotten homework assignment.

3. Under what circumstances, if any, would it be appropriate for a teacher to move directly to the third tier of the hierarchy, use of logical consequences? Justify your answer.

4. Develop logical consequences for each of the following misbehaviours:

    a. The student interrupts while the teacher is talking to a small group of students.
    b. The student steals money from another student's desk.
    c. The student copies a homework assignment from someone else.
    d. The student squirts a water pistol during class.
    e. The student throws spitballs at the blackboard.

    f. The student physically intimidates other students.

    g. Graffiti is found on the restroom wall.

5. List some common teacher verbal interventions that fall under the three types of ineffective verbal communication patterns.

6. Role-play the assertive delivery of "you have a choice."

7. When a teacher uses an aggressive response style, what feelings and behaviours are commonly elicited from the student? What effect does an aggressive response style have on overall teacher effectiveness in both the academic and management domains?

8. When a teacher uses an assertive response style, what feelings and behaviours are commonly elicited from the student? What effect does an assertive response style have on overall teacher effectiveness in both the academic and management domains?

Weblinks

Bridges4Kids
www.bridges4kids.org/news/GRPress8-20-02.html
This website gives suggestions for classroom-management techniques.

Cherryville Elementary School
www.sd22.bc.ca/cherryville/codeofcon.html
Illustrates a very detailed code of conduct where philosophy, responsibilities, and consequences are clearly spelled out.

Vancouver School Board—Code of Conduct
www.vsb.bc.ca/schools/Elementaryschools/03939056/Profile/
schoolcodeofconduct.htm
The site displays the code of conduct for the Vancouver School Board.

Simcoe County District School Board, Code of Conduct
www.scdsb.on.ca/parents/code_of_conduct.cfm?print=true
This is the site for the Simcoe County District School Board; it sets out students' rights and responsibilities.

9

Classroom Interventions for Chronic Problems

Focus on the Principles of Classroom Management

1. When dealing with students who pose chronic behavioural problems, which strategies should teachers use first?
2. What can teachers do to increase the possibility that chronic behavioural problems can be resolved within the classroom?
3. What are the benefits of breaking the cycle of discouragement in which most students with chronic behavioural problems are trapped?
4. Why are private conferences and the use of effective communication skills with students so important for teachers?
5. Why is it important for teachers to use interventions that require students to recognize their inappropriate behaviour and its impact on others?
6. What interventions can be used to promote daily accountability for students with chronic behavioural problems?
7. What interventions can be used to promote gradual but consistent improvement in classroom behaviour?

Introduction

While research, as well as our own experience, indicates that the overwhelming majority of behavioural problems (somewhere in the neighbourhood of 97 percent) can be either prevented or redirected to positive behaviour by the use of a pre-planned hierarchy of non-verbal and verbal interventions (Charney, 1998; Shrigley, 1980), there are some students who pose classroom behavioural problems of a more chronic nature. These students misbehave even after all preventive and intervention, verbal and non-verbal, techniques have been appropriately employed. They disrupt learning, interfere with the work of others, challenge teacher authority, and often try to entice others to misbehave on a fairly consistent basis. These are the students who prompt teachers to say, "If I could only get rid of that Sammy, third period would be a pleasure to teach"; or "Every time I look at that smirk on Jodi's face, I'd like to wring her little neck"; or "If that Greg weren't in this class, I would certainly have a lot more time to spend on helping the other students learn." Jodi, the student described in Case 9.1 on the next page, is a good example.

CASE 9.1 • *"I Just Dropped My Book"*

Jodi, a grade 9 student, entered Mr. Voman's guidance office hesitatingly, sat down, and looked blankly at Mr. Voman.

Mr. Voman: "Well, Jodi, What are you doing here?"

Jodi: "Ms. Kozin sent me out of class and told me not to ever come back. She told me to come see you."

Mr. Voman: "Why did she send you out of class?"

Jodi: "I don't know. I just dropped my book on the floor accidentally!"

Mr. Voman: "Now, come on, Jodi. Ms. Kozin wouldn't put you out of class just for that. Come on now. What did you do?"

Jodi: "Honest, Mr. Voman, you can ask the other kids. All I did was drop my book."

Mr. Voman: "Jodi, I'm going to go and talk to Ms. Kozin about this. Wait here until I get back."

Jodi: "Okay, Mr. Voman, I'll wait here and you'll see that I'm not lying."

Questions to Consider

1. After Mr. Voman talks to Ms. Kozin, what should he say to Jodi?
2. Recently, Jodi has been chronically misbehaving. What are some of the possible underlying causes that may trigger a normally well-behaving student to act out?
3. What else might Ms. Kozin do to help Jodi behave appropriately?

As Mr. Voman discovered when he talked to Ms. Kozin, Jodi had been a constant nuisance for the past month. The book-dropping incident was simply the last straw. Jodi continually talked during lectures; forgot to bring pencils, books, and paper to class; refused to complete homework; didn't even attempt quizzes or tests; and reacted rudely whenever Ms. Kozin approached her. Ms. Kozin had tried non-verbal and verbal interventions, time outs, detentions, and notes to parents. By the time Jodi accidentally dropped her book, Ms. Kozin was completely fed up with her.

Many, though not all, students like Jodi have problems that extend beyond school. Some have poor home lives with few, if any, positive adult role models. Others have no supporters in their lives who really care about them or express real interest in what they are doing. Still others simply view themselves as losers who couldn't succeed in school even if they tried. As a result, they act out their frustrations in class and make life miserable for both their teachers and their peers.

No matter how understandable these students' problems may be, they must learn to control their behaviour. If they do not, they are at risk of continued failure and unhappiness. Furthermore, although teachers are always concerned for the future of the disruptive student, they are also responsible for ensuring that misbehaviour does not deprive the other students of their right to learn. Thus, chronic misbehaviour must not be allowed to continue.

In attempting to deal with chronically disruptive students, classroom teachers often fall into a two-step trap. First, they frequently give in to that natural, fully understandable, human urge to "get even." They scream, punish, and retaliate. When retaliation fails (and it is apt to fail), and because the chronically disruptive student often loves to see the teacher explode, the teacher often feels helpless and seeks outside assistance by sending the student to somebody else. Usually, chronically disruptive students are sent to an administrator or counsellor and sentenced to some form of in-school or out-of-school suspension (Charney, 1998; Tillson, 2000).

Because outside referral removes the disruptive student from the class, the disruptive behaviour does cease. However, this is usually a short-term solution because the student soon returns and, after a brief period of improvement, again disrupts the classroom. The severity and frequency of the misbehaviour after a return to the classroom often increase. It has been hypothesized that misbehaviour increases because the student views the referral either as a further punishment or as a victory over the teacher. When they view referrals as punishments, many disruptive students retaliate as soon as they return to the classroom. When they view referrals as victories, disruptive students often feel compelled to demonstrate even more forcefully their perceived power over the teacher. As a result, in Canada, school administrators are beginning to examine the fundamental causes of problem behaviour and are attempting to incorporate this knowledge into their management strategy (Tillson, 2000).

Porter and Brophy, in a research synthesis on effective teaching, strongly recommend dealing with chronic behavioural problems within the classroom.

> In a study of teachers' strategies for coping with students who presented sustained problems in personal adjustment or behaviour, teachers who were identified as most effective in coping with such problems viewed them as something to be corrected rather than merely endured. Furthermore, although they might seek help from school administrators or mental health professionals, such teachers build personal relationships and work with their problem students, relying on instruction, socialization, cognitive strategy training and other long-term solutions. In contrast, less effective teachers try to turn over the responsibility to someone else (such as the principal, school social worker, or counselor). (1988, 78)

Contrary to popular belief, chronic behavioural problems often can be managed successfully within the confines of the regular classroom and with a minimum of additional effort by the teacher. When such problems are resolved within the conventional classroom setting, the disruptive student, the other students, and the teacher all benefit. The disruptive student learns to control her behaviour without loss of instructional time and without developing the negative attitudes that are often evident in students who have been excluded from the classroom. The teacher gains a more tranquil classroom and additional confidence in her ability to handle all types of behavioural problems successfully. Finally, the other students in the class are again able to concentrate their attention on the learning tasks before them.

In this chapter, we will present two long-term strategies for solving chronic behavioural problems and three specific management techniques in addition to the CALM model that teachers can use. The problem-solving strategies and management techniques are used simultaneously in the classroom; that is, as the teacher is managing the chronic misbehaviour using the management techniques, she is also seeking ways to solve the long-term problems. The two long-term problem-solving strategies—**relationship building** and breaking the **cycle of discouragement**—are described first. This discussion is followed by a section on how to conduct effective private conferences with students. Effective private conferences are an important component of both the long-term problem-solving strategies and the management techniques. In the final section of this chapter, we introduce three specific management techniques: student self-monitoring, which is a student-directed management strategy; anecdotal record keeping, a collaborative management strategy; and behaviour contracting, a teacher-directed management strategy.

Relationship Building

The development of a positive relationship between the teacher and the student with a chronic behavioural problem is one of the most effective strategies for helping such students. Usually, these students do not have positive relationships with their teachers. Indeed, teachers often tend to avoid interaction with such students. This is quite understandable. Students who have chronic behavioural problems are often challenging and cause the teacher to doubt her own competence.

These doubts about competence arise from the misconception that the teacher can *control* a student's behaviour. As we have noted continually in this text, the teacher can only influence a student's behaviour and react to that behaviour. She cannot control anyone's behaviour except her own. If a teacher has the mistaken notion that her job is to control a student's behaviour, she will feel that she is not as competent as she should be every time the student acts inappropriately. Thus, one of the first steps a teacher should take in working with students who have chronic behavioural problems is to recognize that her role is to help these students learn to control their own behaviour. The teacher can only be held accountable for controlling her own behaviour in such a way that it increases the likelihood that the students will learn and want to behave appropriately. Practice of the CALM model cultivates this approach to influencing student behaviour.

To accomplish this, the teacher must disregard any negative feelings she has toward the chronically disruptive student and work at building a positive relationship with that student. We are not suggesting that the teacher must be fond of the student. No teacher honestly likes every student whom she has ever encountered. However, a truly professional teacher does not act on or reveal those negative feelings. Our experience has given us two important insights about working with students who have chronic behavioural problems. First, teachers who look for and are able to find some positive qualities, no matter how small or how hidden, in chronically disruptive students are much more successful in helping those students learn to behave appropriately than those who do not. Second, the primary factor that motivated the vast majority of students who were at one time chronically disruptive to rectify their behaviour was the development of a close, positive relationship with a caring adult. Case 9.2 illustrates the impact that a caring relationship can have on such an individual.

CASE 9.2 • *Jordan*

Jordan, who was born to a single mother in a rundown, crime-ridden neighbourhood in a large Canadian city, was raised by his grandmother, who was the one kind, protective figure in his early life. Despite her efforts to shield him, Jordan was exposed to the availability of drugs, street gangs, and a variety of illegal and often violent activities while he was still in elementary school. Many of the young men in his neighbourhood had a very bad reputation because of the proliferation of guns and shootings.

In high school, Jordan described himself as full of anger and energy, and he became involved in a gang that conducted petty and often violent attacks on other adolescents and adults. As a result, he was eventually sent to a juvenile detention facility and, after he had served the required time, was released. Upon his release, Jordan was assigned to Barbara, a juvenile probation officer.

Barbara was a streetwise veteran in her fifties who had worked with many troubled adolescents. Jordan said to his friends, "She doesn't take any crap." Barbara insisted that Jordan stop his aggressive behaviour and made it clear to him that she thought he was an intelligent young man with the potential to be successful in life if he consciously changed his behaviour. For six years Jordan and Barbara worked together and built a strong interpersonal relationship based on mutual respect and caring. Over this period, Jordan changed dramatically. According to Jordan, "Barbara taught me how to take my anger and aggression and turn them into positive forces in my life. My first successes were on the basketball court and then I began to be successful in the classroom, too." As a result of the close relationship Barbara painstakingly built, Jordan earned passing grades in school, stayed out of trouble, and became a good enough point guard that he earned a scholarship to a small college in the United States. Throughout these years, Barbara's efforts were recognized and supported by Jordan's increasingly proud grandmother. Jordan studied hard, was successful and became a special education teacher. He returned to his hometown expressly hoping to make a difference in the lives of kids like him.

After returning with his strong personal motivation, he saw the need to change the education system itself but felt powerless in his capacity as a teacher to do so. After a few frustrating years, he left teaching and devoted himself to earning a master's degree in counselling, followed by a Ph.D. in curriculum and a principal's certificate. Today, Jordan is a high school principal in the inner city where he was raised. He lives with his wife and young son and spends his time helping inner-city children turn their energy and anger to useful purposes in much the same way Barbara helped him. In fact, he often tells his personal story to kids who are getting into trouble. Jordan and Barbara remain close friends.

Questions to Consider

1. Describe the positive approach that Barbara took with Jordan. Why does such an approach sometimes fail to be effective?

2. What do you think is the most important element of Barbara's relationship with Jordan?

3. Describe Barbara's approach as it might relate to the CALM model.

4. Given what you know, what other solutions might have been helpful for Jordan and other children in his situation if someone like Barbara were not available?

Of course, building positive relationships with students who have chronic behavioural problems is not always an easy task. Many students with chronic behavioural problems have a long history of unsuccessful relationships with adults. Because the adults in these relationships may have ended up being non-supportive or negative in one way or another, many of the students actively resist attempts to build positive relationships. For some students, it becomes safer not to build any relationships at all than to risk another relationship that will result in hurt and disappointment.

Thus, teachers who want to build relationships with such students must be persistent, consistent, and predictable in their own behaviour toward the student (Brendtro, Brokenleg, and Van Bockern, 2002). They must search for positive qualities in the students and work at building the relationship without much initial encouragement or response from the student. As Brendtro, Brokenleg, and Van Bockern note, the desire to build a relationship does not have to spring from a feeling

CASE 9.3 • *Relating to Cindy*

Carol, a student teacher in chemistry, decided to make Cindy "her project." Cindy was an overweight, physically unattractive grade 12 student who did not seem to have any friends at all. She spoke to no one, did not participate in class activities, and had failed every test and quiz from September to late January when Carol took over the class.

Every day in the four minutes before class began, Carol walked back to Cindy's desk and tried to chat with her. For two full weeks, Carol got absolutely no response, not even eye contact. Cindy completely ignored her. Although upset and disappointed, Carol decided to persist. One day during the third week without a response, Carol noticed Cindy reading the college newspaper during class. Instead of viewing this as a behavioural problem, Carol decided to use it as the foundation for a relationship. She had Cindy stay after class and told her that she had seen the newspaper. She asked if Cindy was interested in newspapers. Cindy replied that she wanted to be a journalist. Carol told Cindy she would be happy to bring her a copy of the college newspaper every day as long as Cindy would read it after class.

For the first time, Cindy replied: "That would be great."

Every day for the next 10 weeks, Carol drove 15 minutes out of her way to pick up a newspaper for Cindy. The impact on Cindy was remarkable. She began coming to class early and staying after class each day to speak with Carol. She attended class activities and even participated verbally about once a week or so. Remarkably, she passed every test and quiz from that point until Carol's student teaching experience ended. Given the cumulative nature of the content of chemistry, this academic turnaround astounded Carol, her supervisor (one of the authors), and her co-operating teacher.

Questions to Consider

1. Based on this incident, describe Carol's belief about the role of a teacher.
2. Prior to Carol's presence, describe Cindy's beliefs about herself and her teachers.
3. What was the turning point in Carol's relationship with Cindy and how was this related to the CALM model?
4. What else might Carol have done to gain Cindy's confidence?

of liking or attraction. The teacher simply has to choose to act toward the student in caring and giving ways. Over time, positive feelings of liking and attraction develop. Notice how Carol, the student teacher in Case 9.3, slowly builds a relationship with Cindy. Although such dramatic results do not always or even typically occur, the efforts can be rewarding.

Bob Strachota calls attempts to build positive relationships with students who have chronic behavioural problems "getting on their side" (1996). He notes that teachers need to view themselves as allies rather than opponents of these students and has suggested several steps to help teachers do so. The first step is "wondering why." Strachota points out that many teachers become so preoccupied with techniques for stopping the misbehaviour that they forget to ask such fundamental questions as, (1) Why is the student behaving in this way? and (2) What purpose does it serve or what need does it fulfill? Strachota's underlying assumption is that behaviour is purposeful rather than random and directed at meeting some need even if the goal of the behaviour is faulty or mistaken (see Chapter 3). If the teacher can identify the need, it is often possible to substitute a positive behaviour that will result in fulfillment of the need.

The second step is to develop a sense of empathy and intimacy with the student. Have you ever found yourself in a situation in which you wanted to stop a behaviour but couldn't get control of it? If so, you were presented with a great opportunity to develop a sense of empathy with these students. If you can view yourself and the student in similar terms—wanting to stop a behaviour but not being able to—you are much more likely to be able to work successfully with the student.

The third step is to stay alert for cues and behaviours that reveal other aspects of the student's personality. Sometimes, teachers become so obsessed with the misbehaviour that they do not look at other aspects of the student's behaviour and personality. Students who pose chronic behavioural problems have other, more positive, aspects to their personalities as well, but it takes self-control and persistence to focus on them. When a teacher is controlled and focused enough to see the student's personality and behaviour in its entirety, she is often able to find positive and attractive aspects that can be used as a foundation for building a positive relationship.

Strachota's fourth and final step is for the teacher to monitor carefully her own behaviour in interacting with the student. Strachota points out, "What's going on for me leaks out in the way I talk. I know what I sound like when I am happy, relaxed, curious, flexible, enthusiastic, etc. I know the difference when I feel tense, short, angry, controlling, hurried, sarcastic, or harsh" (1996, 75). Sometimes, teachers unintentionally communicate negative feelings toward disruptive and low-achieving students (see Chapter 5). If a teacher listens closely to what she is saying and observes how she is behaving, she can avoid negative messages and instead offer positive, caring ones.

The teacher's mindset is critical. In most chronic behaviour situations, the teacher sees the student as an opponent in the conflict. Teachers who are successful in resolving chronic behavioural problems see themselves on the student's side, working together to overcome the problem (Novak and Purkey, 2001).

Breaking the Cycle of Discouragement

Many students with chronic behavioural problems suffer from low self-esteem and have a low success-to-failure ratio (see Chapters 3 and 10). Their need for a sense of significance or belonging, competence or mastery, power or independence, and virtue or generosity have not been fulfilled. As we explained in Chapter 3, when these needs are not met, individuals take action to fulfill them. Unfortunately, the student with chronic behavioural problems often takes actions that are inappropriate and negative. These negative behaviours are met with negative teacher responses, punishments, and consequences that further reduce the student's self-esteem and lead to more misbehaviour, negative responses, punishments, and consequences. This cycle of discouragement, which is depicted in Figure 9.1, will continue until a teacher takes action to break it (Cummins, 1998).

Although it is entirely appropriate for these students to receive negative messages about their inappropriate behaviour and to experience the negative consequences of such actions, if that is all that occurs, the cycle of discouragement is simply reinforced. Since it is necessary to stop the misbehaviour, the teacher must also find ways to meet unfulfilled needs and break the cycle of discouragement.

Just as there are students who are caught in the cycle of discouragement, there are those who enjoy their own cycle of encouragement. These students have a high success-to-failure ratio and are having their needs met for feelings of significance, competence, power, and virtue. As a result, they behave in positive and caring ways toward teachers and peers. These positive behaviours are reciprocated, and students are given the message that they are attractive, competent and virtuous, resulting in the cycle of encouragement depicted in Figure 9.2. We believe that the appropriate way to solve chronic behavioural problems is to break the cycle of discouragement by stopping the inappropriate behaviour through management techniques *and* at the same time engaging in behaviours that will help to meet the student's needs for feelings of significance, competence, power, and virtue. Together, these two actions result in the disruption of the cycle of discouragement as shown in Figure 9.3. "A teacher who is en-heartening

FIGURE 9.1   *The Cycle of Discouragement*

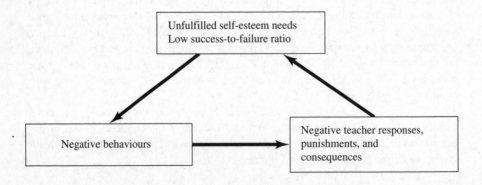

FIGURE 9.2   *The Cycle of Encouragement*

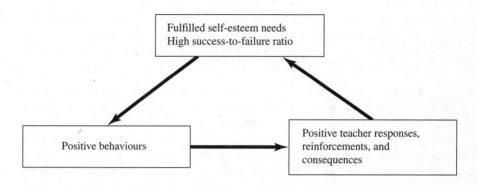

or encouraging is one who communicates hopefulness and a sense of possibility in their interactions with students. If students are to have courage and confidence, they have to see that teachers are at least trying to have confidence in them" (Ellis, Hart, and Small-McGinley, 2001).

FIGURE 9.3   *Disrupting the Cycle of Discouragement*

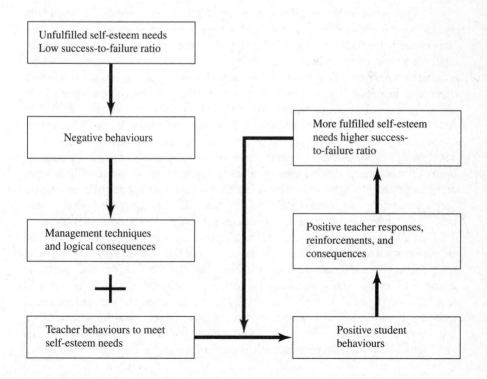

To accomplish this, teachers who are dealing with students with chronic behavioural problems should ask themselves four questions:

1. What can I do to help meet this student's need for significance or belonging?
2. What can I do to help meet this student's need for competence or mastery?
3. What can I do to help meet this student's need for power or independence?
4. What can I do to help meet this student's need for virtue or generosity?

Clearly, behaviour on the part of the teacher that aims to build a positive student–teacher relationship is one powerful tool for meeting a student's need for significance. In the previous section of this chapter, we provided a variety of guidelines and suggestions for building such relationships. Co-operative learning strategies (see Chapters 5 and 6) and other forms of group work help to meet the student's need for feelings of belonging. Student teams that work together productively over time also can help the student to develop a sense of group identity and belonging. Often, students who are chronically disruptive are not well liked by their peers. Thus, putting them in a student-selected group does not usually work and may result in the disruption of the group. The likelihood of positive group interaction can be increased greatly by the teacher's careful selection of the appropriate group for the student. Typically, the optimum group includes students who are good at controlling their own behaviour, are sensitive to the needs of others, and can tolerate some initial conflict. It is also helpful if the teacher uses co-operative learning activities to teach students productive social skills (Elliott and Woloshyn, 1996).

At the elementary level, it is sometimes effective to place those students with chronic behavioural problems in a responsible role—for example, message carrier. This often enhances the student's sense of belonging. In middle school and high school, helping the student to find clubs, intramurals, or other extracurricular activities or out-of-school activities (sometimes a job) in which the student has some interest and talent and then supporting the student's participation in this activity helps to enhance the student's sense of belonging. At all levels, the teacher should make it a point to give the student attention and positive feedback when she engages in appropriate behaviour. The need for a sense of competence can be met by the use of encouragement. Often, students with chronic behavioural problems and their parents receive only negative messages. Showing an interest in those things that the student values and making sure that you, as the teacher, recognize those strengths will help to increase the student's sense of competence. Sometimes, setting short-term goals with the student and then helping the student to keep track of her progress in meeting the goals helps the student to feel more competent.

At all times, feedback to the student with chronic behavioural problems should emphasize what the student can do as opposed to what the student cannot do. Suppose, for example, that a student with chronic behavioural problems takes a valid test of the material the student was supposed to learn, makes a concerted effort to do well, and receives a mark of 67. In most classrooms, the only message that the student would receive was that this was not a good mark, which would reinforce the student's own feelings of incompetence. If we examine the situation more objectively, however, we can see that the student knows twice as much as she does not know. This does not mean that a mark of 67 is good, but rather than communicating that the student is not successful, the teacher can point out that the student has indeed learned and then use that limited success to encourage the student to continue to make the effort to learn. Using encouraging communication, engaging the student in short-term goal setting, stressing effort and improvement, and focusing on the positive aspects of the student's behaviour and performance can increase the student's sense of competence.

We all need to feel that we have control over the important aspects of our lives. When students are deprived of the opportunity to be self-directing and to make responsible choices, they often become bullies or totally dependent on others, unable to control their own lives. A teacher can enhance the student's sense of power by providing opportunities to make choices and by allowing the student to experience the consequences of those choices. There is a wide range of classroom decisions in which, depending on the teacher's philosophy, the student can have a voice. When students are deprived of the opportunity to make choices, especially students with chronic behavioural problems, they often become resentful and challenging of the teacher's authority. It is very important for the teacher not to engage in power contests with these students. Thus, the best course of action for the teacher is to find appropriate opportunities for these students to make responsible choices.

The need for a sense of virtue or generosity revolves around our desire to feel that we are givers as well as takers. When we have a fulfilled sense of virtue, we realize that we are able to give to and nurture others. Elementary teachers often use "book buddies" and cross-grade tutoring opportunities to develop a sense of virtue among their students. Many secondary students have their sense of virtue fulfilled by participating in food drives, marathons, and walkathons for charities, and other types of community service projects. Some of the most successful rehabilitation programs for juvenile offenders engage these adolescents in activities that are beneficial to others in the community (Brendtro, Brokenleg, and Van Bockern, 2002). Although it is sometimes difficult to arrange classroom activities that tap into the need for a sense of virtue, peer tutoring and other opportunities to share talents can enhance a student's sense of virtue or generosity. Before turning to techniques for managing chronic behavioural problems, it should be emphasized that relationship building and breaking the cycle of discouragement require commitment, persistence, patience, and self-control on the part of the teacher. These strategies will not turn things around overnight. Sometimes, they do not result in any tangible benefits for several weeks or months. Persisting with them and ignoring the natural desire to get even or give up constitute the ultimate in professional behaviour. It is extremely hard to do, but it is often the only thing that makes a real difference in the long run to students with chronic behavioural problems.

Private Conferences

Holding private conferences with students who have chronic behavioural problems is the *sine qua non* of the strategies that are intended to manage or solve these behavioural problems. Until the teacher takes the time to sit down with the student to discuss the student's behaviour and to attempt to find ways to help the student behave in more productive ways, the teacher has not begun to attempt to manage or solve the problem. A private conference or a series of conferences with the student accomplishes several important tasks. First, it makes sure that the student is aware that her behaviour is a problem that must be dealt with. Second, sometimes it is one of the basic steps toward building a positive relationship with the student. Thus, it can be an important step toward helping the student to take ownership of the behaviour and find ways to bring it under control.

Receiving Skills

During private conferences, the teacher needs to be aware of the student's perception of the problem and point of view in order to be sure that the intervention focuses on the actual problem. Suppose, for example, the student's chronic misbehaviour is motivated by the student's belief that she doesn't have the ability to do the assigned work. Solutions that ignore the student's underlying feeling of incompetence are not likely to be successful in the long run. Therefore, it is important to be sure you receive the message that the student is sending. The following receiving skills will help to ensure that you receive the student's message:

1. *Use silence and non-verbal attending cues.* Allow the student sufficient time to express her ideas and feelings, and use non-verbal cues such as eye contact, facial expressions, head nodding, and body posture (for example, leaning toward the student) to show that you are interested in and listening to what she is saying. Most important, make sure these cues are sincere—that is, that you really are listening carefully to the student.

2. *Probe.* Ask relevant and pertinent questions to elicit extended information about a given topic, to clarify ideas, and to justify a given idea. Questions such as, "Can you tell me more about the problem with Jerry?" or "What makes you say that I don't like you?" or "I'm not sure I understand what you mean by 'hitting on you'; can you explain what that means?" show that you are listening and want more information.

3. *Check perceptions.* Paraphrase or summarize what the student has said using slightly different words. This acts as a check on whether you have understood the student correctly. This is not a simple verbatim repetition of what the student has said. It is an attempt by the teacher to capture the student's message as accurately as possible in the teacher's words. Usually a perception check ends by giving the student an opportunity to affirm or negate the teacher's perception— for example, "So, as I understand it, you think that I'm picking on you when I give you a detention for not completing your homework, is that right?" or "You're saying that you never really wanted to be in the gifted program anyway, and so you don't care whether you are removed from the program. Do I have that right?"

4. *Check feelings.* Feeling checks refer to attempts to reach student emotions through questions and statements. In formulating the questions and statements, use non-verbal cues (for example, facial expression) and paralingual cues (voice volume,

rate, and pitch) to go beyond the student's statements and understand the emotions behind the words. For instance, "It sounds as if you are really proud of what you're doing in basketball, aren't you?" or "You look really angry when you talk about being placed in the lower section. Are you angry?"

Sending Skills

Individual conferences not only allow the teacher to be sure she understands the problem from the student's vantage point, but also allow the teacher to be sure the student understands the problem from the teacher's point of view. As a teacher, using your sending skills to clearly communicate your thoughts and ideas is a first step toward helping the student gain that insight. Ginott (1972) and Jones (1980) offer the following guidelines for sending accurate messages:

1. *Deal in the here and now.* Don't dwell on past problems and situations. Communicate your thoughts about the present situation and the immediate future. Although it is appropriate to talk about the past behaviour that has created the need for the private conference, there is nothing to be gained by reciting a litany of past transgressions.
2. *Make eye contact and use congruent non-verbal behaviours.* Avoiding eye contact when confronting a student about misbehaviour gives the student the impression that you are uncomfortable about the confrontation. In contrast, maintaining eye contact helps to let the student know that you are confident and comfortable in dealing with problems. Because research indicates that students believe the non-verbal message when verbal and non-verbal behaviour are not congruent (Woolfolk and Brooks, 1983), be sure non-verbal cues match the verbal messages.
3. *Make statements rather than asking questions.* Asking questions is appropriate for eliciting information from the student. However, when the teacher has specific information or behaviours to discuss, the teacher should lay the specific facts out on the table rather than try to elicit them from the student by playing "guess what's on my mind."
4. *Use "I"—take responsibility for your feelings.* You have a right to your feelings. It can be appropriate to be annoyed at students, and it can be appropriate to be proud of students. Students must know that teachers are people who have legitimate feelings and that their feelings must be considered in determining the effects of the student's behaviour on others.
5. *Be brief.* Get to the point quickly. Let the student know what the problem is as you see it and what you propose to do about it. Once you have done this, stop. Don't belabour the issue with unnecessary lectures and harangues.
6. *Talk directly to the student, not about her.* Even if other people are present, talk to the student rather than to parents or counsellors. Use "you" and specifically describe the problem to the student. This behaviour sends the student the powerful message that she, not her parents or anyone else, is directly responsible for her own behaviour.

7. *Give directions to help the student correct the problem.* Don't stop at identifying the problem behaviour. Be specific in setting forth exactly which behaviours must be replaced and in identifying appropriate behaviours to replace them.

8. *Check student understanding of your message.* Once you have communicated clearly what the specific problem is and what steps you suggest for solving it, ask a question to be sure the student has received the message correctly. Often, it is a good idea to ask the student to summarize the discussion. If the student's summary indicates that she has missed the message, the teacher has an opportunity to restate or rephrase the main idea in a way that the student can understand.

With these guidelines for effective communication in mind, we can now consider three specific techniques (*self-monitoring*, *anecdotal record keeping*, and *behaviour contracting*) for managing students with chronic behavioural problems. There are five assumptions underlying these techniques:

1. The number of students in any one class who should be classified as having chronic behavioural problems is small, usually fewer than five. If there are more than five, it is a good indication that the teacher has not done all that could be done to prevent the problems from occurring.

2. The teacher is well prepared for each class, engages the students in interesting learning activities, and uses a variety of effective teaching strategies.

3. The expectations for behaviour are clearly understood by students and enforced on a consistent basis (see Chapter 6).

4. The teacher manages commonplace disruptions with a pre-planned hierarchy of non-verbal and verbal interventions and logical consequences.

5. The teacher attempts to build positive relationships with students who have chronic behavioural problems and attempts to break the cycle of discouragement by helping them to meet their self-esteem needs.

When there are several students who exhibit chronic behavioural problems, they usually fall into one of two categories—those who have the greatest potential for improving their behaviour quickly and those whose behaviour causes the greatest disruption. When there are several students with chronic behavioural problems in one class, the teacher may have to choose to work with one category over another. There are pitfalls in choosing either category. Usually those with the greatest odds for quick improvement are the students with the least severe behavioural problems. Thus, even if the teacher succeeds in helping them, the general level of disruption in the classroom may remain quite high. On the other hand, those students who have the most severe and most disruptive behaviour usually require the longest period of time to improve, but their improvement tends to have a more dramatic impact on the classroom.

There are no clear guidelines as to which category of students teachers should choose. It is really a matter of personal preference. If the teacher is the type of individual who needs to see results quickly in order to persist, she is probably better off choosing those students with the greatest likelihood for quick improvement. If, however, the more serious behaviour is threatening to any individuals, the teacher must begin intervention with those students.

It must be noted that self-monitoring, anecdotal record keeping, or behaviour contracting probably will not be effective in managing chronic behavioural problems if the five assumptions underlying these techniques have not been met. If these assumptions have been met, then the teacher has done all that she can do to prevent behavioural problems from occurring, and the following three management techniques have a reasonably high chance of success.

Management Techniques

Self-Monitoring

Some students who exhibit chronic disruptive behaviours perceive a well-managed private conference as a sign of a teacher's caring and support. Some students leave the conference with a new understanding that their behaviours are interfering with the rights of others and will no longer be tolerated in the classroom. Given the nature and background of chronic behavioural problems, however, most students will need more intensive and frequent intervention techniques. The challenge is to design techniques that are congruent with the belief that students must be given opportunities to learn how to control their own behaviour.

Self-monitoring of behaviour is a student-directed approach that is often effective with students who are really trying to behave appropriately but seem to need assistance to do so. The technique is usually more appropriate for elementary students who have extremely short attention spans or who are easily distracted by the everyday events of a busy classroom. While self-monitoring can be effective with some older students, the teacher must consider the age appropriateness of the self-monitoring instrument that the student will use.

For self-monitoring to be effective, the instrument must clearly delineate the behaviours to be monitored and must be easy for a student to use. The student must also clearly understand the duration of the self-monitoring and the frequency of behavioural checks. Unfortunately, teachers occasionally design an instrument that is too cumbersome to use or is too time consuming. Thus, using the instrument actually interferes with on-task behaviour.

In the beginning, the student may require teacher cues to indicate when it is time to check behaviour and record it on the self-monitoring instrument. These cues may be private, non-verbal signals agreed upon by the teacher and the student. In the beginning, it is a good idea for the teacher to co-monitor the student's behaviour using the same instrument. When this is done, the teacher and the student can compare their monitoring consistency and discuss the proper use of the instrument as well as the progress that is being made.

The effectiveness of self-monitoring relies heavily on how the use of the instrument is explained to the student. If self-monitoring is presented as a technique that students can use to help themselves with the teacher's assistance, support, and encouragement, the likelihood of improved behaviour is high. When teachers have successfully communicated the purpose of the technique and stressed the possible positive outcomes, students have actually thanked them for the opportunity and means to demonstrate on-task behaviour. On the other hand, if the intervention is introduced as a form of punishment, the likelihood of positive behavioural change is diminished.

While other examples of more comprehensive self-monitoring instruments may be found in Chapter 6, Figure 9.4 is an example of a simple self-monitoring instrument for a wide range of behaviours. When a teacher uses this instrument, it is imperative that she and the student clearly understand which behaviours are defined as on task, and therefore coded "1," and which behaviours are off task and coded "0." In addition, a workable coding period needs to be established so that each block represents a predetermined period of time.

As with any intervention that focuses on the improvement of chronic misbehaviour, progress may be slow. Two steps forward and one step backward may be the best a student can do in the beginning. We must remember that chronic misbehaviour does not develop in a day, and it will not be replaced with more appropriate behaviour in a day. It is difficult to learn new behaviours to replace behaviours that have become ingrained and habitual. Therefore, the teacher must be patient and focus on improvements. It is usually best to work on one behaviour at a time. For example, if a student continually talks to neighbours and calls out, the teacher and student should decide on which behaviour to work on first. If the student is successful in managing the selected behaviour, experience has shown that subsequent behaviours are more readily corrected.

As behaviour improves, the teacher should begin to wean the student from self-monitoring. As a first step, once the teacher is convinced that the student is reliably monitoring her own behaviour, the teacher stops co-monitoring and relies solely on the student's report. Next, as behaviours begin to improve, the teacher lengthens the period of time between self-checks. Finally, the teacher removes the student completely from self-monitoring. When this happens, the teacher uses the event to build self-esteem and self-control by making the student aware that she has changed her behaviour

FIGURE 9.4 *Am I on Task?*

		Yes = 1						No = 0			
1	2	3	4	5	6	7	8	9	10	11	12

Score = sum of the cells = _____

on her own and should be quite proud of her accomplishments. Any corresponding improvements in academics or peer interactions should also be noted and tied to the student's improved behaviour.

Figure 9.5 shows a checklist that teachers can use to evaluate the self-monitoring procedures and instruments that they design.

Anecdotal Record Keeping

If the teacher either has tried self-monitoring or has decided not to try this technique because of philosophical objections or the student's refusal to make the required commitments, there is a second option, called **anecdotal record keeping**, for remediating chronic behavioural problems. This method, which is a collaborative approach to managing classroom behaviours (see Chapter 4), has been used successfully by student teachers and veteran teachers alike to handle a variety of chronic behavioural problems at a number of different grade levels (Levin, Nolan, and Hoffman, 1985). It is based on the principles of *Adlerian psychology*, which state that changes in behaviour can be facilitated by making people aware of their behaviour and its consequences for themselves and others (Sweeney, 1981).

Anecdotal record keeping is usually most appropriate for middle and secondary students because students at these levels have better-developed self-regulation. To use the technique, the teacher merely records the classroom behaviour, both positive and negative, of a chronically disruptive student over a period of a few weeks. Although it is preferable to have the student's co-operation, anecdotal record keeping can be employed without it.

The record the teacher has made of the student's behaviour and the measures that have been taken to improve that behaviour form the basis for a private conference with the student. There are nine guidelines that should be followed in conducting this initial conference:

1. The teacher should begin on a positive note.
2. The teacher should help the student to recognize the past behaviour and its negative impact, showing the student the record of past behaviours and discussing it if necessary.

FIGURE 9.5 *Self-Monitoring Checklist*

1. Do the teacher and student clearly understand and agree on the behaviours to be monitored?	_____ Yes	_____ No
2. Is the time period for self-checks clearly specified?	_____ Yes	_____ No
3. Does the student understand how to use the instrument?	_____ Yes	_____ No
4. Have the teacher and student agreed on a meeting time to discuss the self-monitoring?	_____ Yes	_____ No
5. Is the instrument designed so that small increments of improved behaviour will be noted?	_____ Yes	_____ No
6. Is the instrument designed to focus on one behaviour?	_____ Yes	_____ No

3. The teacher should explain that this behaviour is unacceptable and must change.
4. The teacher should tell the student that she will keep a record of the student's positive and negative behaviour on a daily basis and that the student will be required to sign the record at the end of class each day.
5. The teacher should record the student's home phone number on the top of the record and indicate that she will contact the parents/caregivers to inform them of continued unacceptable behaviour. (This option may not be useful for senior high students because parents/caregivers are often not as influential at this age.)
6. The teacher should be positive and emphasize expectations of improvement.
7. The conference should be recorded on the anecdotal record.
8. A verbal commitment for improved behaviour from the student should be sought. This commitment, or the refusal to give it, should be noted on the anecdotal record.
9. The student should sign the anecdotal record at the end of the conference. If the student refuses to sign, the refusal should be recorded.

After the initial conference, the teacher continues the anecdotal record, each day highlighting positive behaviours, documenting negative behaviours, and noting any corrective measures taken. Keeping this systematic record enables the teacher to focus on the behaviour (the deed) rather than on the student (the doer) (Ginott, 1972). The teacher reinforces the student's improved behaviours and, if possible, clarifies the connection between improved behaviours and academic achievement. Thus, the teacher "catches the student being good" (Canter, 1989; Jones, 1980) and demonstrates the concept of encouragement (Dreikurs, Grundwald, and Pepper, 1998). To illustrate the concept of student accountability, the teacher must be consistent in recording behaviours, sharing the record with the student, and obtaining the student's signature on a daily basis (Brophy, 1988). If the student refuses to sign the record on any day, the teacher simply makes note of this fact on the record. Figure 9.6 is the anecdotal record used with one grade 10 student over a three-week period. The technique succeeded after the management hierarchy had been used with little improvement in the student's behaviour. Note that the teacher highlighted positive behaviours to "catch the student being good."

While teachers may think that this technique will consume a lot of instructional time, it does not. If the documentation occurs in the last few minutes of class, perhaps when students are doing homework or getting ready for the next class, the two or three minutes required for it compare favourably to the enormous amount of time wasted by unresolved chronic behavioural problems. Thus, this technique actually helps to conserve time by making more efficient use of classroom time.

In studying the use of anecdotal record keeping, Levin, Nolan, and Hoffman (1985) requested teachers to log their views on the effectiveness of the procedure. On page 226 are two representative logs by secondary teachers.

FIGURE 9.6 *An Anecdotal Record*

Student's Name _____

Home Phone _____

Date	Student Behaviour	Teacher Action	Student Signature
4/14	Talking with Van Out of seat three times Refused to answer question	Verbal reprimand Told her to get back Went on	
4/16	Had private conference Rhonda agreed to improve	Explained anecdotal record Was supportive	
4/17	Stayed on task in lab	Positive feedback	
4/20	Late for class Worked quietly	Verbal reminder Positive feedback	
4/21	Worked quietly Wrestling with Jill	Positive feedback Verbal reprimand	
4/22	No disruptions Volunteered to answer	Positive feedback Called on her three times	
4/23	Late for class Left without signing	Detention after school Recorded it on record	
4/24	Missed detention	Two days' detention	
4/27	Stayed on task all class	Positive feedback	
4/28	Listened attentively to film	Positive feedback	
4/29	Worked at assignment well	Positive feedback	
4/30	Participated in class No disruptions Left without signing	Called on her twice Positive feedback Recorded it	
5/1	Conference to discontinue anecdotal records		

Teacher's Log—Grade 11 English

About a week and a half ago, I implemented the anecdotal record in one of my classes. Two male students were the subjects. The improvement shown by one of these students is very impressive.

On the first day that I held a conference with the student, I explained the procedure, showed him my records for the day, and asked for his signature. He scribbled his name and looked at me as if to say, "What a joke." On the second day, his behaviour in class was negative again. This time, when I spoke to him and told him that one more day of disruptive behaviour would result in a phone call to his parents, he looked at me as if to say, "This joke isn't so funny any more." From that moment on, there was a marked improvement in his behaviour. He was quiet and attentive in class. After class, he would come up to me and ask me where he was supposed to sign his name for the day. And he "beamed" from my remarks about how well behaved he was that day. Only one time after that did I have to speak to him for negative behaviour. I caught him throwing a piece of paper. As soon as he saw me looking at him, he said, "Are you going to write that down in your report?" Then, after class, he came up to me with a worried expression on his face and asked, "Are you going to call my parents?" I didn't, because of the previous days of model behaviour.

I must say that I was sceptical about beginning this type of record on the students. It seemed like such a lengthy and time-consuming process. But I'll say what I'm feeling now. If the anecdotal record can give positive results more times than not, I'll keep on using it. If you can get one student under control, who is to say you can't get five or ten students under control? It truly is a worthwhile procedure to consider.

Teacher's Log—Grade 8 Science

Day 1

I discovered a method with which to deal with some major behavioural problems in one of my classes. It uses an anecdotal record, which is a record of student actions and student behaviours. I think it will probably work because it holds the student accountable for her behaviours. If something must be done, the student has nobody to blame but herself.

Day 2

Today, I set up private conferences with anecdotal record students. I wonder if they'll show up—and if they do, how will they respond?

Day 3

Two students (of three) showed up for their anecdotal record conferences. The third is absent. Both students were very co-operative and made a commitment to better behaviour. One student even made the comment that she thought this idea was a good one for her. The way things look, this will work out fairly well. We'll see . . .

Day 8

One of the students on anecdotal record has improved in behaviour so much that I informed her that if her good behaviour kept improving, I'd take her off the record next Wednesday. I think it will be interesting to see how her behaviour will be; will it keep improving or will it backtrack again?

Implementing any new strategy may be difficult, and anecdotal record keeping is no exception. The teacher must expect that a handful of students will be quite hostile when the procedure is introduced. Some may adamantly refuse to sign the record; others may scribble an unrecognizable signature. The teacher must remain calm and positive and simply record these behaviours. This action communicates to the student that she is solely responsible for her behaviour and that the teacher is only an impartial recorder of the behaviour. Student behaviour will usually improve, given time. Since improved behaviour becomes a part of the record, the anecdotal record reinforces the improvement and becomes the basis for a cycle of improvement.

When the student's behaviour has improved to an acceptable level, the teacher informs her that it will no longer be necessary to keep the anecdotal record because of the improvement in her behaviour. It is important, as suggested earlier, to connect the improved behaviour to academic success and improved grades, if possible. The teacher must also make clear to the student that her fine behaviour is expected to continue. Because continued attention is a key link in the chain of behaviours that turn disruptive class members into students who behave appropriately, the teacher must continue to give the student attention when she behaves appropriately. If the student's behaviour shows no improvement, it may be time to discontinue the process.

It can be quite difficult to decide when to stop recording behaviour. There are no hard and fast rules, but there are some helpful guidelines. If the student has displayed acceptable behaviour for a few days to a week, the record may be discontinued. If the student's behaviour remains disruptive continuously for a week, the anecdotal record keeping should be discontinued and the student told why. If the misbehaviour is somewhat reduced, it may be advisable to have a second conference with the student to determine whether to continue record keeping.

Behaviour Contracting

The third technique is behaviour contracting. **Behaviour contracting** is a teacher-directed strategy (see Chapter 4). This technique is grounded in the principles of operant conditioning, which state that a behaviour that is reinforced is likely to be repeated and that a behaviour that is not reinforced will disappear.

This technique involves the use of a written agreement, known as a *behaviour contract*, between the teacher and student. This contract commits the student to behave appropriately and offers a specified reward when the commitment is met. The contract details the expected behaviour, a time period during which this behaviour must be exhibited, and the reward that will be provided. The purposes of the contract are to manage behaviour that is not managed by normal classroom procedures, to encourage self-discipline, and to foster the student's sense of commitment to appropriate classroom behaviour. Although behaviour contracting can be used with students at any grade level, it often is more appropriate and effective with elementary and middle school students since older students often resent what they are likely to see as an obvious attempt to manipulate their behaviour. This technique is frequently and effectively used in special education classes (Dworet and Rathgeber, 1998).

Because an integral part of behaviour contracting is the use of rewards—often extrinsic, concrete rewards—some teachers may be philosophically opposed to the technique. These teachers often overcome their philosophical objections by replacing concrete, extrinsic rewards with those more focused on learning activities, such as additional computer time, library passes, or assignment of special classroom duties and responsibilities. Teachers who feel that students should not be rewarded for behaviour that is normally expected should keep in mind the fact that this technique has been shown to be effective and is one of the last possible strategies that can be used within the classroom. However, if there are strong philosophical objections to the technique, the teacher should not use it because the likelihood of its successful use is diminished if its philosophical underpinnings are in contradiction to the teacher's (see Chapter 4).

Teachers who decide to use behaviour contracting should remember that it is unlikely that one contract will turn a chronically disruptive student into the epitome of model behaviour. Usually, the teacher must use a series of short-term behaviour contracts that result in steady, gradual improvement in the student's behaviour. A series of short-term behaviour contracts allow the student to see the behaviour changes as manageable and receive small rewards after short intervals of improvement. In other words, a series of contracts provides the student with the opportunity to be successful. Manageable changes in behaviour, shorter time intervals, and frequent opportunities for success make it more likely that the student will remain motivated.

In designing the series of contracts, the teacher should keep three principles in mind. First, design the contracts to require specific, gradual improvements in behaviour. For example, if a student normally disrupts learning six times a period, set the initial goal at four disruptions or fewer per day. Over time, increase the goal until it is set at zero disruptions per day. Second, gradually lengthen the time period during which the contract must be observed in order to gain the reward. For instance, the set time is one day for the first contract, a few days for the second contract, a week for the third contract, and so on. Third, move little by little from more tangible, extrinsic rewards to less tangible, more intrinsic rewards. Thus, a pencil or other supplies are the rewards under the first few contracts, and free time for pleasure reading is the reward under a later contract. Using these three principles takes advantage of a behaviour-modification technique called *behaviour shaping* and gradually shifts management of the student's behaviour from the teacher to the student, where it rightfully belongs.

Before writing the contract, the teacher should make a record of the student's past misbehaviours and the techniques that were used to try to ameliorate these transgressions. The teacher should use all available evidence, including documents and personal recollections, and try to be as accurate and neutral as possible. This record will help the teacher to decide which specific behaviours must be changed and how much change seems manageable for the student at one time. It also ensures that all appropriate management techniques have been used before the implementation of the behaviour contract process. Once the record is compiled, the teacher holds a private conference with the student. It is best to begin the conference on a positive note. The teacher should communicate to the student that she has the potential to do well and to succeed if she can learn to behave appropriately. In doing this, the teacher is using the concept of encouragement (Dreikurs, Grundwald, and Pepper, 1998). The teacher should then attempt to get the student to acknowledge that her behaviour has been inappropriate and to recognize its negative impact on everyone in the classroom. Stressing the effect of the student's behaviour on others promotes the development of higher moral reasoning (Tanner, 1978). To help the student recognize that her behaviour has been unacceptable, the teacher may want to use questions similar to these: "What have you been doing in class?"; or "How is that affecting your chances of success?"; or "How would you like it if other students treated you like that?"; or "How would you like it if you were in a class you really liked but never got a chance to learn because other students were always causing trouble?" Thereafter, the teacher should tell the student that her behaviour, no matter what the explanation for it, is unacceptable and must change. This is followed by a statement such as, "I'd like to work out a plan with you that will help you to behave more appropriately in class."

The teacher must clearly state how the plan works. Because a contract is an agreement between two people, if the student refuses to make a commitment to the contract, the technique cannot be used. If, however, the student commits herself to improvements in classroom behaviour for a specified period of time, some positive consequences or rewards result. The reward may be free time for activities of special interest; a letter, note, or phone call to parents/caregivers describing the improvements in behaviour; or supplies, such as posters, pencils, and stickers. The most important consideration in deciding which particular reward to use is whether the student perceives it as motivating. For that reason, it is often a good idea to allow the student to suggest possible rewards or to discuss rewards with the student. If the student's parents/caregivers are co-operative, it is sometimes possible to ask them to provide a reward at home that is meaningful to the student. At this point, the teacher should draw up the contract, setting forth the specific improvements in behaviour, the time period, and the reward. Both the teacher and student should then sign the contract and each should receive a copy. In the case of young students, it is often a good idea to send a copy of the contract home to parents/caregivers as well. It might also be deemed appropriate for parents/caregivers to sign the contract, particularly with younger students. The conference should end as it began, on a positive note. The teacher, for example, might tell the student that she is looking forward to positive changes in the student's behaviour.

Figure 9.7 on the next page is an example of a behaviour contract and a behaviour contract checklist that may be used by teachers to evaluate the quality of contracts that they draw up. The sample contract was the third in a series between Jessica and her grade 5 teacher, Ms. Jones. Before the behaviour contract intervention, Jessica spent the vast majority of each day's 40-minute social studies period wandering around the room. The first two contracts resulted in her being able to remain seated for roughly half the period.

FIGURE 9.7 *Third Contract Between Jessica and Ms. Jones*

1. *Expected behaviour*
    Jessica remains in her seat for the first 30 minutes of each social studies period.

2. *Time period*
    Monday, February 27 to Friday, March 3.

3. *Reward*
    If Jessica remains in her seat for the first 30 minutes of each social studies period,
    a. she can choose the class's outdoor game on Friday afternoon, March 3, or
    b. Ms. Jones will telephone her parents to tell them of the improvement in Jessica's behaviour on Friday afternoon, March 3.

4. *Evaluation*
    a. After each social studies period, Ms. Jones records whether Jessica did or did not get out of her seat during the first 30 minutes.
    b. Jessica and Ms. Jones will meet on Friday, March 3 at 12:30 p.m. to determine whether the contract has been performed and to write next week's fourth contract.

Student _____

Teacher _____

Date _____

Behaviour Contract Checklist

1. Is the expected behaviour described specifically?	_____ Yes	_____ No
2. Is the time period specified clearly?	_____ Yes	_____ No
3. Has the reward been specified clearly?	_____ Yes	_____ No
4. Is the reward motivating to the student?	_____ Yes	_____ No
5. Is the evaluation procedure specified?	_____ Yes	_____ No
6. Has a date been set to meet to review the contract?	_____ Yes	_____ No
7. Has the student understood, agreed to, and signed the contract?	_____ Yes	_____ No
8. Has the teacher signed the contract?	_____ Yes	_____ No
9. Do both the teacher and student have copies?	_____ Yes	_____ No
10. Did the student's parents get a copy of the contract?	_____ Yes	_____ No

Once the contract is made, the teacher should record the behaviour of the student each day regarding the terms specified in the contract. At the end of the contract period, the teacher can use this record to conduct a conference with the student. If the student has kept her commitment, the teacher should provide the reward. If the student's behaviour needs further improvement, the teacher can draw up a new contract that specifies increased improvement over a longer time period. If at the end of the contract the student's behaviour has improved sufficiently to conform to final expectations, the teacher can inform the student that a behaviour contract is no longer needed. If possible, the teacher should point out to the student the direct relationship between the improved behaviour and the student's academic success in the classroom. The teacher also should make clear that she expects acceptable behaviour and success to continue. Of course, the teacher must continue to give the student attention after the contract has ended. This consistent attention helps the student to recognize that positive behaviour results in positive consequences and usually helps to maintain appropriate behaviour over a long period of time.

If at the end of the contract period the student has not kept the commitment, the teacher should accept no excuses. During the conference, the teacher should assume a neutral role, explaining that the reward cannot be given because the student's behaviour did not live up to the behaviour specified in the contract. The teacher should point out to the student that the lack of reward is simply a logical consequence of the behaviour. This helps the student to see the cause-and-effect relationship between behaviour and its consequences. If the student learns only this, she has learned an extremely valuable lesson.

At this point, the teacher must decide whether or not it is worth trying a new contract with the student. If the teacher believes that the student tried to live up to the contract, a new contract that calls for a little less drastic improvement or calls for improvement over a slightly shorter time frame may be worthwhile.

If the student has not made a sincere effort to improve, obviously the contracting is not working. It is time to try another option. Nothing has been lost in the attempt except a little bit of time, and the teacher has accumulated additional documentation, which will be helpful if it is necessary to seek outside-the-classroom assistance.

There is one final technique for the teacher to try when these classroom management techniques do not work. This is the exclusion of the student from the classroom until she makes a written commitment to improve her behaviour.

Prior to exclusion, the teacher tells the student that she is no longer welcome in the class because of her disruptive behaviour, which is interfering with the teacher's right to teach and the students' right to learn. The teacher then tells the student to report to a specified location in the school where appropriate classroom assignments involving reading and writing will be given. The student is also told that she will be held accountable for the completion of all assignments in an acceptable and timely manner, the same as required in the regular classroom. The teacher stresses that the student may return to the classroom at any time by giving a written commitment to improve her behaviour. This written commitment must be in the student's own words and must specify the changed behaviour that will be evident when the student returns to the classroom. Of course, exclusion presupposes that the administration is supportive of such a technique and has made appropriate arrangements for the setting.

Our experience has shown that those few students who have been excluded from the classroom and have then made the written commitment and returned have remained in the classroom with acceptable behaviour. Exclusion finally demonstrates to the student that her behaviour will no longer be tolerated and that the entire responsibility for the student's behaviour is on the student and only the student.

If a student does not make the written commitment within a reasonable period of time, usually no more than a few days, outside assistance (in the form of parents, counsellor, principal, or outside agency) must be sought (see Chapter 10, "Seeking Outside Assistance"). If it is necessary to seek outside assistance, the teacher's use of self-monitoring, anecdotal record keeping, or behaviour contracting will provide the documented evidence needed to make an appropriate referral.

Summary

In this chapter, we have discussed the strategies that can be used in working with students who have chronic behavioural problems. We discussed two long-term strategies for resolving chronic problems: building positive relationships and breaking the cycle of discouragement. In addition, we introduced three techniques for managing students with chronic behavioural problems: self-monitoring, anecdotal record keeping, and behavioural contracting. Of the three techniques, self-monitoring is most compatible with the student-directed philosophy; anecdotal record keeping is most compatible with the collaborative philosophy; and behavioural contracting is most compatible with the teacher-directed philosophy. We also discussed *when*, *how*, and *with which* students to use these strategies and techniques. We divided the communication skills needed for a private conference, an essential component of any strategy for working with students who have chronic behavioural problems, into receiving skills and sending skills. Finally, we presented the technique of exclusion from the classroom—the final step between in-class teacher management and outside referral.

Key Terms

anecdotal record keeping: the teacher records positive and negative classroom behaviour of a chronically disruptive student over a period of a few weeks.

behaviour contracting: involves the use of a written agreement, known as a *behaviour contract*, between the teacher and student.

cycle of discouragement: often occurs when students suffer from low self-esteem and a low success-to-failure ratio.

relationship building: the conscious attempt by a teacher to build a positive relationship with students.

self-monitoring: student-directed approach; often effective with students who are trying to behave appropriately but need assistance to do so.

Exercises

1. Think of the teachers you had in school who were most successful in building positive relationships with students. What qualities did these teachers possess? How was their behaviour toward students different from the behaviour of teachers who were not good at building relationships? What implications do these differences have for building positive relationships with students who have chronic behavioural problems?

2. In this chapter, we suggest that teachers should attempt to empathize with students who have chronic behavioural problems. Does this mean that disruptive behaviour should be excused or condoned?

3. In this chapter, we present several ideas for breaking the cycle of discouragement by helping to meet students' self-esteem needs. In each of the following four categories of self-esteem needs, suggest additional behaviours that a teacher might use to enhance student self-esteem: (a) the need for significance, (b) the need for competence, (c) the need for power, (d) the need for virtue.

4. Form a triad with two other classmates. Designate a letter (A, B, or C) for each of you. Role-play three conferences between a teacher and a chronically disruptive student. In each instance, the individual playing the teacher will create the scenario that has led to the conference. During each conference, the person who plays the role of teacher should practise using effective receiving and sending skills. The process observer will give feedback to the teacher on her use of effective communication. Divide the roles for the three conferences according to the following format:

	Person A	Person B	Person C
Conference 1	Teacher	Student	Process observer
Conference 2	Process observer	Teacher	Student
Conference 3	Student	Process observer	Teacher

5. Design a self-monitoring instrument that is appropriate for elementary children and that monitors (a) calling out, (b) talking to neighbours, and (c) staying focused on seat work.

6. This chapter classified self-monitoring as a student-directed approach to the management of chronic behavioural problems. Do you agree? If so, what makes it a student-directed approach? If not, how should it be classified? If not, is it possible to have a student-directed technique to manage chronic behavioural problems?

7. Should chronically disruptive students receive special rewards for behaviours that are typically expected of other students? Justify your answer.

8. Make a list of rewards under the regular classroom teacher's control that could be used in behaviour contracts for students at each of the following levels: (a) elementary, (b) middle or junior high, (c) senior high.

9. Develop a list of learning-focused positive consequences that could be substituted for the use of concrete, extrinsic rewards in behaviour contracts.

10. Design an initial behaviour contract for the following situation: Jonathan, a grade 6 middle school student who loves sports, has during the past three weeks refused to do homework, started fights on three different occasions, and disrupted class two or three times each day.

11. We classify anecdotal record keeping as a collaborative approach to classroom management. Do you agree? If so, what makes it a collaborative approach? If not, how should it be classified?

12. Examine the sample anecdotal record in Figure 9.6 on page 225. Explain whether you concur with the following decisions made by the teacher: (a) to continue the intervention after 4/23 and 4/24; (b) to stop the record after 4/30. Justify your answers.

13. Which types of misbehaviour constitute sufficient grounds for exclusion from the classroom? Justify your answers.

*Weblinks*_____

Centre for Addiction and Mental Health
www.camh.net
This site provides useful resources related to students who are disruptive in the class-room and the possible underlying causes. Links are provided for the *Journal of Addiction and Mental Health.*

Facts About Corporal Punishment Worldwide(NCACPS)
www.stophitting.com/disatschool/facts.php
Offers facts and links to information about corporal punishment in Canada and around the world.

The National Crime Prevention Strategy
www.publicsafety.gc.ca/prg/cp/ncps-en.asp
A Government of Canada site that provides many resources and articles offering information about how to effectively interact with students.

Intervention Central
www.interventioncentral.org
"Intervention Central offers free tools and resources to help school staff and parents to promote positive classroom behaviours and foster effective learning for all children and youth."

10

Seeking Outside Assistance

Focus on the Principles of Classroom Management

1. What actions should professional teachers initiate when they recognize that some chronic misbehaviour problems are beyond their expertise?
2. When is a multidisciplinary team the most effective approach to manage chronic misbehaviour problems?
3. What techniques are essential to ensure parental support and co-operation with the school when attempting to manage a student who chronically misbehaves?

Introduction

Even when teachers use all of the strategies suggested in this text to prevent, cope with, and solve behavioural problems, there are some students who simply cannot behave appropriately without some type of specialized **outside assistance** or intervention. In these cases, the most rigorous step of the CALM model must be applied. Indeed, students who exhibit unmanageable behavioural problems are capable of overshadowing the positive educational climate of the classroom to such an extent that teachers can begin to question their own professional competence. Thus, it is very important for teachers to acknowledge that there are certain circumstances under which they should and must seek outside support and expertise. In fact, the mark of skilled professionals is to recognize the limits of their expertise and to make the necessary and appropriate consultations and referrals without any sense of professional inadequacy. In Canada, each board/school has a set of procedures that describe the appropriate steps for teachers to take when confronted by patterns of extreme student behaviours. Teachers are expected to be familiar with the board/school policies.

Sometimes, the first referral teachers make is to the student's parents or caregivers. They may do this through written correspondence or a phone conversation. Teachers should make this contact when (1) the misbehaviour is a minor surface behaviour that continues after the teacher has used the strategies discussed in this text and (2) the teacher is confident that parental input is all that is needed to assist in managing the misbehaviour. The contact should be made only after the student has been given a choice between improving his behaviour or having his parents/caregivers informed of his behaviour. The teacher should point out that the primary responsibility for controlling his behaviour rests with the student, not his parents or caregivers. Often, this in itself will bring the desired change. If not, parental contact is made and often results in consequences at home that are enough to motivate a change in school behaviour.

At other times, the behaviour is such that the teacher decides parental contact will not be sufficient to remedy the problem and that he needs outside expertise to understand and cope with the student. In these cases, parental contact comes after consultation with other professional staff members. Consultation ensures that the student's parents will have an adequate description of the problem, an explanation of the intervention strategies attempted, and a comprehensive proposed plan of action.

Whether parental contact is the first step or a later step in seeking outside assistance, it is critical that the contact sets the stage for a co-operative home–school relationship. For this to occur, it is often necessary to overcome negative, defensive parental perceptions and attitudes toward the school and/or the teacher. Thus, any parental contact must be preceded by careful planning and preparation. In addition to the student's parents/caregivers, the teacher may consult with the school's administrators, psychologists, learning specialists, and social workers. By doing this, specialized expertise is brought to bear on understanding and working with both the student who is displaying unremitting misbehaviour and his family. In some cases, referrals outside the school may be necessary.

In this chapter, we discuss the nature of persisting misbehaviour, the point at which a teacher needs to seek outside assistance, preparing for and conducting parent conferences, and the roles of other school staff members. In the penultimate section, "Symptoms of Serious Problems" on pages 248 and 249, we detail behaviours that may not be disruptive but that teachers must be aware of. These behaviours may be symptomatic of other serious problems that require outside referrals.

The Nature of Persisting Misbehaviour

In Chapter 3, which dealt exclusively with why children misbehave, we noted that much of the daily disruptive behaviour observed in children is characteristic of the developmental stages that all children go through and a normal reaction to society and recent societal changes. Obviously, some children display disruptive behaviour more frequently or more defiantly than others, but again, most of this behaviour is within the range of normal child and adolescent behaviour and usually can be influenced through the techniques and strategies suggested in this text. However, there are some students who display deviant behaviours that resist all attempts at modification.

These students often are reacting to negative influences within their environment. These influences may be quite obvious and identifiable, or they may be rather subtle. When a teacher is trying to understand a long-term pattern of misbehaviour, environmental influences must be viewed in a summative manner. Long-term behaviour is not understood by examining one or two snapshots of specific environmental influences. A history of influences must be considered.

One concept that is especially helpful in understanding historical influences is the success–failure ratio. This is a ratio of the amount of success a student experiences in his daily life to the amount of failure he experiences. Most students exhibit adaptive, productive behaviour and feel good about themselves when they are successful. Students who do not meet with a reasonable degree of success become frustrated and discouraged, and their behaviour becomes maladaptive and destructive (Glasser, 1969). Although students with chronic behaviour difficulties may appear hard and defiant, they are often very damaged and vulnerable. Frequently, negative experiences have left them unresponsive to the normal classroom reinforcements intended to increase the success–failure ratio. What are the influences that cause students to have a low success–failure ratio?

Failure in the Classroom Environment

Some students simply are not—or cannot find a way to be—successful at school in academic, social, and/or extracurricular activities. For these students, school is a daily source of failure that significantly reduces their overall success–failure ratio. Success in school and behaviour are so interrelated that it has been concluded that many misbehaving students do not feel successful in school (Wolfgang, 1999). In some cases, social failure can cause the child to resort to bullying or, conversely, could result in the child being bullied. In either case, the child is experiencing social failure that, in turn, can interfere with successful learning (Marini, Spear, and Bombay, 1999; Marini, Fairbain, and Zuber, 2001; Pepler and Craig, 1994). In some cases, careful observation and evaluation will uncover a learning or behavioural disability. The disability may have gone undiagnosed because it did not become apparent until the child moved toward higher grade levels, where behavioural expectations and the conceptual demands of the curriculum increased. These students are not involved or interested in what they learn. Their misbehaviour serves as a protection from further hurt and feelings of inadequacy (Wolfgang, 1999). In other cases, students may possess personality traits that cause classmates to either torment or ignore them. The behavioural difficulties that these students display may be understood as an expression of their frustration and discouragement, which many times escalate into the observable behaviours of anger and retaliation. For these students, reward and gratification stem more from their success at focusing attention on themselves than from meeting appropriate behavioural and instructional expectations.

Failure Outside the Classroom Environment

Some students exhibit extreme behaviours that seem to have little to do with the day-to-day realities of the class environment. Extreme apprehension, distrust, disappointment, hurt, anger, or outrage can be triggered in them under the most benign circumstances or with the slightest provocation. A teacher may find such a student reacting to him as if he were abusive or rejecting. These distorted emotional responses are reactions that often have been shaped outside the classroom and reflect problems that exist within the home and family or long-standing problems with peers. Some studies have concluded that 50 percent of children who experience behavioural problems at school also experience them at home (Johnson, Bolstad, and Lobitz, 1976; Day and Hrynkiw-Augimeri, 1996; Patterson, 1974). Some students with long-standing interpersonal relationship difficulties find the normal social pressures of the classroom too much to tolerate. Just as failure within the classroom lowers a student's perceived success–failure ratio, so, too, does failure outside the classroom.

Failure as a Result of Primary Mode of Conduct

For some students, misbehaviour seems to be the natural state of affairs. Their behaviour seems to be an expression of their own internal tension, restlessness, and discomfort rather than a reaction to any apparent environmental influence. These students' difficulties emerge during the preschool and kindergarten years. Their teachers view them as immature, emotionally volatile, inattentive, demanding, overly aggressive, and self-centred. They are usually quick to react with anger to any sort of stress or frustration. Unfortunately, their behaviour is too often explained simplistically as the natural expression of the "difficult child" temperament. For some, there is a significant improvement with age; for others, the problems intensify as negative reactions to home and school further reduce the success–failure ratio. Many of these children are eventually diagnosed with attention deficit hyperactivity disorder (ADHD) or oppositional defiant disorder (ODD).

When Outside Assistance Is Needed

How do teachers decide when to seek outside consultation or referral? Although there are no rules, two general guidelines can assist with the decision. First, referral is warranted when teachers recognize that a developing problem is beyond their professional expertise. When true professionals recognize this, they act to identify and contact specialized professional assistance. Second, the more deviant, disruptive, or frequent the behaviour, the more imperative it is to make referrals. In other words, referral is necessary when

1. A misbehaving student does not improve after the hierarchical interventions described in this text have been exhausted, or
2. The hierarchical approach has resulted in improvement, but the student continues to manifest problems that disrupt either teaching or learning. This is the kind of case where the CALM model is an important approach for the teacher to take. Clearly, some action is necessary as learning/teaching are being affected negatively.

There are some students who are not behavioural problems but show signs that may be symptoms of serious problems that require the attention of professionals with specialized training. Symptoms of social difficulty, illness, anxiety, depression, learning difficulty, abuse, substance abuse, suicide, and family discord become apparent to the knowledgeable and sensitive teacher. We include a more detailed discussion of these symptoms in the "Symptoms of Serious Problems" section later in this chapter.

The Referral Process

When outside assistance is warranted, the teacher must have access to a network of school support personnel who are trained to cope with children with unremitting problematic classroom behaviour. Most often, the first referral is to an administrator (typically a principal in elementary school and a vice-principal at the secondary level). Contact with the appropriate administrator helps to ensure that parents are not called in before the school has explored all the possible interventions at its disposal. Except for serious problems, parents/caregivers should be contacted only when it is apparent that the school has no other alternatives (Jones and Jones, 1995).

Parents are apt to be responsive and co-operative if they can see a history of teacher and school interventions. Working closely with the parents of students who exhibit chronic behavioural problems is so critical that it will be discussed in depth later in this chapter (see the section entitled, "Working with Parents" on pages 241 to 248). First, what role does the administrator play?

The Role of the Learning Specialist

In schools where there is a learning specialist on the professional staff, teachers should contact him as soon as the decision has been made to seek outside assistance. Teachers should be prepared to present documented data on the student's misbehaviour and all approaches used in the attempt to manage the disruptive behaviour (Weber and Bennett, 1999). Anecdotal records and behaviour contracts (see Chapter 9) are excellent sources for this information.

In difficult situations, a teacher may become stuck, repetitively applying strategies that do not work. As an outside observer, the learning specialist is quite useful. He is a neutral onlooker with a fresh view from outside the classroom who may be able to suggest modifications in the strategies or techniques the teacher has tried. The learning specialist may want to explore further the student's behaviour, the teacher's style, the nature of the teacher–student interaction, and the learning environment by visiting the classroom or by scheduling further conferences with the student and/or teacher, either alone or together. Once this has been done, the learning specialist may be able to provide objective feedback and offer suggestions for new approaches. He may also work closely with the student to help develop more acceptable in-class behaviours.

The learning specialist also can help to improve the strained teacher–student relationship by acting as an intermediary, thus assisting the teacher and the student simultaneously. He can offer support to the teacher, who must cope with the stress of managing a child who exhibits chronically disruptive behaviour, and he can discuss with the student classroom problems that arise from behaviour, academics, or social interactions. Often, problems are adequately handled at this level. However, in those cases in which this is not sufficient, additional consultants are called on. Typically, they include an administrator, parents, or representatives from appropriate outside agencies.

The Role of the Administrator

In many cases of chronic misbehaviour, certain in-school strategies or decisions require the authoritative and administrative power of the principal or vice-principal. For example, decisions to remove a student from a classroom for an extended period of time, to change a student's teacher, and to implement in-school or out-of-school suspensions must be approved and supported by an administrator. An administrator's approval often is needed to refer a student to a learning specialist.

Very deviant behaviour may require action at the school board level. In cases of expulsion or recommendations for placement in specialized educational settings outside the school, the administrator will be expected to provide testimony at any hearings that may be held and, thus, must be thoroughly familiar with the student's history.

The Role of the School Board Psychologist

If there are indications that a student's problems are rooted in deeper and more pervasive personality disturbances or family problems, the clinical resources of the school board psychologist should be sought. The initial role of the school board psychologist, which in some cases includes a psychometrist, is one of evaluation and diagnostic study. Although this team will apply independent observational, interview, and testing techniques, these are really an extension of the day-to-day data that may have already been accumulated by the classroom teacher(s), other in-school learning specialists, and the administrator(s). The results of these evaluative studies may lead to recommendations for further study, specialized programming, or referral to outside resources.

The Role of the Consultative Team

Once the administrator(s) and possibly a learning specialist or psychologist are involved, a **consultative team** has been created. Although a team approach is not formalized in many schools, it can be quite effective in delineating responsibilities and keeping the lines of communication open and clearly defined. The team approach facilitates group problem solving, offers a multidisciplinary perspective, and reduces the possibility that any one individual will become overburdened with a sense of responsibility for "the problem." As with any team, a leader is needed to coordinate the team's efforts. The learning specialist may be a good coordinator because he is thoroughly familiar with the student and has quick access to all members of the team (Weber and Bennett, 1999).

Most school boards have come to realize that teachers cannot be expected to possess the expertise necessary to manage effectively all the learning and behavioural problems found in today's classrooms. To provide support in addressing these problems, school-based consultation teams that follow systematic models of assistance and/or intervention have been implemented. These teams, made up of classroom teachers, instructional support specialists, principals, parents/caregivers, and others, work together to modify the regular classroom environment to increase student achievement and improve behaviour before a student can be referred for testing for possible placement in special education. In Ontario, such a team is called the Identification, Placement, and Review Committee (IPRC); New Brunswick has Collaborative Educational Planning or Students with Exceptionalities; and British Columbia has Individual Educational Plans. At the secondary level, these teams are often made up of teachers, guidance counsellors, principals, and others who provide assistance to students who are having serious personal, behavioural, and/or academic difficulties.

Working with Parents

When it is apparent that the teacher and school have explored all the interventions at their disposal, the student's parents should be contacted. It is essential to have the support and co-operation of parents in working effectively with a chronically misbehaving student (Lam and Peake, 1997). Unfortunately, parental contacts often are characterized by negative reactions and defensiveness on the part of parents and the teacher. It is imperative to minimize negativity and maximize positive support and co-operation. This takes careful planning and a great deal of skill in interpersonal interaction and conferencing techniques on the part of the consultative team members (Canter and Canter, 2001). If the teacher has started to build a positive relationship with parents before the problem really begins, parental contacts concerning problems are likely to result in much greater parental co-operation. Many teachers send a beginning-of-the-year letter home to parents. This letter explains a little bit about the teacher and his academic and behavioural goals and hopes for the coming year. In addition to providing information about how to contact the teacher, the letter also spells out opportunities for parental involvement in the classroom and suggestions for how parents can help their child to be successful. Many effective teachers follow up on this beginning-of-the-year letter with positive messages to parents in the form of emails, telephone calls, and "good news notes."

When Parents Should Be Contacted

Under the following conditions, parents should be contacted concerning behavioural problems:

1. When the student displays unremitting misbehaviour after the teacher and the school have employed all available interventions.
2. When the consultative team decides that the student needs a change in teacher or schedule.
3. When the consultative team decides that the student should be removed from a class for an extended period of time or from school for even one day.
4. When the consultative team decides that the student needs to be tested for learning, emotional, or physical difficulties.
5. When the consultative team decides that outside specialists such as psychiatrists, physicians, and social workers are required.

The Importance of Working with Parents

When the school has exhausted its alternatives in attempting to manage a chronically misbehaving student, it is essential for the student's parents to be contacted and made members of the consulting team. After all, whether a student exhibits disruptive behaviour or not, all parents have the right to be informed of their child's behavioural and academic progress. Furthermore, parental support of the school has a major impact on a child's positive attitude toward school (Jones, 1980; Weber and Bennett, 1999). When a student's parents feel good about the teacher and school, the student usually receives encouragement and reinforcement for appropriate school behaviour (Jones and Jones, 1995). Parents can, in fact, be one of the teacher's strongest allies, which is particularly helpful when the student exhibits chronic behavioural problems (Brookover and Gigliotti, 1988). Thus, parental support and co-operation must be cultivated by the teacher and other school staff members. To this end, programs such as parent visitation; meet-the-teacher nights; parent–teacher organizations; parent advisory boards, such as school councils; and volunteer programs have been widely instituted. As we have noted, individual teachers complement such school-wide efforts by communicating positive aspects of children's education to their parents by sending notes and phone calls, inviting parents to call when they have any questions, and requiring students to take home graded assignments and tests.

CASE 10.1 • *In Order to Drive, You Must Speak French*

Dawn is 16 years old. Her grades have gone from Bs to Ds in French and history. The decline in her academic performance is a result of inattentiveness and poor study habits. After the teacher and guidance counsellor speak to Dawn without any noticeable improvement, her parents are called.

During a conference, Dawn explains that she doesn't like French or history and doesn't see why she needs these subjects anyway. Her teachers try to explain why these subjects are important, especially in today's world, but have little success. Finally, her parents intervene and point out to Dawn that she has scheduled driver's education for the spring semester. If she expects to be able to drive, they say, she must demonstrate responsibility and discipline and one way to do so is to do well in all school subjects. They finally give Dawn a choice: either

her grades improve or she will not be allowed to take driver's education and obtain her learner's permit.

Her teachers and parents keep in contact; by the end of the fall semester, Dawn's grades are again Bs.

Questions to Consider

1. What lesson(s) did Dawn learn from this experience?
2. What other methods might have been used to motivate Dawn? Discuss the likelihood of success.
3. How could/should the parents and teachers have reacted if Dawn had said that she did not care about driver's education, but that if they did not let her enrol, she would move away from home and into a friend's apartment?
4. How does the CALM model apply to this case? Discuss how it could be effective.

Frequently, these children, especially when they are adolescents, are not motivated or are unresponsive to the encouragements a school can provide. Their parents, on the other hand, can provide a wider variety of more attractive encouragements. Indeed, a system of home consequences contingent on school behaviour can be an effective means for modifying classroom behaviour (Ayllon, Garber, and Pisor, 1975). Such a system is illustrated in Case 10.1. Thus, because parents usually care greatly about their children, they represent an interested party that can provide an inexpensive, continuous treatment resource to augment school efforts. The school's positive working relationship with parents often is the most critical component for effectively influencing a disruptive student.

Understanding Parents

For all the positive help parents or caregivers may be able to offer, teachers and other school personnel often feel uncomfortable contacting them. Many parents harbour negative feelings toward their child's teachers and school. School personnel often complain that contacting parents necessitates using time, usually before or after school, that could be put to better use. Teachers also complain that they often feel intimidated by parents who think that teachers should be able to maintain control of their child without parental help. Also, because education is funded by tax dollars, parents sometimes appear to believe they should be able to judge and monitor teacher performance. However, as professionals, teachers and other school staff must not allow these feelings to jeopardize the opportunity to gain the support and co-operation of parents.

If parental contacts result in distrust, apprehension, and dissatisfaction for both parents and teachers, efforts to assist the disruptive student probably will fail. In time, the parents' sense of alienation from the school will be passed onto the child, further lessening the possibility of the school working with the parents to find a means to redirect the student toward acceptable behaviour. Therefore, the members of the consultative team must create an atmosphere that facilitates a change of negative parental perceptions and assumptions into positive ones. This is more easily accomplished when team members understand the parents' perspectives (Waters, 2002).

Many children who exhibit chronic misbehaviour in school display similar behaviours at home. Often, their parents have been frustrated by their own failures in raising their child. Since parents consider their children as extensions of themselves and products of their parenting, they are not anxious to be reminded of how inadequate they have been. Sometimes, there has been a long history of negative feedback from teachers and administrators that has created a feeling of powerlessness and humiliation. Because these parents feel everyone is blaming them for their child's misbehaviour, they are quite wary of any sort of school contact and react by withdrawing, resisting, or angrily counterattacking and blaming the school for the problems. This does not have to happen. Through careful planning and the use of proper conferencing skills, the school consultative team can gain the needed support and co-operation from parents (Minke and Anderson, 2003).

A review of research on parental involvement in schools by Hoover-Dempsey and Sandler (1997) suggests that three major factors influence parents' decisions about whether to become involved in their child's education or not. Parents' beliefs about their role as parents as it relates to providing home support for school endeavours is one key factor. A second key factor is parents' sense of efficacy concerning their ability to help their child be successful in school. The third key factor is the parents' perceptions of the general invitation for parental involvement in the school and classroom. Schools can influence parental choice of involvement by engaging in activities that influence these three perceptions. Consistently advocating that parental involvement is a critical factor in school success can have an impact on parental role perception. Conducting workshops, classes, and courses on parental effectiveness can increase parents' sense of efficacy (Rosenthal and Sawyers, 1996). Finally, making sure that both the general school climate and individual classroom climate welcome parental involvement can influence parents to become more actively involved in their child's education. Welcoming climates are marked by a variety of factors, including frequent positive parental contact, face-to-face interaction at times that are convenient for parents, and opportunities for parents to influence decisions that will affect their children.

Conducting Parent Conferences

When the consultative team determines that conditions warrant parental (or caregiver) involvement, the school principal or team coordinator usually makes the first contact. The tone of this initial contact is extremely important in developing a co-operative working relationship. The principal or team coordinator should expect some degree of defensiveness on the part of the parent, especially if the student has had a history of school misbehaviour. This attitude should be understood and not taken personally. The cause of the school's concern should be stated clearly and honestly. The climate of the conversation should be, "How can we work as a team to best meet your child's needs?" rather than "Here we go again!" or "We've done everything we can. Now, it's up to you."

Once a conference has been scheduled, the team must decide who will attend the conference. Should all the members of the consultative team be in attendance? Should the student be at the conference (Lam and Peake, 1997)? The answers depend on the particular problem, the amount of expertise needed to explain the situation, the approaches that have been tried, and who will need to be available to answer any questions that may arise. In addition, the conference must be conducted in a positive manner that is least threatening to the parents. This often means the fewer people present, the less threatening the conference appears to parents. In most circumstances, the initial conference is conducted by the team coordinator. Unless the problem includes discussing behaviour or other signs that indicate serious health, emotional, or legal problems, the student may be present.

The conference should begin by introducing all in attendance, thanking the parents for their willingness to attend, and outlining the goal of the conference. Throughout the conference, everyone should have an equal chance to express his or her viewpoint. School personnel also look for any signs that indicate that the conference is deteriorating into a debate or blaming session and act rapidly to defuse the situation by directing the conference back to the major purpose of how best to meet the student's needs.

Obviously, appropriate interpersonal and conferencing skills must be familiar to and practised by all professionals in attendance (Rosenthal and Sawyers, 1996). Some of these skills are to be friendly, to be supportive, and to use active listening (which includes paraphrasing) to ensure proper understanding by all (see Chapter 9). The teacher should be prepared to have some positive things to say about the student. Information should be elicited through the use of questions rather than directive statements aimed at the student or parents/caregivers. Neither the child nor the parents should be attacked, disparaged, or blamed. However, sometimes parents and the student attack, disparage, and blame the teacher or other school officials. If this occurs, it is important to remember that one does not defend one's professional competence with words, but with behaviour.

One of the best means to demonstrate professional competence is through the use of previously collected data that illustrate and demonstrate the concerns of the school and the need for the conference. The data should include a history of objective and specific information about the student's behaviours and the actions taken by the teacher and the school to manage them. Anecdotal records are an excellent source for this data (see Chapter 9). The use of these data reduces the likelihood of the conference turning into a debate, illustrates that the problem is not exaggerated, and defuses any attempt by the parent to suggest that the school did not take appropriate and necessary actions.

Throughout the conference, the parents' and student's feelings, viewpoints, and suggestions should be actively solicited. The outcome of the conference, it is hoped, will be either an agreed-upon course of action or the decision that the school will contact the parents in the near future with a suggested course of action. The meeting ends on an optimistic note with a summary, a show of appreciation, and an encouraging statement that with both the home and school working as a team, a successful outcome is likely.

With some students, it may be decided to try additional school and/or classroom strategies with little additional parental involvement. This decision is usually a result of new information that allows the school to design additional appropriate strategies or because the parents, like Sharon's mother in Case 10.2 on the next page and following, clearly demonstrate their lack of interest. Sharon's mother is atypical, not because she is uninterested but because she openly and honestly admits it. Sometimes, when parents are uninterested, there is a tendency on the part of the school personnel to give up and adopt an attitude that "if they don't care, then we've done what we can." However, children should never be denied access to potentially effective school intervention programs because their parents are uninterested, uncooperative, or unsupportive (Walker, 1979).

When it is obvious that parental involvement will probably improve the child's behaviour significantly or there is evidence of a deficiency in parenting skills, increased parental involvement will be requested. Some school boards now provide information about parenting classes held in their community.

Concentric Case Study Kaleidoscope

CASE 10.2 • *"I'm Not Much Help to Her"*

The Story

Sharon is in grade 10. Her behaviour is excellent. She is of average intelligence, always completes assignments and consistently achieves average marks. In addition, she is rarely absent, is well dressed and has a number of friends. Overall, she appears to be a typical happy grade 10 student. However, she always asks one of her teachers if she can stay in order to help with anything. If there is nothing for her to do, she merely sits and talks. She seems quite content to spend her spare time in this way and the teachers have become used to her patterns of behaviour. As the term end approaches and her marks are compiled, Sharon's teachers are startled to discover that she will receive all Ds and Fs rather than her usual Cs and Bs.

As Sharon's new slate of marks emerges, her teachers begin to speak to her about the sudden change in her achievement levels. One of them also refers her to the vice-principal for counselling. Throughout all discussions, Sharon maintains that she is happy and that nothing is wrong. In an attempt to help Sharon, extra remedial help is offered but there is no evidence of improved achievement.

Before report cards are issued, the vice-principal schedules a conference with Sharon, her mother, and her teachers. The VP is concerned that Sharon is failing, and she wants to make sure that her mother is apprised of the situation before the report card arrives home.

When Sharon's mother arrives, she appears well dressed, well spoken, and somewhat concerned about Sharon's drop in achievement. As each teacher present talks about Sharon's poor performance in the class, Sharon's mother appears to listen carefully and looks very serious. When it is her turn to respond she says, "Sharon's dad left us ten years ago. Since then, I have been a single mother devoting myself to raising my daughter. But now she is older—I need to focus on my own life, look after myself, and get things moving in the right direction. Now I am busy. I have a career and I do a lot of internet dating. To be perfectly honest, I buy Sharon's clothes and make sure that she eats properly, but that is all the time I have. I owe something to myself now and I am not getting any younger." There is a short silence and Sharon's mother continues earnestly, "I would really appreciate anything you can do for Sharon because I know that I'm not much help to her at this time. I have to go now, as I have an important date. Sorry about that."

When she leaves, there is a silence. One of the teachers asks, "What can we do for Sharón?"

Sharon's Perspective

I really like school and I really like my teachers! I know that I am one of the few students who wish that the day would not end. Most of my teachers seem to like me, and if I stay around them after school, they will talk to me. This part of the afternoon is very important for me and I finally go home feeling good about my day. When I get home, my mother is usually too busy to really talk to me. She always gets dinner and we eat together, but the phone usually rings and she talks to her boyfriends during dinner. I wish she would talk to me more. Sometimes, I think she forgets that I am in the house.

I know I have been neglecting my homework and my studying this past term.

I am not sure why, but I just don't feel like working hard. It does not seem to be worth the effort at this point. Whether I get good marks or not doesn't seem to matter to anyone, so why should I care? I really don't think my mother would notice one way or the other. In any case, she never asks me about my work and never reminds me to do my homework like she used to.

I miss my old relationship with my mother. We used to talk and laugh and she used to tell me what to do. I didn't always like it but at least she paid attention to me. I know she has been called to the school to talk about the fact that I am not doing very well in my classes. She is going to have to think about me, anyway. In fact, in a way I am glad that the school called her—she seems to have forgotten that I have to do my work if I am going to get good marks.

Sharon's Mother

The school has called to ask me to come and talk about Sharon's marks. I know I should pay more attention to Sharon, but right now I have to think about my own future. I am really tired of struggling as a single mother and feeling so lonely. Sharon is now in high school and I have given her 15 years of my life. I am not getting any younger or more attractive. This may be my last chance to find happiness in a good relationship. I have determined to put my focus there now and I am going to succeed. I feel good about myself for the first time in years.

At times, I feel a bit guilty about neglecting Sharon, but she is older now and should be able to run her own life and do her homework without constant reminders and interaction with me. I look after the bills; she has a roof over her head and food on the table. She should be fine.

I wonder why she is not doing as well as usual in school. I guess the school will want me to take responsibility for her marks as well. No one really understands how hard

it is to be in charge of everything. Am I supposed to sacrifice my whole life for the sake of my daughter? Why is it my fault if a mature child cannot take responsibility for her work? After all, I have taken responsibility for her for most of her life. It is her turn now.

I can sense that the teachers are concerned and that they are being judgmental about my decisions to have fun while I can. I don't care. They are the professionals. They are the ones who are supposed to understand adolescents. It is their job to teach her. I am doing my half and expect them to do theirs. I am glad I was open and honest with them so they will know exactly how I feel.

One of Sharon's Teachers

I like Sharon and I'm disappointed in her marks this term. I know that when she stays behind after school she wants to talk. For some reason, she appears to need attention which did not appear to be her typical behaviour prior to this term. I wonder what has changed in her life. Also, I see that all her marks are lower. Something is certainly going on in her life, which is causing her to react negatively. I'm glad we decided to call her mother in for a talk about this issue.

Now that I see Sharon's mother, I am shocked. She has obviously been paying a very great deal of attention to her appearance. She's trying to look younger than her daughter; instead, she just looks silly. After hearing her talk about her desire to date and find a new relationship, it's obvious that she is paying little attention to Sharon's needs. Although Sharon's physical needs are being met, it is equally clear that there's an emotional hole in her life. I feel bad about that.

I am really too busy with my own issues, my own children, and my own career to take over the kind of relationship that Sharon needs. I believe that parents rely on the school too much to do parenting as well as teaching. I simply do not have the time and I'm not paid to take care of other people's children. If I tried to help all neglected children, I would have no life of my own and my family would suffer. Sharon will have to find another way to cope and perhaps there is someone else she can talk to. I wonder if I should call a counsellor.

Another of Sharon's Teachers

I like Sharon and am sorry to see that she has been less effective as a student this past term. Clearly, something is wrong in her life and I'm really glad that we have called a meeting to address the problem with her mother before it's too late to remedy the problem.

I am shocked by Sharon's mother's appearance, as she's clearly done herself up to look very young and to attract attention. The mother feels she has spent enough time raising her daughter and now wants to go forward in her own life. I wish her luck, although I am not sure she is going about attaining her goals in a sensible manner. If anything is going to change for Sharon and her emotional needs are to be met, it will clearly have to be by someone other than her mother.

I think that I will have to respond to this situation by trying to help Sharon. I wonder if there is a Big Sister program in the area, and if the school board has a counsellor who can help. Maybe Sharon has a grandmother who is in the area. I wonder what I can do.

Questions to Consider

1. Whose responsibility is it to see that Sharon's emotional needs are met?

2. What specific actions would you take in this case if Sharon were your student?

3. What should the school vice-principal do next?

4. Do you think students such as Sharon are frequently found in our schools? Explain.

5. Set up a role-playing scenario similar to the one discussed in this case and construct a dialogue between the two teachers.

Symptoms of Serious Problems

Some students display symptoms of serious problems that may or may not be accompanied by disruptive and/or academic difficulties. These problems may be related to physical or emotional health or associated with an abusive home or with substance abuse. All of these areas may fall outside the expertise and domain of the school. An aware teacher often recognizes these symptoms and notifies the appropriate school official, usually the principal, who then decides on the proper step.

Some of the signs that may be significant include the following:

1. *Changes in physical appearance.* Often, students reveal their underlying problems through sudden changes in their physical appearance. Posture, dress, and grooming habits are reflections of underlying mood and self-image, and a student's deterioration in these habits should be noted with concern. More striking changes such as rapid weight loss or gain, particularly in light of the dramatic increase in eating disorders among high school students, should be investigated. While unusual

soreness, bruises, cuts, or scarring are signs of possible neglect or abuse, they may also indicate self-mutilation or other self-destructive tendencies.

2. *Changes in activity level.* Teachers need to be aware of the significance of changes in activity level. Excessive tardiness, lethargy, absenteeism, and a tendency to fall asleep in class may result from a variety of problems, including depression and substance abuse. Hyperactivity, impulsivity, lowered frustration and tolerance thresholds, and overaggressiveness also may represent the student's effort to deal with emotional unrest and discomfort.

3. *Changes in personality.* Emotional disturbances in children and adolescents are sometimes reflected in very direct forms of expression and behaviour. The seemingly well-adjusted child who is suddenly sad, easily agitated, or has angry outbursts uncharacteristic of his prior behaviour should be closely observed and monitored.

4. *Changes in achievement status.* A decline in a student's ability to focus on his work, persist at his studies, or produce or complete work successfully is often an indication of the draining effects of emotional turmoil or significant changes in the home environment.

5. *Changes in health or physical abilities.* Complaints of not being able to see or hear, when it appears the student is paying attention, should be referred to health professionals for follow-up. Complaints of frequent headaches, stomach aches, dizziness, sores that will not heal, skin rashes, and frequent bathroom use are signs that you should be concerned about the student's health.

6. *Changes in socialization.* Children who spend most of the time by themselves, seem to have no friends, and are socially withdrawn are not often identified as problem students because their symptoms do not have a disturbing impact on the classroom. These students may drift from one grade to another without appropriate attention and concern. However, they often leave a sign of their underlying misery in their behaviour, artwork, and creative writing samples.

In most cases of serious problems, schools are able to arrange for or make referrals to a host of specialized professionals, including psychologists, psychiatrists, nutritionists, medical doctors, social workers, and legal authorities. However, appropriate intervention rests with the aware and concerned teacher who must make the initial observations and referral.

Legal Aspects of Seeking Outside Assistance

There are some legal issues that must be considered to protect children's and parents' or caregivers' rights when seeking outside assistance. Most school boards are aware of these laws and have developed appropriate procedures to abide by them. In addition, all provinces have laws that require teachers to report any signs of child abuse. Many of these laws have provisions that impose penalties on school personnel who fail to meet this responsibility.

Summary

Some students simply do not experience the degree of success in the classroom that supports the development and maintenance of appropriate behaviour. Their conduct problems remain unremitting despite the application of appropriate hierarchical strategies, or they show other signs and symptoms indicative of serious underlying disturbances. In these cases, some type of specialized or out-of-school assistance may be required.

A team approach, which may include the student, parents, teacher(s), learning specialist, administrator(s), and outside specialists, is an effective means for expanded evaluation and for the development of specific interventions that may extend beyond the normal classroom. The support and co-operation of parents is critical to increase the likelihood of successful intervention. Any negative parental attitudes must be defused. This is best accomplished through careful planning and the skilled use of conferencing techniques when working with parents. Protecting students' rights throughout any process focused on managing misbehaviour is paramount.

Key Terms

consultative team: a team approach that facilitates group problem solving, offers a multidisciplinary perspective, and reduces the possibility that any one individual will become overburdened with a sense of responsibility for "the problem."

outside assistance: needed when a teacher recognizes that a problem is beyond his expertise and outside referral and consultation are necessary.

Exercises

1. The student's success–failure ratio is an extremely important variable that influences student behaviour. There are many areas in which students experience success and failure, including academic, social, and extracurricular areas. List several specific areas in a school setting in which students can experience success or failure.

2. The importance of success in specific areas depends on the student's age. Using the list of specific areas for success developed in the first exercise, rate each area's importance for students in elementary, middle, junior high, and senior high school.

3. Develop a list of symptoms that could be added to the list of potentially serious problems that may warrant outside assistance. Be able to justify why each symptom should be included on the list.

4. Are there any dangers associated with using a list similar to the one developed in the third exercise? Before answering, consider such areas as contextual setting, duration and severity of behaviour, and so on. If there are dangers, what can a teacher do to minimize them?

5. Even when students are not exhibiting behavioural problems, it is important for teachers to gain the support of parents. In what ways can teachers develop such support?

6. Compose a beginning-of-the-school-year letter that you could send to parents. In the letter, be sure to include information about yourself, your classroom, your hopes and goals for the coming year, and ideas about how parents can become involved in supporting their child's success. Also include contact information so parents can reach you. Make sure that the letter is free of educational jargon.

7. Sometimes teachers may decide to contact the parents before consulting a student's administrators. When should parents be contacted before the administrators?

8. In consultation with your instructor, contact a school (use your own school if you are currently teaching) and identify all the resources available to assist teachers with seriously misbehaving students.

9. Children with attention deficit hyperactivity disorder (ADHD) and oppositional defiant disorder (ODD) are in mainstreamed classrooms. Research the behaviours these children exhibit, and suggest or research strategies that are effective in managing these children.

10. It has been said that if a teacher is a good teacher for difficult children, he will be an excellent teacher for all the children in his class. Explain what this means.

Weblinks

The Canadian Home and School Federation
www.canadianhomeandschool.com
The website describes the role of parents in education today.

Centre for Addiction and Mental Health
www.camh.net
This site has many resources—one article is entitled, "Mischief or a Cry for Help? Disciplining Students Demands Awareness of Underlying Distress."

Children and Adolescents with Conduct Disorder: Parent Training and Peer Group Interventions
www.cmho.org/pdf_files/CD_W3_Parent%20training.pdf
This document describes a number of family programs designed to address and modify conduct disorders among children.

Edmonton Public Schools Board Policies and Regulations
www.epsb.ca/policy/ig.bp.shtml
From the Edmonton School Board, this is an example of students' rights and responsibilities.

Iterative Case Study Analysis

Fourth Analysis

Considering the concepts discussed in Parts III and IV, reanalyze your third analysis. What has changed and what has stayed the same since your last analysis? Once again, consider why the students may be choosing to behave inappropriately and how you might intervene to influence the students to stop the disruptive behaviour and resume appropriate on-task behaviour.

Elementary School Case Study

During silent reading time in my grade 4 class, I have built in opportunities to work individually with students. During this time, the students read to me and practice word work with flash cards. One student has refused to read to me but instead wants only to work with the flash cards. After a few sessions, I suggested we work with word cards this time and begin reading next time. He agreed. The next time we met, I reminded him of our plan, and he screamed, "I don't remember! I want to do word cards!" At this point, I tried to find out why he didn't like reading and he said, "There's a reason, I just can't tell you," and he threw the word cards across the room, some of them hitting other students. What should I do?

Middle School Case Study

I can't stop thinking about a problem I'm having in class with a group of 12-year-old boys. They consistently use vulgar language toward one another and some of the shyer kids in the class, especially the girls. In addition, they are always pushing and shoving each other. I've tried talking to them about why they keep using bad language when they know it's inappropriate. The response I get is that "it makes me look cool and funny in front of my friends." I have asked them to please use more appropriate language in the classroom but that has not worked. I haven't even started to address the pushing and shoving. What should I do?

High School Case Study

This past week, I had a student approach me about a problem he was experiencing in our class. The grade 11 student had recently "come out" as being gay. He said he was tired and upset with the three boys who sit near him. These boys frequently call him a "homo" and a "fag" every time they see him, both in and out of class. What should I do?

252

Appendix

The Discipline Problem Analysis Inventory (DPAI)

The discipline problem analysis inventory is a tool the classroom teacher can use to reflect on inappropriate student behaviour and its prevention, causes, and solutions. The inventory presents questions teachers can ask themselves regarding the development of hierarchical management plans or a particular student misbehaviour. Part A of the inventory contains questions regarding the prevention of misbehaviour. Part B contains questions regarding the resolution of misbehaviour.

Part A: Have I Done All I Can to Prevent Misbehaviour?

Chapter 1: The Foundations

1. Do I consider how my behaviour affects student behaviour?
2. Am I familiar with the principles of classroom management as presented in this book?
3. Do I employ a professional decision-making approach to classroom management?

Chapter 2: The Nature of Behavioural Problems

1. Do the behaviours I am trying to correct constitute discipline problems as defined in the text? Do they interfere with teaching or the rights of others to learn? Are they psychologically or physically unsafe? Do they destroy property?
2. Do my behaviours contribute to any discipline problems?
3. Do my behaviours maximize the time students spend on learning?
4. Do I deal with non-discipline behaviour problems after the rest of the class is involved in the learning activities?

Chapter 3: Understanding Why Children Misbehave

1. Is the misbehaviour a result of unmet physiological needs (for example, nourishment, rest, temperature, ventilation, noise, lighting)?

2. Is the misbehaviour a result of unmet safety and security needs (for example, fear of other students, teachers, staff members, parents, other adults; insecurity about rules and expectations)?

3. Is the misbehaviour a result of unmet needs for belonging and affection?

4. Do I provide opportunities for students to feel significant, competent, powerful, and have a sense of virtue?

5. Is the misbehaviour a result of a mismatch between the student's cognitive developmental level and instructional goals, tasks, or methods?

6. Is the misbehaviour a result of a mismatch between the student's moral developmental level and my management plan?

7. Is the misbehaviour a result of striving to meet the faulty goals of attention, power, revenge, or inadequacy?

8. Am I trying not to personalize students' misbehaviours?

Chapter 4: Philosophical Approaches to Classroom Management

1. Have I analyzed which power base(s) I employ to manage classroom behaviour?

2. Have I asked myself the nine basic questions to analyze which theory of classroom management is consistent with my beliefs about teaching and learning?

3. Do I employ the power base(s) that is/are consistent with my beliefs about teaching and learning?

4. Are my management behaviours consistent with the power base(s) and theory of management I want to use?

Chapter 5: The Professional Teacher

1. Do I plan my lessons to include findings from effective teaching research by
   a. including an introduction?
   b. clearly presenting the content?
   c. checking for student understanding?
   d. providing for coached and solitary practice?
   e. providing for closure and summarization?
   f. conducting periodic reviews?

2. Do I increase student motivation to learn by considering student interests, student needs, instruction novelty and variety, student success, student attributions, tension, feeling tone, feedback, and encouragement?

3. Do I communicate high expectations for learning and behaviour by equalizing response opportunities, providing prompt and constructive feedback, and treating each student with personal regard?

4. Do I use questioning to involve students actively in the learning process by asking questions at different cognitive levels and using probing questions, wait time, a variety of techniques to elicit response, and a variety of positive reinforcements?

5. Do I maximize both allocated and engaged time in learning?

6. Do I teach for deep understanding, emphasizing topics that are important, at the appropriate developmental level, and related to students' lives and interests outside of school?

7. Do I use the five components of authentic instruction?

8. Do I use all five of the teaching frameworks described in *dimensions of learning*?

9. Do I use cooperative learning activities that contain all three essential elements of cooperative learning?

10. Do I teach in ways that allow students to demonstrate their knowledge using all seven types of human intelligence?

11. Do I use personal goal setting and appropriate attributions for student success and failure to increase student motivation and promote positive feelings of self-efficacy?

Chapter 6: Structuring the Environment

1. Do I make my room physically comfortable by considering lighting, ventilation, and noise reduction?

2. Do I design seating arrangements to accommodate the various learning activities?

3. Does the seating arrangement ensure that each student can see the instructional activities, that the teacher has close proximity to each student, and that seats are not placed in high traffic areas or close to distractions?

4. Do I use my bulletin boards to recognize students and provide students with active participation?

5. Do I develop and teach procedures for everyday routines?

6. Do I analyze the classroom environment to determine the rules needed to protect teaching, learning, safety, and property?

7. Do I clearly communicate the rules and their rationales to students?

8. Do I attempt to obtain student commitments to abide by the rules?

9. Do I teach and evaluate student understanding of the rules?

10. Do I develop and enforce each rule with a natural or logical consequence?

11. Do I consider my students' cultural values, norms, and behavioural expectations in setting classroom rules and guidelines and in interpreting student behaviour?

12. Do I use cooperative learning activities and teach social skills to my students in order to create group norms that will promote prosocial behaviour and engagement in learning activities?

Part B: Am I Effectively Resolving Behaviour?

Chapter 7: Managing Common Behaviour Problems: Non-verbal Interventions

1. Do I meet the six prerequisites to appropriate student behaviour?
   a. Am I well prepared to teach?
   b. Do I provide clear directions and expectations?
   c. Do I ensure student understanding of evaluation criteria?
   d. Do I clearly communicate, rationalize, and consistently enforce behavioural expectations?
   e. Do I demonstrate enthusiasm and encouragement and model expected behaviour?
   f. Do I establish positive relationships with students?

2. Do I effectively employ proactive coping skills by changing the pace of instructions, removing seductive objects, boosting interest, redirecting behaviour through non-punitive time out, reinforcing appropriate behaviour, and providing cues?

3. Do I consider the five intervention guidelines when deciding which coping skill to employ?
   a. Does the intervention provide students with opportunities for self-control?
   b. Is the intervention less disruptive than the students' behaviour?
   c. Does the intervention lessen the probability that students will become confrontational?
   d. Does the intervention protect students and the teacher from physical or psychological harm?
   e. Does the intervention maximize the number of management alternatives available to the teacher?

4. Do I effectively use the remedial coping skills (planned ignoring, signal interference, and proximity interference) in a hierarchical order?

Chapter 8: Managing Common Behaviour Problems: Verbal Interventions and Use of Logical Consequences

1. Do I follow the guidelines for using verbal interventions?
   a. Do I keep them as private as possible?
   b. Do I make them brief?
   c. Do I speak to the situation, not the person?

d. Do I set limits on behaviours, not feelings?

e. Do I avoid sarcasm and belittlement?

2. Do I monitor my verbal interventions for ineffective communication patterns?

3. Do I use verbal interventions in a hierarchical manner (adjacent reinforcement, calling on student, humour, awareness questioning, direct appeal, "I message," positive phrasing, "are not for" rule reminders, triplets, explicit redirection, "broken record")?

4. Do I use natural and/or logical consequences using "You have a choice"?

5. When I use consequences, do I consistently follow through or do I use them as threats?

Chapter 9: Classroom Interventions for Chronic Problems

1. Do I build positive relationships with students who exhibit chronic behaviour problems?

2. Do I attempt to disrupt the cycle of discouragement and replace it with a cycle of encouragement?

3. Do I effectively use appropriate receiving skills during private conferences with students?

   a. Do I use non-verbal attending cues?

   b. Do I use probing questions?

   c. Do I check perceptions?

   d. Do I check feelings?

4. Do I effectively use appropriate sending skills during private conferences with students?

   a. Do I deal in the present?

   b. Do I make eye contact?

   c. Do I make statements rather than ask questions?

   d. Do I use "I" to relate my feelings?

   e. Am I brief?

   f. Do I talk directly to the students?

   g. Do I give the student directions on how to correct the problem?

   h. Do I check for understanding?

5. Have I reviewed the self-monitoring checklist to ensure that I have developed and employed an effective self-monitoring technique?

   a. Do teacher and student understand/agree on behaviours?

   b. Is the time period specified?

   c. Does the student understand the instrument's use?

   d. Have the teacher and student agreed on a meeting/discussion time?

   e. Will the instrument facilitate the noting of small increments of progress?

   f. Does the instrument focus on one behaviour?

6. Have I reviewed the guidelines for initiating and employing anecdotal record keeping to ensure that I have effectively implemented the procedure?

   a. Am I positive?
   b. Do I help the student recognize the past behaviour and its negative impact?
   c. Do I explain that the behaviour is unacceptable?
   d. Do I explain the anecdotal record-keeping procedure?
   e. Do I communicate an expectation for improvement?
   f. Do I attempt to obtain the student's commitment for improved behaviour?
   g. Do I record the conference and obtain the student's signature?

7. Have I reviewed the behaviour contract checklist to ensure that I have effectively developed and employed the behaviour contract?

   a. Do I specify the behaviour, time period, reward, and evaluation?
   b. Do I provide a motivating reward?
   c. Do I ensure that the student understood, agreed to, and signed the contract?
   d. Do I sign the contract?
   e. Do I, the student, and the student's parents get copies?

8. Do I exclude the student from the classroom and require a written statement of better behaviour before allowing the student to return to class?

Chapter 10: Seeking Outside Assistance

1. Do I provide many opportunities for the student to be successful in the classroom?

2. Does the behaviour warrant outside consultation?

3. Do I consult with a counsellor or an administrator about the chronically misbehaving student?

4. Should parents be contacted?

   a. Does the student display unremitting misbehaviour?
   b. Has the consultative team decided that the student needs a change of schedule or teacher; should be removed from class or school for a period of time; should be tested for learning, emotional, or physical difficulties; should be referred to outside specialists?

5. Do I employ the behaviours that allow me to work positively with parents and gain their support and cooperation?

6. Does the student show any behaviours or signs that may be symptomatic of other serious problems?

   a. Has the student undergone changes in physical appearance, activity level, personality, achievement status, health or physical abilities, or socialization?

7. Do I protect student rights?

References

Chapter 1

Anderson, S. (2002). Teachers talk about instruction. *Orbit, 32*(4), 22–26.

Bandura, A. (1977). *Social Learning Theory*. New York: General Learning Press.

Bembenutty, H., and Chen, P. P. (2005). Self-efficacy and delay of gratification. *Academic Exchange Quarterly, 9*(4), 78–86.

Boudourides, M.A. (2003). Constructivism, education, science, and technology. *Canadian Journal of Learning and Technology, 29*(3) Fall/automne.

Boyan, N. J., and Copeland, W. D. (1978). *Instructional Supervision Training Program*. Columbus, OH: Merrill.

Brophy, J. (1988). Research on teacher effects: Uses and abuses. *The Elementary School Journal, 89*(1), 3–21.

Dixon-Krauss, L. (1996). *Vygotsky in the Classroom: Mediated Literacy Instruction and Assessment*. White Plains, NY: Longman.

Emmer, E. T., Evertson, C. M., Clements, B. S., and Worsham, M. E. (1997). *Classroom Management for Secondary Teachers* (4th ed.). Boston: Allyn & Bacon.

Evertson, C. M., Emmer, E. T., Clements, B. S., and Worsham, M. E. (1997). *Classroom Management for Elementary Teachers* (4th ed.). Boston: Allyn & Bacon.

Glasersfeld, E. von (1996). Aspectos del constructivismo radical (Aspects of radical constructivism). In M. Pakman (Ed.) *Construcciones de la Experiencia Humana* (23–49). Barcelona, Spain: Gedisa Editorial.

Goldman, D. (1996). *Emotional Intelligence*. London: Bloomsbury.

Haberman, M. (1995). *Star Teachers of Children in Poverty*. West Lafayette, IN: Kappa Delta Pi.

Keating D. P., and Matthews D. J. (1999). What we are learning about how children learn and what this means for teachers. *Education Canada, 39*(1), 35–37.

Martin, J., and Sugarman, J. (1993). *Models of Classroom Management: Principles, Applications and Critical Perspectives* (2nd ed.). Calgary, AB: Detselig.

Morgan, N., and Saxton, J. (1991). *Teaching Questioning and Learning*. New York: Routledge.

Murdoch-Morris, P. (1993). The peaceful school: An elementary school perspective. *Orbit, 24*(1), 27–28.

Piaget, J. (1975). *The Development of Thought: Equilibration of Cognitive Structures*. New York: Viking.

Redl, F., and Wineman, D. (1952). *Controls from Within: Techniques for Treatment of the Aggressive Child*. New York: Free Press.

Shrigley, R. L. (1985). Curbing student disruption in the classroom—teachers need intervention skills. *National Association of Secondary School Principals Bulletin, 69*(479), 26–32.

Sweeney, T. J. (1981). *Adlerian Counseling: Proven Concepts and Strategies* (2nd ed.). Muncie, IN: Accelerated Development.

Tauber, R. T., and Mester, C. S. (1994). *Acting Lesson for Teachers*. Westport, CT: Praeger.

Vygotsky, L. S. (1978). *Mind in Society*. Cambridge, MA: Harvard University Press.

Watts, R. E. (Ed.) (2003). *Adlerian, Cognitive, and Constructivist Therapies. An Integrative Dialogue*. New York: Springer Publishing Company.

Chapter 2

A quarter of Nova Scotia teachers who responded to a recent survey said they faced physical violence at work. (2003, February 14). Canadian Press Newswire. Retrieved Apr. 21, 2003, from the Canadian Business and Current Affairs (CBCA) database through www.brocku.ca/library/databases. (While only those with access to Brock's online library can gain access to the CBCA through this URL, many libraries offer access to the CBCA database.)

Angus Reid Group. (1999). Canadian teens voice their opinions on violence in their schools. Retrieved April 15, 2003, from www.angusreid.com/search/pdf/media/pr990503%5F1.pdf.

Baker, K. (1985). Research evidence of a school discipline problem. *Phi Delta Kappan, 66*(7), 482–488.

Benn, R. (2002). Bullying behaviour not tolerated says school board. Retrieved March 14, 2007, from www.peacefulcommunities.ca/2002/October/oct11.htm.

Bonta, J. and Hanson, R. K. (1994). *Gauging the Risk of Violence: Measurement, Impact and Strategies for Change*. Ottawa, ON: Solicitor General of Canada.

Brendtro, L. K., Brokenleg, M., and Van Bockern, S. (1990). *Reclaiming Youth at Risk: Our Hope for the Future*. Bloomington, IN: National Educational Service.

Brophy, J. (1988). Research on teacher effects: Uses and abuses. *The Elementary School Journal, 89*(1), 3–21.

Canadian Teachers' Federation. (2002). National study confirms CTF concerns about teacher recruitment and retention. Retrieved April 15, 2003, from www.ctf-fce.ca/e/press/2002/pr02-2.htm.

Canter, L. (1989). Assertive discipline: More than names on the board and marbles in a jar. *Phi Delta Kappan, 71*(1), 57–61.

Charach, A., Pepler, D., and Ziegler, S. (1995). Bullying at school: A Canadian perspective. *Education Canada, 35*, 12–18.

Craig, W. M., Peters, R. D., and Konarski, R. (1998). Bullying and victimization among Canadian school children. Retrieved April 2, 2003, from www.hrdc-drhc.gc.ca/sp-ps/arb-dgra/publications/research/abw-98-28e.shtml.

Crux, S. C. (1993). Why is violence in our schools? *Brock Education, 3*(1), 23–24.

Department of the Solicitor General of Canada. (2002). School-based violence prevention in Canada: Results of a national survey of policies and programs. Retrieved April 2, 2003, from www.sgc.gc.ca/publications/corrections/199502_e.asp.

DiPrete, T., Muller, C., and Shaeffer, N. (1981). *Discipline and Order in American High Schools*. Washington, DC: National Center for Education Statistics.

Doyle, W. (1978). Are students behaving worse than they used to behave? *Journal of Research and Development in Education, 11*(4), 3–16.

Dreikurs, R. (1964). *Children the Challenge*. New York: Hawthorn.

Duquette, C. (2001). *Students at Risk: Solutions to Classroom Challenges*. Markham, ON: Pembroke Publishers Ltd.

Feitler, F., and Tokar, E. (1992). Getting a handle on teacher stress: How bad is the problem? *Educational Leadership, 49*, 456–458.

Fitzpatrick, C. (1994). *Violence Prevention: A Working Paper and Proposal for Action*. St. John's, NL: Avalon Consolidated School Board.

Hawes, J. M. (1971). *Children in Urban Society: Juvenile Delinquency in Nineteenth Century America*. New York: Oxford University Press.

Holt, R. (2007). Edmonton public schools student behaviour and conduct policy. Retrieved March 14, 2007, from www.epsb.ca/datafiles/parents/English_Student_Conduct_Brochure.pdf.

Housego, B. E. J. (1990). Student teachers' feelings of preparedness to teach. *Canadian Journal of Education, 15*(1), 37–56.

Huber, J. D. (1984). Discipline in the middle school—parent, teacher, and principal concerns. *National Association of Secondary School Principals Bulletin, 68*, 471, 74–79.

Ipsos-Reid. (1999). Canadians' assessment and views of the education system. Retrieved April 15, 2003, from www.ipsos-reid.com/pdf/publicat/RRtoc_9903.pdf.

James, J. M. (1993). Conflict resolution: Programs and strategies at the secondary level. *Orbit, 24*(1), 26–27.

Kounin, J. (1970). *Discipline and Group Management in Classrooms*. New York: Holt, Rinehart and Winston.

Leger Marketing. (2002). How Canadians feel about the educational system. Retrieved April 15, 2003, from www.queensu.ca/cora/polls/2002/September16-Perception_of_Education_System.pdf.

Levin, J. (1980). Discipline and classroom management survey: Comparisons between a suburban and urban school. Unpublished report, Pennsylvania State University, University Park.

Levin, J., Hoffman, N., Badiali, B., and Neuhard, R. (1985). Critical experiences in student teaching: Effects on career choice and implications for program modification. Paper presented to the Annual Conference of the American Educational Research Association, Chicago.

MacDougall, J. (1993). *Violence in the School: Programs and Policies for Prevention.* Toronto, ON: Canadian Education Association.

Marini, Z., Spear, S., and Bombay, K. (1999). Peer victimization in middle childhood: Characteristics, causes and consequences of school bullying. *Brock Education, 9,* 32–47.

Martin, J. M., Dworet, D. H., and Davis, C. (1997). The secondary student with behaviour disorders: a puzzle worth solving. *Exceptionality Education Canada, 6*(3 and 4), 183–201.

Mennell, R. M. (1973). *Thorns and Thistles: Juvenile Delinquents in the United States 1825–1940.* Hanover, NH: The University Press of New England.

Novak, J. M. and Purkey, W. W. (2001). *Invitational Education.* Bloomington, IN: Phi Delta Kappa Educational Foundation.

O'Connell, P., Pepler, D., and Craig, W. (1999). Peer involvement in bullying: Insights and challenges for intervention. *Journal of Adolescence, 22*(4), 437–452.

Olweus, D. (1991). Bully/victim problems among school children: Some basic facts and effects of a school-based intervention program. In D. Pepler and K. Rubin (Eds.), *The Development and Treatment of Childhood Aggression* (411–438), Hillsdale, NJ: Erlbaum.

Patus, M. (1993). Managing aggressive tendencies in adolescents. *Brock Education, 3*(1), 19–22.

Pepler, D., and Craig, W. (1995). A peek behind the fence: Naturalistic observations of aggressive children with remote audiovisual recording. *Developmental Psychology, 31,* 548–553.

Roher, E. M. (1993). Violence in a school setting. *Brock Education, 3*(1), 1–4.

Roy, I. (1993). Violence is preventable: How some schools are educating students to be peacemakers. *Brock Education, 3*(1), 16–18.

Schlossman, S. L. (1977). *Love and the American Delinquent: The Theory and Practice of "Progressive" Juvenile Justice, 1825–1920.* Chicago: University of Chicago Press.

Shrigley, R. L. (1979). Strategies in classroom management. *The National Association of Secondary School Principals Bulletin, 63*(428), 1–9.

Smith, O. B. (1969). Discipline. In R. L. Ebel, *Encyclopedia of Educational Research* (4th ed.). New York: Macmillan.

Statistics Canada. (1999). Education indicators in Canada: Report of the Pan-Canadian Education Indicators Program, 1999. Retrieved June 3, 2003, from www.statcan.ca/english/freepub/81-582-XIE/free.htm.

Statistics Canada. (2003). Tech and teens: Access and use. Retrieved February 12, 2003, from www.statcan.ca/english/freepub/11-008-XIE/0010311-008-XIE.pdf.

Statistics Canada. (2004). Youth court statistics, 2002/03. Ottawa. Retrieved March 14, 2007, from http://142.206.72.67/04/04b/04b_002b_e.htm.

Stipek, D. J. (1998). *Motivation to Learn: From Theory to Practice* (3rd ed.). Boston: Allyn & Bacon.

Taylor, A. (1996). Understanding children's behaviour: The key to effective guidance. Canadian Child Care Federation, 3. Retrieved April 21, 2003, from www.cfc-efc.ca/docs/cccf/00009_en.htm.

Thomas, G. T., Goodall, R., and Brown, L. (1983). Discipline in the classroom: Perceptions of middle grade teachers. *The Clearinghouse, 57*(3), 139–142.

Vittetoe, J. O. (1977). Why first-year teachers fail. *Phi Delta Kappan, 58*(5), 429.

Walker, H. M. (1979). *The Acting-Out Child: Coping with Classroom Disruption.* Boston: Allyn & Bacon.

Walker, H. M., and Buckley, N. K. (1973). Teacher attention to appropriate and inappropriate classroom behaviour: An individual case study. *Focus on Exceptional Children, 5,* 5–11.

Walker, H. M., and Buckley, N. K. (1974). *Token Reinforcement Techniques: Classroom Applications for the Hard to Teach Child.* Eugene, OR: E-B Press.

Walsh, D. (1983). Our schools come to order. *American Teacher, 68,* 1.

Wayson, W. W. (1985). The politics of violence in school: Doublespeak and disruptions in public confidence. *Phi Delta Kappan, 67*(2), 127–132.

Weber, T. R., and Sloan, C. A. (1986). How does high school discipline in 1984 compare to previous decades? *The Clearinghouse, 59*(7), 326–329.

Weiner, B. (1980). A cognitive (attribution)–emotion–action, model of motivated behaviour: An analysis of judgments of help-giving. *Journal of Personality and Social Psychology, 39,* 186–200.

Winzer, M. (2002). *Children with Exceptionalities in Canadian Classrooms* (6th ed.). Don Mills, ON: Prentice Hall.

Chapter 3

Adler, I. (1966, December). Mental growth and the art of teaching. *The Mathematics Teacher, 59,* 706–715.

Alphonso, C. (2003, November 19). Schoolyard bullies ape violence on TV, study for teachers finds. *The Globe and Mail,* 1.

American Psychological Association. (1993). *Violence and Youth: Psychology's Response,* Vol. 1. Washington, DC.

Bandura, A. (1973). *Aggression: A Social Learning Analysis.* Englewood Cliffs, NJ: Prentice Hall.

Bayh, B. (1978). Seeking solutions to school violence and vandalism. *Phi Delta Kappan, 59*(5), 299–302.

Bloodshed, butchery and video games: Parental control, not government intervention, may be the best answer, (1994, January 17). *Western Report, 8* (51), 32–33. Retrieved April 27, 2003, from the Canadian Business and Current Affairs (CBCA) database through www.brocku.ca/library/databases. (While only those with access to Brock's online library can gain access to the CBCA through this URL, many libraries offer access to the CBCA database.)

Bouthilet, P. D., and Lazar, J. (Eds.). (1982). *Television and Behaviour: Ten Years of Scientific Progress and Implications for the Eighties.* Washington, DC: U.S. Department of Health and Human Services, National Institute of Mental Health.

Canada says education is key to combating global poverty. (2001, April 29). Department of Finance Canada, 2001–2004. Retrieved May 7, 2003, from www.fin.gc.ca/news01-044e.html.

Canadian Council on Social Development (2002). Percentage and number of persons in low income/poverty, by age, sex and family characteristics, Canada, 1990 and 1999. Retrieved May 7, 2003, from www.ccsd.ca/factsheets/fs_pov9099.htm.

Canadian Press (2003). The Roadrunner made me do it. Retrieved April 10, 2007, from www.ctv.ca/servlet/ArticleNews/story/CTVNews/20030309/tv_ciolence_030309?s_name=&no_ads=.

Canadian Teachers' Federation, The. (2003). Kids take on media. Retrieved on September 11, 2007, from www.ctf-fce.ca/e/resources/MERP/TeachersandStudentsGuide.pdf.

Chandler, K. A., Chapman, C. D., Rand, M. R., and Taylor, B. M. (1998). *Students' Reports of School Crime: 1989 and 1995.* U.S. Departments of Education and Justice. NCES 98-241/NCJ-169607. Washington, DC.

Charles, C. M., Senter, G. W., and Barr, K. B. (1995). *Building Classroom Discipline* (5th ed.). New York: Longman.

Clarizio, H. F., and McCoy, G. F. (1983). *Behaviour Disorders in Children* (3rd ed.). New York: Harper & Row.

Congressional Quarterly. (1993). TV violence. *CQ Researcher, 3*(12), 165–187.

Coopersmith, S. (1967). *The Antecedents of Self-Esteem.* San Francisco: W. H. Freeman.

Dewey, J. (1916). *Democracy and Education.* New York: Macmillan.

Dreikurs, R., Grundwald, B., and Pepper, F. (1982). *Maintaining Sanity in the Classroom: Classroom Management Techniques* (2nd ed.). New York: Harper & Row.

Dubelle, S. T., and Hoffman, C. M. (1984). *Misbehaving—Solving the Disciplinary Puzzle for Educators.* Lancaster, PA: Technomic.

Elliott, A., Bosacki, S., Woloshyn, V., and Richards, M. (2001). Exploring preadolescents' media and literacy choices. *Language and Literacy, 3*(2), 1–13.

Elliot, D. S., and Voss, H. L. (1974). *Delinquency and Dropout.* Lexington, MA: Lexington.

Feldhusen, J. F. (1978). Behaviour problems in secondary schools. *Journal of Research and Development in Education, 11*(4), 17–28.

Feldhusen, J. F., Thurston, J. R., and Benning, J. J. (1973). A longitudinal study of delinquency and other aspects of children's behaviour. *International Journal of Criminology and Penology, 1*, 341–351.

French, J. R. P., and Raven, B. (1960). In D. Cartwright and A. Zander (Eds.), *Group Dynamics: Research and Theory*. Evanston, IL: Row-Peterson.

Fullan, M.G. (1993). Why teachers must become change agents. *Educational Leadership, 50*(6), 12–17.

Fullan, M. G. (2001). *Leading in a Culture of Change*. San Francisco: Jossey-Bass.

Gabay, J. (1991, January). ASCD Update.

Gelfand, D. M., Jenson, W. R., and Drew, C. J. (1982). *Understanding Child Behaviour Disorders*. New York: Holt, Rinehart & Winston.

Gilliland, H. (1986). Self-concept and the Indian student. In J. Reyhner (Ed.), *Teaching the Indian Child*. Billings, MT: Eastern Montana College.

Glasser, W. (1978). Disorders in our schools: Causes and remedies. *Phi Delta Kappan, 59*(5), 321–333.

Goertzel, V., and Goertzel, M. (1962). *Cradles of Eminence*. Boston: Little, Brown.

Gorman, R. M. (1972). *Discovering Piaget: A Guide for Teachers*. Columbus, OH: Merrill.

Green, A., Campbell, L., Stirtzinger, R., DeSouza, C., and Dawe, I. (2001). Multimodal school-based intervention for at-risk, aggressive, latency-age youth. *Canadian Journal of School Psychology 17*(1), 27–46.

Hargreaves, A. (1994). *Changing Teachers, Changing Times: Teachers' Work and Culture in the Post-Modern Age*. New York: Teachers College Press.

Health Canada. (2002). Trends in the health of Canadian youth. Retrieved May 8, 2003, from www.hc-sc.gc.ca/dca-dea/pdfa-zenglish.html#t16.

Jenkins, J., Simpson, A., Dunn, J., Rasbash, J., and O'Connor, T. (2005). Mutual influence of marital conflict and children's behavior problems: Shared and nonshared family risks. *Child Development, 76*(1), 24–39.

Jessor, J., and Jessor, S. L. (1977). *Problem Behaviour and Psychosocial Development*. New York: Academic.

Karplus, R. (1977). *Science Teaching and the Development of Reasoning*. Berkeley: University of California Press.

Kindsvatter, R. (1978). A new view of the dynamics of discipline. *Phi Delta Kappan, 59*(5), 322–325.

Knowles, J. G. and Cole, A. L. (1994). *Through Preservice Teachers' Eyes*. Don Mills, ON: Maxwell Macmillan Canada Inc.

Kohlberg, L. (1969). *Stages in the Development of Moral Thought and Action*. New York: Holt, Rinehart & Winston.

Kohlberg, L. (1975). The cognitive-developmental approach to moral education. *Phi Delta Kappan, 56*(10), 610–677.

Kounin, J. S. (1970). *Discipline and Group Management in Classrooms*. New York: Holt, Rinehart & Winston.

Levin, J., and Shanken-Kaye, J. (1996). *The Self-Control Classroom: Understanding and Managing the Disruptive Behaviour of All Students Including Students with ADHD*. Dubuque, IA: Kendall-Hunt.

Levine, V. (1984, August). Time use and student achievement: A critical assessment of the National Commission Report. *Forum* (College of Education, Pennsylvania State University), *11*, 12.

Livingstone, S., and Bovill, M. (1999). *Young People, New Media: Summary*. London: London School of Economics and Political Science.

Luke, C. (1999). Media and cultural studies in Australia. *Journal of Adolescent and Adult Literacy, 42*(8), 622–637.

MacDonald, I. (1997). Violence in school: Multiple realities. *Alberta Journal of Educational Research, XLIII*(2/3), 142–156.

Mahoney, J. (2007, March 14). Population growth will likely be all immigration by 2030. *The Globe and Mail*.

Manley-Casimir, M. E., and Luke, C. (1987). *Children and Television*. New York: Praeger.

Marini, Z., Fairbain, L., and Zuber, R. (2001). Peer harassment in individuals with developmental disabilities: Towards the development of a multi-dimensional bullying identification model. *Developmental Disabilities Bulletin, 29*(2), 170–195.

Marini, Z., Spear, S., and Bombay, K. (1999). Peer victimization in childhood: Characteristics, causes and consequences of school bullying. *Brock Education, 9*, 32–47.

Maslow, A. (1968). *Toward a Psychology of Being*. New York: D. Van Nostrand.

McMillan, S. J., and Morrison, M. (2006, February). Coming of age with the internet: A qualitative exploration of how the internet has become an integral part of young people's lives. *New Media Society, 8*(1), 73–95.

Media Awareness Network. (2005). Young Canadians in a wired world. Retrieved April 10, 2007, from / www.media-awareness.ca/english/research/YCWW/phaseII.

Menacker, J., Weldon, W., and Hurwitz, E. (1989). School order and safety as community issues. *Phi Delta Kappan, 71*(1), 39.

Morgan, M., Shanahan, J., and De-Guise, J. (2001). Television and its viewers: Cultivation theory and research. *Canadian Journal of Communication, 26*(4), 568–570.

Ng, S. M. (2006). Literacy and diversity: Challenges of change. In A. McKeough, L. Phillips, V. Timmons, and J. L. Lupart (Eds.) *Understanding Literacy Development*. Mahwah, NJ: Lawrence Erlbaum Associates, Publishers.

Novak, J. M. and Purkey, W. W. (2001). *Invitational Education*. Bloomington, IN: Phi Delta Kappa Educational Foundation.

Ontario: Where everyone looks the same? (1999, February 2). Canadian Press Newswire. Retrieved. Apr. 27, 2003, from Canadian Business and Current Affairs (CBCA) database through www.brocku.ca/library/databases. (While only those with access to Brock's online library can gain access to the CBCA through this URL, many libraries offer access to the CBCA database.)

Parke, R. D. (1978). Children's home environments: Social and cognitive effects. In I. Altman and J. F. Wohlwill (Eds.), *Children and the Environment*. New York: Plenum.

Pearl, D. (1984). Violence and aggression. *Society, 21*(6) 15–16.

Pearl, D., Bouthilet, L., and Lazar, J. (Eds.). (1982). *Television and Behaviour: Ten Years of Scientific Progress and Implications for the Eighties*, Vol. 2. Washington, DC: U.S. Government Printing Office.

Pepler, R., and Craig, W. (1994). About bullying. *Orbit, 25*(3), 43–44.

Piaget, J. (1965). *The Moral Judgment of the Child*. Glencoe, IL: Free Press.

Piaget, J. (1970). Piaget's theory. In P. H. Mussen (Ed.), *Carmichael's Manual of Child Psychology*, Vol. 1. New York: John Wiley & Sons.

Purkey, W. W., and Novak, J. M. (1996). *Inviting School Success: A Self-Concept Approach to Teaching, Learning and Democratic Practice* (3rd ed.). Belmont, CA: Wadsworth.

Rice, M. L., Huston, A. C., and Wright, J. C. (1982). The forms and codes of television: Effects on children's attention, comprehension and social behaviour. In D. Pearl, L. Bouthilet, and J. Lazar (Eds.), *Television and Behaviour: Ten Years of Scientific Progress and Implications for the Eighties*, Vol. 2. Washington, DC: U.S. Government Printing Office.

Rice, P. F. (1981). *The Adolescent Development, Relationships, and Culture* (3rd ed.). Boston: Allyn & Bacon.

Rosenberg, J., and Barbara, J. S. (2007). Media and entertainment violence and children. Retrieved April 1, 2007, from www.Fradical.Com/Physicians_For_Global_Survival_Canada.htm.

Rutter, M. (1978). Family, area, and school influences in the genesis of conduct disorders. In L. Herson, M. Berger, and D. Shaffer (Eds.), *Aggression and Anti-Social Behaviour in Childhood and Adolescence*. Oxford, UK: Pergamon.

Seeds of violence, The. (2001, October). *Canada and the World Backgrounder, 67*(2), 17, Retrieved April 27, 2003, from the Canadian Business and Current Affairs (CBCA) database through www.brocku.ca/library/databases. (While only those with access to Brock's online library can gain access to the CBCA through this URL, many libraries offer access to the CBCA database.)

Singer, J. L., Singer, D. G., and Rapaczynski, W. S. (1984). Family patterns and television viewing as predictors of children's beliefs and aggression. *Journal of Communications, 34*(2), 73–89.

Smith, R., Bertrand, L., Arnold, B., and Hornick, S. (1995). *A Study of the Level and Nature of Youth Crime and Violence in Calgary*. Ottawa, ON: Solicitor General of Canada.

Statistics Canada. (2001). Average hours per week of television viewing. Retrieved January 27, 2004, from http://0-www.statcan.ca.brain.biblio.brocku.ca/english/Pgdb/arts23.htm.

Statistics Canada. (2002a). Divorce. *The Daily*. Retrieved May 4, 2003, from www.statcan.ca/Daily/English/021202/d021202f.htm.

Statistics Canada. (2002b). Selected dwelling characteristics and household equipment. Retrieved January 27, 2004, from 0-www.statcan.ca.brain.biblio.brocku.ca/english/Pgdb/famil09c.htm.

Statistics Canada. (2006). Canadian internet use survey. *The Daily*. Retrieved April 9, 2007, from www.statcan. ca/Daily/English/060815/d060815b.htm.

Stinchcombe, A. L. (1964). *Rebellion in a High School*. Chicago: Quadrangle.

Stipek, D. J. (1993). *Motivation to Learn, from Theory to Practice* (2nd ed.). Boston: Allyn & Bacon.

Subrahmanyam, K., Kraut, R. E., Greenfield, P. M., and Gross, E. F. (2000). The impact of home computer use on children's activities and development. *Children and Computer Technology, 10*(2), 123–145.

Sweeney, J. J. (1981). *Adlerian Counseling: Proven Concepts and Strategies* (2nd ed.). Muncie, IN: Accelerated Development.

Tanner, L. N. (1978). *Classroom Discipline for Effective Teaching and Learning*. New York: Holt, Rinehart & Winston.

Toffler, A. (1970). *Future Shock*. New York: Random House.

Turkel, S. (1996). *Life on the Screen*. New York: Simon & Schuster.

Visher, E. B., and Visher, J. S. (1978). Common problems of stepparents and their spouses. *American Journal of Orthopsychiatry, 48*, 252–262.

Waterloo Region District School Board (2007). Balanced school day. Retrieved April 1, 2007, from www.wrdsb.on.ca/balanced_school.php.

Williams, C. (2001, Fall). Family disruptions and childhood happiness. Canada Social Trends, Statistics Canada. Retrieved May 4, 2003, from 0-www.statcan.ca.brain.biblio.brocku.ca/english/indepth/11-008/feature/star2001062000s3a01.pdf.

Withall, J. (1969, March). Evaluation of classroom climate. *Childhood Education, 45*(7), 403–408.

Withall, J. (1979). Problem behaviour: Function of social–emotional climate? *Journal of Education, 161*(2), 89–101.

Zillman, D., and Weaver, J. B., III (1999). Effects of prolonged exposure to gratuitous media violence on provoked and unprovoked hostile behaviour. *Journal of Applied Social Psychology, 29*, 145–165.

Chapter 4

Alberta Department of Education. (2003). Curriculum by subject. Retrieved July 16, 2003, from ednet.edc.gov.ab.ca/k_12/curriculum/bySubject.

Alberto P. A., and Troutman A. C. (1999). *Applied Behavior Analysis for Teachers* (5th ed.). Upper Saddle River, NJ: Merrill.

Axelrod, S. (1983). Behaviour Modification for the Classroom Teacher. New York: McGraw-Hill.

Berne, E. (1964). *Games People Play: The Psychology of Human Relations*. New York: Avon.

Boekaerts, M., and Corno, L. (2005). Self-regulation across domains of applied psychology: Is there an emerging consensus? *Applied Psychology (Special Issue), 54*(2), 199–231.

Cangelosi, J. S. (1997). *Classroom Management Strategies: Gaining and Maintaining Students' Cooperation*. New York: Longman.

Canter, L., and Canter, M. (1992). *Assertive Discipline: Positive Behaviour Management for Today's Classrooms* (rev. ed.). Santa Monica, CA: Canter Associates.

Charney, R. (1992). *Teaching Children to Care: Management in the Responsive Classroom*. Greenfield, MA: Northeast Foundation for Children.

Curwin, R. L., and Mendler, A. (1988). *Discipline with Dignity*. Alexandria, VA: Association for Supervision and Curriculum Development.

Drake, S. M. (1998). *Creating Integrated Curriculum*. Thousand Oaks, CA: Corwin Press Inc.

Dreikurs, R., Grundwald, B., and Pepper, F. (1998). *Maintaining Sanity in the Classroom: Classroom Management Techniques* (2nd ed.). Washington, DC: Taylor and Francis.

Elliott, A., and Woloshyn, V. (1996). Adopting collaborative strategies in the classroom. *The Canadian School Executive 15*(9), 3–9.

Erchul, W. P., Raven, B. H., and Whichard, S. M. (2001). School psychologist and teacher perceptions of social power in consultation. *Journal of School Psychology 39*(6), 483–497.

Fast, L., Elliott, A., Hunter, R., and Bellamy, J. (2002). Perspectives from the other side of the (new teacher's) desk. *Brock Education 12*(12), 1–16.

Forton, M. B. (1998). Apology of action. *Responsive Classroom, 10*(1), 6–7.

French, J. R. P., and Raven, B. (1960). The bases of social power. In D. Cartwright and A. Zander (Eds.), *Group Dynamics: Research and Theory*. Evanston, IL: Row-Peterson.

Ginott, H. (1972). *Between Teacher and Child*. New York: Wyden.

Glasser, W. (1992). *The Quality School: Managing Students without Coercion*. New York: HarperCollins.

Gordon, T. (1989). *Teaching Children Self-Discipline at Home and in School*. New York: Random House.

Harris, T. (1969). *I'm O.K., You're O.K.: A Practical Guide to Transactional Analysis*. New York: Harper & Row.

Housego, B. E. J. (1992). Monitoring student teachers' feelings of preparedness to teach: Personal teaching efficacy and teaching efficacy in a new secondary teacher education program. *The Alberta Journal of Educational Research XXXVIII*(1), 49–64.

Kerr, M. M., and Nelson, C. M. (1998). *Strategies for Managing Behaviour Problems in the Classroom* (3rd ed.). Scarborough, ON: Prentice Hall.

Kohn, A. (1996). *Beyond Discipline: From Compliance to Community*. Alexandria, VA: Association for Supervision and Curriculum Development.

Lasley. T. J. (1989). A teacher development model for classroom management. *Phi Delta Kappan, 71*(1), 36–38.

Lepper, M., and Green, D. (1978). *The Hidden Costs of Reward: New Perspectives on Human Motivation*. Hillsdale, NJ: Erlbaum.

Martin, J., and Sugarman, J. (1993). *Models of Classroom Management* (2nd ed.). Calgary, AB: Detselig Enterprises Ltd.

Newfoundland and Labrador Department of Education. (2003). Curriculum and related documents. Retrieved July 16, 2003, from www.gov.nf.ca/edu/sp/main.htm.

Novak, J. M. (2002). *Inviting Educational Leadership: Fulfilling Potential and Applying an Ethical Perspective to the Educational Process*. Don Mills, ON: Pearson Canada.

Ontario Ministry of Education. (2003). Curriculum and policy. Retrieved July 16, 2003, from www.edu.gov.on.ca/eng/document/curricul/curricul.html.

Putnam, J., and Burke, J. (1992). *Organizing and Managing Classroom Learning Communities*. New York: McGraw-Hill.

Ryan, R. M., and Deci, E. L. (2000). Self-determination theory and the facilitation of intrinsic motivation, social development, and well-being. *American Psychologist, 55*(1), 68–78.

Schwartz, S., and Pollishuke, M. (2002). *Creating the Dynamic Classroom*. Toronto, ON: Irwin.

Strachota, R. (1996). *On Their Side: Helping Children Take Charge of Their Learning*. Greenfield, MA: Northeast Foundation for Children.

Valentine, M. (1987). *How to Deal with Discipline Problems in the Schools: A Practical Guide for Educators*. Dubuque, IA: Kendall-Hunt.

Wolfgang, C., and Glickman, C. (1995). *Solving Discipline Problems: Methods and Models for Today's Teachers* (2nd ed.). Boston: Allyn & Bacon.

Winter, S. (1983). Rewarding work output of a child with poor attention: You get what you reward. *Behavioural Approaches with Children, 7*(4), 12–16.

Chapter 5

Akey, T. M. (2006). School context, student attitudes and behavior, and academic achievement: An exploratory analysis. Retrieved May 22, 2007, from www.mdrc.org/publications/419/full.pdf#search=%22School%20Context%2C%20Student%20Attitudes%20and%20Behavior%2C%20and%20Academic%20Achievement%3A%20An%20Exploratory%20Analysis%22.

The American Heritage® New Dictionary of Cultural Literacy (3rd ed.). Definition of *digital divide* retrieved September 24, 2007, from the following Dictionary.com URL: http://dictionary.reference.com/browse/digitaldivide.

Ames, R., and Ames, C. (Eds.). (1984). *Research on Motivation in Education*, Vol. 1: *Student Motivation*. New York: Academic.

Anderson, L. M. (1989). Classroom instruction. In M. C. Reynolds (Ed.), *Knowledge Base for the Beginning Teacher*. New York: Pergamon.

Anderson, S. E. (2002). Teachers talk about instruction. *Orbit 32*(4), 22–26.

Armstrong, T. (1994). *Multiple Intelligences in the Classroom*. Alexandria, VA: Association for Supervision and Curriculum Development.

Auditor General of Canada. (1999). Indian and Northern Affairs Canada: Elementary and secondary education. Report to the House of Commons, Chapter 4. Ottawa, ON: Minister of Public Works and Government Services Canada.

Bandura, A. (1986). *Social Foundations of Thought and Action: Social Cognition Theory*. Englewood Cliffs, NJ: Prentice Hall.

Battiste, M., and Barman, J. (1995). *First Nations Education in Canada: The Circle Unfolds*. Vancouver: UBC Press.

Brandt, R. (1993). On teaching for understanding: A conversation with Howard Gardner. *Educational Leadership, 50*(7), 4–7.

Brophy, J. E. (1987). Synthesis of research strategies on motivating students to learn. *Educational Leadership, 45*(2), 40–48.

Brophy, J. E. (1988a). Educating teachers about managing classrooms and students. *Teaching and Teacher Education, 4*(1), 1–18.

Brophy, J. E. (1988b). Research on teacher effects and abuses. *Elementary School Journal, 89*(1), 3–21.

Brophy, J. E. (1993). Probing the subtleties of subject matter teaching. *Educational Leadership, 49*(7), 4–8.

Brophy, J. E., and Good, T. L. (1974). *Teacher–Student Relationships: Causes and Consequences*. New York: Holt, Rinehart & Winston.

Brophy, J. E., and Good, T. L. (1986). Teacher behavior and student achievement. In M. C. Wittrock (Ed.), *Handbook of Research on Teaching* (3rd ed.). New York: Macmillan.

Brualdi, A. C. (1996). Multiple intelligences: Gardner's theory. ERIC Digest [online]. Retrieved May 22, 2007, from www.eric.ed.gov/contentdelivery/servlet/ERICServlet?accno=ED410226.

Bruner, J. (1986). *Actual Minds, Possible Worlds*. Cambridge, MA: Harvard University Press.

Castellano, M. B., Davis, L., and Lahache, L. (Eds.). (2000). *Aboriginal Education: Fulfilling the Promise*. Vancouver: UBC Press.

Cecil, N. L. (1995). *The Art of Inquiry: Questioning Strategies for K–6 Classrooms*. Winnipeg, MB: Peguis Publishers.

Cope B., and Kalantzis, M. (2000). *Mutliliteracies: Literacy Learning and the Design of Social Futures*. New York: Routledge.

Drake, S. M. (1998). *Creating Integrated Curriculum*. Thousand Oaks, CA: Corwin Press Inc.

Dreikurs, R. (1964). *Children the Challenge*. New York: Hawthorne.

Duke, D. E. (1982). *Helping Teachers Manage Classrooms*. Alexandria, VA: Association for Supervision and Curriculum Development.

Elliott, A., Woloshyn, V., Bajovic, M., and Ratkovic, S. (2007). Promoting teacher candidates' awareness of the role of critical literacy in the curriculum: Lunchtime conversations. *The Reading Professor*, July.

Evertson, C. M. (1989). Classroom organization and management. In M. C. Reynolds (Ed.), *Knowledge Base for the Beginning Teacher*. New York: Pergamon.

Feathers, N. (1982). *Expectations and Actions*. Hillsdale, NJ: Erlbaum.

Gardner, H. (1983). *Frames of Mind: The Theory of Multiple Intelligences*. New York: Basic Books.

Gibson, B. P. and Govendo, B. L. (1999). Encouraging constructive behavior in middle school classrooms: A multiple-intelligences approach. *Intervention in School & Clinic 35*(1), 16–21.

Good, T. L. (1987, July–August). Two decades of research on teacher expectations: Findings and future directions. *Journal of Teacher Education 1987*, 32–47.

Good, T. L., and Brophy, J. E. (1972). Behavioural expression of teacher attitudes. *Journal of Educational Psychology, 63*, 617–624.

Good, T. L., and Brophy, J. E. (1997). *Looking in Classrooms* (4th ed.). New York: Harper & Row.

Good, T. L., and Brophy, J. E. (2000). *Looking in Classrooms* (8th ed.). New York: Longman.

Hunter, M. (1982). *Mastery Teaching.* El Segundo, CA: TIP Publications.

Janes, R. C. (1996). An examination of the relationship between teacher expectations, attribution theory and student achievement. *Morning Watch: Education & Social Analysis 24*(1/2), 1–12.

Johnson, D. W., Johnson, R. T., and Holubec, E. J. (1993). *Cooperation in the Classroom* (rev. ed.). Edina, MN: Interaction Book Company.

Kagan, S. (1994). *Cooperative Learning: Resources for Teachers.* San Juan Capistrano, CA: Resources for Teachers.

Khalid, T. (2003). Pre-service high school teachers' perceptions of three environmental phenomena. *Environmental Education Research 9*(1), 35–50.

Laughlin, M. A., Hartoonian, H. M., and Berci, M. (1999). Challenges of social studies instruction in middle and high schools. *Canadian Social Studies 33*(4), 128–129.

Lieberman, A., and Denham, C. (1980). *Time to Learn.* Sacramento, CA: California Commission for Teacher Preparation and Licensing.

Lytton, H., and Pyryt, M. C. (1998). Predictors of achievement in basic skills: A Canadian effective schools study. *Canadian Journal of Education 23*(3), 281–301.

Martin, J., and Sugarman, J. (1993). *Models of Classroom Management* (2nd ed.). Calgary, AB: Detselig Enterprises Ltd.

Marzano, R. J. (1992). *A Different Kind of Classroom: Teaching with Dimensions of Learning.* Alexandria, VA: Association for Supervision and Curriculum Development.

Maslow, A. (1968). *Toward a Psychology of Being.* New York: D. Van Nostrand.

Mastropieri, M. A., and Scruggs, T. (2005). *Effective Instruction for Special Education* (3rd ed.). Austin, TX: Allyn & Bacon.

Mazurek, J. (2002). Instructional intelligence: A snapshot. *Orbit 32*(4), 16–21.

McKenzie, J. (2002). Questions as technology: Questions and questioning may be the most powerful technologies of all. *Orbit 32*(4), 35–39.

Millar, G. (1991). The power of questioning: An enabling strategy to enhance learning. *AGATE 5*(1), 26–38.

Mollica, A. (1994). Planning for successful teaching: Questioning strategies. *Mosaic 1*(4), 18–20.

Morgan, N., and Saxton, J. (1991). *Teaching Questioning and Learning.* New York: Routledge.

Newmann, F., and Wehlage, G. (1993). Five standards of authentic instruction. *Educational Leadership, 50*(7), 8–12.

Ng, S. M. (2006). Literacy and diversity: Challenges of change. In A. McKeough, L. Phillips, V. Timmons, and J. L. Lupart (Eds.) *Understanding Literacy Development.* Mahwah, NJ: Lawrence Erlbaum Associates, Publishers.

Novak, J. M., and Purkey, W. W. (2001). *Invitational Education.* Bloomington, IN: Phi Delta Kappa Educational Foundation.

Olafson, L. J., and Field, J. C. (1999). Understanding resistance in students at risk. *Canadian Journal of Education 24*(1), 70–76.

O'Reilly, R. R. (1999). Getting serious about literacy in schools: Canada and Australia. *Education Canada 39*(2), 28–29.

Perkins, D., and Blythe, T. (1994). Putting understanding up front. *Educational Leadership, 51*(5), 4–7.

Pintrich, P. R., Marx, R. W., and Boyle, P. (1993). Beyond conceptual change: The role of motivational beliefs and classroom contextual factors in conceptual change teaching. *Review of Educational Research, 63*(2), 167–200.

Postman, N. (1979). *Teaching as a Conserving Activity.* New York: Delacorte Press.

Prawat, R. S. (1993). From individual differences to learning communities. *Educational Leadership, 49*(7), 9–13.

Rosenshine, B., and Stevens, R. (1986). Teaching functions. In M. C. Wittrock (Ed.). *Handbook of Research on Teaching* (3rd ed.). New York: Macmillan.

Rosenthal, R., and Jacobson, L. (1968). *Pygmalion in the Classroom: Teacher Expectations and Pupils' Intellectual Development*. New York: Holt, Rinehart & Winston.

Scardamalia, M., and Bereiter, C. (1991). Higher levels of agency for children in knowledge building: A challenge for the design of new knowledge media. *Journal of the Learning Sciences 1*(1), 37–68.

Schwartz, S., and Pollishuke, M. (2002). *Creating the Dynamic Classroom*. Toronto, ON: Irwin.

Slavin, R. E. (1989–90). Research on cooperative learning: Consensus and controversy. *Educational Leadership, 47*(4), 52–54.

Sloan, L. V., and Toews, R. J. (1984). Good questioning techniques. *Canadian School Executive 3*(9), 20–21.

Starnes, B. A., and Paris, C. (2000). Choosing to learn. *Phi Delta Kappan, 81*(5), 392–397.

Statistics Canada (2005). Characteristics of individuals using the internet. Retrieved May 24, 2007, from www40.statcan.ca/l01/cst01/comm15.htm.

Stepien, W., and Gallagher, S. (1993). Problem-based learning: As authentic as it gets. *Educational Leadership, 50*(7), 17–20.

Stipek, D. (1993). *Motivation to Learn: From Theory to Practice* (2nd ed.). Boston: Allyn & Bacon.

Taylor, M. C., and Blunt, A. (2001). A situated cognition perspective on literacy discourses: Seeing more clearly through a new lens. *Canadian Journal for the Study of Adult Education, 15*(2), 79–103.

Tombari, M. L. and Borich, G. D. (1998). *Authentic Assessment in the Classroom: Applications and Practice*. Englewood Cliffs, NJ: Prentice Hall.

Vygotsky, L. S. (1978). *Mind and Society*. Cambridge, MA: Harvard University Press.

Wang, M. C., and Palinscar, A. S. (1989). Teaching students to assume an active role in their learning. In M. C. Reynolds (Ed.), *Knowledge Base for the Beginning Teacher*. New York: Pergamon.

Wineburg, S. (1987). The self-fulfillment of the self-fulfilling prophecy. *Educational Researcher, 16*(9), 28–36.

Woloshyn, V., and Elliott, A. (1998). Providing seventh- and eighth-grade students with reading and writing strategy instruction: Comparing explicit-strategy and implicit-strategy programs. *The Reading Professor 20*(2), 59–79.

Chapter 6

Abi-Nader, J. (1993). Meeting the needs of multicultural classrooms: Family values and the motivation of minority students. In M. J. O'Hair and S. J. Odell (Eds.), *Diversity and Teaching: Teacher Education Yearbook 1*. Fort Worth, TX: Harcourt, Brace, Jovanovich College Publications.

Andrews, J., and Lupart, J. (2000). *The Inclusive Classroom* (2nd ed.). Scarborough, ON: Nelson.

Banks, J. A. (1995). Multicultural education: Its effects on students' racial and gender-role attitudes. In J. A. Banks and C. A. Banks (Eds.), *Handbook of Research on Multicultural Education* (pp. 617–627). New York: Macmillan.

Blades, D., Johnston, I., and Simmt, E. (2000, June). Cultural diversity and secondary school curricula. Canadian Race Relations Foundation, Toronto. Retrieved July 4, 2003, from www.crr.ca/en/Publications/ResearchReports/doc/ePub_FinalBladesRpt.pdf.

Brophy, J. (1988a). Educating teachers about managing classrooms and students. *Teaching and Teacher Education, 4*(1), 1–18.

Brophy, J. (1988b). Research on teaching effects: Uses and abuses. *The Elementary School Journal, 89*(1), 3–21.

Canter, L. (1989). Assertive discipline—More than names on the board and marbles in a jar. *Phi Delta Kappan, 71*(1), 57–61.

Clarizio, H. F. (1980). *Toward Positive Classroom Discipline* (3rd ed.). New York: John Wiley & Sons.

Confederation College (2004). Charter of students' rights and responsibilities. Retrieved February 12, 2007, from www.confederationc.on.ca/academicpolicies/documents/Chapter5/5-5-03b.pdf.

Cummins, J. (1986). Empowering minority students. *Harvard Educational Review, 17*(4), 18–36.

Curwin, R., and Mendler, A. (1999). *Discipline with Dignity*. Upper Saddle River, NJ: Merrill Prentice Hall.

Dreikurs, R. (1964). *Children the Challenge*. New York: Hawthorne.

Dreikurs, R., Grundwald, B. B., and Pepper, F. C. (1998). *Maintaining Sanity in the Classroom: Classroom Management Techniques* (2nd ed.). New York: Taylor and Francis.

Dreikurs, R., Cassel, P., Ferguson, E. D. (2004). *Discipline without Tears*. Toronto: John Wiley & Sons.

Elementary Teachers' Federation of Ontario. (2000). *Classroom Beginnings*. Toronto, ON: Elementary Teachers' Federation of Ontario.

Elliott, A., and Woloshyn, V. (1996). Adopting collaborative learning strategies in the classroom. *The Canadian School Executive, 15*(9), 3–9.

Emmer, E. T., Evertson, C. M., Worsham, M. E. (2003). *Classroom Management for Secondary Teachers* (6th ed.). Boston: Allyn & Bacon.

Epstein, C. (1979). *Classroom Management and Teaching: Persistent Problems and Rational Solutions*. Reston, VA: Reston.

Evans, G., and Lovell, B. (1979). Design modification in an open-plan school. *Journal of Educational Psychology, 71*, 41–49.

Evertson, C. M., and Emmer, E. T. (1982). Preventive classroom management. In D. L. Duke (Ed.), *Helping Teachers Manage Classrooms* (pp. 2–31). Alexandria, VA: Association for Supervision and Curriculum Development.

Good, T., and Brophy, J. (1987). *Looking in Classrooms* (4th ed.). New York: Longman.

Harris, J. R. (1998). The nurture assumption. New York: Simon & Schuster.

Heitzman, A. J. (1983). Discipline and the use of punishment. *Education, 104*(1), 17–22.

Hyman, I. A., and Snook, P. A. (1999). *Dangerous Schools: What Can We Do About the Physical and Emotional Abuse of Our Children?* San Francisco: Jossey-Bass.

Irvine, J. J. (1990). *Black Students and School Failure: Policy, Practices, Prescriptions*. Westport, CT: Greenwood.

Johnson, D. W., Johnson, R. T., and Holubec, E. J. (1993). *Cooperation in the Classroom* (6th ed.). Edina, MN: Interaction Book Company.

Johnson, S. M., Boadstad, D. D., and Lobitz, G. K. (1976). Generalization and contrast phenomena in behavior modification with children. In E. J. Mash, L. A. Hamerlynck, and L. C. Handy (Eds.), *Behavior Modification and Families*. New York: Brunner/Mazell.

Jones, V. F., and Jones, L. S. (2003). *Comprehensive Classroom Management: Creating Positive Learning Environments and Solving Problems* (7th ed.). Boston: Allyn & Bacon.

Kazdin, A. E., and Bootzin, R. R. (1972). The token economy: An evaluative review. *Journal of Applied Behavior Analysis, 5*, 343–372.

Kohn, A. (1999). *Punished by Rewards*. Boston: Houghton Mifflin.

Ladson-Billings, G. (1994). *The Dreamkeepers: Successful Teachers of African American Children*. San Francisco: Jossey Bass.

Madsen, C. H., Becker, W., and Thomas, D. R. (1968). Rules, praise and ignoring: Elements of elementary classroom control. *Journal of Applied Behavior Analysis, 1*, 139–150.

Manitoba Human Rights Commission. (2007). Human rights in the school. Retrieved February 12, 2007, from www.gov.mb.ca/hrc/english/publications/school/chap1.html.

Martin, J., and Sugarman, J. (1993). *Models of Classroom Management* (2nd ed.). Calgary, AB: Detselig Enterprises Ltd.

National Clearing House of Educational Facilities. (2006). Classroom design. Retrieved December 20, 2006, from www.edfacilities.org/rl/classroom_design.cfm.

National Post. Spanking is not abuse (editorial). Retrieved August 6, 2003, from http://proquest.umi.com/pqdweb?index=2&did=000000347477191&SrchMode=1&sid=1&Fmt=3&VInst=PROD&VType=PQD&RQT=309&VName=PQD&TS=1060198475&clientId=17280.

O'Brien, A., and Pietersma, E. G. (2000). The Section 43 debate: The teacher's perspective. *Education Canada, 40*(2) 44–45.

Ritchie, P. J., Rinholm, J., Flewelling, R., Kelly, M. J., and Sammon, J. (1999). The fine art of teaching and behaviour management. *Education Forum, 25*(3), 19–22.

Schwartz, S., and Pollishuke, M. (2002). *Creating the Dynamic Classroom*. Toronto, ON: Irwin.

Smith, A. B., Gollop, M. M., Taylor, N. J., and Marshall, K.A. (2003). The discipline and guidance of children: Messages from research. Retrieved December 22, 2006, from www.occ.org.nz/childcomm/content/download/840/4422/file/discipline.pdf.

Sweeney, T. J. (1981). *Adlerian Counseling: Proven Concepts and Strategies* (2nd ed.). Muncie, IN: Accelerated Development.

Technology and Instruction: Educ 204/504/531. (2006). Learning environment design. Retrieved December 20, 2006, from www.coastal.edu/education/ti/environment.html.

Walker, H. M. (1979). *The Acting-Out Child: Coping with Classroom Disruption.* Boston: Allyn & Bacon.

Zine, J. (2003). Dealing with September 12th: The chapters with anti-Islamophobia education. *Orbit, 33*(3), 39–41.

Chapter 7

Brophy, J. (1988). Educating teachers about managing classrooms and students. *Teaching and Teacher Education, 4*(1), 1–18.

Canter, L. (1989). Assertive discipline—more than names on the board and marbles in a jar. *Phi Delta Kappan, 71*(1), 57–61.

Huber, J. D. (1984). Discipline in the middle school: Parent, teacher, and principal concerns. *National Association of Secondary School Principals Bulletin, 68*(471), 74–79.

Kerr, M. M., and Nelson, C. M. (2002). *Strategies for Addressing Behaviour Problems in the Classroom* (4th ed.). Don Mills, ON: Prentice Hall.

Kounin, J. (1970). *Discipline and Group Management in Classrooms.* New York: Holt, Rinehart & Winston.

Lasley, T. J. (1989). A teacher development model for classroom management. *Phi Delta Kappan, 71*(1), 36–38.

Levin, J. (1980). *Discipline and Classroom Management Survey: Comparison Between a Suburban and Urban School.* Unpublished report, Pennsylvania State University, University Park.

Redl, F., and Wineman, D. (1952). *Controls from Within.* New York: Free Press.

Ritchie, P. J., Rinholm, J., Flewelling, R., Kelly, M. J., and Sammon, J. (1999). The fine art of teaching and behaviour management. *Education Forum 25*(3), 19–22.

Schwartz, S., and Pollishuke, M. (2002). *Creating the Dynamic Classroom.* Toronto, ON: Irwin.

Shrigley, R. L. (1980). *The Resolution of 523 Classroom Incidents by 54 Classroom Teachers Using the Six-Step Intervention Model.* University Park: Pennsylvania State University, College of Education, Division of Curriculum and Instruction.

Shrigley, R. L. (1985). Curbing student disruption in the classroom—Teachers need intervention skills. *National Association of Secondary School Principals Bulletin, 69*(479), 26–32.

Thomas, G. T., Goodall, R., and Brown, L. (1983). Discipline in the classroom: Perceptions of middle grade teachers. *The Clearinghouse, 57*(3), 139–42.

Weber, T. R., and Sloan, C. A. (1986). How does high school discipline in 1984 compare to previous decades? *The Clearinghouse, 59*(7), 326–329.

Chapter 8

Bandura, A. (1977). *Social Learning Theory.* Englewood Cliffs, NJ: Prentice Hall.

Brophy, J. (1988). Educating teachers about managing classrooms and students. *Teaching and Teacher Education, 4*(1), 1–8.

Canter, L., and Canter, M. (1992). *Assertive Discipline: Positive Behaviour Management for Today's Classrooms* (rev. ed.). Santa Monica, CA: Canter Associates.

Dreikurs, R., Grundwald, B. B., and Pepper, F. C. (1998). *Maintaining Sanity in the Classroom: Classroom Management Techniques* (2nd ed.). New York: Taylor and Francis.

Ginott, H. (1972). *Between Teacher and Child.* New York: Peter H. Wyden.

Glasser, W. (1969). *Schools Without Failure.* New York: Harper & Row.

Gordon, T. (1989). *Teaching Children Self-Discipline at Home and in School.* New York: Random House.

Lasley, T. J. (1989). A teacher development model for classroom management. *Phi Delta Kappan, 71*(1), 30–38.

Levin, J., Nolan, J., and Hoffman, N. (1985). A strategy for the classroom resolution of chronic discipline problems. *National Association of Secondary School Principals Bulletin, 69*(7), 11–18.

Martin, J., and Sugarman, J. (1993). *Models of Classroom Management* (2nd ed.). Calgary, AB: Detselig Enterprises Ltd.

Novak, J. M., and Purkey, W. W. (2001). *Invitational Education.* Bloomington, IN: Phi Delta Kappa Educational Foundation.

Shrigley, R. (1985). Curbing student disruption in the classroom—Teachers need intervention skills. *National Association of Secondary School Principals Bulletin, 69*(7), 26–32.

Sugai, G., and Horner, R. H. (1999). Discipline and behavioral support: Practices, pitfalls, & promises. *Effective School Practices, 17*(4), 10–22.

Valentine, M. R. (1987). *How to Deal with Discipline Problems in the School: A Practical Guide for Educators.* Dubuque, IA: Kendall/Hunt.

Chapter 9

Brendtro, L., Brokenleg, M., and Van Bockern, S. (2002). *Reclaiming Youth at Risk: Our Hope for the Future* (2nd ed.). Bloomington, IN: National Educational Services.

Brophy, J. (1988). Educating teachers about managing classrooms and students. *Teaching and Teacher Education, 4*(1), 1–18.

Canter, L. (1989). Assertive discipline: More than a few names on the board and marbles in a jar. *Phi Delta Kappan, 71*(1), 57–61.

Charney, R. S. (1998, March). Got the "Kids who blurt out" blues? How one teacher curbs disruptions and keeps learning running smoothly. *Instructor, 107.*

Cummins, K. K. (1998). *The Teacher's Guide to Behavioral Interventions: Intervention Strategies for Behavioral Problems in the Educational Environment.* Columbia, MO: Hawthorne Educational Services.

Dreikurs, R., Grundwald, B. B., and Pepper, F. C. (1998). *Maintaining Sanity in the Classroom: Classroom Management Techniques* (2nd ed.). New York: Harper & Row.

Dworet, D., and Rathgeber, A. (1998). Confusion reigns: Definitions of behavioural exceptionalities in Canada. *Exceptionality Education Canada 8*(1), 3–19.

Elliott, A., and Woloshyn, V. (1996). Adopting collaborative learning strategies in the classroom. *The Canadian School Executive 15*(9), 3–9.

Ellis, J., Hart, S., and Small-McGinley, J. (2001). Encouraging the discouraged: Students' views for elementary classrooms. *Analytic Teaching, 22*(1). Retrieved September 19, 2003, from www.mentorship.ualberta. ca/jed.html.

Ginott, H. G. (1972). *Teacher and Child.* New York: Macmillan.

Jones, V. F. (1980). *Adolescents with Behavioural Problems.* Boston: Allyn & Bacon.

Levin, J., Nolan, J., and Hoffman, N. (1985). A strategy for the classroom resolution of chronic discipline problems. *National Association of Secondary School Principals Bulletin, 69*(479), 11–18.

Novak, J. M., and Purkey, W. W. (2001). *Invitational Education.* Bloomington, IN: Phi Delta Kappa Educational Foundation.

Porter, A. C. and Brophy, J. (1988). Synthesis of research on good teaching: Insights from the work of the IRT. *Educational Leadership 45*(8), 74–83.

Shrigley, R. L. (1980). *The Resolution of 523 Classroom Incidents by 54 Classroom Teachers Using the Six-Step Intervention Model.* University Park: Pennsylvania State University, College of Education, Division of Curriculum and Instruction.

Strachota, R. (1996). *On Their Side: Helping Children Take Charge of Their Learning.* Greenfield, MA: Northeast Foundation for Children.

Sweeney, T. J. (1981). *Adlerian Counseling: Proven Concepts and Strategies.* Muncie, IN: Accelerated Development.

Tillson, T. (2000). Mischief or a cry for help? Disciplining students demands awareness of underlying distress. *The Journal of Addiction and Mental Health*. Retrieved September 19, 2003, from www.cfcefc. ca/docs/cccf/00009_en.htm.

Tanner, L. N. (1978). *Classroom Discipline for Effective Teaching and Learning*. New York: Holt, Rinehart & Winston.

Woolfolk, A., and Brooks, D. (1983). Nonverbal communication in teaching. In E. W. Gordon (Ed.), *Review of Research in Education, 10*. Washington, DC: American Educational Research Association.

Chapter 10

Ayllon, T., Garber, S., and Pisor, K. (1975). The elimination of discipline problems through a combined school–home motivation system. *Behaviour Therapy, 6*, 616–626.

Brookover, W. B., and Gigliotti, R. J. (1988). *Parental Involvement in the Public Schools*. Alexandria, VA: National School Boards Association.

Canter, L., and Canter, M. (2001). *Assertive Discipline: Positive Behaviour Management for Today's Classrooms* (rev. ed.). Los Angeles, CA: Canter Associates.

Day, D. M., and Hrynkiw-Augimeri, L. (1996). *Serving Children at Risk for Juvenile Delinquency: An Evaluation of the Earlscourt Under 12 Outreach Project (ORP)*. Final Report submitted to the Department of Justice, September 1996.

Glasser, W. (1969). *Schools Without Failure*. New York: Harper & Row.

Hoover-Dempsey, K., and Sandler, H. (1997). Why do parents become involved in their children's education? *Review of Educational Research, 67*(1), 3–42.

Johnson, S. M., Bolstad, O. D., and Lobitz, G. K. (1976). Generalization and contrast phenomena in behaviour modification with children. In E. J. Marsh, L. A. Hamerlynck, and L. C. Handy (Eds.), *Behaviour Modification and Families*. New York: Brunner/Mazell.

Jones, V. F. (1980). *Adolescents with Behavioural Problems*. Boston: Allyn & Bacon.

Jones, V. F., and Jones, L. S. (1995). *Comprehensive Classroom Management: Creating Positive Learning Environments for All Students* (4th ed.). Boston: Allyn & Bacon.

Lam, J., and Peake, D. (1997). Triad conference: Is it a more effective way of involving parents and students? *McGill Journal of Education, 32*, 249–272.

Marini, Z., Fairbain, L., and Zuber, R. (2001). Peer harassment in individuals with developmental disabilities: Towards the development of a multi-dimensional bullying identification model. *Developmental Disabilities Bulletin 29*(2), 170–195.

Marini, Z., Spear, S., and Bombay, K. (1999). Peer victimization in childhood: Characteristics, causes and consequences of school bullying. *Brock Education, 9*, 32–47.

Minke, K., and Anderson, K. (2003). Restructuring routine parent–teacher conferences: The family–school conference model. *The Elementary School Journal, 104*(1), 49–69.

Patterson, G. R. (1974). Intervention for boys with conduct problems: Multiple settings, treatments and criteria. *Journal of Consulting and Clinical Psychology, 42*, 471–81.

Pepler, R., and Craig, W. (1994). About bullying. *Orbit 25*(3), 43–44.

Rosenthal, D. M., and Sawyers, J. Y., (1996). Building successful home–school partnerships. *Childhood Education, 72*(4), 194–200.

Walker, H. M. (1979). *The Acting-Out-Child: Coping with Classroom Disruption*. Boston: Allyn & Bacon.

Waters, P. (2002). Defining roles: The role of the parent in education today to improve education performance. Retrieved October 3, 2003, from cap.ic.gc.ca/chsptf/education/roleofparent.pdf.

Weber, K., and Bennett, S. (1999). *Special Education in Ontario Schools* (4th ed.). Thornhill, ON: Highland Press.

Wolfgang, G. H. (1999). *Solving Discipline Problems: Methods and Models for Today's Teachers* (4th ed.). Boston: Allyn & Bacon.

Index